UNIVERSITY OF NOTTINGHAM
D0511677
LIBRARY
THE NEW
PALGRAVE
ONE WEEK LOAN
ALLOCATION, INFORMATION
UNIVERSITY LIBRARY
above
10013

ALLOCATION, INFORMATION AND MARKETS

EDITED BY

JOHN EATWELL · MURRAY MILGATE · PETER NEWMAN

MACMILLAN
REFERENCE
BOOKS

First published in
The New Palgrave: A Dictionary of Economics
Edited by John Eatwell, Murray Milgate and Peter Newman
in four volumes, 1987

Published in the United Kingdom by
THE MACMILLAN PRESS LIMITED, 1989
London and Basingstoke
Associated companies in Auckland, Delhi, Dublin, Gaborone,
Hamburg, Harare, Hong Kong, Johannesburg, Kuala Lumpur, Lagos,
Manzini, Maseru, Melbourne, Mexico City, Nairobi, New York,
Singapore, Tokyo.

Paperback reprinted 1990

British Library Cataloguing in Publication Data

The new Palgrave: allocation information and markets
1. Economics. Markets
I. Eatwell, John II. Milgate, Murray
338.5

ISBN 0-333-49538-1
ISBN 0-333-49539-X Pbk

Sept 89

Printed in Hong Kong

Contents

Acknowledgements

R. Wilson (Exchange) wishes to acknowledge support from Stanford University, Stanford; research support from the National Science Foundation (SES83-08723) and the Office of Naval Research (N00014-79C0865).

General Preface

The books in this series are the offspring of *The New Palgrave*: *A Dictionary of Economics*. Published in late 1987, the *Dictionary* has rapidly become a standard reference work in economics. However, its four heavy tomes containing over four million words on the whole range of economic thought is not a form convenient to every potential user. For many students and teachers it is simply too bulky, too comprehensive and too expensive for everyday use.

By developing the present series of compact volumes of reprints from the original work, we hope that some of the intellectual wealth of *The New Palgrave* will become accessible to much wider groups of readers. Each of the volumes is devoted to a particular branch of economics, such as econometrics or general equilibrium or money, with a scope corresponding roughly to a university course on that subject. Apart from correction of misprints, etc. the content of each of its reprinted articles is exactly the same as that of the original. In addition, a few brand new entries have been commissioned especially for the series, either to fill an apparent gap or more commonly to include topics that have risen to prominence since the dictionary was originally commissioned.

As *The New Palgrave* is the sole parent of the present series, it may be helpful to explain that it is the modern successor to the excellent *Dictionary of Political Economy* edited by R.H. Inglis Palgrave and published in three volumes in 1894, 1896 and 1899. A second and slightly modified version, edited by Henry Higgs, appeared during the mid-1920s. These two editions each contained almost 4,000 entries, but many of those were simply brief definitions and many of the others were devoted to peripheral topics such as foreign coinage, maritime commerce, and Scottish law. To make room for the spectacular growth in economics over the last 60 years while keeping still to a manageable length, *The New Palgrave* concentrated instead on economic theory, its originators, and its closely cognate disciplines. Its nearly 2,000 entries (commissioned from over 900 scholars) are all self-contained essays, sometimes brief but never mere definitions.

Apart from its biographical entries, *The New Palgrave* is concerned chiefly with theory rather than fact, doctrine rather than data; and it is not at all clear how theory and doctrine, as distinct from facts and figures, *should* be treated in an encyclopaedia. One way is to treat everything from a particular point of view. Broadly speaking, that was the way of Diderot's classic *Encyclopédie raisonée* (1751–1772), as it was also of Léon Say's *Nouveau dictionnaire d'économie politique* (1891–2). Sometimes, as in articles by Quesnay and Turgot in the *Encyclopédie*, this approach has yielded entries of surpassing brilliance. Too often, however, both the range of subjects covered and the quality of the coverage itself are seriously reduced by such a self-limiting perspective. Thus the entry called '*Méthode*' in the first edition of Say's *Dictionnaire* asserted that the use of mathematics in economics 'will only ever be in the hands of a few', and the dictionary backed up that claim by choosing not to have any entry on Cournot.

Another approach is to have each entry take care to reflect within itself varying points of view. This may help the student temporarily, as when preparing for an examination. But in a subject like economics, the Olympian detachment which this approach requires often places a heavy burden on the author, asking for a scrupulous account of doctrines he or she believes to be at best wrong-headed. Even when an especially able author does produce a judicious survey article, it is surely too much to ask that it also convey just as much enthusiasm for those theories thought misguided as for those found congenial. Lacking an enthusiastic exposition, however, the disfavoured theories may then be studied less closely than they deserve.

The New Palgrave did not ask its authors to treat economic theory from any particular point of view, except in one respect to be discussed below. Nor did it call for surveys. Instead, each author was asked to make clear his or her own views of the subject under discussion, and for the rest to be as fair and accurate as possible, without striving to be 'judicious'. A balanced perspective on each topic was always the aim, the ideal. But it was to be sought not *internally*, within each article, but *externally*, between articles, with the reader rather than the writer handed the task of achieving a personal balance between differing views.

For a controversial topic, a set of several more or less synonymous headwords, matched by a broad diversity of contributors, was designed to produce enough variety of opinion to help form the reader's own synthesis; indeed, such diversity will be found in most of the individual volumes in this series.

This approach was not without its problems. Thus, the prevalence of uncertainty in the process of commissioning entries sometimes produced a less diverse outcome than we had planned. 'I can call spirits from the vasty deep,' said Owen Glendower. 'Why, so can I,' replied Hotspur, 'or so can any man;/ But will they come when you do call for them?' In our experience, not quite as often as we would have liked.

The one point of view we did urge upon every one of *Palgrave*'s authors was to write from an historical perspective. For each subject its contributor was asked to discuss not only present problems but also past growth and future prospects. This request was made in the belief that knowledge of the historical development of any theory enriches our present understanding of it, and so helps to construct better theories for the future. The authors' response to the request was generally so positive that, as the reader of any of these volumes will discover, the resulting contributions amply justified that belief.

John Eatwell
Murray Milgate
Peter Newman

Preface

In the early 1950s, Arrow, Debreu, McKenzie and other economists brilliantly reformulated the Walrasian system of competitive equilibrium in such a way as to permit general and straightforward proofs of its logical consistency. The results of their investigations are often summarized in the phrase 'competitive equilibrium exists', which is harmless enough provided one realizes that what they proved was an assertion not about economic reality but about the coherence of a theoretical system. 'Equilibrium' is necessarily a theoretical concept, and so its presence or absence must be a property not of phenomena themselves but of ways of thinking about them.

Such considerations are especially relevant to the particular reformulation that came to be called the Arrow–Debreu (A–D) model of competitive general equilibrium. Anticipated in varying degrees by Fisher, Hayek and Hicks, and perhaps not so methodologically self-conscious at first as they became later, the eponymous authors gave fresh meanings to the basic concepts of 'commodity' and 'equilibrium' that were of such breathtaking scope as to constitute something fundamentally new. For example they invented contingent commodities, which are contracts for purchase *now* specifying a deal to take place at some stipulated future date contingent upon what state of nature will prevail *then*; and these were quite unknown before at this level of generality.

The upshot was a model of such scope and flexibility that at first it swept all before it, in a triumph which was only enhanced by the rapid rediscovery and final proof of Edgeworth's conjecture, that with a suitably infinite number of agents the core of an economy coincides with the set of competitive allocations. By the mid-1960s the A–D model really did appear, what many people still consider it to be, the keystone of modern neoclassical economics.

But its very virtues were, in a sense, its undoing. For by setting out in explicit detail the conditions underlying its basic theorems – existence, efficiency, 'pricing out', core equivalence, local uniqueness, etc. – the model made it easy for critics to discover its limitations. To put the matter more positively (as it should be), the triumph of the A–D model pointed the way forward to a well-defined research programme, the identification and analysis of those situations where it fails.

No one was more conscious of this than Arrow himself, and no one welcomed it more. Indeed, two decades ago his famous but obscurely published paper on 'The Organization of Economic Activity: Issues Pertinent to the Choice of Market versus Nonmarket Allocation' (reprinted in Volume 2 of his *Collected Papers*) listed a series of problems that read now like the post A–D research agenda that, as shown in the present volume, was actually followed over the next twenty years. Among the limitations to the scope of the A–D model that he mentioned, for example, were asymmetric information and its discontents such as adverse selection, moral hazard, and agency; strategic behaviour; increasing returns; and, above all, incomplete markets.

At the same time he took a sensibly conservative approach to the original model, showing that by suitable reinterpretation of the meaning of an A–D commodity several problems of 'externality' can be formally accomodated within its framework. Since, however, 'markets for externalities usually involve small numbers of buyers and sellers' so that 'even if a competitive equilibrium could be defined, there would be no force driving the system to it', this particular victory seemed Pyrrhic. As Joan Robinson said in a related context almost fifty years ago: 'If the world were such that perfect competition were possible, it would be such that the demarcation of commodities would present no difficulty' (*Economica*, 1941).

It is much too early to say how successful the implementation of the post-A–D research programme will be. At present, like post-Modernist architecture, it looks fragmentary, complicated and incomplete, with unification and simplification still indefinitely far away. But that is only to be expected given the intrinsic difficulties. One disquieting theme running through many recent contributions is logical discomfort with what Frank Knight used to call 'the irrational passion for dispassionate rationality', and a consequent though reluctant disposition to accept some unspecified form of bounded rationality as substitute. This is unsatisfactory if only because, as with *non*-linearity and *non*-convexity and *in*finity, one can be non-rational and irrational in innumerable ways.

The Editors

Efficient Allocation

STANLEY REITER

Analysis of efficiency in the context of resource allocation has been a central concern of economic theory from ancient times, and is an essential element of modern microeconomic theory. The ends of economic action are seen to be the satisfaction of human wants through the provision of goods and services. These are supplied by production and exchange and limited by scarcity of resources and technology. In this context efficiency means going as far as possible in the satisfaction of wants within resource and technological constraints. This is expressed by the concept of Pareto optimality, which can be stated informally as follows: a state of affairs is Pareto optimal if it is within the given constraints and it is not the case that everyone can be made better off in his own view by changing to another state of affairs that satisfies the applicable constraints.

Because knowledge about wants, resources and technology is dispersed, efficient outcomes can be achieved only by coordination of economic activity. Hayek (1945) pointed out the role of knowledge or information, particularly in the context of prices and markets, in coordinating economic activity. Acquiring, processing and transmitting information are costly activities themselves subject to constraints imposed by technological and resource limitations. Hayek pointed out that the institutions of markets and prices function to communicate information dispersed among economic agents so as to bring about coordinated economic action. He also drew attention to motivational properties of those institutions, or incentives. In this context, the concept of efficiency takes account of the organizational constraints on information processing and transmission in addition to those on production of ordinary goods and services. The magnitude of resources devoted to business or governmental bureaucracies, and to some of the functions performed by industrial salesmen, attests to the importance of these constraints. Economic analysis of efficient allocation has formally imposed only the constraints on production and exchange, and until recently recognized organizational constraints only in an informal way. But it is these constraints that motivate the pervasive and enduring interest in decentralized modes of economic organization, particularly the competitive mechanism.

It is necessary to limit the scope of this essay so that it is not coextensive with microeconomic theory. The main limitation imposed here is to confine attention to models in which either the role of information is ignored, or in which agents do not behave strategically on the basis of private information. In so doing, a large and important class of models involving problems of efficient allocation in the presence of incentive constraints is excluded.

The main ideas of efficient resource allocation are present in their simplest form in the linear activity analysis model of production. We begin with that model.

EFFICIENCY OF PRODUCTION: LINEAR ACTIVITY ANALYSIS

The analysis of production can to some extent be separated from that of other economic activity. The concept of efficiency appropriate to this analysis descends from that of Pareto optimality, which refers to both productive and allocative efficiency in the full economy in which production is embedded. It is useful to begin with a model in which technological possibilities afford constant returns to scale, that is, with the (linear) activity analysis model of production pioneered by Koopmans (1951a, 1951b, 1957), and closely related to the development of linear programming associated with Dantzig (1951a, 1951b) and independently with the Russian mathematician Kantorovitch (1939, 1942) and Kantorovitch and Gavurin (1949).

The two primitive concepts of the model are *commodity* and *activity*. A list of n commodities is postulated; a commodity *bundle* is given by specifying a sequence of n numbers $a_1, a_2, \ldots, a_n$. Technological possibilities are thought of as knowledge of how to transform commodities. Such knowledge may be described in terms of collections of activities called *processes*, much as knowledge of how to prepare food is described by recipes. A recipe commonly has two parts, a list of ingredients or inputs and of the output(s) of the recipe, and a description of how the ingredients are to be combined to produce the output(s). In the activity analysis model the description of productive activity is suppressed. Only the specification of inputs and outputs is retained; this defines the production process.

Commodities are classified into 'desired', 'primary' and 'intermediate' commodities. Desired commodities are those whose consumption or availability is the recognized goal of production; they satisfy wants. Primary commodities are those available from nature. (A primary commodity that is also desired is listed separately among the desired commodities and must be transformed by an act of production into its desired form.) Intermediate commodities are those that merely pass from one stage of production to another. Each commodity can exist in any non-negative amount (*divisibility*). Addition and subtraction of the numbers measuring the amount of a commodity represent joining and separating corresponding amounts of the commodity.

An activity is characterized by a *net output number* for each commodity, which is positive if the commodity is a net output, negative if it is a net input and zero if it is neither. The term *input–output vector* is also used for this ordered array of numbers. Activity analysis postulates a finite number of basic activities from which all technologically possible activities can be generated by suitable combination. Allowable combinations are as follows. If two activities are known to be possible, then the activity given by their algebraic sum is also possible, i.e. if $a=(a_1,a_2,\ldots,a_n)$ and $b=(b_1,b_2,\ldots,b_n)$, then $a+b=(a_1+b_1,a_2+b_2,\ldots,a_n+b_n)$ is also possible. Thus, additivity embodies an assumption of non-interaction between productive activities, at least at the level of knowledge. Furthermore, if an activity is possible, then so is every non-negative multiple of it (*proportionality*), i.e. if $a=(a_1,a_2,\ldots,a_n)$ is possible, then so is $\mu a=(\mu a_1,\mu a_2,\ldots,\mu a_n)$ for any non-negative real number μ. This expresses the assumption of constant returns to scale. The family of activities consisting of all non-negative multiples of a given one forms a process. Since there is a finite number of basic activities, there is also a finite number of basic processes, each intended to describe a basic method of production capable of being carried out at different levels, or intensities.

The assumptions of additivity and proportionality determine a linear model of technology that can be given the following form. Let A be an n by k matrix whose jth column is the input–output vector representing the basic activity that defines the jth basic process, and let $x=(x_1,x_2,\ldots,x_n)$ be the vector whose jth component x_j is the scale (level or intensity) of the jth basic process. Let $y=(y_1,y_2,\ldots,y_n)$ be the vector of commodities. Technology is represented by a linear transformation mapping the space of activity levels into the commodity space, i.e.

$$y=Ax \qquad x\geqslant 0.$$

With the properties assumed, a process can be represented geometrically in the commodity space by a halfline from the origin including all non-negative multiples of some activity in that process. The finite number of halflines representing basic processes generate a convex polyhedral cone consisting of all activities that can be expressed as sums of activities in the basic processes, or equivalently, as non-negative linear combinations of the basic activities, sometimes called a *bundle of basic activities*. This cone is called the *production set*, or set of *possible productions*.

Two other assumptions are made about the production set itself, rather than just the individual activities. First, there is no activity, whether basic or derived, in the production set with a positive net output of some commodity and non-negative net outputs of all commodities. This excludes the possibility of producing something from nothing, whether directly or indirectly. Second, it is assumed that the production set contains at least one activity with a positive net output of some commodity.

If the availability of primary commodities is subject to a bound, the technologically possible productions described by the production set are subject to another restriction; only those possible productions that do not require primary inputs in amounts exceeding the given bounds can be produced. Furthermore, because intermediate commodities are not desired in themselves, their net output is required to be zero. (Strictly speaking, the technological constraint on intermediate commodities is that their net output be non-negative. The requirement that they be zero can be viewed as one of elementary efficiency, excluding accumulation or necessity to dispose of unwanted goods.) With these restrictions the model can be written

$$y = Ax,\ x \geqslant 0,\ y_i = 0 \quad \text{if } i \text{ is an intermediate commodity, and}$$

$$y_i \geqslant r_i \quad \text{if } i \text{ is a primary commodity,}$$

where r_i is the (non-positive) limit on the availability of primary commodity i. This leads to the concept of an *attainable* activity.

A bundle of basic activities is *attainable* if the resulting net outputs are non-negative for all desired commodities, zero for intermediate commodities and non-positive for primary commodities, and if the total inputs of primary commodities do not exceed (in absolute amount) the prescribed bounds of availability of those commodities. The set of activities satisfying these conditions is a truncated convex polyhedral cone in the commodity space called the *set of attainable productions.*

The concept of productive efficiency in this model is as follows. An activity (a bundle of basic activities) is *efficient* if it is attainable and if every activity that provides more of some desired commodity and no less of any other is not attainable.

This concept can be seen to be a specialization of Pareto optimality. If for each desired commodity there is at least one consumer who is not satiated in that commodity, at least in the range of production attainable within the given resource limitations, then increasing the amount of any desired commodity without decreasing any other can improve the state of some non-satiated consumer without worsening that of any other.

CHARACTERIZING EFFICIENT PRODUCTION IN TERMS OF PRICES

Efficient production can be characterized in terms of *implicit prices,* also called *shadow prices,* or in the context of linear programming, *dual variables.* Efficient activities are precisely those that maximize profit for suitably chosen prices. The profit returned by a process carried out at the level x is

$$x \textstyle\sum_i p_i a_i,$$

where the prices are $p = (p_1, \ldots, p_n)$, and $a = (a_1, \ldots, a_n)$ is the basic activity defining the process; the profit on the bunble of activities Ax at prices p is given by the inner product $py = pAx$.

This characterization is the economic expression of an important mathematical fact about convex sets in n-dimensional Euclidean space, namely that through every point of the space not interior to the convex set in question there passes a hyperplane that contains the set in one of its two halfspaces (Fenchel, 1950; Nikaido, 1969, 1970). (A hyperplane in n dimensional space is a level set of a linear function of n variables, and thus is a translate of an $n-1$

dimensional linear subspace. A hyerplane is given by an equation of the form $c_1x_1 + c_2x_2 + \ldots + c_nx_n = k$, where the x's are variables, the c's are coefficients defining the linear function and k is a constant identifying the level set. A hyperplane divides the space into two halfspaces corresponding to the two inequalities $c_1x_1 + c_2x_2 + \ldots + c_nx_n \gtreqless k$ respectively.) It can also be seen that a point of a convex set is a boundary point if and only if it maximizes a linear function on the (closure of the) set. These facts can be used to characterize efficient production because the attainable production set is convex and efficient activities are boundary points of it. Because the efficient points are those, roughly speaking, on the 'north-east' frontier of the set, the linear functions associated with them have non-negative coefficients, interpreted as prices. On the other hand, if a point of the attainable set maximizes a linear function with strictly positive coefficients (prices), then it is on the 'north-east' frontier of the set.

In Figure 1 the set enclosed by the broken line and the axes is the projection of the attainable set on the output coordinates; inputs are not shown. The point y' in the figure is efficient; the point y'' is not; both y' and y'' maximize a linear function with non-negative coefficients (the level set containing y' is labelled a and also contains y''). However, y' maximizes a linear function with positive coefficients (one such, whose level set through y' is labelled b, is shown), while y'' does not.

These implicit, or efficiency prices arise from the logic of efficiency or maximization when the relevant sets are convex, not from any institutions such as markets or exchange. An important reason for interest in them is the possibility of achieving efficient performance by decentralized methods. As described above, under the assumptions of additivity and constant returns to scale the production set can be seen to be generated by a finite number of basic processes, each of which consists of the activities that are non-negative multiples of a basic activity,

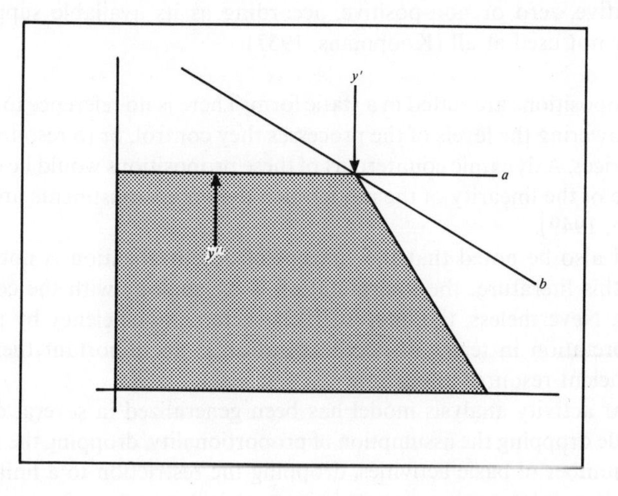

Figure 1

the multiple being the scale (level, or intensity) at which the process is operated. Following the presentation of Koopmans (1957), each basic process is controlled by a manager, who decides on its level. The manager of a process is assumed to know only the input–output coefficients of his process. Each primary resource is in the charge of a resource holder, who knows the limit of its availability. Efficiency prices are used to guide the choices of managers and resource holders. (Under constant returns to scale, if an activity yields positive profit at a given system of prices, then increasing the scale of the process containing that activity increases the profit. Since the scale can be increased without bound, if the profitability of a process is not zero or negative, then, in the eyes of its manager, who does not know the aggregate resource constraints, it can be made infinite. Therefore, the systems of prices that can be considered for the role of efficiency prices must be restricted to those *compatible with the given technology*, namely prices such that no process is profitable and at least one process breaks even.) Two propositions characterize efficient production by prices and provide the basis for an interpretation in terms of decentralized control of production.

> In a given linear activity analysis model, if there is a given system of prices compatible with the technology, in which the prices of all desired commodities are positive, then any attainable bundle of basic activities selected only from processes that break even and which utilizes all positively priced primary commodities to the limit of their availability and does not use negatively priced primary commodities at all, is an efficient bundle of activities.

> In a given linear activity analysis model, each efficient bundle of activities has associated with it at least one system on prices compatible with the technology such that every activity in that bundle breaks even and such that prices of desired commodities are positive, and the price of a primary commodity is non-negative, zero or non-positive, according as its available supply is full, partly, or not used at all (Koopmans, 1957).

These propositions are stated in a static form. There is no reference to managers raising or lowering the levels of the processes they control, or to resource holders adjusting prices. A dynamic counterpart of these propositions would be of interest, but because of the linearity of the model such dynamic adjustments are unstable (Samuelson, 1949).

It should also be noted that the concept of decentralization is not explicitly defined in this literature; the interpretation is by analogy with the competitive mechanism. Nevertheless, the interest in characterizing efficiency by prices and their interpretation in terms of decentralization is an important theme in the study of efficient resource allocation.

The linear activity analysis model has been generalized in several directions. These include dropping the assumption of proportionality, dropping the restriction to a finite number of basic activities, dropping the restriction to a finite number of commodities and dropping the restriction to a finite number of agents. Perhaps the most directly related generalization is to the nonlinear activity analysis, or nonlinear programming, model.

EFFICIENCY OF PRODUCTION: NONLINEAR PROGRAMMING

In the nonlinear programming model there is, as in the linear model, a finite number of basic processes. Their levels are represented by a vector $x = (x_1, x_2, \ldots, x_k)$, where k is the number of basic processes. Technology is represented by a nonlinear transformation from the space of process levels to the commodity space (still assumed to be finite dimensional), written

$$y = F(x),\ x \geqslant 0.$$

The production set in this model is the image in the commodity space of the non-negative orthant of the space of process levels. Under the assumptions usually made about F, the production set is convex, though, of course, not a polyhedral cone.

In this model as in the linear activity analysis model a central result is the characterization of efficient production in terms of prices. The simplest case to begin with is that of one desired commodity, say, one output, with perhaps several inputs. In this case the (vector-valued) function F can be written

$$F(x) = [f(x), g_1(x), g_2(x), \ldots, g_m(x)],$$

where the value of f is the output, and $g_1, \ldots, g_m$ correspond to the various inputs. Resource constraints are expressed by the conditions

$$g_j(x) \geqslant 0, \quad \text{for} \quad j = 1, 2, \ldots, m,$$

and non-negativity of process levels by the condition, $x \geqslant 0$. (Here the resource constraints $r_j \leqslant h_j(x) \leqslant 0$ are written more compactly as $h_j(x) - r_j = g_j(x) \geqslant 0$.)

In this model the definition of efficient production given in the linear model amounts to maximizing the value of f subject to the resource and non-negativity constraints just mentioned.

Problems of constrained maximization are intimately related to saddle-point problems. Let L be a real valued function defined on the set $X \times Y$ in R^n. A point (x^*, y^*), in $X \times Y$ is a *saddle point* of L if

$$L(x, y^*) \leqslant L(x^*, y^*) \leqslant L(x^*, y), \text{ for all } x \text{ in } X \text{ and all } y \text{ in } Y.$$

The concept of a concave function is also need. A real valued function f defined on a convex set X in R^n is a *concave function* if for all x and y in X and all real numbers $0 \leqslant a \leqslant 1$

$$f(ax + (1-a)y) \geqslant af(x) + (1-a)f(y).$$

The following mathematical theorem is fundamental.

Theorem (Kuhn and Tucker, 1951; Uzawa, 1958): Let f and $g_1, g_2, \ldots, g_m$ be real valued concave functions defined on a convex set X in R^n. If f achieves a maximum on X subject to $g_j(x) \geqslant 0$, $j = 1, 2, \ldots, m$ at the point x^* in X, then there exist non-negative numbers $p_0^*, p_0^*, \ldots, p_m^*$, not all zero, such that $p_0^* f(x) + p^* g(x) \leqslant p_0^* f(x^*)$ for all x in X, and furthermore, $p^* g(x^*) = 0$. (Here the vectors $p^* = (p_1^*, p_2^*, \ldots, p_m^*)$, and $g(x) = [g_1(x), g_2(x), \ldots, g_m(x)]$.) The vector p^* may be chosen so that

$$\sum_0^m p_j^* = 1.$$

An additional condition (Slater, 1950) is important. (It ensures that the coefficient p_0 of f is not zero.)

Slater's Condition: There is a point x' in X at which $g_j(x') > 0$ for all $j = 1, 2, \ldots, m$.

If attention is restricted to concave functions, as in the Kuhn–Tucker–Uzawa Theorem, the relation between constrained maxima and saddle points can be summarized in the following theorem.

Theorem: If f and g_j, $j = 1, 2, \ldots, m$ are concave functions defined on a convex subset X in R^n, and if Slater's Condition is satisfied, then x^* in X maximizes f subject to $g_j(x) \geqslant 0$, $j = 1, 2, \ldots, m$, if and only if there exists $\lambda^* = (\lambda_1^*, \lambda_2^*, \ldots, \lambda_m^*)$, $\lambda_j^* \geqslant 0$ for $j = 1, 2, \ldots, m$, such that (x^*, λ^*) is a saddle point of $L(x, \lambda) = f(x) + \lambda g(x)$ on $X \times R_+^n$.

This theorem is easily seen to cover the case where some constraints are equalities, as in the case of intermediate commodities. The sufficiency half of this theorem holds for functions that are not concave.

The auxiliary variables $\lambda_1, \lambda_2, \ldots, \lambda_m$, called *Lagrange multipliers*, play the role of efficiency prices, or shadow prices; they evaluate the resources constrained by the condition $g(x) \geqslant 0$. The maximum characterized by the theorem is a global one, as in the case of linear activity analysis.

If the functions involved are differentiable, a saddle point of the Lagrangean can be studied in terms of first-order conditions. The first-order conditions are necessary conditions for a saddle point of L. If the functions f and the g's are concave on a convex set X, then the first-order conditions at a point (x^*, λ^*) are also sufficient; that is, they imply that (x^*, λ^*) is a saddle point of L. Thus,

Theorem: If $f, g_1, g_2, \ldots, g_m$ are concave and differentiable on an open convex set X in R^n, and if Slater's Condition is satisfied, then x^* maximizes f subject to $g_j(x) \geqslant 0$ for $j = 1, 2, \ldots, m$ if and only if there exists numbers $\lambda_1^*, \lambda_2^*, \ldots, \lambda_m^*$ such that the first-order conditions for a saddle point of $L(x, \lambda) = f(x) + \lambda g(x)$ are satisfied at (x^*, λ^*).

If there are non-negativity conditions on the x's,

$$g_j(x) \geqslant 0, \quad x \geqslant 0, \quad x \text{ in } R^n$$

and the first-order conditions can be written

$$f_x^* + \lambda^* g_x^* \leqslant 0, (f_x^* + \lambda^* g_x^*)x^* = 0$$

$$\lambda^* g(x^*) = 0, g(x^*) \geqslant 0, g(x^*) \geqslant 0,$$

$$\lambda^* \geqslant 0 \quad \text{and} \quad \lambda^* g(x^*) = 0,$$

where f_x^* denotes the derivative of f evaluated at x^*. In more explicit notation, the conditions $f_x^* + \lambda^* g_x^* = 0$ can be written as

$$\partial f/\partial x_i + \sum_{j=1}^{m} \lambda_j^* \partial g_j/\partial x_i = 0 \qquad i = 1, 2, \ldots, n$$

When the assumption of concavity is dropped, it is no longer possible to ensure that the local maximum is also a global one. However, it is still possible to analyse local constrained maxima in terms of local saddle-point conditions. In this case a condition is needed to ensure that the first-order conditions for a saddle point are indeed necessary conditions. The Kuhn–Tucker Constraint Qualification is such a condition. Arrow, Hurwicz and Uzawa (1961) have found a number of conditions, more useful in application to economic models, that imply the Constraint Qualification.

The case of more than one desired commodity leads to what is called the *vector maximum problem*, Kuhn and Tucker (1951). This may be defined as follows. Let $f_1, f_2, \ldots, f_k$ and $g_1, g_2, \ldots, g_m$ be real valued functions defined on a set X in R^n. We say x^* in X achieves a (global) *vector maximum* of $f = (f_1, f_2, \ldots, f_k)$ subject to $g_j(x) \geqslant 0, j = 1, 2, \ldots, m$ if,

(I) $g_j(x^*) \geqslant 0, j = 1, 2, \ldots, m,$

(II) there does not exist x' in X satisfying $f_i(x') \geqslant f_i(x^*)$ for $i = 1, 2, \ldots, k$ with $f_i(x') > f_i(x^*)$ for some value of i, and $g_j(x') \geqslant 0$ for $j = 1, 2, \ldots, m$.

This is just the concept of an efficient point expressed in the present notation.

A vector maximum has a saddle-point characterization similar to that for a scalar valued function.

Theorem: Let $f_1, f_2, \ldots, f_k$ and $g_1, g_2, \ldots, g_m$ be real valued concave functions defined on a convex X set in R^n. Suppose there is x^0 in X such that $g_j(x^0) > 0$, $j = 1, 2, \ldots, m$ (Slater's Condition). If x^* achieves a vector maximum of f subject to $g(x) \geqslant 0$ then there exist $a = (a_1, a_2, \ldots, a_k)$ and $\lambda^* = (\lambda_1^*, \lambda_2^*, \ldots, \lambda_m^*)$ with $a_j \geqslant 0$ for all j, $a \neq 0$ and $\lambda \geqslant 0$ such that (x^*, λ^*) is a saddle point of the Lagrangean $L(x, \lambda) = af(x) + \lambda g(x)$.

Several different 'converses', to this theorem are known. One states that if x^* maximizes $L(x, \lambda^*)$ for some strictly positive vector a and non-negative λ^*, and if $\lambda^* g(x^*) = 0$ and $g(x^*) \geqslant 0$, then x^* gives a vector maximum of f subject to $g(x) \geqslant 0$, and x in X. Another, parallel to the result for the case of one desired commodity, is the following.

Theorem: Let f and g be functions as in the theorem above. If there are positive real numbers $a_1, a_2, \ldots, a_k$ and if (z^*, λ^*) is a saddle point of the Lagrangean L

(defined as above) then (I) x^* achieves a maximum of f subject to $g(x) \geqslant 0$ on X, and (II) $\lambda^* g(x^*) = 0$.

The positive numbers $a_1, \ldots, a_k$ are interpreted as prices of desired commodities, and the non-negative numbers λ_j^* are prices of the remaining commodities. The condition $\lambda^* g(x^*) = 0$ which arises in these theorems states that the value of unused resources at the efficiency prices λ^* is zero; that is, resources not fully utilized at a vector maximum have a zero price.

The connection between vector maxima and Pareto optima is as follows. Because a vector maximum is an efficient point (for the vectorial ordering of the commodity space), it is a Pareto optimum for appropriately specified (non-satiated) utility functions, as was already pointed out in the case of the linear activity analysis model. Furthermore, if the functions $f_1, \ldots, f_k$ are themselves utility functions, and the variable x denotes allocations, with the constraints g defining feasibility, then a vector maximum of f subject to the constraints $g(x) \geqslant 0$ and x in X is a Pareo optimum, and vice versa. Hence the saddle-point theorems give a characterization of Pareto optima by prices. The interpretation of prices in terms of decentralized resource allocation described in the linear activity analysis model also applies in this nonlinear model. The proofs of these theorems reveal an important logical role played by the principle of marginal cost pricing.

The basic theorems of nonlinear programming, especially the Kuhn–Tucker–Uzawa Theorem in the setting of the vector maximum problem, have been extended to the case of infinitely many commodities. (Hurwicz, 1958, first obtained the basic results in this field.) Technicalities aside, the theorems carry over to certain infinite dimensional spaces, namely linear topological spaces, or in the case of first-order conditions, Banach spaces.

Dropping the restriction to a finite number of basic processes leads to classical production or transformation function models of production, whose properties depend on the detailed specifications made.

Samuelson (1947) used Lagrangean methods to analyse interior maxima subject to equality constraints in the context of production function models, as well as that of optimization by consumers. He also gave the interpretation of Lagrange multipliers as shadow prices.

EFFICIENT ALLOCATION IN AN ECONOMY WITH CONSUMERS AND PRODUCERS

In an economy with both consumption and production decisions, efficiency is concerned with distribution as well as production. Data about restrictions on consumption and the wants of consumers must be specified in addition to the data about production. The elements of the models are as follows.

The commodity space is denoted X; it might be l-dimensional Euclidean space, or a more abstract space such as an additive group in which, for example, some coordinates are restricted to have integer values. There is a (finite) list of consumers $1, 2, \ldots, n$, and a similar list of producers, $1, 2, \ldots, m$. A *state* of the economy is an array consisting of a commodity bundle for each agent in the economy, consumer or producer. This may be written $(\langle x^i \rangle, \langle y^j \rangle)$, where

$\langle x^i \rangle = (x^1, x^2, \ldots, x^n)$ and $\langle y^j \rangle = (y^1, y^2, \ldots, y^m)$ and x^i and y^j are commodity bundles. Absolute constraints on consumption are expressed by requiring that the allocation $\langle x^i \rangle$ belong to a specified subset X of the space X^n of allocations. Examples of such constraints are:

1. The requirement that the quantity of a certain commodity be non-negative.
2. The requirement that a consumer requires certain minimum quantities of commodities in order to survive.

Each consumer i has a preference relation, denoted $\succsim_i$, defined on X. This formulation admits externalities in consumption, including physical externalities and externalities in preferences; for example, preferences that depend on the consumption of other agents, termed non-selfish preferences. The consumption set of the ith consumer is the projection X^i of X onto the space of commodity bundles whose coordinates refer to the holdings of the ith consumer.

Technology is specified by a production set Y, a subset of X^m, consisting of those arrays $\langle y^j \rangle$ of input–output vectors that are jointly feasible for all producers. The production set of the jth producer, denoted Y^j, is the projection of Y onto the subspace of X^m whose coordinates refer to the jth producer.

The (aggregate) initial endowment of the economy is denoted by w, a commodity bundle in X.

These specifications define an *environment*, a term introduced by Hurwicz (1960) in this usage and according to him suggested by Jacob Marschak. This term refers to the primitive or given data from which analysis begins. Each environment determines a set of *feasible* states. These are the states $(\langle x^i \rangle, \langle y^j \rangle)$ such that $\langle x^i \rangle$ is in X, $\langle y^j \rangle$ is in Y and $\Sigma x^i - \Sigma y^j \leqslant w$.

An environment determines the set of states that are Pareto optimal for that environment. Explicitly, they are the states $(\langle x^{*i} \rangle, \langle y^{*j} \rangle)$ that are feasible in the given environment, and such that if any other state $(\langle x^i \rangle, \langle y^j \rangle)$ has the property that $\langle x^i \rangle \succsim_i \langle x^{*i} \rangle$ for all i with $\langle x^{i'} \rangle \succ_{i'} \langle x^{*i'} \rangle$ for some i', then $(\langle x^i \rangle, \langle y^j \rangle)$ is not feasible in the given environment.

It is important to note that the set of feasible states and the set of Pareto optimal states are completely determined by the environment; specification of economic organization is not involved.

At this level of generality, where externalities in consumption and production are admitted as possibilities, and where commodities may be indivisible, no general characterization of Pareto optima in terms of prices is possible. (Indeed, Pareto optima may not exist. Conditions that make the set of feasible allocations non-empty and compact and preferences continuous suffice to ensure the existence of Pareto optima.) In environments with externalities, or other non-neoclassical features, Pareto optima are generally not attainable by decentralized processes (Hurwicz, 1966).

If the class of environments under consideration is restricted to the neoclassical environments, the fundamental theorems of welfare economics provide a characterization of Pareto optimal states via efficiency prices. That characterization has a natural interpretation in terms of a decentralized mechanism for allocation of resources.

The framework for these results is obtained by restricting the class of environments specified above as follows. The commodity space is to be Euclidean space of l dimensions, i.e. $X = R^l$. The consumption set for the economy is to be the product of its projections, i.e. $X = X^1 \times X^2 \times \ldots \times X^n$. This expresses the fact that if each agent's consumption is feasible for him, the total array is jointly feasible. Furthermore, each agent is restricted to have selfish preferences; that is, agent i's preference relation depends only on the coordinates of the allocation that refer to his holdings. In that case the preference relation $\succsim_i$ may be defined only on X^i, for each i. Similarly, externalities are ruled out in production, i.e. $Y = Y^1 \times Y^2 \times \ldots \times Y^m$.

The concept of an *equilibrium relative to a price system* (Debreu, 1959) serves to characterize Pareto optima by prices. A price system, denoted p, is an element of R^l; the environment $e = [(X^i), (\succsim_i), (Y^j), w]$ is of the restricted type specified above (free of externalities and indivisibilities).

A state $[(x^{*i}), (y^{*i})]$ of e is an *equilibrium relative to price system* p if:

1. For every consumer i, x^{*i} maximizes preference $\succsim_i$ on the set of consumption bundles whose value at the prices p does not exceed the value of x^{*i} at those prices, i.e., if x^i is in $\{x^i \text{ in } X^i : px^i \leqslant px^{*i}\}$ then $x^i \precsim_i x^{*i}$.
2. For every producer j, y^{*j} maximizes profit py^i on Y^j.
3. Aggregate supply and demand balance, i.e.

$$\sum_i x^{*i} - \sum_j y^{*j} = w.$$

An equilibrium relative to a price system differs from a competitive equilibrium (see below) in that the former does not involve the budget constraints applying to consumers in the latter concept. In an equilibrium relative to a price system the distribution of initial endowment and of the profits of firms among consumers need not be specified.

The first theorem of neoclassical welfare economics states, subject only to the exclusion of externalities and a mild condition that excludes preferences with thick indifference sets, that a state of an environment e that is an equilibrium relative to a price system p is a Pareto optimum of e (Koopmans, 1957).

The second welfare theorem is deeper and holds only on a smaller class of environments, sometimes referred to in the literature as the *classical environments* (called neoclassical above). One version of this theorem is as follows. Let $e = [(X^i), (\succsim_i), (Y^i), w]$ be an environment such that for each i

1. X^i is convex.
2. The preference relation $\succsim_i$ is continuous.
3. The preference relation $\succsim_i$ is convex.
4. The set $\Sigma_j Y^j$ is convex.

Let $[(x^{*i}), (y^{*j})]$ be a Pareto optimum of e such that there is at least one consumer who is not satiated at x^{*i}. Then there is a price system p, with not all components equal to 0, such that (except for Arrow's (1951) 'exceptional case', where p is such that for some i the expenditure px^{*i} is a minimum on the consumption set X^i) the state $[(x^{*i}), (y^{*j})]$ is an equilibrium relative to p.

(The condition that preferences are convex and not satiated is sufficient to exclude 'thick' indifference sets. A preference relation on X^i is convex if whenever x' and x'' are points of X^i with x' strictly preferred to x'' then the line segment connecting them (not including the point x'') is strictly preferred to x'. The consumption set X^i must be convex for this property to make sense. A preference relation is not satiated if there is no consumption preferred to all others.)

Hurwicz (1960) has given an alternative formalization of the competitive mechanism in which Arrow's exceptional case presents no difficulties.

If the exceptional case is not excluded, then it can still be said that:

1. x^{*i} minimizes expenditure at prices p on the upper contour set of x^{*i}, for every i, and

2. y^{*j} maximizes 'profit' py^j on the production set Y^j, for every j.

The state (x^*, y^*) together with the prices p, constitute a *valuation equilibrium* (Debreu, 1954).

As in the case of efficiency prices in pure production models, these prices have in themselves no institutional significance. They are, however, in the same way as other efficiency prices, suggestive of an interpretation in terms of decentralization.

If, in addition to the restriction to classical environments, the economic organization is specified to be that of a system of markets in a private ownership economy, and if agents are assumed to take prices as given, then the welfare theorems can translate into the assertion that the set of Pareto optima of an environment e and the set of competitive equilibria for e (subject to the possible redistribution of initial endowment and ownership shares) are identical. More precisely, the specification of the environment given above is augmented by giving each consumer a bundle of commodities, his initial endowment, denoted w^i. The total endowment is $w = \Sigma_i w^i$. Furthermore, each consumer has a claim to a share of the profits of each firm; the claims for the profit of each firm are assumed to add up to the entire profit. When prices and the production decisions of the firms are given, the profits of the firms are determined and so is the value of each consumer's initial endowment. Therefore, the income of each consumer is determined. Hence, the set of commodity bundles a consumer can afford to buy at the given prices, called his *budget set*, is determined; this consists of all bundles in his consumption set whose value at the given prices does not exceed his income at the given prices. Competitive behaviour of consumers means that each consumer treats the prices as given constants and chooses a bundle in his budget set that maximizes his preference; that is, a bundle x^i that is in X^i and such that if any other bundle x'^i is preferred to it, then x'^i is not in his budget set.

Competitive behaviour of firms is to maximize profits computed at the given prices p, regarded by the firms as constants; that is, a firm chooses a production vector y^j in its production set with the property that any other vector affording higher profits than py^i is not in the production set of firm j.

A *competitive equilibrium* is a specification of a commodity bundle for each consumer, a production vector for each firm and a price system, together denoted $[(x^{*i}), (y^{*j}), p^*]$, where p^* has no negative components, satisfying the following conditions:

1. For each consumer i the bundle x^{*i} maximizes preference on the budget set of i;
2. For each firm j the production vector y^{*j} maximizes profit p^*y^j on the production set Y^j;
3. For each commodity, the total consumption does not exceed the net total output of all firms plus the total initial endowment, i.e. $\Sigma_i x^{*i} - \Sigma_j y^{*j} \leqslant w = \Sigma_i w^i$;
4. For those commodities k for which the inequality in 3 is strict; that is, the total consumption is less than initial endowment plus net output, the price p_k^* is zero.

The welfare theorems stated in terms of equilibrium relative to a price system translate directly into theorems stated in terms of competitive equilibrium. Briefly, every competitive equilibrium allocation in a given classical environment is Pareto optimal in that environment, and every Pareto optimal allocation in a given classical environment can be made a competitive equilibrium allocation of an environment that differs from the given one only in the distribution of the initial endowment. (Arrow (1951), Koopmans (1957), Debreu (1959) and Arrow and Hahn (1971) give modern and definitive treatment of the classical welfare theorems.)

It should be noted that the equilibria involved must exist for these theorems to have content. Sufficient conditions for existence of competitive equilibrium, which, since a competitive equilibrium is automatically an equilibrium relative to a price system, are also sufficient for existence of an equilibrium relative to a price system, include convexity and continuity of consumption sets and preferences and of production sets, as well as some assumptions which apply to the environment as a whole, restricting the ways in which individual agents may fit together to form an environment (Arrow and Debreu, 1954; Debreu, 1959; McKenzie, 1959).

The second welfare theorem involves redistribution of initial endowment. This is essential because the set of competitive equilibria from a given initial endowment is small (essentially finite, see Debreu, 1970), while the set of Pareto optima is generally a continuum. The set of Pareto optima cannot in general be generated as competitive allocations without varying the initial point. If redistribution is done by an economic mechanism, then it should be a decentralized one to support the interpretation given of the second welfare theorem. No such mechanism has been put forward as yet. Redistribution of initial endowment by lump-sum taxes and transfers has been discussed. A customary interpretation views these as brought about by a process outside economics, perhaps by a political process; no claim is made that such processes are decentralized. Some economists consider dependence on redistribution unsatisfactory because information about initial endowment is private; only the individual agent knows his own endowment. Consequently the expression of that information through political or other action can be expected to be strategic. The theory of second-best allocations has been proposed in this context. Redistribution of endowment is excluded, and the mechanism is restricted to be a price mechanism, but the price system faced by consumers is allowed to be different from that faced by producers; all agents behave according to the rules of the (static) competitive mechanism. The allocations that satisfy these conditions, when the price systems are variable, are maximal allocations in the sense that they are Pareto optimal within the restricted class just defined. These are so-called *second-best* allocations. This analysis was pioneered by Lipsey and Lancaster (1956) and Diamond and Mirrlees (1971).

EFFICIENT ALLOCATION IN NON(NEO)CLASSICAL ENVIRONMENTS

The term *nonclassical* refers to those environments that fail to have the properties of classical ones; there may be indivisible commodities, nonconvexities in consumption sets, preferences or production sets, or externalities in production or consumption. An example of nonconvex preference would arise if a consumer preferred living in either Los Angeles or New York to living half the time in each city, or living half-way between them, depending on the way the commodity involved is specified. A production set representing a process that affords increasing returns to scale is an example of nonconvexity in production. A large investment project such as a road system is an example of a significant indivisibility. Phenomena of air or water pollution provide many examples of externalities in consumption and production.

The characterization of optimal allocation in terms of prices provided by the classical welfare theorems does not extend to nonclassical environments. If there are indivisibilities, equilibrium prices may fail to exist. Lerner (1934, 1947) has proposed a way of optimally allocating resources in the presence of indivisibilities. It would typically require adding up consumers' and producers' surplus'.

Increasing returns to scale in production generally results in non-existence of competitive equilibrium, because of unbounded profit when prices are treated as given. Nash equilibrium, a concept from the theory of games, can exist even in cases of increasing returns. The difficulty is that such equilibria used need not be optimal. Similar difficulties occur in cases of externalities.

Failure of the competitive price mechanism to extend the properties summarized in the classical welfare theorems to nonclassical environments has led economists to look for alternative ways of achieving optimal allocation in such cases. Such attempts have for the most part sought institutional arrangements that can be shown to result in optimal allocation. Ledyard (1968, 1971) analysed a mechanism for achieving Pareto optimal performance in environments with externalities. The use of taxes and subsidies advocated by Pigou (1932) to achieve Pareto optimal outcomes in cases of externalities is such an example. In a similar spirit Davis and Whinston (1962) distinguish externalities in production that leave marginal costs unaffected from those that do change marginal costs. In the former case they propose a pricing scheme, but one that involves lump-sum transfers. Marginal cost pricing, including lump-sum transfers to compensate for losses, which was extensively discussed as a device to achieve optimal allocation in the presence of increasing returns (Lerner, 1947; Hotelling, 1938; and many others) is another example of a scheme to realize optimal outcomes in nonclassical environments in a way that seeks to capture the benefits associated with decentralized resource allocation. In the case of production under conditions of increasing returns, the use of nonlinear prices has been suggested in an effort to achieve optimality with at least some of the benefits of decentralization. (See Arrow and Hurwicz, 1960; Heal, 1971; Brown and Heal, 1982; Brown, Heal, Khan and Vohra, 1985; Jennergren, 1971; Guesnerie, 1975.)

In the case of indivisibilities, and in the context of productive efficiency, integer programming algorithms exist for finding optima in specific problems, but a general characterization in terms of prices such as exists for the classical environments is not available. A decentralized process, involving the use of randomization, whose equilibria coincide with the set of Pareto optima has been put forward by Hurwicz, Radner and Reiter (1975). This process has the property that the counterparts of the classical welfare theorems hold for environments in which all commodities are indivisible, and the set of feasible allocations is finite, or in which there are no indivisible commodities, or externalities, but there may be nonconvexities in production or consumption sets, or in preferences. This, of course, includes the possibility of increasing returns to scale in production.

The schemes and processes that have been proposed, including many not described here, are quite different from one another. If attention is confined to pricing schemes without additional elements, such as lump-sum transfers, it may be satisfactory to proceed on the basis of an informal intuitive notion of decentralization. This amounts in effect to identifying decentralization with the competitive mechanism, or more generally with price or market mechanisms. If a broader class of processes is to be considered, including some already mentioned in this discussion, then a formal concept of decentralized resource allocation process is needed.

EFFICIENT ALLOCATION THROUGH INFORMATIONALLY DECENTRALIZED PROCESSES

A formal definition of a concept of *allocation process* was first given by Hurwicz (1960). He also gave a definition of *informational decentralization* applying to a broad class of allocation mechanisms, based in part on a discussion by Hayek (1945) of the advantages of the competitive market mechanism for communicating knowledge initially dispersed among economic agents so that it can be brought to bear on the decisions that determine the allocation of resources. Hurwicz's formulation is as follows.

There is an initial dispersion of information about the environment; each agent is assumed to observe directly his own characteristic, e^i, but to know nothing directly about the characteristics of any other agent. In the absence of externalities, specifying the array of individual characteristics specifies the environment, i.e. $e = (e^1, \dots, e^n)$. When there are externalities, an array of individual characteristics, each component of which corresponds to a possible environment, may not together constitute a possible environment. In more technical language, when there are externalities the set of environments is not the Cartesian product of its projections onto the sets of individual characteristics.

The goal of economic activity, whether efficiency, Pareto optimality or some other desideratum such as fairness, can be represented by a relation between the set of environments and the set of allocations, or outcomes. This relation assigns to each environment the set of allocations that meet the criterion of desirability. In the case of the Pareto criterion, the set of allocations that are Pareto optimal in a given environment is assigned to that environment. Formally, this relation is a correspondence (a set-valued function) from the set of environments to the set of allocations.

An allocation process, or mechanism, is modelled as an explicitly dynamic process of communication, leading to the determination of an outcome. In formal organizations standardized forms are frequently used for communication; in organized markets like the Stock Exchange, these include such things as order forms; in a business, forms on which weekly sales are reported; in the case of the Internal Revenue Service, income tax forms. A form consists of entries or blanks to be filled in a specified way. Thus, a form can be regarded as an ordered array of variables whose values come from specified sets. In the Hurwicz model, each agent is assumed to have a *language*, denoted M^i for the ith agent, from which his (possibly multi-dimensional) *message*, m^i, is chosen. The *joint message* of all the agents, $m = (m^1, \dots, m^n)$ is in the *message space* $M = M^1 \times \dots \times M^n$. Communication takes place in time, which is discrete; the message $m_t = (m_t^1, \dots, m_t^n)$ denotes the message at time t. The message an agent emits at time t can depend on anything he knows at that time. This consists of what the agent knows about the environment by direct observation, by assumption (*privacy*), his own characteristics, e^i for agent i, and what he has learned from others via the messages received from them. The agents' behaviour is represented by *response functions*, which show how the current message depends on the information at hand. Agent i's message at time t is

$$m_t^i = f^i(m_{t-1}, m_{t-2}, \dots; e^i), \qquad i = 1, \dots, n, \quad t = 0, 1, 2, \dots$$

If it is assumed that memory is finite, and bounded, it is possible without loss of generality to take the number of past periods remembered to be one. (If memory is unbounded, taking the number of periods remembered to be one excludes the possibility of a finite dimensional message space.) In that case the response equations become a system of first order temporally homogeneous difference equations in the messages. Thus:

$$m_t^i = f_i(m_{t-1}; e^i) \qquad i = 1, \dots, n, \quad t = 0, \dots,$$

which can be written more compactly as

$$(*) \qquad m_t = f(m_{t-1}; e).$$

(This formulation can accommodate the case of directed communication, in which some agents do not receive some messages; if agent i is not to receive the message of j, then f^i is independent of m^j, although m^j appears formally as an argument.) Analysis of informational properties of mechanisms is to begin with separated from that of incentives. When the focus is on communication and complexity questions, the response functions are not regarded as chosen by the agent, but rather by the designer of the mechanism.

The iterative interchange of messages modelled by the difference equation system (*) eventually comes to an end, by converging to a stationary message. (It is also possible to have some stopping rule, such as to stop after a specified number of iterations.) The stationary message, which will be referred to as an *equilibrium message*, is then translated into an outcome, by means of the *outcome function*:

$$h: M \to Z,$$

where Z is the space of outcomes, usually allocations or trades. An allocation mechanism so modelled is called an *adjustment process*; it consists of the triple (M, f, h). Since no production or consumption takes place until all communication is completed, these processes are *tâtonnement* processes.

A more compact and general formulation was given by Mount and Reiter (1974) by looking only at message equilibria when attention is restricted to static properties. A correspondence is defined, called the *equilibrium message correspondence*. It associates to each environment the set of equilibrium messages for that environment. In order to satisfy the requirement of privacy, namely that each agent's message depend on the environment only through the agent's characteristic, the equilibrium message correspondence must be the intersection of individual message correspondences, each associating a set of messages acceptable to the individual agent as equilibria in the light of his own characteristic. Thus the equilibrium message correspondence

$$\mu: E \to M,$$

is given by

$$\mu(e) = \bigcap_i \mu^i(e^i),$$

where $\mu^i: E^i \to M$ is the individual message correspondence of agent i. Note that here the message space M need not be the Cartesian product of individual languages. In the case of an adjustment process, the equilibrium message correspondence is defined by the conditions

$$\mu^i(e^i) = \{m \text{ in } M \mid f^i(m; e^i) = m^i\}, \qquad i = 1, \ldots, n$$

together with the condition that μ is the intersection of the μ^i. Specification of the outcome function $h: M \to Z$ completes the model, (M, μ, h).

The performance of a mechanism of this kind can be characterized by the mapping defined by the composition of the equilibrium message correspondence

μ and the outcome function h. The mapping $h\mu: E \to Z$, possibly a correspondence, specifies the outcomes that the mechanism (M, μ, h) generates in each environment in E. A mechanism, whether in the form of an adjustment process, or in the equilibrium form, is called *Pareto-satisfactory* (Hurwicz, 1960) if for each environment in the class under consideration, the set of outcomes generated by the mechanism coincides with the set of Pareto optimal outcomes for that environment. Allowance must be made for redistribution of initial endowment, as in the case of the second welfare theorem. (A formulation in the framework of mechanisms is given in Mount and Reiter, 1977.)

The competitive mechanism formalized as a static mechanism is as follows. (Hurwicz, 1960, has given a different formulation, and Sonnenschein, 1974, has given an axiomatic characterization of the competitive mechanism from a somewhat different point of view.) The message space M is the space of prices and quantities of commodities going to each agent (it has dimension $n(l-1)$ when there are n agents and l commodities, taking account of budget constraints and Walras' Law), the individual message correspondence μ^i maps agent i's characteristic e^i to the graph of his excess demand function. The equilibrium message is the intersection of the individual ones, and is therefore the price–quantity combinations that solve the system of excess demand equations. The outcome function h is the projection of the equilibrium message onto the quantity components of M. Thus $h\mu(e)$ is a competitive equilibrium allocation (or trade) when the environment is e. The classical welfare theorems state that for each e in E_c, $h[\mu(e)] = P(e)$, where E_c denotes the set of classical environments and P is the Pareto correspondence. (Allowance must be made for redistribution of initial endowment in connection with the second welfare theorem. Explicit treatment of this is omitted to avoid notational complexity. The decentralized redistribution of initial endowment is, as in the case of the second welfare theorem, not addressed.) The welfare theorems can be summarized in the Mount–Reiter diagram (Figure 2; see Reiter, 1977).

The welfare theorems state that this diagram *commutes* in the sense that starting from any environment e in E_c one reaches the same allocations via the mechanism, that is, via $h\mu$, as via the Pareto correspondence P.

With welfare theorems as a guide, the class of environments E_c can be replaced by some other class E, and the Pareto correspondence can be replaced by a

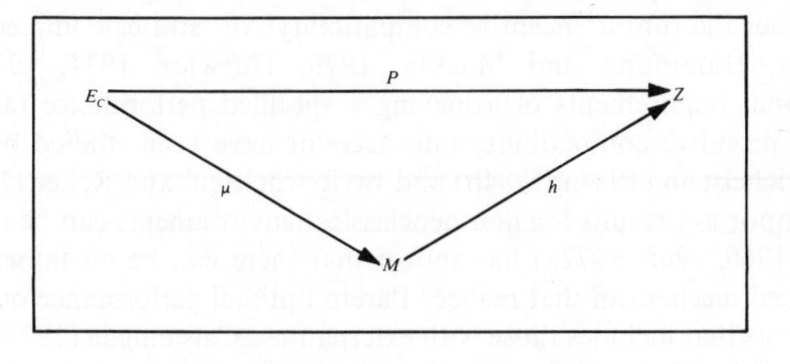

Figure 2

correspondence, P, embodying another criterion of optimality, and one can ask whether there is a mechanism, (M, μ, h) that makes the diagram commute, or, in other words, *realizes* P? Without further restrictions on the mechanism, this is a triviality, because one agent can act as a central agent to whom all others communicate their environmental characteristics; the central agent then has the information required to evaluate P.

The concept of an *informationally decentralized mechanism* defined by Hurwicz (1960) makes explicit intuitive notions underlying the view that the price mechanism is decentralized.

Informationally decentralized processes are a subclass of so-called *concrete processes*, introduced by Hurwicz (1960). These are processes that use a language and response rules that allow production and distribution plans to be specified explicitly. The informationally decentralized processes are those whose response rules permit agents to transmit information only about their own actions, and which in effect require each agent to treat the rest of the economy either as one aggregate, or in a symmetrical way that, like the aggregate, gives anonymity to the other agents.

In the case of static mechanisms, the requirements for informational decentralization boil down to the condition that the message space have no more than a certain finite dimension, and in some cases only that it be of finite dimension. In the case of classical environments this can be seen to include the competitive mechanism, and to exclude the obviously centralized one mentioned above.

Without going deeply into the matter, an objective of this line of research is to analyse explicitly the consequences of constraints on economic organization that come from limitations on the capacity of economic agents to observe, communicate and process information. One important result in this field is that there is no mechanism (M, μ, h) where μ preserves privacy, that uses messages smaller (in dimension) than those of the competitive mechanism (Hurwicz, 1972b; Mount and Reiter, 1974; Walker, 1977; Osana, 1978). Similar results have been obtained for environments with public goods, showing that the Lindahl mechanism uses the minimal message space (Sato, 1981). Another objective is to analyse effects on incentives arising from private motivations in the presence of private information; that is, information held by one agent that is not observable by others, except perhaps at a cost. (There is a large literature on this subject under the rubric 'incentive compatibility', or 'strategic implementation' (Dasgupta, Hammond and Maskin, 1979; Hurwicz, 1971, 1972a). The informational requirements of achieving a specified performance taking some aspects of incentive compatibility into account have been studied by Hurwicz (1976), Reichelstein (1984a, 1984b) and by Reichelstein and Reiter (1985).

Some important results for non-neoclassical environments can be mentioned. Hurwicz (1960, 1966, 1972a) has shown that there can be no informationally decentralized mechanism that realizes Pareto optimal performance on a class of environments that includes those with externalities. Calsamiglia (1977, 1982) has shown in a model of production that if the set of environments includes a sufficiently rich class of those with increasing returns to scale in production, then the dimension of the message space of any mechanism that realizes efficient production cannot be bounded.

EFFICIENT ALLOCATION WITH INFINITELY MANY COMMODITIES

An infinite dimensional commodity space is needed when it is necessary to make infinitely many distinctions among goods and services. This is the case when commodities are distinguished according to time of availability and the time horizon in the model is not bounded or when time is continuous, or according to location when there is more than a finite number of possible locations; differentiated commodities provide other examples, and so does the case of uncertainty with infinitely many states. The bulk of the literature deals with the infinite horizon model of allocation over time, though recently more attention is given to models of product differentiation. Ramsey (1928) studied the problem of saving in a continuous time infinite horizon model with one consumption good and an infinitely lived consumer. He used as the criterion of optimality the infinite sum (integral) of undiscounted utility. Ramsey's contribution was largely ignored, and rediscovered when attention returned to problems of economic growth. A model of maximal sustainable growth based on a linear technology with no unproduced inputs was formulated by von Neumann (1937 in German; English translation, 1945–6). This contribution was unknown among English-speaking economists until after World War II. Study of intertemporal allocation by Anglo-American economists effectively began with the contributions of Harrod (1939) and Domar (1946). These models were concerned with stationary growth at a constant sustainable rate (stationary growth paths) rather than full intertemporal efficiency. Malinvaud (1953) first addressed this problem in a pioneering model of intertemporal allocation with an infinite horizon.

Efficient allocation over (discrete) time would be covered by the finite dimensional models described above if the time horizon were finite. It might be thought that a model with a sufficiently large but still finite horizon would for all practical purposes be equivalent to one with an infinite horizon, while avoiding the difficulties of infinity, but this is not the case, because of the dependence of efficient or optimal allocations on the value given to final stocks, a value that must depend on their uses beyond the horizon.

Malinvaud (1953) formulated an important infinite horizon model, which is the infinite dimensional counterpart of the linear activity analysis model of Koopmans. In Malinvaud's model time is discrete. The time horizon consists of an infinite sequence of time periods. At each date there are finitely many commodities. All commodities are desired in each time period, and no distinction is made between desired, intermediate and primary commodities. As in the activity analysis model, there is no explicit reference to preferences of consumers. Productive efficiency over time is analysed in terms of the output available for consumption, rather than the resulting utility levels.

Technology is represented by a production set X^t for each time period

$t=1,2,\ldots$, an element of X^t being an ordered pair (a^t, b^{t+1}) of commodity bundles where a^t represents inputs to a production process in period t, and b^{t+1} represents the outputs of that process available at the beginning of period $t+1$. Here both a^t and b^{t+1} are non-negative. The set X^t is the aggregate production set for the economy during period t. The net outputs available for consumption are given by

$$y^t = b^t - a^t, \qquad \text{for } t \geqslant 1,$$

where b^1 is the initial endowment of resources available at the beginning of period 1. A *programme* is an infinite sequence $\langle (a^t, b^{t+1}) \rangle$; it is a *feasible programme* if (a^t, b^{t+1}) is in X^t, and $b^t - a^t \geqslant 0$ for each $t \geqslant 1$, given b^1. The sequence $y = \langle y^t \rangle$ is called the *net output programme* associated with the given programme; it is a *feasible net output programme* if it is the net output programme of a feasible programme. A programme is *efficient* if it is (1) feasible and (2) there is no other programme that is feasible, from the same initial resources b^1, and provides at least as much net output in every period and a larger net output in some period. This is the concept of efficient production, already seen in the linear activity analysis model, now extended to an infinite horizon model. The main aim of this research is to extend to the infinite horizon model the characterization of efficient production by prices seen in the finite model. This goal is not quite reached, as is seen in what follows.

The main difficulties presented by the infinite horizon are already present in a special case of the Malinvaud model with one good and no consumers. Let Y be the set of all non-negative sequences $y=(y_t)$ that satisfy $0 \leqslant y_t = f(a_{t-1}) - a_t$ for $t \geqslant 1$, and $0 \leqslant y^0 = b^1 - a^0, b^1 > 0$, where f is a real-valued continuous concave function on the non-negative real numbers (the production function), $f(0)=0$, and b^1 is the given initial stock. The set Y is the set of all feasible programmes. A programme $y' - y > 0$. A price system is an infinite sequence $p = (p^t)$ of non-negative numbers. Denote by P the set of all price systems.

Malinvaud recognized the possibility that an efficient net output programme (y^i) need not have an associated system of non-zero prices (p^t) relative to which the production programme generating y satisfies the condition of intertemporal profit maximization, namely that

$$p^{t+1} f(a^t) - p^t a^t \geqslant p^{t+1} f(a) - p^t a$$

for all t and every $a \geqslant 0$. (Here (a^t) is the sequence of inputs producing y.) A condition introduced by Malinvaud, called *nontightness*, is sufficient for the existence of such nonzero prices. Alternative proofs of Malinvaud's existence theorem were given by Radner (1967) and Peleg and Yaari (1970). (An example showing the possibility of non-existence given by Peleg and Yaari (1970) is as follows. Suppose f is as shown in Figure 3.

At an interior efficient, and therefore value maximizing, programme the first-order necessary conditions for a maximum imply $p^{t+1} f'(a^t) = p^t$. If there is a time at which $a^t = a^*$, in an efficient programme, then, since $f'(a^*) = 0$, it

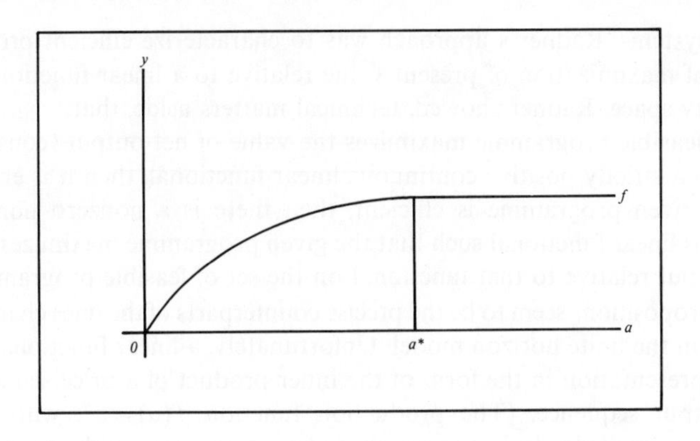

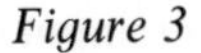
Figure 3

follows that prices at all prior and future times are 0. Nontightness rules out such examples.)

On the side of sufficiency, Malinvaud showed that inter-temporal profit maximization relative to a strictly positive price system p is not enough to ensure that a feasible programme is efficient. An additional (transversality) condition is needed. In the present model the following is such a condition;

$$\lim_{t \to \infty} p^t y^t = 0.$$

Cass (1972) has given a criterion that completely characterizes the set of efficient programmes in a one-good model with strictly concave and smooth production technology that satisfies end-point conditions $0 \leqslant f'(\infty) < 1 < f'(x) < \infty$ for some $x > 0$. Cass's criterion, states that a programme is *inefficient* if and only if the associated competitive prices – that is, satisfying $p^{t+1} f'(a^t) = p^t$ – also satisfy $\Sigma_{t=1}^{\infty} (1/p^t) < \infty$. This criterion may be interpreted as requiring the terms of trade between present and future to deteriorate sufficiently fast. Other similar conditions have been presented (Benveniste and Gale, 1975; Benveniste, 1976; Majumdar, 1974; Mitra, 1979). It is hard to see how any transversality condition can be interpreted in terms of decentralized resource allocation.

An alternate approach to characterizing efficient programmes was taken by Radner (1967), based on value functions as introduced in connection with valuation equilibrium by Debreu (1954). (Valuation equilibrium was discussed in connection with Arrow's exceptional case, above.) The value function approach was followed up by Majumdar (1970, 1972) and by Peleg and Yaari (1970). A price system defines a continuous linear functional, a real-valued linear function, on the commodity space. This function assigns to a programme its present value. The present value may not be well-defined, because the infinite sequence that gives it diverges. This creates certain technical problems passed over here. A more important difficulty is that linear functionals exist that are not defined by price systems. Radner's approach was to characterize efficient programmes in terms of maximization of present value relative to a linear functional on the commodity space. Radner showed, technical matters aside, that:

1. If a feasible programme maximizes the value of net output (consumption) relative to a strictly positive continuous linear functional, then it is efficient.
2. If a given programme is efficient, then there is a nonzero non-negative continuous linear functional such that the given programme maximizes the value of net output relative to that functional on the set of feasible programmes.

These propositions seem to be the precise counterparts of the ones characterizing efficiency in the finite horizon model. Unfortunately, a linear functional may not have a representation in the form of the inner product of a price sequence with a net output sequence. (The production function $f(a)=a^{\beta}$, with $0<\beta<1$ provides an example. It is known that the programme with constant input sequence $x_t=(1/\beta)^{\beta/\beta-1}$ and output sequence $y_t=(1/\beta)^{\beta/\beta-1}-(1/\beta)^{1/\beta-1} t=1,2,\ldots$, is efficient, and therefore there is a continuous linear functional relative to which it is value maximizing. But there is no price sequence (p^t) that represents that linear functional.) This presents a serious problem, because in the absence of such a representation it is unclear whether this characterization has an interpretation in terms of decentralized allocation processes; profit in any one period can depend on 'prices at infinity'.

This approach has the advantage that it is applicable not only to infinite horizon models, but to a broader class in which the commodity space is infinite dimensional. Bewley (1972), Mas-Colell (1977) and Jones (1984) among others discuss Pareto optimality and competitive equilibrium in economies with infinitely many commodities. Hurwicz (1958) and others analysed optimal allocation in terms of nonlinear programming in infinite dimensional spaces. Theorems of programming in infinite dimensional spaces are also used in some of the models mentioned in this discussion.

The basic difficulties encountered in the one-good model, apart from the numerous technical problems that tend to make the literature large and diverse as different technical structures are investigated, are on the one hand the fact that transversality conditions are indispensable, and on the other the possibility that linear functionals, even when they exist, may not be representable in terms of price sequences. These problems raise strong doubt about the possibility of achieving efficient intertemporal resource allocation by decentralized means, though they leave open the possibility that some other decentralized mechanism, not using prices, might work. Analysis of this possibility has just begun, and is discussed below.

The difficulties seen in the one-good production model persist in more elaborate ones, including multisectoral models with efficiency as the criterion, and models with consumers in which Pareto optimality is the criterion. McFadden, Mitra and Majumdar (1980) studied a model in which there are firms, and overlapping generations of consumers, as in the model first investigated by Samuelson (1958). Each consumer lives for a finite time and has a consumption set and preferences like the consumers in a finite horizon model. A model with overlapping generations of consumers presents the fundamental difficulty that consumers cannot trade with future consumers as yet unborn. This difficulty can appear even in a finite horizon model if there are too few markets. The economy is closed in the sense that there are no nonproduced resources; the von Neumann growth model is an example of such a model. Building on the results of an earlier investigation (Majumdar, Mitra and McFadden, 1976), these authors introduced several notions of price systems, of competitive equilibrium, efficiency and optimality, and sought to establish counterparts of the classical welfare theorems. To summarize, in the 1976 paper they strengthen an earlier result of Bose (1974) to the effect that the problem of proper distribution of goods is essentially a short-run problem, and that the only long-run problem, one created by the infinite horizon, is that of inefficiency through overaccumulation of capital. In the 1980 paper the focus is on the relationships among various notions of equilibrium and Pareto optimality. The force of their results is, as might be expected, that the difficulties already seen in the one-good model without consumers persist in this model. A tranversality condition is made part of the definition of competitive equilibrium in order to obtain the result that an equilibrium is optimal. A partial converse requires some additional assumptions on the technology (reachability) and on the way the economy fits together (nondecomposability). These results certainly illuminate the infinite horizon model with overlapping generations of consumers and producers, but the possibility of efficient or optimal resource allocation by decentralized means is not different from that in the one-good Malinvaud model.

Recently, Hurwicz and Majumdar in an unpublished manuscript dated 1983, and later Hurwicz and Weinberger (1984), have addressed this issue directly, building on the approach of mechanism theory.

Hurwicz and Majumdar have studied the problem of efficiency in a model with an infinite number of periods. In each period there are finitely many commodities, one producer who is alive for just one period, and no consumers' choices. The criterion is the maximization of the discounted value of the programme (well-defined in this model). The producer alive in any period knows only the technology in that period. The question is whether there is a (static) privacy preserving mechanism using a finite dimensional message space whose equilibria coincide with the set of efficient programmes. The question can be put as follows. In each period a message is posted. The producer alive in that period responds 'Yes' or 'No'. If every producer over the entire infinite horizon answers 'Yes', the programme is an outcome corresponding to the equilibrium consisting of the infinite succession of posted messages. Since each producer knows only the technology prevailing in the period when he is alive, the process preserves privacy. If in addition the message posted in each period is finite dimensional, the process is informationally decentralized. Period-by-period profit maximization using period-by-period prices is a mechanism of this type; the message posted in each period consists of the vector of prices for that period, and the production plan for that period, both finite dimensional. The object is to characterize all efficient programmes as equilibria of such a mechanism. This would be an analogue of the classical welfare theorems, but without the restriction to mechanisms that use prices in their messages.

The main result is in the nature of an impossibility theorem. If the technology is constant over time, and that fact is common knowledge at the beginning, the problem is trivial since knowledge of the technology in the first period automatically means knowledge of it in every period. On the other hand, if there is some period whose technology is not known in the first period, then there is no finite dimensional message that can characterize efficient programmes, and in that sense, production cannot be satisfactorily decentralized over time.

Hurwicz and Weinberger (1984) have studied a model with both producers and consumers. As with producers, there is a consumer in each period, who lives for one period. The consumer in each period has a one-period utility function, which is not known by the producer; similarly the consumer does not know the production function. The criterion of optimality is the maximization of the sum of discounted utilities over the infinite horizon. Hurwicz and Weinberger show that there is no privacy preserving mechanism of the type just described whose equilibria correspond to the set of optimal programmes. It should be noted that their mechanism requires that the first-period actions (production, consumption and investment decisions) be made in the first period, and not be subject to revision after the infinite process of verification is completed. (On the other hand, under tâtonnement assumptions it may be possible to decentralize. In this model tâtonnement entails reconsideration 'at infinity'.)

If attention is widened to efficient programmes, and if technology is constant over time, there is an efficient programme with a fixed ratio of consumption to investment. This programme can be obtained as the equilibrium outcome of a mechanism of the specified type. However, this corresponds to only one side of the classical welfare theorems. It says that the outcome of such a mechanism is efficient; but it does not ensure that every efficient programme can be realized as the outcome of such a mechanism. The latter property fails in this model.

BIBLIOGRAPHY

Arrow, K. 1951. An extension of the basic theorems of classical welfare economics. In *Proceedings of the Second Berkeley Symposium on Mathematical Statistics and Probability*, ed. J. Neyman, Berkeley: University of California Press.

Arrow, K. and Debreu, G. 1954. Existence of an equilibrium for a competitive economy. *Econometrica* 22, July, 265–90.

Arrow, K. and Hahn, F. 1971. *General Competitive Analysis*. San Francisco: Holden-Day.

Arrow, K. and Hurwicz, L. 1960. Decentralization and computation in resource allocation. In *Essays in Economics and Econometrics*, ed. R.W. Pfouts, Chapel Hill: University of North Carolina Press, 34–104.

Arrow, K., Hurwicz, L. and Uzawa, H. 1961. Constraint qualifications in maximization problems. *Naval Research Logistics Quarterly* 8(2), June, 175–91.

Benveniste, L. 1976. Two notes on the Malinvaud condition for efficiency of infinite horizon programs. *Journal of Economic Theory* 12, 338–46.

Benveniste, L. and Gale, D. 1975. An extension of Cass' characterization of infinite efficient

production programs. *Journal of Economic Theory* 10, 229–38.
Bewley, T. 1972. Existence of equilibria in economies with infinitely many commodities. *Journal of Economic Theory* 4, 514–40.
Bose, A. 1974. Pareto optimality and efficient capital accumulation. Discussion Paper No. 74–4, Department of Economics, University of Rochester.
Brown, D. and Heal, G. 1982. Existence, local-uniqueness and optimality of a marginal cost pricing equilibrium in an economy with increasing returns. Cal. Tech. Social Science Working Paper No. 415.
Brown, D., Heal, G., Ali Khan, M. and Vohra, R. 1985. On a general existence theorem for marginal cost pricing equilibria. Cowles Foundation Working Paper No. 724. Reprinted in *Journal of Economic Theory* 38, 1986, 111–19.
Calsamiglia, X. 1977. Decentralized resource allocation and increasing returns. *Journal of Economic Theory* 14, 263–83.
Calsamiglia, X. 1982. On the size of the message space under non-convexities. *Journal of Mathematical Economics* 10, 197–203.
Cass, D. 1972. On capital over-accumulation in the aggregative neoclassical model of economic growth: a complete characterization. *Journal of Economic Theory* 4(2), April, 200–23.
Dantzig, G.B. 1951a. The programming of interdependent activities. In *Activity Analysis of Production and Allocation*, ed. T. Koopmans, Cowles Commission Monograph No. 13, New York: Wiley, ch. 2, 19–32.
Dantzig, G.B. 1951b. Maximization of a linear function of variables subject to linear inequalities. In *Activity Analysis of Production and Allocation*, ed. T. Koopmans, Cowles Commission Monograph No. 13, New York: Wiley, ch. 21, 339–47.
Dasgupta, P., Hammond, P. and Maskin, E. 1979. The implementation of social choice rules: some general results on incentive compatibility. *Review of Economic Studies* 46, 185–216.
Davis, O.A. and Whinston, A.B. 1962. Externalities welfare and the theory of games. *Journal of Political Economy* 70, 214–62.
Debreu, G. 1954. Valuation equilibrium and Pareto optimum. In *Proceedings of the National Academy of Sciences of the USA* 40(7), 588–92.
Debreu, G. 1959. *Theory of Value*. New York: Wiley.
Debreu, G. 1970. Economies with a finite set of equilibria. *Econometrica* 38(3), May, 387–92.
Diamond, P. and Mirrlees, J. 1971. Optimal taxation and public production. I: Production efficiency; II: Tax rules. *American Economic Review* 61, 8–27; 261–78.
Domar, E. 1946. Capital expansion, rate of growth, and employment. *Econometrica* 14, April, 137–47.
Fenchel, W. 1950. Convex cones, sets, and functions. Princeton University (hectographed).
Guesnerie, R. 1975. Pareto optimality in non-convex economies. *Econometrica* 43, 1–29.
Harrod, R.F. 1939. An essay in dynamic theory. *Economic Journal* 49, 14–33.
Hayek, F. von. 1945. The use of knowledge in society. *American Economic Review* 35, 519–53. Reprinted in F. von Hayek, *Individualism and Economic Order*, Chicago: University of Chicago Press, 1949, 77–92.
Heal, G. 1971. Planning, prices and increasing returns. *Review of Economic Studies* 38, 281–94.
Hotelling, H. 1938. The general welfare in relation to problems of taxation and of railway and utility rates. *Econometrica* 6, 242–69.
Hurwicz, L. 1958. Programming in linear spaces. In *Studies in Linear and Non-Linear*

Programming, ed. K. Arrow, L. Hurwicz and H. Uzawa, Stanford: Stanford University Press.

Hurwicz, L. 1960. Optimality and informational efficiency in resource allocation processes. In *Mathematical Methods in the Social Sciences, 1959*, ed. K.J. Arrow, S. Karlin and P. Suppes, Stanford: Stanford University Press.

Hurwicz, L. 1971. Centralization and decentralization in economic processes. In *Comparison of Economic Systems: Theoretical and Methodological Approaches*, ed. A. Eckstein, Berkeley: University of California Press, ch. 3.

Hurwicz, L. 1972a. On informationally decentralized systems. In *Decision and Organization*, ed. C. McGuire and R. Radner, Amsterdam, London: North-Holland, ch. 14, 297–336.

Hurwicz, L. 1972b. On the dimensional requirements of informationally decentralized Pareto-satisfactory processes. Presented at the Conference Seminar in Decentralization, Northwestern University. In *Studies in Resource Allocation Processes*, ed. K.J. Arrow and L. Hurwicz, Cambridge and New York: Cambridge University Press, 1977.

Hurwicz, L. 1976. On informational requirements for nonwasteful resource allocation systems. In *Mathematical Models in Econometrics: Papers and Proceedings of a US–USSR Seminar, Moscow*, ed. S. Shulman, New York: National Bureau of Economic Research.

Hurwicz, L., Radner, R. and Reiter, S. 1975. A stochastic decentralized resource allocation process. *Econometrica* 43: Part I, 187–221; Part II, 363–93.

Hurwicz, L. and Weinberger, H. 1984. Paper presented at IMA seminar in Minneapolis.

Jennergren, L. 1971. Studies in the mathematical theory of decentralized resource-allocation. PhD dissertation, Stanford University.

Jones, L. 1984. A competitive model of commodity differentiation. *Econometrica* 52, 507–30.

Kantorovitch, L. 1939. *Matematicheskie metody organizatii i planirovania proizvodstva* (Mathematical methods in the organization and planning of production). Izdanie Leningradskogo Gosudarstvennogo Universiteta, Leningrad. Trans. in *Management Science* 6(4), July 1960, 363–422.

Kantorovitch, L. 1942. On the translocation of masses. (In English.) *Comptes Rendus (Doklady) de l'Academie des Sciences d l'URSS* 37(7–8).

Kantorovitch, L. and Gavurin, M. 1949. Primenenie matematicheskikh metodov v voprosakh analyza grusopotokov (The application of mathematical methods to problems of freight flow analysis). In *Problemy Povysheniia Effektivnosty Raboty Transporta* (Problems of raising the efficiency of transportation), ed. V. Zvonkov, Moscow and Leningrad: Izdatel'stvo Akademii Nauk SSSR.

Koopmans, T.C. 1951a. Analysis of production as an efficient combination of activities. In *Activity Analysis of Production and Allocation*, ed. T. Koopmans, Cowles Commission Monograph No. 13, New York: Wiley, ch. 3, 33–97.

Koopmans, T.C. 1951b. Efficient allocation of resources. *Econometrica* 19, 455–65.

Koopmans, T.C. 1957. *Three Essays on the State of Economic Science*. New York: McGraw-Hill, 66–104.

Kuhn, H. and Tucker, A. 1951. Nonlinear programming. In *Proceedings of the Second Berkeley Symposium on Mathematical Statistics and Probability*, ed. J. Neyman, Berkeley: University of California Press, 481–92.

Ledyard, J. 1968. Resource allocation in unselfish environments. *American Economic Review* 58, 227–37.

Ledyard, J. 1971. A convergent Pareto-satisfactory non-tâtonnement adjustment process for a class of unselfish exchange environments. *Econometrica* 39, 467–99.

Lerner, A. 1934. The concept of monopoly and measurement of monopoly power. *Review*

of Economic Studies 1(3), June, 157–75.
Lerner, A. 1944. *The Economics of Control*. New York: Macmillan.
Lipsey, R. and Lancaster, K. 1956. The general theory of second best. *Review of Economic Studies* 24, 11–32.
McFadden, D., Mitra, T. and Majumdar, M. 1980. Pareto optimality and competitive equilibrium in infinite horizon economies. *Journal of Mathematical Economics* 7, 1–26.
McKenzie, L. 1959. On the existence of general equilibrium for a competitive market. *Econometrica* 27(1), January, 54–71.
Majumdar, M. 1970. Some approximation theorems on efficiency prices for infinite programs. *Journal of Economic Theory* 2, 399–410.
Majumdar, M. 1972. Some general theorems of efficiency prices with an infinite dimensional commodity space. *Journal of Economic Theory* 5, 1–13.
Majumdar, M. 1974. Efficient programs in infinite dimensional spaces: a complete characterization. *Journal of Economic Theory* 7, 355–69.
Majumdar, M., Mitra, T. and McFadden, D. 1976. On efficiency and Pareto optimality of competitive programs in cooled multisector models. *Journal of Economic Theory* 13, 26–46.
Malinvaud, E. 1953. Capital accumulation and efficient allocation of resources. *Econometrica* 21, 233–68.
Mas-Colell, A. 1977. Regular nonconvex economies. *Econometrica* 45, 1387–407.
Mitra, T. 1979. On optimal economic growth with variable discount rates: existence and stability results. *International Economic Review* 20, 133–45.
Mount, K. and Reiter, S. 1974. The informational size of message spaces. *Journal of Economic Theory* 8, 161–92.
Mount, K. and Reiter, S. 1977. Economic environments for which there are Pareto satisfactory mechanisms. *Econometrica* 45, 821–42.
Nikaido, H. 1969. *Convex Structures and Economic Theory*. New York: Academic Press.
Nikaido, H. 1970. *Introduction to Sets and Mappings in Modern Economics*. Trans. K. Sato, Amsterdam: North-Holland (Japanese original, Tokyo, 1960).
Osana, H. 1978. On the informational size of message spaces for resource allocation processes. *Journal of Economic Theory* 17, 66–78.
Peleg, B. and Yaari, M. 1970. Efficiency prices in an infinite dimensional commodity space. *Journal of Economic Theory* 2, 41–85.
Pigou, A. 1932. *The Economics of Welfare*. 4th edn, London: Macmillan; New York: St. Martin's Press, 1952.
Radner, R. 1967. Efficiency prices for infinite horizon production programs. *Review of Economic Studies* 34, 51–66.
Ramsey, F. 1928. A mathematical theory of saving. *Economic Journal* 38, 543–59.
Reichelstein, S. 1984a. Dominant strategy implementation, incentive compatibility and informational requirements. *Journal of Economic Theory* 34(1), October, 32–51.
Reichelstein, S. 1984b. Information and incentives in economic organizations. PhD dissertation, Northwestern University.
Reichelstein, S. and Reiter, S. 1985. Game forms with minimal strategy spaces. Discussion Paper No. 663, The Center for Mathematical Studies in Economics and Management Science, Northwestern University, Evanston, Ill.
Reiter, S. 1977. Information and performance in the (new)^2 welfare economics. *American Economic Review* 67, 226–34.
Samuelson, P. 1947. *Foundations of Economic Analysis*. Cambridge, Mass.: Harvard University Press.

Samuelson, P. 1949. Market mechanisms and maximization, I, II, III. Hectographed memoranda, The RAND Corporation, Santa Monica.
Samuelson, P. 1958. An exact consumption-loan model of interest with or without the social contrivance of money. *Journal of Political Economy* 66, December, 467–82.
Sato, F. 1981. On the informational size of message spaces for resource allocation processes in economies with public goods. *Journal of Economic Theory* 24, 48–69.
Slater, M. 1950. Lagrange multipliers revisited: a contribution to non-linear programming. *Cowles Commission Discussion Paper*, Math. 403, also RM-676, 1951.
Sonnenschein, H. 1974. An axiomatic characterization of the price mechanism. *Econometrica* 42, 425–34.
Uzawa, H. 1958. The Kuhn–Tucker Theorem in concave programming. In *Studies in Linear and Non-Linear Programming*, ed. K. Arrow, L. Hurwicz and H. Uzawa, Stanford: Stanford University Press.
Von Neumann, J. 1937. A model of general economic equilibrium. *Ergebnisse eines mathematischen Kolloquiums*, No. 8. Trans. from German, *Review of Economic Studies* 13(1), (1945–6), 1–9.
Walker, M. 1977. On the informational size of message spaces. *Journal of Economic Theory* 15, 366–75.

Adverse Selection

CHARLES WILSON

Consider a market in which products of varying quality are exchanged. Both buyers and sellers rank products of different quality in the same way, but only the sellers can observe the quality of each unit of the good they sell. Buyers can observe at most the *distribution* of the quality of the goods previously sold. Without some device for the buyers to identify good products, bad products will always be sold with the good products. Such a market illustrates the problem of *adverse selection.*

Economists have long recognized that the problem of adverse selection can interfere with the effective operation of a market. However, the modern theoretical treatment of the problem began with a paper by George Akerlof, 'The Market for Lemons' (1970). As the title suggests, he considered a stylized market for used cars. The set of cars is indexed by a quality parameter q uniformly distributed between 0 and 1. For a car of quality q, he assumed that the reservation value of a buyer is $(3/2)q$ while the reservation value for a seller is just q. He then addressed the problem of determining the market price and the volume of trade in a situation where the number of potential buyers exceeds the number of sellers.

If both sides can observe the quality of cars in such a market, efficiency requires that all cars be exchanged and, if the market is competitive, cars of quality q are exchanged at a price of $(3/2)q$. Akerlof assumed, however, that buyers can observe only the *average* quality of a car for sale at any price p. Since, in this case, any seller with a car of quality p or less offers the car for sale, the average quality of the cars for sale at any price p is equal to $q/2$. Given this relation between price and average quality, buyers value any car offered for sale at only $(3/4)p$. Consequently, the only market clearing price is 0 with no transactions occurring at all.

Akerlof's example presents the most extreme consequence of the problem of adverse selection. In general, not all trade is eliminated. Nevertheless, the market allocation is almost always inefficient. Briefly, the reason is as follows. Since sellers offer any good for exchange whose value is less than the price, the value to the sellers of the *average* product offered for sale is generally lower than the price. In contrast, the uninformed buyers purchase the product to the point where the value to them of the average product offered for sale is equal to the price. Consequently, in any Walrasian equilibrium, the value of the *marginal* car to the buyer exceeds its value to the seller. Furthermore, all buyers purchase from the same pool of products. To the extent that some buyers are willing to pay more for products of higher quality, a second source of inefficiency results.

Akerlof's analysis was generalized by Wilson (1980). He showed that when the buyers have heterogeneous preferences, there may be multiple Walrasian equilibria which can be ranked by the Pareto criterion. His argument is based on the following observation. If the average quality of the goods offered for sale increases sufficiently with the price, some buyers may actually prefer to buy at higher prices. Consequently, even in the absence of income effects, the demand curve may be upward sloping over some range of prices. If the demand and supply curves intersect more than once, multiple Walrasian equilibria result. Furthermore, since the supply curve must be upward sloping, demand must also be higher at higher equilibrium prices. It then follows by revealed preference that some buyers must also be better off at these prices. In fact, if the buyers have a constant marginal rate of substitution between the quality of the car and the consumption of other goods, Wilson showed that every buyer prefers a higher equilibrium price to a lower equilibrium price. Since sellers always prefer to sell at a higher price, it follows immediately that higher equilibrium prices are Pareto superior to lower equilibrium prices. It is also possible to construct examples where a price floor is Pareto superior to any equilibrium price even if the excess supply is rationed at random.

Based on these observations Wilson went on to argue that, in the presence of adverse selection, market forces may not lead to a single price. In fact, the nature of the equilibrium will generally depend on the nature of the institution or convention used to set the price. Akerlof's analysis implicitly assumed some kind of Walrasian mechanism. That is, in equilibrium all goods are exchanged at a single price which clears the market. Suppose instead, that each buyer must announce a price and then wait for offers. Then, if any buyer prefers a price which is higher than the Walrasian price, an equilibrium may result with excess supply which must be rationed. To increase the average quality of the product, sellers may prefer a price which is so high that supply exceeds demand, so that some suppliers are unable to sell their product.

This idea has been used by Stiglitz and Weiss (1981) to explain credit rationing. They considered a competitive banking system in which the supply of loanable funds is an increasing function of the deposit rate. Each borrower requires the same amount of funds and is indistinguishable to the banks from any other borrower. However, because of the possibility of default, borrowers differ in the expected return banks will earn at any given interest rate. In this model the banks assume the role of the uninformed buyers in Akerlof's used car example and the borrowers assume the role of the informed sellers. Stiglitz and Weiss then demonstrated that for a robust class of parameters, the market equilibrium implies an excess demand for loans.

I will illustrate their argument with a simple example. Suppose there are two types of borrowers. Both types use funds B to finance an investment project with the same expected return. Each of the n low risk borrowers earn a zero return with probability 1/2 and a return 2B with probability 1/2. Each of the n high risk borrowers earn a zero return with probability 3/4 and a return 4B with probability 1/4. In order to borrow the funds, banks require that firms put up collateral $C = B/2$. Then, at any (gross) interest rate r, a borrower repays the loan only if his return exceeds $[r-(1/2)B]$. Otherwise, he defaults and the bank collects whatever the firm earns plus the collateral.

Now consider the demand curve for loans. So long as this expected return exceeds the interest rate, a borrower will stay in the market. However, because of the differences in their distributions, the two types have different reservation values. Low risk borrowers earn non-negative profits only when $r \leqslant 3/2$, while high risk borrowers earn non-negative profits so long as $r \leqslant 5/2$. Consequently, the demand for loans is $2n$B for $0 < r \leqslant 3/2$, nB for $3/2 < r \leqslant 5/2$, and 0 for $r > 5/2$.

Finally, consider the supply of loanable funds. Since a bank is equally likely to lend to either a low or a high risk borrower when $r \leqslant 3/2$, for $0 < r \leqslant 3/2$, the expected (gross) rate of return to a bank is $[3r + (5/2)]/8$. For $3/2 \leqslant r \leqslant 5/2$, only the high risk borrowers are serviced, resulting in an expected rate of return $[2r + 3]/8$. Now suppose that the level of loans supplied by banks is $(16/13)n$B times the gross rate of return. Then we obtain a 'supply' curve of $n(16/13)$B$[3r + (5/2)]/8$ for $r \leqslant 3/2$ and $n(16/13)$B$[2r + 3]/8$ for $3/2 < r \leqslant 5/2$. Note that this supply curve is upward sloping everywhere except at $r = 3/2$ at which point it falls discontinuously from $n(14/13)$B to $n(12/13)$B. Consequently, 'supply' is equal to demand at loan rate $r = 7/4$. At this loan rate, only high risk borrowers demand loans and the average rate of return to each bank is 13/16.

Although an interest rate of 7/4 clears the market, this is not the outcome we would expect if profit-maximizing banks could set their own interest rates, even in a competitive market. Since the interest rate is above 3/2, the least risky borrowers have dropped out of the market. Consequently, by lowering the interest rate to 3/2 and attracting the low risk borrowers, it is possible for a bank to raise its expected rate of return even though it earns a lower rate of return on each high risk borrower. In this example, any bank which lowers its interest rate to 3/2 and attracts an equal number of both types of consumers will increase its expected rate of return to 7/8. Since every borrower prefers the lower interest rate, the higher 'market clearing' rate is not sustainable. The result is an equilibrium rate of return with an excess demand for loans.

In his *Bell Journal* paper, Wilson suggested that a different equilibrium might emerge if the informed agents were the price setters. Refer back to the used car example. If it is easy to show that the higher the reservation value of the seller, the smaller is the decrease in price he is willing to accept in order to increase his chances of finding a buyer. This observation suggests that it may be possible to sustain an equilibrium with a distribution of prices. Sellers of high-quality products announce high prices which attract only a few buyers. Sellers of low-quality products announce low prices which attract more buyers. Buyers are willing to purchase at both prices because the quality of the cars offered increases with the price. The quality of cars increases with the price because more buyers purchase at low prices than at high prices. This tradeoff between price and the probability of selling has also been exploited by Samuelson (1984) and others in the design of optimal mechanisms for allocating goods in environments with adverse selection.

Both of the non-Walrasian equilibria discussed above are the consequence of individual agents trying to exploit the relation between quality and price to avoid the problem of adverse selection. Indeed, the study of how agents try to compensate for the problems of adverse selection makes up a large part of the literature on markets with imperfect information. One of the most important ideas to come out of this line of research is the concept of market signalling first investigated by Michael Spence (1973). The idea is that sellers of higher-quality products will try to reveal themselves by undertaking some activity which is less costly to them than to sellers with lower-quality products. In his example, more productive workers signal their productivity by purchasing education. In product markets, firms use guarantees to signal product reliability. In credit markets, lenders use collateral to signal credit worthiness (Bester, 1984).

BIBLIOGRAPHY

Akerlof, G. 1970. The market for lemons. *Quarterly Journal of Economics* 84(3), August, 488–500.

Bester, H. 1984. Screening versus rationing in credit markets with imperfect information. University of Bonn Discussion Paper No. 136, May.

Samuelson, W. 1984. Bargaining under asymmetric information. *Econometrica* 52(4), July, 995–1005.

Spence, M. 1973. Job market signalling. *Quarterly Journal of Economics* 87(3), August, 355–74.

Stiglitz, J. and Weiss, A. 1981. Credit rationing in markets with imperfect information. *American Economic Review* 71, June, 393–410.

Wilson, C. 1980. The nature of equilibrium in markets with adverse selection. *Bell Journal of Economics* 11, Spring, 108–30.

Asymmetric Information

A. POSTLEWAITE

The Arrow–Debreu model is the basic model in which the two classical welfare theorems of economics are expressed. Under quite general assumptions, it can be shown that, first, a competitive equilibrium allocation, or Walrasian allocation, is Pareto efficient (Pareto optimal); second, under somewhat different assumptions, any Pareto efficient allocation will be a competitive equilibrium allocation after some suitable redistribution of initial endowments. Implicitly or explicitly, the statement of the first welfare theorem assumes that all economic agents have the same information about all economic variables. This is not to say that uncertainty is ruled out; there may be uncertainty as long as all agents are identically uncertain. If this assumption of symmetric information is violated, the competitive outcome will no longer be guaranteed to be Pareto efficient. The introduction of asymmetric information into various economic problems has given us new insight into how market failures might arise and whether there may be governmental, or other non-market, corrections which can improve welfare. Several examples illustrating this are given below.

There may be a good which can vary in quality and whose quality will be known only by the owner. As an example, one can think of the objects being sold as used cars. Potential buyers will realize that there are good and bad quality cars and will rationally pay a price based on the average quality. This means that some cars will be underpriced (the highest quality cars), but which ones will be known only to the owner. Some underpriced cars may be so much underpriced that the owners will not be willing to sell them at the price based on the average quality. But the withdrawal of these quality cars causes the average quality of the cars in the market to decrease and consequently, potential buyers will rationally lower the price they are willing to pay for a car randomly drawn from those remaining. This in turn may lead to another round of withdrawal of some of the better remaining cars and a further lowering of the price buyers will pay. In the extreme, the equilibrium of this process may have no cars sold even in the case that all would have been sold had the quality of goods been symmetrically known, that is, when either everyone or no one could determine the quality. This problem is essentially that analysed by Akerlof (1970).

Asymmetric information has been introduced into a labour-management model to illustrate how it may distort the optimal labour contract. Assume that the demand function facing the firm is known to the firm but not to the workers. An optimal contract would generally be characterized by a constant labour force and a variable wage, lower wages being associated with lower levels of demand. This may not be feasible given the asymmetry, however. The firm would announce that the state of demand is low regardless of the truth since this lowers its wage bill without cost. The optimal contract with the asymmetry will typically involve a lower amount of labour employed when the firm announces that demand is low. Since this is more costly when demand is high (and the marginal revenue product of an additional hour is high), than when demand is low, optimal contracts in the presence of this sort of asymmetric information often take this form. Rosen (1985) surveys the literature on this problem.

A third area in which asymmetric information has been successfully introduced into traditional economic problems is that of industrial organization. As an example, it can be assumed that there are several firms within an industry and that each may know more about its own cost structure than about its competitor's (or potential competitor's). Equilibria in such models conform better to what is generally believed to be involved in predatory pricing and limit pricing than equilibria in models without asymmetric information. (Examples of such arguments can be found in Milgrom and Roberts, 1982a, 1982b.) It has also been shown that if small amounts of asymmetric information are introduced into the finitely played prisoners' dilemma game and into the chain store paradox, the paradoxes associated with these games disappear (see, e.g., Kreps et al., 1982).

In public economics, models have been investigated in which individuals know their own valuation for public goods but know nothing about other individuals' valuations. These models provide explanations of how and why governments may want to provide public goods. These explanations improve upon the explanations provided by models without asymmetric information; in addition, they provide a clearer understanding of the nature of the improvement in welfare that a government can effect. (Bliss and Nalebuff (1984) give an insight into the problem of public goods with asymmetric information.)

The above examples focus on positive models which encompass asymmetric information. That is, they provide models which depend upon asymmetries in information to explain phenomena which are generally believed, but which are difficult to reconcile with optimizing behaviour in the absence of such asymmetries. There is extensive use of asymmetric information in normative models as well. We may want to devise governmental or non-governmental mechanisms to augment, alter or replace markets; if so, we presumably want to do so in an 'optimal' manner, whatever notion of optimality we may want to rely on. To the extent that there is asymmetry among the agents in the economy in question, we must be able to predict the outcome after our augmentation, alteration or replacement in the face of this asymmetry. This approach has been used extensively in optimal taxation. Suppose one feels that a given amount of tax revenue must be raised and that it is fairest to raise more revenue from those who are most able (most productive). If the ability of an agent is known to himself but not to anyone else, this asymmetry of information has to be taken into account. We must maximize social welfare subject to the constraint that it must be in the individuals' interest to reveal, indirectly or directly, these privately known abilities. In this manner, it is possible to derive characteristics of an optimal tax schedule under asymmetric information. In a similar manner we can determine the qualitative characteristics of other types of taxes to be levied in environments with asymmetric information. Atkinson and Stiglitz (1980) is an excellent reference to the literature in this area.

Similar normative models have been used to investigate the nature of optimal policy for many problems such as regulatory policy, anti-trust policy, monetary policy and other problems in which asymmetric information may play a role.

The common technique in analysing both normative and positive problems with asymmetric information is to model them as games with incomplete information and to use the Bayesian–Nash solution concept. This captures both the asymmetric information and the problems raised by economic agents sometimes having incentives to misrepresent the information they have. This modelling technique is not wholly satisfactory, however. Embedded in the technique is the assumption that the information structure is common knowledge. This is an assumption that while an agent may not know the exact information that another agent has, he knows the probability distribution of the information. Further, the second agent knows that the first knows this, the first knows that the second agent knows that he knows, and so on ad infinitum. The assumption that the information structure is common knowledge is extremely strong and the results of models using the assumption are correspondingly less convincing. Myerson (1979) is the standard reference here.

Much of the use of asymmetric information in economic models was motivated by a desire to understand seeming (Pareto) inefficiencies in particular market situations. The integration of asymmetric information into economic models accomplished this. In addition, the formalization of the asymmetry in the information among agents helped to clarify the notion of welfare in such circumstances as well. The question of whether or not a change from one allocation to another might make all agents better off is unambiguous in the case that there there is no uncertainty. With uncertainty which is identical for all agents, it is also simple; each agent makes the comparison between the two allocations by taking the expected utility of the allocations using the commonly accepted probability distribution. When each agent has different information the problem becomes more complicated. Some agents may know that certain events cannot happen while others may not know this. What probabilities should be used to calculate an agent's expected utility – his own beliefs, those of the best informed agent, the totality of the information held by all agents or some entirely different probability? Holmstrom and Myerson (1983) provide a careful analysis of welfare judgements in the face of asymmetric information.

The introduction of asymmetric information into models in which agents behave strategically made it necessary to consider not only what agents knew, but what they thought other agents knew, what they thought other agents knew about what they knew and so forth. Addressing this directly resolved many of the dilemmas posed by welfare comparisons in an environment with asymmetric information.

BIBLIOGRAPHY

Akerlof, G. 1970. The market for lemons. *Quarterly Journal of Economics*, August, 488–500.

Atkinson, A. and Stiglitz, J. 1980. *Lectures on Public Economics*. New York: McGraw-Hill.

Bliss, C. and Nalebuff, B. 1984. Dragon-slaying and ballroom dancing: the private supply of a public good. *Journal of Public Economics* 25, August, 1–12.

Hölmstrom, B. and Myerson, R. 1983. Efficient and durable decision rules with incomplete information. *Econometrica* 51, November, 1799–1820.

Kreps, D., Milgrom, P., Roberts, J. and Wilson, R. 1982. Rational cooperation in the finitely repeated prisoners' dilemma. *Journal of Economic Theory* 27, August, 245–52.

Milgrom, P. and Roberts, J. 1982a. Predation, reputation, and entry deterrence. *Journal of Economic Theory* 27, August, 280–312.

Milgrom, P. and Roberts, J. 1982b. Limit pricing and entry under incomplete information: an equilibrium analysis. *Econometrica* 50, 443–59.

Myerson, R. 1979. Incentive compatibility and the bargaining problem. *Econometrica* 47, 61–74.

Rosen, S. 1985. Implicit contracts: a survey. *Journal of Economic Literature* 23, September, 1144–75.

Auctions

VERNON L. SMITH

Herodotus reports the use of auctions as early as 500 BC in Babylon (see Cassady, 1967, pp. 26–40 for references to this and the following historical notes). The Romans made extensive use of auctions in commerce and the Roman emperors Caligula and Aurelius auctioned royal furniture and heirlooms to pay debts. Roman military expeditions were accompanied by traders who bid for the spoils of war auctioned *sub hasta* (under the spear) by soldiers. In AD 193 the Praetorian Guard seized the crown from the emperor Pertinax and auctioned it to the highest bidder, Didius, who, upon paying each guardsman the winning bid, 6250 drachmas, was declared emperor of Rome. It would appear that the Romans used the 'English' progressive method of auctioning, since the word auction is derived from the Latin root *auctus* (an increase).

TYPES OF AUCTION INSTITUTIONS

Auctions may be for a single object or unit, as in the unique object auctioning of paintings and antiques at Sotheby's and Christie's in London, or a lot or package of non-identical items, as in the family groups sold in the slave auctions of the antebellum South. Alternatively, auctions may be for multiple units where many units of a homogeneous standardized good are to be sold, such as gold bullion in the auctions conducted by the International Monetary Fund and the US Treasury in the 1970s, and in the weekly auctioning of 91-day and 182-day securities by the Treasury.

Auctions may also be classified according to the different institutional rules governing the exchange. Since the seminal work of Vickrey (1961), it has been recognized that these rules are important because they can affect bidding incentives, and therefore the terms and the efficiency of an exchange. The literature (Cassady, 1967; Arthur, 1976) has identified many different auction institutions throughout the world, but, following Vickrey (1961), it has become standard to distinguish four primary types of auctions which can be used either in single object or multiple (identical or non-identical) unit auctions.

English Auction. The auction customarily begins with the auctioneer soliciting a first bid for the object from the crowd of would-be buyers, or (where permitted by the auction house rules) announcing the seller's reservation price. Any bid, once recognized by the auctioneer, becomes the standing bid which cannot be withdrawn. Any new bid is admissible if and only if it is higher than the standing bid. The auction ends when the auctioneer is unable to call forth a new higher bid, and the item is 'knocked down' to the last (and highest) bidder at a price equal to the amount bid.

Where multiple units of identical, or nearly identical (close substitute), items are sold by one or more sellers at English auction, individual lots or units are put up for sale in some sequence with each lot or unit sold as a single object. Examples include livestock in the United States and wool in Australia. When there are Q strictly identical items to be sold in a progressive auction, the following alternative procedure has been suggested: '... the items are auctioned simultaneously, with up to (Q) bids permitted at any given level, the rule being that once (Q) bids have been made equal to the highest bid, any further bid must be higher than this' (Vickrey, 1976, p. 14).

Dutch Auctions. Under this procedure, originally called 'mineing', the price begins at some level thought to be somewhat higher than any buyer is willing to pay, and the auctioneer decreases the price in decrements until the first buyer accepts by shouting 'mine'. The item is then awarded to that buyer at the price accepted. Many years ago this procedure was automated by an electrical clock mechanism which is used widely in Holland for the sale of produce and cut flowers. The clock is normally located in a large amphitheatre (Cassady, 1967, p. 194) with buyers sitting at desks facing the clock. An indicator hand on the clock decreases counterclockwise through a series of descending prices. Any buyer can stop the indicator hand by pressing a button when the descending indicated price is acceptable.

The descending offer procedure is used in the sale of fish in England and Israel, in the sale of tobacco in Canada, and a variant of the procedure is used regularly to mark down clothing in Filene's department store in Boston. When the descending offer procedure is applied to multiple units, the first bidder exercises his option to take part of the quantity offered. The offer price then continues its descent until the next bidder accepts and so on. Thus in fish markets in British ports, the auctioneer accepts 'book' bids for specified quantities. If the offer price reached this level before anyone accepts from the floor, the book bid is filled with any remaining quantity offered at descending prices to the crowd.

First Price Auction. This is the common form of 'sealed' or written bid auction, in which the highest bidder is awarded the item at a price equal to the amount bid. The multiple unit generalization of this procedure is called a *discriminative* auction. Thus if Q identical units are offered, the highest bids for the first Q units are all accepted at the prices and quantities stated in the bids tendered. The weekly primary auction of new short-term US. Treasury securities has used this institution for about fifty years.

Second Price Auction. This is a sealed bid auction in which the highest bidder is awarded the item at a price equal to the bid of the second highest bidder. The procedure is not common although it is used in stamp auctions. For example, the London stamp auction uses English oral bidding, but buyers not present may submit written 'book' bids. An award to a book bidder is made at one price interval or unit above the floor bid, or the second highest book bid, whichever is the largest. If the auctioneer has two book bids he starts the bidding at a unit interval above the second highest of the book bids. If the bid is not raised on the floor he declares it sold to the highest book bidder at this (approximately) second highest bid price.

The multiple unit extension of the second price sealed bid auction is called a *competitive* (or uniform price auction). Under this procedure if Q identical units of a good are offered, the highest bids for the first Q units are all accepted at one market clearing price equal to the bid for $Q+1$st unit. The procedure was used experimentally by the US Treasury in the 1970s to sell long-term bonds, and in one gold bullion sale. Exxon Corporation has sold bonds (usually to registered brokers and dealers) by this method on several occasions since the US Treasury experiments. Since 1978 Citicorp has been auctioning commercial paper weekly using the method, but the institution has not found general acceptance. These auctions are referred to as 'Dutch' auctions in the financial trade literature, but this is a misnomer because the long established 'mineing' procedure, known as the Dutch auction, follows a discriminative, not a uniform, multiple unit pricing procedure.

Tâtonnement. A summary of auction institutions should not omit some comment on the Walrasian *tâtonnement* hypothesis, which has long served the need of equilibrium price theory for a path independent process that precludes contracting at non-equilibrium prices. It appears that the only naturally occurring organized markets using a procedure similar to a Walrasian *tâtonnement* are the gold and silver bullion price 'fixing', or determining, markets (Jarecki, 1976). In the London Gold Market, representatives of the dealers in this market meet twice daily, and establish a price as follows: the chairman of the meeting begins with an initial starting price, and each representative indicates whether he is a seller, a buyer or neither at that price. Each dealer has orders from clients all over the world. To be a buyer means that at the trial price the volume of his client's buy orders exceeds the volume of the sell orders. If at the starting price there are no sellers, the price is raised by varying amounts until one or more of the traders indicates that he is a seller at the standing price. Similarly, the price is moved down if there are no buyers at the starting price. At this juncture the chairman asks for 'figures'; i.e. for the net quantites each trader wishes to buy or sell. If the total indicated purchase quantity does not match the quantity offered by the traders the price is further adjusted until a match occurs. This Walrasian market also has a unanimity stopping rule. Each trader has a small Union Jack in front of him. When a trader is satisfied with the standing price, and has no further orders that require price adjustment, he puts the flag down. The chairman announces that the price is 'fixed' if and only if all flags are down.

THEORY OF AUCTIONS

The following analysis of auctions will adopt five principal assumptions: (1) Each bidder desires to purchase a single unit of the commodity. (2) Buyer i associates a cash value, v_i, with the item which represents i's maximum willingness to pay. In some auctions, notably the English institution, v_i can be interpreted as the cash equivalent of an uncertain item value. (3) The value v_i to i is independent of the value, v_j, to any j; i.e. v_i would not change if i had knowledge of v_j for all i and j. (4) Each i knows the value v_i, but has no certain knowledge of the values of others. (5) Transactions costs, including the cost of thinking, calculating, deciding and bidding, are negligible. Without loss of generality we can number the agents so that $v_1 > v_2 > \ldots > v_N$. An auction allocation is efficient (Pareto optimal) if it awards the offered unit(s) to the buyer(s) that value it most highly. When $Q = 1$ unit is offered, the allocation is efficient if it goes to buyer 1 with value v_1. If $Q = 7$ is offered, an efficient allocation requires buyers 1 to 7 each to receive one unit.

The English and Dutch systems are *continuous auctions* (in time) in which an agent may alter his/her bid in response to the bids of others, or the failure of a bid to be accepted; i.e. bid information is made available continuously by the process until the auction stopping rule is invoked. In *sealed bid* auctions each agent submits one bid message to a centre, which processes the messages according to the rules of the institution, then announces some form of aggregate or summary information describing the outcome. Either type of auction may be repeated over time, thereby generating a history of outcome information, but continuous auctions provide a message history between successive contracts, while sealed-bid auctions do not.

In auction theory it is convenient to define formal concepts of environment, institution, and agent behaviour (*see* EXPERIMENTAL METHODS IN ECONOMICS). The *environment*, $E = (E^1, \ldots, E^N)$, where each agent's characteristics, $E^i = (u^i, w^i, T^i)$, are defined by his preferences or utility (u^i), endowment (w^i) and state of knowledge (T^i). In the English or Second Price auction, $E^i = (v_i, N > 1)$ for agent i, indicating that i's preferences and endowment are defined by his/her value for one unit of the commodity, that i knows that there is at least one other bidder, and (by omission) that i knows nothing about any $v_j, j \neq i$.

The institution specifies (1) a language, $M = (M^1, \ldots, M^N)$, consisting of message elements $m = (m^1, \ldots, m^N)$, where M^i is the set of messages that can be sent by i, and m^i is the message sent by i; (2) a set of allocation rules $h = [h^1(m), \ldots, h^N(m)]$, and a set of cost imputation rules $c = [c^1(m), \ldots, c^N(m)]$, where $h^i(m)$ is the commodity allocation to agent i, and $c^i(m)$ is the payment required of i, given all the messages, m; (3) a set of adjustment process rules, $g(t_0, t, T)$, consisting of a starting rule, $g(t_0, \cdot, \cdot)$, a transition rule, $g(\cdot, t, \cdot)$, and a stopping rule, $g(\cdot, \cdot, T)$, after which the allocation and cost imputation rule become effective. Hence, an *institution* is defined by $I = (I^1, \ldots, I^N)$ where $I^i = [M^i, h^i(m), c^i(m)\, g(t_0, t, T)]$. In all auctions the messages are bids; i.e. $m^i \equiv b_i$, where b_i is a bid by agent i. Let the bids be numbered from highest to lowest $b_1 > b_2 > \ldots > b_N$ (the order and numbering of the bids need not be the same as for the values). In an English auction the process starts with some bid $b_j(t_0)$ by some agent j. This is the standing bid until, under the transition rule, some agent announces a higher bid which becomes the new standing bid, and so on in sequence. The process stops with a bid $b_1(T)$ when the auctioneer is unable to solicit a higher bid. Hence, $b_1(T)$ becomes the final message, and in the English auction institution, $I_e = (I_e^1, \ldots, I_e^N)$, the outcome rules are

$$I_e = [\cdot, h^1(m) = 1, c^1(m) = b_1; h^i(m) = 0, c^i(m) = 0, \quad \text{for all} \quad i > 1, \cdot]$$

indicating that the last (and highest) bidder wins the item, pays the amount bid, and all others receive and pay nothing. In the Second Price sealed-bid auction the starting and stopping rules merely define the pre-auction time interval within which bids are to be tendered, and there is no transition rule. The bids are all examined at once, and the Second Price institution specifies $I_s = [h^1(m) = 1, c^1(m) = b_2; h^i(m) = 0, c^i(m) = 0$, for all $i > 1]$, indicating that the high bidder is awarded the item at a price equal to the next highest bid, with all others receiving and paying nothing.

Within this framework we define *agent behaviour* as a function that carries each agent's characteristics, E^i, given the institution, I, into the (final) message m^i sent by i, $m^i = \beta(E^i | I)$. A *theory* of agent behaviour has the objective of specifying β as a *hypothesis* about the observed message responses of agents in alternative institutions such as the English and Second Price auctions.

English. Let $b_k(t)$ be the tth standing bid (in some sequence), announced by agent k. Then it is a dominant strategy for any $i \neq k$ to raise the bid if $v_i > b_k(t)$; i.e. this strategy is *best* for i whatever might be the response of any other agent. Note that since the winning bidder must pay the amount bid it is never optimal for any i to raise her own bid. If the auction has a standard bid increment, δ, assumed to be smaller than the distance between any two adjacent values, then i is motivated to bid $b_i(t+1) = b_k(t) + \delta$ if and only if $v_i \geqq b_i(t+1)$. Clearly, this process must stop with the Tth bid, when (eventually) agent 1 bids $b_1(T)$, where $v_2 - \delta < b_1(T) \leqq v_2 + \delta$, and agent 2 is unable to raise the bid without bidding in excess of v_2. Hence, in the English auction we have $m^i \equiv b_i = \beta(v_i, N > 1 | I_e) \equiv v_i$ for $i = 2, 3, \ldots, N$; i.e. each $i \neq 1$ is motivated to reveal demand by bidding up to his value v_i, with agent 1 *discovering* that she does not need to bid v_1, but at most $v_2 + \delta$ to obtain the award. It follows that the equilibrium price, p_e, must satisfy $v_2 - \delta < p_e \leqq v_2 + \delta$, and the award to agent 1 will be efficient.

Because individual units are sold sequentially in typical multiple unit English auctions ($N > Q > 1$), a theory of this case would require some hypothesized expansion of agent information sets which allows each i to weigh formally the prospect of underbidding v_i by some amount in earlier auctions in anticipation of possible lower prices in later auctions. But Vickrey's generalization (quoted above) of the English auction to multiple identical units, which preserves the information properties of the single unit case, does lead to determinate results: once the bidders with the Q highest values match bids at $b(T) \in (v_{Q+1} - \delta, v_{Q+1} + \delta)$, then no bidder will be motivated to raise this standing bid. Hence, the price for any Q units ($N > Q \geqq 1$) must satisfy $v_{Q+1} - \delta < p_e \leqq v_{Q+1} + \delta$, and the award to agents $1, 2, \ldots, Q$ will be efficient.

Second Price. In this auction the surplus obtained by the winning bidder depends upon the bid of the highest among the other $N - 1$ losing bidders; i.e. if i is the winner and j the highest losing bid, the surplus to i is $v_i - b_j$. Hence the optimal bid is the bid that maximizes the probability of winning a positive surplus. This occurs only if each i bids v_i. To bid less than v_i is to reduce the chance of being the high bidder, without affecting the surplus $v_i - b_j$. To bid more than v_i is to risk (without compensating benefit) winning at a price $b_j > v_i$, yielding a negative surplus. If each i *reasons* in this manner, then $m^i \equiv b_i = \beta(v_i, N > 1 | I_s) \equiv v_i$ for *all i*. It follows that the award will be to agent 1, which is efficient, and the price will be $p_s = b_2 = v_2$. This argument extends to the multiple unit case in which N bidders each submit a bid for one of Q identical units ($N > Q > 1$). It is a dominant strategy for each i to bid v_i, the award will be to agents $1, 2, \ldots, Q$, and the competitive price paid by all Q winning bidders will be $p_c = b_{Q+1} = v_{Q+1}$.

In comparing the English and Second Price institutions it is seen that in the limit, as δ becomes small, the two institutions are isomorphic; that is, they lead to the same price and allocations. In the language of game theory these institutions are equivalent in the sense that they have the same normal form. They have quite different extensive (sequential process) forms. Analysis of the richer extensive form of the English auction leads to the conclusion that the high bidder wins with a bid of v_2 which makes the theoretical auction outcome identical to that of the Second Price auction, although the institutions have distinct cost imputaton rules. It should be noted from our discussion in section I that the Second Price procedure appears to have arisen in practice in the British stamp (and some fish) markets which permitted 'book' bids at English auction. It is easy to see that in such circumstances auctioneers might soon 'discover' the equivalence of the English and Second Price procedure without having to resort to formal analysis.

The First Price and Dutch auctions use the same allocation and cost imputation rules that are used in the English auction; they are like the Second Price auction in that the auction is over before the bidders obtain informative data about their rivals from the auction itself. In these auctions it is of importance what each bidder assumes about the values and bidding behaviour of his rivals. In the analysis below we will follow Vickrey (1961) in supposing that the values are assumed by each agent to be independent occurrences from a constant density on the interval [0, 1]. Any bids and values can be mapped into this interval by expressing them as fractions of the largest possible value. Thus, if the maximum value is $\bar{v}$, a bid of b' and value v', can be represented by $b=(b'/\bar{v})$ and $v=(v'/\bar{v})$. With these assumptions about agent knowledge the environment is $E^i=[v_i; P(v)=v, N>1]$ indicating that each i knows with certainty his/her own value $v_i \in [0, 1]$ for a single unit, that the other agent's values have the probability distribution, $\text{Prob}\{x<b\} \equiv P(v)=v$ and that there are N bidders.

First Price. Vickrey (1961) showed that if all agents are risk neutral the noncooperative (or Nash) equilibrium bid function in the First Price auction is

$$m^i \equiv b_i = \beta[v_i; P(v)=v, N|I_f] \equiv \left(\frac{N-1}{N}\right)v_i.$$

If all bidders have the same strictly concave utility function for surplus, say $u(v_i-b_i)$, the resulting bid function $b_A(v_i)$ will have the property

$$b_A(v_i) > \left(\frac{N-1}{N}\right)v_i$$

(Holt, 1980). In both of these cases, since the equilibrium bid function depends only on value, and not upon which agent has any particular value, any given ordering of the values induces the same ordering on the bids. Hence the highest value bidder will submit the highest bid, and the allocation is efficient. However, if each bidder i has constant relative risk averse (CRRA) utility, $(v_i-b_i)^{r}i$, $r_i \in (0, 1)$, then it can be shown (Cox et al., 1982) that the Vickrey bid function generalizes to

$$b_i = \left(\frac{N-1}{N-1+r_i}\right)v_i, \qquad \text{for} \qquad b_i < \bar{b} = \frac{N-1}{N}.$$

Consequently, in this case (and in general when utility functions are distinct) the highest value bidder is not necessarily the highest bidder, since if he is less risk averse than the second, or third, highest bidder, his bid may be lower than theirs. All these results have been further generalized to the multiple unit discriminative auction $(N>Q>1)$ (see Vickrey, 1962; Harris and Raviv, 1981; Cox et al., 1984).

Dutch. The Dutch auction starting rule is to announce (or display on the clock) an initial asking price, $a(t_0)$. If the clock speed, measured in dollars, is s (\$ per second), then the transition rule states that at time t the asking price is $a(t)=a(t_0)-st$. If at T, agent i is the first to accept the standing offer (the stopping rule), then i's bid, and the price paid is, $b_i=a(t_0)-sT$. Each bidder must decide when to stop the descending offer price. Vickrey was the first to argue that the Dutch and First Price auctions are isomorphic; i.e. that a bidder i who would bid b_i in the First Price auction would stop the clock at T such that $b_i=a(t_0)-sT$ in the Dutch auction. This was demonstrated formally in Cox et al. (1982) by proving the equivalence of a pre-auction planning model of the Dutch (and First Price) auction with a Bayesian model of participation in the Dutch auction. The Bayesian model shows that the information at time t on the Dutch clock (no bidder by time t has stopped the clock) is non-informative; i.e. it provides no rational basis for modifying the optimal bid given any pre-auction postulated environment, such as $E^i = [v_i, P(v), N > 1]$. Hence, a Nash model of the Dutch auction (assuming CRRA utility) yields the behavioural hypothesis that

$$m^i \equiv b_i = \beta[v_i; r_i; P(v) = v, N > 1 | I_d] \equiv \left(\frac{N-1}{N-1+r_i}\right) v_i,$$

where each i is defined by the characteristics (v_i, r_i).

Because the Dutch auction has such a rich extensive form, containing parameters such as $a(t_0)$ and s that do not enter into the First Price auction, it would be surprising if these two auction procedures produced the same results in any particular parametric implementation. One can easily imagine an s so large that the standing price is not discernible on a Dutch clock, with a bidder having to guess at the bid price at which she is stopping the clock. Similarly, s might be so small that the waiting cost is significant leading to higher bids in the Dutch than in the First Price auction. The Dutch–First Price equivalence theorem abstracts from these extensive form parametric differences and analyses each institution as a mathematical game in normal form.

Theoretical behaviour in the standard single object auctions can be compared using the following compact representation:

$$b_i = \beta(E^i | I)$$
$$= \begin{cases} b_1 \in (v_2 - \delta, v_2 + \delta) \text{ for } i = 1, \text{ and } b_i \leqq v_i, \text{ for } i > 1, \\ \quad \text{if } E^i = (v_i),\ I = I_e \\ v_i, \text{ for all } i, \text{ if } E^i = (v_i;\ N > 1),\ I = I_s \\ \left(\dfrac{N-1}{N-1+r_i}\right) v_i, \text{ for all } i, \\ \quad \text{if } E^i = [v_i, r_i;\ \Phi(r),\ P(v) = v,\ N > 1],\ I = I_f \text{ or } I_d. \end{cases} \tag{1}$$

These results generalize for multiple units, giving

$$b_i = \beta(E^i | I)$$
$$= \begin{cases} b_Q \in (v_{Q+1} - \delta, v_{Q+1} + \delta) \text{ for } i \leqq Q, \\ \quad \text{and } b_i \leqq v_i \text{ for } i > Q, \text{ if } E^i = (v_i),\ I = I_e \\ v_i, \text{ for all } i, \text{ if } E^i = (v_i;\ N > Q \geqq 1), \\ \quad I = I_{Q+1}\ (Q+1 \text{ price auction}) \\ b_a(v_i, r_i | E(r),\ N > Q \geqq 1), \\ \quad \text{if } E^i = [v_i, r_i;\ \Phi(r),\ P(v) = v,\ N > Q \geqq 1], \\ \quad I = I_D\ (\text{discriminative auction}), \end{cases} \tag{2}$$

where b_a is the CRRA bid function for multiple units [see Cox et al. (1984) and the references therein for the formula and its derivation], $\Phi(r)$ is the population distribution of the CRRA risk parameter and $E(r)$ is its expected value.

If we let $E[P(I)]$ be the (mathematical) expected selling price in a single object auction under institution I, using (1) it is easy to compare the four standard auctions in terms of this outcome measure (Vickrey, 1961) if we assume risk neutrality; i.e. $E^i = (v_i, r_i = 1;\ P(v) = v,\ N > 1)$:

$$E[P(I)] = \begin{cases} E(b_1) \in \left[\left(\dfrac{N-1}{N+1}\right) - \delta, \left(\dfrac{N-1}{N+1}\right) + \delta\right], & \text{if } I = I_e, \\ E(b_2) = \left(\dfrac{N-1}{N+1}\right), & \text{if } I = I_s, \\ E(b_1) = \left(\dfrac{N-1}{N+1}\right), & \text{if } I = I_f \text{ or } I_d, \end{cases} \tag{3}$$

since $E(v_2) = (N-1)/(N+1)$. It follows that for $\delta = 0$, all four auctions give the same expected selling price. It is also easy to show that if the bidders are risk averse, then $E[P(I_e)] = E[P(I_s)] < E[P(I_f)] = E[P(I_d)]$. Thus a testable outcome implication of the above models of bidding behaviour is that observed mean prices will be ordered

$$\bar{P}(I_e) = \bar{P}(I_s) = \left(\frac{N-1}{N+1}\right) \leq \bar{P}(I_f) = \bar{P}(I_d).$$

Also, efficiency, measured by the percentage (probability) of awards to the highest value bidder will be 100 per cent in all the auctions if bidders are risk neutral or all have the same concave utility for surplus. But if bidders have CRRA utility with different parameters, r_i, then this measure of efficiency, ζ, will be ordered $100 = \zeta_e = \zeta_s > \zeta_f = \zeta_d$ in the English, Second, First and Dutch auctions respectively.

Experimental Tests of Auction Market Behaviour. Several studies (see Cox et al., 1984 and its citations) have tested the above models and various extensions of them using experimental methods. In all of the experiments summarized below, values are assigned from a uniform probability function whose parameters are common knowledge to all the participants. Each participant understands that he/she will be paid in cash the difference between the value assigned, and the price paid, conditional upon being a winning bidder in any particular auction.

From the numerous experimental studies reporting the results of perhaps 1500–2000 auctions, the following brief summary is offered:

1. The behaviour of prices in the four standard auctions is illustrated by the representative charts in Figures 1 and 2 comparing I_e and I_d prices using eight bidders, and I_f and I_s prices using five bidders. In these experiments, in each auction, a random sample of N values are assigned to the bidders from the

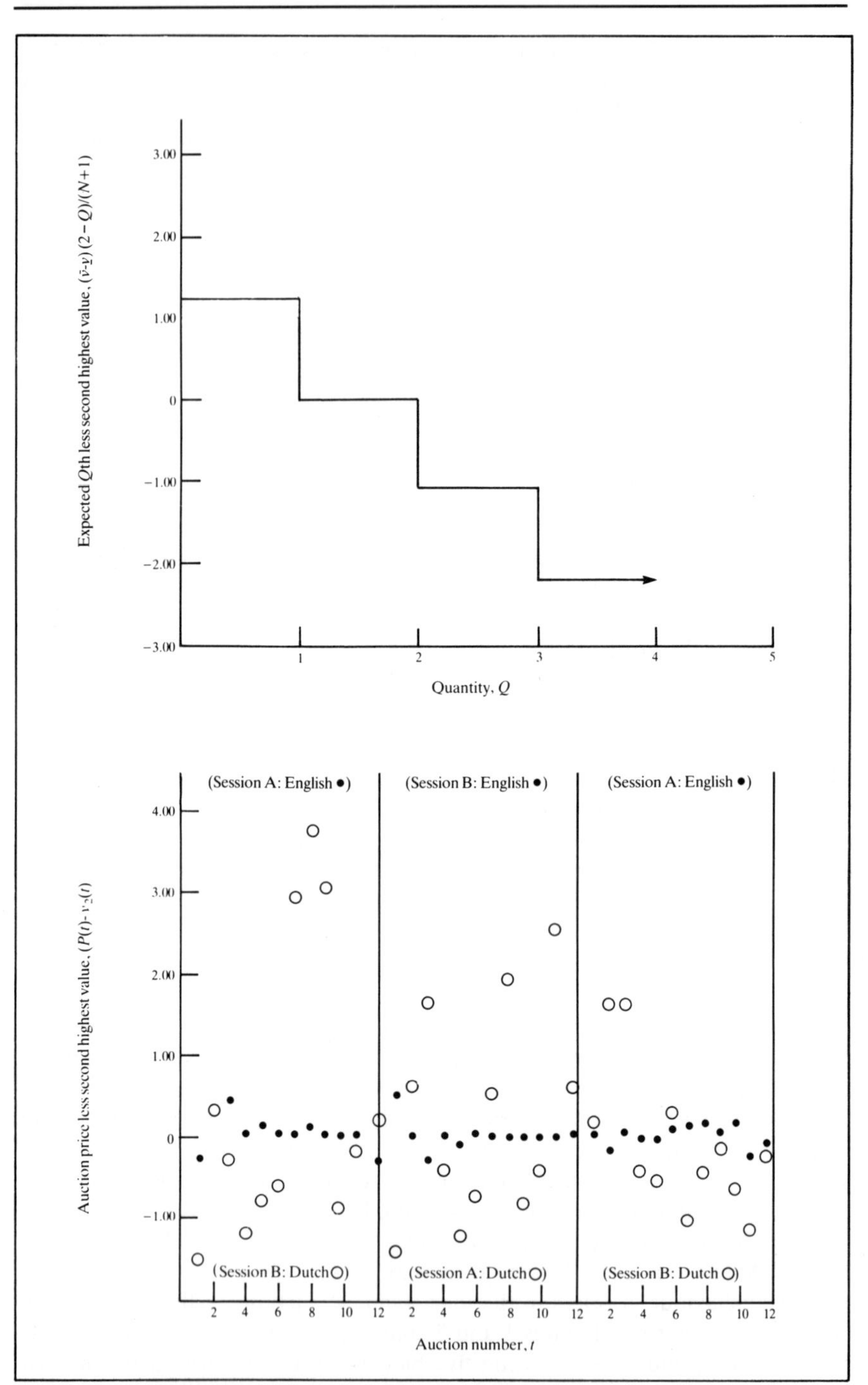

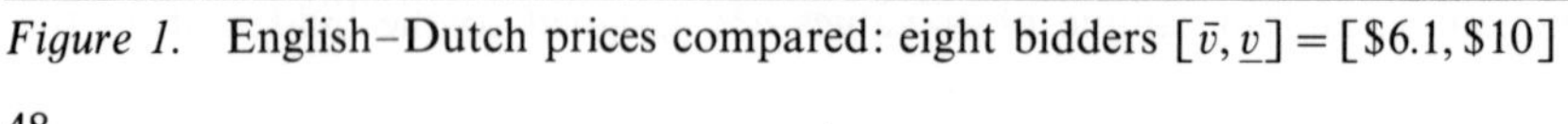
Figure 1. English–Dutch prices compared: eight bidders $[\bar{v}, \underline{v}] = [\$6.1, \$10]$

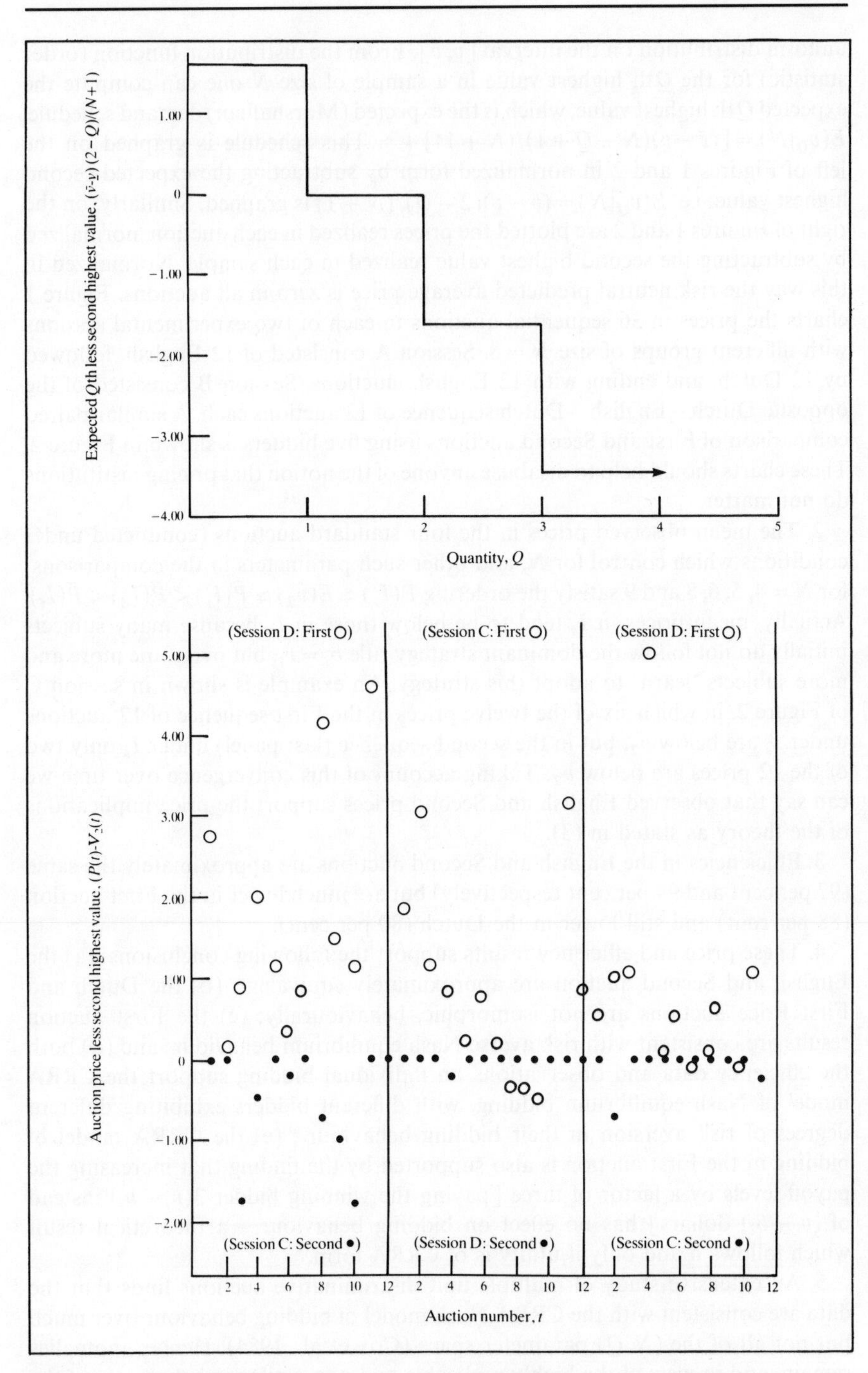

Figure 2. First–Second prices compared: 5 Bidders $[\bar{v}, \underline{v}] = [\$0.1, \$10]$

uniform distribution on the interval $[\underline{v}, \bar{v}]$. From the distribution function (order statistic) for the Qth highest value in a sample of size N one can compute the expected Qth highest value, which is the expected (Marshallian) demand schedule, $E(v_Q|N) = [(\bar{v} - \underline{v})(N - Q + 1)/(N + 1)] + \underline{v}$. This schedule is graphed on the left of Figures 1 and 2 in normalized form by subtracting the expected second highest value; i.e. $E(v_Q|N) = (\bar{v} - \underline{v})(2 - Q)/(N + 1)$ is graphed. Similarly, on the right of Figures 1 and 2 are plotted the prices realized in each auction, normalized by subtracting the second highest value realized in each sample. Normalized in this way the risk neutral predicted average price is zero in all auctions. Figure 1 charts the prices in 36 sequential auctions in each of two experimental sessions with different groups of size $N = 8$. Session A consisted of 12 English, followed by 12 Dutch, and ending with 12 English, auctions. Session B consisted of the opposite Dutch – English – Dutch sequence of 12 auctions each. A similar paired comparison of First and Second auctions using five bidders is shown in Figure 2. These charts should help to disabuse anyone of the notion that pricing institutions do not matter.

2. The mean observed prices in the four standard auctions (conducted under conditions which control for N, and other such parameters in the comparisons) for $N = 4, 5, 6, 8$ and 9 satisfy the ordering $\bar{P}(I_e) \simeq E(v_2) \simeq \bar{P}(I_s) < \bar{P}(I_d) < \bar{P}(I_f)$. Actually, mean prices in I_s tend to be below those in I_e because many subjects initially do not follow the dominant strategy rule $b_i = v_i$, but over time more and more subjects 'learn' to adopt this strategy. An example is shown in session C of Figure 2, in which six of the twelve prices in the First sequence of 12 auctions under I_s are below v_2, but in the second sequence (last panel) under I_s only two of the 12 prices are below v_2. Taking account of this convergence over time we can say that observed English and Second prices support the price implications of the theory as stated in (3).

3. Efficiencies in the English and Second auctions are approximately the same (97 per cent and 94 per cent respectively) but are much lower in the First auction (88 per cent) and still lower in the Dutch (80 per cent).

4. These price and efficiency results support the following conclusions: (a) the English and Second auction are approximately equivalent; (b) the Dutch and First Price auctions are not isomorphic, behaviourally; (c) the First auction results are consistent with risk averse Nash equilibrium behaviour; and (d) both the efficiency data and observations on individual bidding support the CRRA model of Nash equilibrium bidding, with different bidders exhibiting different degrees of risk aversion in their bidding behaviour ; (e) the CRRA model of bidding in the First auction is also supported by the finding that increasing the payoff levels by a factor of three [paying the winning bidder $3(v_i - b_i)$ instead of $(v_i - b_i)$ dollars] has no effect on bidding behaviour – a theoretical result which follows if and only if utility is of CRRA form.

5. An extensive study of multiple unit discriminative auctions finds that the data are consistent with the CRRA Nash model of bidding behaviour over much but not all of the (N, Q) parameter space (Cox et al., 1984). Hence, anomalies remain, and in view of the highly replicable and non-artifactual character of the

empirical results there is the strong implication that the resolution of these anomalies is an unfinished theoretical task.

6. The Second Price auction results do not extend to the multiple unit uniform price auction. Apparently, with multiple units, in those parameter cases that have been studied, the market is less effective in disciplining (with failure experiences) those strategies that depart from the dominant strategy.

ENRICHING THE ENVIRONMENT: DEPENDENCE, INFORMATION, COLLUSION AND COMBINATORIAL CONSIDERATIONS

Once replicable experimental results have been established and the strengths and weaknesses of a theory have been assessed, it is natural to extend both the theoretical and the empirical inquiry to richer environments. The required theoretical advances have been more difficult to achieve than the creation of richer environments in the laboratory (Kagel et al., 1983).

A limiting feature of the above theories is the assumption that agent values are independent. Consequently, each agent's willingness-to-pay as might be revealed in the open English auction has no information value to any other agent. Milgrom and Weber (1982) capture this important postulated property of some commodities by introducing the concept of positively dependent (affiliated) values. In this environment the English auction is no longer isomorphic to the Second Price auction; instead, prices in the former exceed those in the latter. Milgrom and Weber (1982) also argue that the Dutch–First isomorphism continues to hold when values are positively dependent, but this extension is of more limited scientific significance (than the extension of English–Second auction theory) since the experimental evidence is inconsistent with this implication in the independent values environment. Any theoretical implication found to be robust with respect to some generalization of the environment is a moot discovery if that implication is contrary to the evidence in the more special environment.

An important application of the case in which individual values are affiliated is to the sealed-bid auctions of oil exploration and development leases by the government. In this case we can think of each v_i as i's estimate of the value of the lease after obtaining seismic and other sample data providing information on the existence of possible oil bearing geological structures. This application is often referred to as the common value of mineral rights model, since the analysis has assumed that all companies place the same value on any petroleum that might be discovered on the tract. This assumption is much too limiting since there is an active market for existing or proven petroleum reserves, and one cannot account for such exchanges if private values are indeed common. Hence petroleum exploration and development leases are best viewed as a case in which the commodity exhibits differing, but affiliated, private values. The first experimental study of 'common value' auctions (Kagel et al., 1983) reports bidding behaviour in which the bids are too high to be consistent with risk neutral utility functions and too diverse among individuals to be consistent with the implication of symmetrical bid functions. In effect these results, when values are affiliated, imply rejection of the common values model, and serve to establish the robustness of the experimental results when values are independent (Cox et al., 1984). These findings heavily underline the methodological point that evidence contrary to a postulate (e.g. symmetry) in any environment requires modification of the theory if one is to obtain empirically useful and observationally disciplined extensions of the theory to more complex environments.

The different standard auctions are not equivalent in terms of their collusive potential. The open-bid English auction is particularly vulnerable to collusion since a subset of $n < N$ buyers have only to agree not to bid against each other in order to reduce the expected price that will be paid. Furthermore, the English auction process assures that the agreement will be easy to monitor.

It is an open question whether a seller, such as the government in the sale of mineral leases, should publicize each bidder's bid every time a sealed-bid auction is conducted. It serves to reinforce the credibility of the auction process by allowing each bidder to verify that his bid was processed honestly. But if a buyers' ring is operating, such information makes it easy for the ring to monitor the bids of its members, and to determine the identity of outside bidders and the conditions under which the ring loses the auction.

Sealed-bid auctions are vulnerable to collusion between the auctioneer and one or more buyers, and between the auctioneer and the seller. Thus, in the First Price auction, the terms of agreement between the auctioneer and a buyer might be that if the buyer enters the highest bid, then his bid is to be reentered slightly in excess of the second highest bid.

The Dutch auction is perhaps effective against all of the above examples of collusion. In this auction, since none of the losing bids is known to anyone, they cannot even be leaked, let alone announced, and these types of conspiracies are not feasible.

A new proposed auction institution which has yet to be implemented in practice, but has been subjected to limited testing in the laboratory is the combinatorial auction (Rassenti et al., 1982). This is a sealed-bid auction which allows bidders to submit bids for one or more combinations of non-identical items in a multiple unit auction. The problem was originally suggested in the context of designing a market for airport landing or takeoff slots. Airport slots are an extreme example of a resource whose productive value is enhanced in specified combinations. Thus a slot at New York's Kennedy International has no productive value except in combination with a flight compatible slot at Chicago's O'Hare Field.

BIBLIOGRAPHY

Amihud, Y. (ed.) 1976. *Bidding and Auctioning for Procurement and Allocation.* New York: New York University Press.

Arthur, H. 1976. The structure and use of auctions. In Amihud (1976).

Cassady, R. 1967. *Auctions and Auctioneering.* Berkeley: University of California Press.

Cox, J., Roberson, B. and Smith, V. 1982. Theory and behavior of single unit auctions. In *Research in Experimental Economics*, Vol. 2, Greenwich, Conn.: JAI Press.

Cox, J., Smith, V. and Walker, J. 1984. Theory and behavior of multiple unit discriminative auctions. *Journal of Finance* 39(4), September, 983–1010.

Harris, M. and Raviv, A. 1981. Allocation mechanisms and the design of auctions. *Econometrica* 49(6), November, 1477–99.

Holt, C. 1980. Competitive bidding for contracts under alternative auction procedures. *Journal of Political Economy* 88(3), June, 433–45.

Jarecki, H. 1976. Bullion dealing, commodity exchange trading and the London gold fixing. In Amihud (1976).

Kagel, J., Levin, J., Battalio, R. and Meyer, D. 1983. Common value auctions: some initial experimental results. University of Houston Working Paper, November.

Milgrom, P. and Weber, R. 1982. A theory of auctions and competitive bidding. *Econometrica* 50(5), September, 1089–122.

Rassenti, S., Smith, V. and Bulfin, R. 1982. A combinatorial auction mechanism for airport time slot allocation. *Bell Journal of Economics* 13(2), Autumn, 402–17.

Vickrey, W. 1961. Counterspeculation, auctions, and competitive sealed tenders. *Journal of Finance* 16(1), March, 8–37.

Vickrey, W. 1962. Auctions and bidding games. In *Recent Advances in Game Theory*, Proceedings of a Conference, Princeton: Princeton University Press.

Vickrey, W. 1976. Auctions, markets and optimal allocation. In Amihud (1976).

Bidding

ROBERT WILSON

Auctions are studied because they are market institutions of practical importance. Their simple procedural rules to resolve multilateral bargaining over the terms of trade enjoy enduring popularity. They also present simply several basic issues of price determination: the role of private information, the consequences of strategic behaviour and the effect of many traders. These issues have influenced the subject since the initial work of Vickrey (1961), the early contribution of Griesmer, Levitan, and Shubik (1967), and the influential dissertation by Ortega-Reichert (1968). Useful introductory surveys are by Engelbrecht-Wiggans (1980), Engelbrecht-Wiggans, Shubik and Stark (1983), Milgrom (1985), and MacAfee and McMillan (1986); bibliographies are in MacAfee and McMillan (1986) and Stark and Rothkopf (1979); and Cassady (1967) provides an historical perspective.

This note supplements the essay on Auctions by summarizing some additional theoretical contributions to these issues. This literature relies on the game-theoretic perspective that emphasizes the implications of complete optimizing behaviour. Omitted here are the experimental studies that offer alternative predictions of bidder behaviour. It remains to determine which better describes the behaviour of experienced, savvy bidders in the major auction markets. Although general equilibrium models of closed economies have been studied (Schmeidler, 1980; Shapley and Shubik, 1977; Wilson, 1978), we focus on partial equilibrium models with bids and offers denominated in money terms. Also omitted are studies of markets with intermediaries such as brokers and specialists; models without private information (Dubey, 1982; Milgrom, 1986); and auctions in which losers also pay, as in price wars and wars of attrition.

In the traditional view, price determination is a consequence of market clearing: prices equate supply and demand. This clearing process is especially transparent in the case of auction markets. Essentially, auctions are markets with explicit trading rules that specify precisely how market clearing determines prices. For example, in a sealed-bid auction of one or more identical indivisible items, the (interval of) clearing prices is determined by intersecting the seller's supply schedule (reflecting the number of units available and announced reservation prices) with the demand schedule formed by arraying the buyers' bids in descending order. Non-discriminatory pricing sets the price at the highest rejected bid, discriminatory pricing charges each successful bidder the amount of his bid, and various intermediate cases are possible. Double auctions operate similarly except that the supply schedule is constructed by arraying the sellers' offers in ascending order. With divisible commodities, the aggregate schedules are obtained by constructing the sums of the traders' demand and supply schedules at each price. Oral auctions, such as the English auction, find a clearing price by calling for bids in ascending order. An oral double auction, or 'bid–ask' market, allows free outcry of bids and offers that can be accepted immediately and therefore depends on participants' judgments about the likely clearing price.

The variety of possible procedural rules is large, so theoretical studies emphasize the characterization of efficient trading rules, such as rules that are optimal for the buyers or the sellers. The design of trading rules is subject to the incentive compatibility constraints induced by the traders' private information and the option of any trader to forego participation or trade. Auctions are especially restrictive trading mechanisms because their rules are specified independently of information about the distribution of traders' attributes, even if this information is common knowledge. On the other hand, auctions have been important market institutions for millennia precisely because they are efficient or nearly so in a wide variety of environments.

Much of the theory of efficient trading rules studies 'direct revelation' games in which, in equilibrium, each trader's action consists of a direct report of his private information. This approach loses no generality in static models but the resulting optimal rules depend on the distribution of traders' attributes: only in special cases can they be implemented fully as auctions. (In the extreme case of highly correlated private information, an *optimal* trading rule can be designed by the seller to extract most or all of the potential revenue (Crémer and McLean, 1985; Myerson, 1981).) The theory therefore divides between the study of auctions, in which traders' strategies take account of the distribution of attributes, and the study of optimal direct revelation games, in which the trading rule incorporates this data. We concentrate on auctions here, but mention intersections with the general theory.

A trading rule specifies each trader's feasible actions and the prices and trades resulting from their joint actions. Models also specify each trader's information and preferences. Typically each trader i knows privately an observation s_i affecting his preferences, and the restrictive assumption is adopted that the joint probability distribution of these observations and any salient unobserved random variable v is common knowledge among the participants. (The observation s_i is often taken to be real valued for simplicity; it could be the bidder's posterior certainty-equivalent valuation of the item based on his private information.) A strategy therefore specifies a trader's actions depending on his observation and any further observations (such as others' bids) made in process. Trader i's expected utility u_i depends on the received quantity q_i, the price(s) p_i at which these units are traded, his observation s_i, the array $S_i = \{s_j | j \neq i\}$ of others' observations, and possibly on other variables v.

Interesting special cases of the probabilistic structure are: independent and identically distributed (iid) observations; conditionally iid observations given v; and more generally, affiliated observations (e.g., nonnegative correlation on any rectangle). In each case assume that the (conditional) distribution of an observation satisfies the monotone hazard rate or likelihood ratio property. Most of the familiar probability distributions satisfy these assumptions; e.g., lognormal distributions are often used in applications to oil-lease bidding.

Interesting special cases of the preference structure for a single item include: private values, $u_i = s_i - p_i$; a common value, $u_i = v - p_i$; mixed values, $u_i = u(s_i, v) - p_i$, where u is increasing; and private-value cases with common risk aversion, $u_i = U(s_i - p)$, where U is increasing and concave. Relevant features are summarized in the expected utility $\bar{u}(s_i, S_i) = \mathscr{E}\{u(s_i, v) | s_i, S_i\}$.

Other features are also addressed in some formulations: the seller's optimal reservation price, a trader's option to obtain costly further observations to improve his information, bids submitted jointly by syndicates of traders, and entry fees and auxiliary contingent payments such as royalties. (Bidding on the royalty rather than the price has been used in auctions of oil leases.) Uncertainty about the number of bidders is easily included if this number is independent of the bidders' observations; however, somewhat different comparative statics results ensue. If there are bid preparation costs, exposure constraints (total amount of bids submitted) or portfolio motives, then participation in an auction is itself a strategic action and may involve randomization if there are too many potential bidders for all to expect to recoup their costs. If information is costly and subject to choice then, even with many bidders, there is typically an upper bound on the bidders' total expenditures and each bidder may choose to collect relatively little information (Matthews, 1984). Repeated auctions introduce novel features, such as reputation effects, that severely alter the results; e.g., one bidder with privileged information can win systematically (Bikhchandani, 1985).

Most theoretical studies assume that the traders' strategies form a Nash equilibrium, or in dynamic formulations, a sequential equilibrium: each strategy in each contingency is optimal for the remainder of the game. For many auction models the equilibrium strategies can be characterized elegantly in terms of the joint distribution of observations and bids (Milgrom and Weber, 1985). If the bidders (on the same side of the market) are positioned symmetrically *ex ante* then one focuses on the symmetric equilibrium in which all bidders use the same strategy, which is an increasing function of one's observation. A large class of symmetric discriminatory auctions have *only* symmetric equilibria (Maskin and Riley, 1986); they are usually characterized by differential equations, as illustrated for various cases in Milgrom and Weber (1982), Reece (1978), Wilson (1977, 1985). In non-discriminatory auctions a single equation specifies the optimal bid as the most one would be willing to pay conditional on one's observation being the most optimistic. Results about symmetric equilibria are fairly robust: examples indicate that under- or over-bidding by one participant engenders a similar but muted response by others, and the difference from the symmetric equilibrium varies smoothly. In sealed-bid discriminatory auctions with iid private values, one's bid is essentially the conditional expectation of the highest rejected valuation given that one's valuation is acceptable. An analogous property applies to mixed-value preferences. The important asymmetric cases occur when some bidders' information is superior to others' (e.g., direct information about v); in these cases any bidder with strictly inferior information obtains expected profits of at most zero, and bidders may use randomized strategies. If all bidders have private information (with a positive density satisfying technical restrictions) then typically equilibrium strategies are not randomized and positive expected profits result.

We summarize results mainly for the special probabilistic and preference structures mentioned above, and for symmetric equilibria. Also, multiple-item auctions introduce few novelties when there is a single seller offering a fixed supply of identical items and each bidder wants at most one, so we focus on the single item case. An exception is a 'share auction', in which bidders offer demand schedules for shares of a divisible item in fixed supply: in this case there can be a continuum of symmetric equilibria, and the seller's expected revenue can be unaffected by more bidders (Wilson, 1979).

A main effect of risk aversion is to increase bids in symmetric discriminatory auctions with iid private values. The seller can enhance this effect by imposing an entry fee (preferably decreasing in the amount of the bid and ultimately negative for the highest bids) (Matthews, 1983; Maskin and Riley, 1984). Risk aversion induces bidders to bid higher under discriminatory pricing, and in fact this rule makes the winning bid a less risky random variable. The seller therefore prefers discriminatory pricing, and more so if he too is risk averse. However, if bidders have decreasing absolute risk aversion (ARA), they have the reverse preference (Matthews, 1987). With constant (or zero) ARA, a bidder's higher price with discriminatory pricing is exactly balanced by the riskier price associated with non-discriminatory pricing. With affiliated observations, the bidders prefer discriminatory pricing if they have constant ARA, and will be indifferent again at some degree of decreasing ARA. Affiliation biases the seller's preferences in the opposite direction, towards non-discriminatory pricing.

Hereafter we assume no risk aversion. Then, in the iid private-values model of bidders' preferences, the seller's expected revenue is the same for discriminatory and non-discriminatory pricing (Harris and Raviv, 1981a, 1981b; Myerson, 1981; Riley and Samuelson, 1981). Moreover, subject to a technical restriction, either of these is optimal among all possible trading rules provided the seller adopts an optimal reservation price (Harris and Raviv, 1981a, 1981b; Myerson, 1981). With more general preferences, whenever $\bar{u}$ is increasing affiliation produces a distinct preference of the seller for (and the bidders against) non-discriminatory pricing *vs.* discriminatory; indeed, the seller further prefers an oral auction (Milgrom and Weber, 1982). This illustrates the 'linkage principle': the seller wants to reduce the bidders' profits from their private information, and auction rules that reveal affiliated information publicly (inferences from bids in the case of oral auctions) or otherwise positively link one bidder's price to another's bid (non-discriminatory pricing) are advantageous when observations are affiliated and therefore positively correlated. Similarly, the seller prefers to reveal publicly and relevant affiliated information he has so as to reduce the bidders' informational advantages *vis-à-vis* each other. (However, revealing non-affiliated information may be disadvantageous, and in particular this applies to the number of bidders, even when it is independent of other data (Matthews, 1987).) The seller can gain further by conditioning payments *ex post* on realized values, as in the case of a royalty (Riley, 1986).

The main results about bidders' strategies in single-item sealed-bid discriminatory auctions can be summarized for bidders with symmetric conditionally iid mixed-value preferences. *Ex ante* each bidder has an equal chance of winning and the bidder with the most optimistic observation is predicted to win, namely i wins in the event $W(s_i) \equiv \{s_i > \max S_i | s_i\}$. (Failure to recognize that winning is an informative event, signalling that others' observations were less optimistic, is called the winner's curse (Capen, Clapp and Campbell, 1971); it is distressingly common in practice as well as in experiments. The implications of the fact that the maximum of several unbiased estimates is biased upward are apparently difficult to appreciate.) The most that i can profitably bid is therefore $\hat{u}(s_i) = \mathscr{E}\{\bar{u}(s_i, S_i) | W(s_i)\}$, whereas the optimal bid is less than this, by a percentage that is of the order of $1/n$ when there are n bidders, reflecting the bidder's monopoly rent both in terms of the limited number of bidders and the advantage of his private information, which are the two sources of bidders' expected profits. (In a nondiscriminatory auction, i bids $\hat{u}(s_i)$ computed from $\hat{W}(s_i) \equiv \{s_i = \max S_i | s_i\}$ but in equilibrium pays $\hat{u}(\max S_i)$ if he wins.) With many bidders these rents are dissipated and, remarkably, the winning bid conveys essentially all the information about v contained in $\max_i s_i$. In the common value model, the winning bid is a consistent estimator of the value whenever *any* consistent estimator exists that is a function of $\max_i s_i$: the winning bid is asymptotically as good an estimator as is possible from extrema of the bidders' observations. In particular, if the relative likelihood of a large observation is small for smaller values of v, then the maximum bid converges in probability to v as the number of bidders increases (Milgrom, 1979a, 1979b; Palfrey, 1985; Wilson, 1977).

These features are reflected in the detailed calculations reported for models of oil-lease bidding (Reece, 1978). Other examples are shown in Table 1, which exhibits the equilibrium strategies for a model that roughly approximates firms' bidding for oil leases. Each bidder i observes $s_i = (s_{i1}, s_{i2})$ and $u(s_i, v) = s_{i1} v$, where s_{i1} represents a private factor (e.g., price or discount factor), and s_{i2} represents an estimate of the common factor v. Assume that, conditional on a location parameter $\bar{s}_1$, the private factors are conditionally independent and $\ln s_{i1}$ has mean $\ln \bar{s}_1$ and variance σ_1^2; and marginally $\ln \bar{s}_1$ has variance $\bar{\sigma}_1^2$. Similarly, conditional on v the estimates are conditionally independent and $\ln s_{i2}$ has mean $\ln v$ and variance σ_2^2; and marginally $\ln v$ has variance $\bar{\sigma}_2^2$. Consider the case adapted to the empirical fact that for Gulf of Mexico oil leases the logarithm of the bids typically has conditional variance about 1.0 whereas the estimating precision implies a variance of about 0.36, given that the prior variances $(\bar{\sigma}_1^2, \bar{\sigma}_2^2)$ are comparatively so large that they can be considered infinite: assume that the conditional variance of the private factors accounts for the difference. In this case, the symmetric equilibrium bidding strategy specifies that each firm submits a bid that is a specified fraction (the bid factor) of the product of its private factor and its posterior expectation of the common factor given its estimate. The tabulation shows the percentage bid factor for four numbers n of bidders, assuming the seller's reservation price is zero, and it shows the winning bidder's expected percentage profit. The seemingly low bid factors are necessary to avoid the winner's curse; whereas the surprisingly large profit percentages reflect the role of the private valuation factors.

Table 1. Examples of Equilibrium Bidding Strategies Lognormal Distributions

$u_i = s_{i1}v$, $\sigma_1^2 + \sigma_2^2 = 1.0$, $\sigma_2^2 = 0.36$

Number of Bidders	(n)	2	4	8	16
Bid Factor	(%)	30.9	39.0	40.5	39.6
Expected Profit	(%)	53.45	33.85	23.78	17.82

Analogous models in which a bidder can increase the precision of his information at increasing cost differ in that, even though bidders' total expenditures converge to a positive level as the number of bidders increases, each bidder's expenditure converges to zero. In this case the winning bid is not a consistent estimator of the common value v and the seller's expected revenue is reduced by the amount of the bidders' total expenditure on information, since in equilibrium this is necessarily recouped in expectation by the participating bidders (Matthews, 1984). An important policy conclusion is that bidders' expenditures on information are inefficiently large.

Single-item auctions with dynamic rules add a few new aspects. In a Dutch auction an exogenously specified price is lowered until a bidder accepts. This rule induces a game that for the bidders is strategically equivalent to a sealed-bid auction; it is also payoff equivalent unless they are impatient to trade, in which case a bidder is concerned about the sum of the interest rate and the hazard rate that trade will be usurped by a competitor. For the seller it differs if he cannot commit himself to forego trading by stopping the price at a reservation price exceeding his valuation. In the iid private-values model of preferences, a generalized multi-item Dutch auction is an optimal selling strategy for a monopolist seller whenever potential demand exceeds supply (Harris and Raviv, 1981a, 1981b). Auctions with exogenously ascending prices, in which the items are awarded to the remaining bidders at the price at which the last of the others drops out, are a form of nondiscriminatory auction; but with affiliated observations, a bidder's strategy accounts for the learning enabled by seeing the prices at which others drop out – an instance of the linkage principle.

Double auctions have been studied only for the case of iid private values and non-discriminatory pricing. The price chosen is the midpoint of the interval of clearing prices derived from intersecting the schedules of bids (arrayed in descending order) and offers (arrayed in ascending order). Such an auction is actually an *ex ante* efficient trading rule for the case of one buyer and one seller with values distributed uniformly on the same interval (Chatterjee and Samuelson, 1983; Myerson and Satterthwaite, 1983); and by implication from the previous results for auctions, for one buyer *or* one seller. With several buyers and sellers and fairly general distributions, the *ex ante* efficient trading rule bears a strong resemblance to a double auction and has the remarkable property that the expected efficiency losses (compared to *ex post* efficiency) from strategic behaviour decline nearly quadratically to zero as the numbers of traders increase (Gresik and Satterthwaite, 1984). The weaker criterion of *interim* efficiency requires that no other trading rule is sure to improve every trader's expected gains from trade: a double auction satisfies this criterion if there are sufficiently many buyers and sellers (Wilson, 1985).

Oral multi-item discriminatory double auctions, allowing free outcry of bids and offers, are the most important practically (e.g. commodity markets) and the most challenging theoretically. Since trades are consummated in process at differing prices, 'market clearing' is dynamic and, for example, traders with extra-marginal valuations in the static sense can obtain gains from trade early on. Since traders are continually motivated to estimate the distribution of subsequent bids and offers, the learning process is a key feature. Theoretical studies have been attempted for both complete equilibrium models (Wilson, 1987) and others invoking some plausible behavioral assumptions (Easley and Ledyard, 1982; Friedman, 1984). These studies aim to explain the dramatic efficiency attained in experiments and the tendency for transaction prices to approximate or converge to the static Walrasian clearing prices (Smith, 1982; Plott and Sunder, 1982), especially with replication, even when the subjects lack a base of common knowledge about distributional features. The efficiency realized in experimental settings is a major puzzle deserving better theoretical explanations.

In summary, auctions are important market institutions that ensure market clearing via explicit trading rules that are independent of the distribution of preferences and information among the participants. Over wide ranges of models of preferences and information, these trading rules are *ex ante* or *interim* efficient or nearly so, and both practically and experimentally they are evidently robust. The theory elaborates these properties and demonstrates the role of private information and strategic behaviour. The explicit construction of equilibrium strategies establishes the magnitudes of these effects and enables comparisons of trading rules, preference structures, informational conditions and the number of participants; and additionally it explains phenomena such as the winner's curse that stem from adverse selection effects when there is dispersed information. Some models predict that the choice of pricing rule is inconsequential because bidders alter their strategies to compensate: the market clearing condition is the main determinant of welfare consequences.

In relation to the general economic theory of markets, the theory of auctions addresses the special case of markets with explicit market-clearing trading rules and elaborates in fine detail the determination of prices and the efficiency and distributional consequences of particular assumptions about the attributes of participants. This endeavour is a useful step in the construction of a general theory of the micro-structure of markets that encompasses the full range from bilateral bargaining to 'perfectly competitive' markets.

BIBLIOGRAPHY

Bikhchandani, S. 1985. Reputation in repeated second price auctions. Research Paper 815, Stanford Business School, July 1985; also in 'Market games with few traders', PhD dissertation, 1986.

Capen, E., Clapp, R. and Campbell, W. 1971. Competitive bidding in high-risk situations. *Journal of Petroleum Technology* 23, 641–53.

Cassady, R. Jr. 1967. *Auctions and Auctioneering*. Berkeley: University of California Press.

Chatterjee, K. and Samuelson, W. 1983. Bargaining under incomplete information. *Operations Research* 31, 835–51.

Crémer, J. and McLean, R. 1985. Optimal selling strategies under uncertainty for a discriminating monopolist when demands are interdependent. *Econometrica* 53, 345–63.

DeBrock, L. and Smith, J. 1983. Joint bidding, information pooling, and the performance of petroleum lease auctions. *Bell Journal of Economics* 14, 395–404.

Dubey, P. 1982. Price–quantity strategic market games. *Econometrica* 50, 111–26.

Easley, D. and Ledyard, J. 1982. A theory of price formation and exchange in oral auctions. Discussion Paper 461, Northwestern University, 1982.

Engelbrecht-Wiggans, R. 1980. Auctions and bidding models: a survey. *Management Science* 26, 119–42.

Engelbrecht-Wiggans, R., Milgrom, P.R. and Weber, R.J. 1983. Competitive bidding and proprietary information. *Journal of Mathematical Economics* 11, 161–9.

Engelbrecht-Wiggans, R., Shubik, M. and Stark, R. (eds) 1983. *Auctions, Bidding, and Contracting: Uses and Theory*. New York: New York University Press.

Friedman, D. 1984. On the efficiency of double auction markets. *American Economic Review* 74, 60–72.

Griesmer, J., Levitan, R. and Shubik, M. 1967. Towards a study of bidding processes, Part Four: Unknown competitive costs. *Naval Research Logistics Quarterly* 14, 415–33.

Gresik, T. and Satterthwaite, M. 1984. The rate at which a simple market becomes efficient as the number of traders increases: an asymptotic result for optimal trading mechanisms. Discussion Paper 641, Northwestern University, 1984.

Harris, M. and Raviv, A. 1981a. A theory of monopoly pricing schemes with demand uncertainty. *American Economic Review* 71, 347–65.

Harris, M. and Raviv, A. 1981b. Allocation mechanisms and the design of auctions. *Econometrica* 49, 1477–99.

Harris, M. and Townsend, R. 1981. Resource allocation under asymmetric information. *Econometrica* 49, 33–64.

Holt, C.A., Jr. 1979. Uncertainty and the bidding for incentive contracts. *American Economic Review* 69, 697–705.

Holt, C.A., Jr. 1980. Competitive bidding for contracts under alternative auction procedures. *Journal of Political Economy* 88, 433–45.

MacAfee, E.P. and McMillan, J. 1987. Auctions and bidding. *Journal of Economic Literature* 25.

Maskin, E. and Riley, J. 1984a. Monopoly with incomplete information. *Rand Journal of Economics* 15, 171–96.

Maskin, E. and Riley, J. 1984b. Optimal auctions with risk averse buyers. *Econometrica* 52, 1473–518.

Maskin, E. and Riley, J. 1986. Existence and uniqueness of equilibrium in sealed high bid auctions. Discussion Paper 407, University of California at Los Angeles, March 1986.

Matthews, S. 1983. Selling to risk averse buyers with unobservable tastes. *Journal of Economic Theory* 30, 370–400.

Matthews, S. 1984a. Information acquisition in discriminatory auctions. In *Bayesian Models in Economic Theory*, ed. M. Boyer and R. Kihlstrom, Amsterdam: North-Holland.

Matthews, S. 1984b. On the implementability of reduced form auctions. *Econometrica* 52, 1519–22.

Matthews, S. 1987. Comparing auctions for risk averse buyers: a buyer's point of view. *Econometrica* 55.

Milgrom, P.R. 1979a. *The Structure of Information in Competitive Bidding*. New York: Garland Publishing Co.

Milgrom, P.R. 1979b. A convergence theorem for competitive bidding with differential information. *Econometrica* 47, 679–88.

Milgrom, P.R. 1981. Rational expectations, information acquisition, and competitive bidding. *Econometrica* 49, 921–43.

Milgrom, P.R. 1985. The economics of competitive bidding: a selective survey. In *Social Goals and Social Organization*, ed. L. Hurwicz, D. Schmeidler and H. Sonnenschein, Cambridge: Cambridge University Press.

Milgrom, P.R. 1986. Auction theory. In *Advances in Economic Theory 1985*, ed. T. Bewley, Cambridge: Cambridge University Press.

Milgrom, P.R. and Weber, R.J. 1982a. A theory of auctions and competitive bidding. *Econometrica* 50, 1089–122.

Milgrom, P.R. and Weber, R.J. 1982b. The value of information in a sealed-bid auction. *Journal of Mathematical Economics* 10, 105–14.

Milgrom, P.R. and Weber, R.J. 1985. Distributional strategies for games with incomplete information. *Mathematics of Operations Research* 10, 619–32.

Moore, J. 1984. Global incentive constraints in auction design. *Econometrica* 52, 1523–5.

Myerson, R.B. 1981. Optimal auction design. *Mathematics of Operations Research* 6, 58–73.

Myerson, R.B. and Satterthwaite, M.A. 1983. Efficient mechanisms for bilateral trading. *Journal of Economic Theory* 29, 265–81.

Ortega-Reichert, A. 1968. *Models for Competitive Bidding Under Uncertainty*. Technical Report 8, Operations Research Department Stanford University.

Palfrey, T.R. 1985. Uncertainty resolution, private information aggregation and the Cournot competitive limit. *Review of Economic Studies* 52, 69–83.

Plott, C.R. and Sunder, S. 1982. Efficiency of experimental security markets with insider information: an application of rational expectations models. *Journal of Political Economy* 90, 663–98.

Reece, D.K. 1978. Competitive bidding for offshore petroleum leases. *Bell Journal of Economics* 9, 369–84.

Reece, D.K. 1979. Alternative bidding mechanisms for offshore petroleum leases. *Bell Journal of Economics* 10, 659–69.

Riley, J. 1986. Ex post information in auctions. Discussion Paper 367, University of California at Los Angeles, March.

Riley, J. and Samuelson, W. 1981. Optimal auctions. *American Economic Review* 71, 381–92.

Schmeidler, D. 1980. Walrasian analysis via strategic outcome functions. *Econometrica* 48, 1585–93.

Shapley, L. and Shubik, M. 1977. Trade using one commodity as a means of payment. *Journal of Political Economy* 85, 937–68.

Smith, V. 1982. Microeconomic systems as experimental science. *American Economic Review* 72, 923–55.

Stark, R.M. and Rothkopf, M.H. 1979. Competitive bidding: a comprehensive bibliography. *Operations Research* 27, 364–90.

Vickrey, W. 1961. Counterspeculation, auctions and competitive sealed tenders. *Journal of Finance* 16, 8–37.

Vickrey, W. 1962. Auctions and bidding games. In *Recent Advances in Game Theory*, ed. O. Morgenstern and A. Tucker, Princeton: Princeton University Press.

Wilson, R. 1977. A bidding model of 'perfect' competition. *Review of Economic Studies* 44, 511–18.

Wilson, R. 1978. Competitive exchange. *Econometrica* 46, 557–85.

Wilson, R. 1979. Auctions of shares. *Quarterly Journal of Economics* 93, 675–89.

Wilson, R. 1985. Incentive efficiency of double auctions. *Econometrica* 53, 1101–16.

Wilson, R. 1987. Equilibria of bid–ask markets. In *Arrow and the Ascent of Economic Theory: Essays in Honour of Kenneth J. Arrow*, ed. G. Feiwel, London: Macmillan.

The Coase Theorem

ROBERT D. COOTER

Anyone who has taught the Coase Theorem to fresh minds has experienced first hand the wonder and admiration which it inspires, yet Coase never wrote it down, and, when others try, it probably turns out to be false or a tautology. The proposition, or propositions, called the Coase Theorem was originally developed through a series of examples (Coase, 1960). Like a judge, Coase steadfastly refused to articulate broad generalizations in his original paper. Like a judge's opinion, for every interpretation of his paper there is a plausible alternative. Instead of trying to arrive at the ultimate answer, I will offer several conventional interpretations of the Coase Theorem and illustrate them with one of his examples. After more than twenty years of debate the conventional interpretations appear to have exhausted its meanings.

A central insight in microeconomics is that free exchange tends to move resources to their highest valued use, in which case the allocation of resources is said to be Pareto efficient. Besides ownership of resources, the law creates many other entitlements, such as the right to use one's land in a certain way, the right to be free from a nuisance, the right to compensation for tortuous accidents, or the right to performance on a contract. Coase can be regarded as having generalized propositions about the exchange of resources to cover propositions about the exchange of legal entitlements. Under this interpretation, the Coase Theorem states that *the initial allocation of legal entitlements does not matter from an efficiency perspective so long as they can be freely exchanged.* In other words, misallocation of legal entitlements by law will be cured in the market by free exchange.

This interpretation suggests that insuring the efficiency of law is a matter of removing impediments to the free exchange of legal entitlements. Legal entitlements often suffer from vagueness, which makes their value difficult to assess. Furthermore, the courts are not always willing to enforce contracts for the sale of legal entitlements. Consequently, under the 'free exchange interpretation', the efficiency of law is to be secured by defining entitlements clearly and enforcing private contracts for their exchange.

Besides freedom of exchange, there are other conditions which economists usually regard as necessary for markets to allocate resources efficiently. One such condition concerns the elusive, but unavoidable, concept of transaction costs. Narrowly conceived, transaction costs refer to the time and effort required to carry out a transaction. In some circumstances these costs can be very high, as when a deal involves several parties at different locations. High transaction costs can block the workings of markets which would otherwise be efficient. Broadly conceived, transaction costs refer to any use of resources required to negotiate and enforce agreements, including the cost of information needed to formulate a bargaining strategy, the time spent higgling, and the cost of preventing cheating by the parties to the bargain. Stressing the 'transaction cost interpretation', the Coase Theorem can be regarded as stating that *the initial allocation of legal entitlements does not matter from an efficiency perspective so long as the transaction costs of exchange are nil.*

Like a frictionless plane in physics, a costless transaction is a logical construction, rather than something encountered in life. Keeping this fact in mind, the policy prescription following from the transaction cost interpretation of the Coase Theorem is to use a law to minimize transaction costs, not eliminate them. According to this line of reasoning, rather than allocating legal entitlement efficiently in the first place, lawmakers are more likely to achieve efficiency by lubricating their exchange. Legal procedure is rife with devices whose purpose is to avoid litigation by encouraging private agreements involving an exchange of legal entitlement.

The 'transaction costs' interpretation focuses attention on some obstacles to exchanging legal entitlement, specifically the cost of negotiating and enforcing private agreements. When 'transaction costs' are given a reasonably circumspect definition, there are additional obstacles to private exchange besides transaction costs. The theory of regulation has developed a finer, richer classification based upon deviations from perfect competition (Schultze, 1977). To illustrate, a monopolist can increase his profits by supplying less than the competitive amount of the good and forcing the price up. Thus monopoly is a form of market failure which is usually distinguished from transaction costs. Stressing this 'market failures interpretation', the Coase Theorem can be regarded as stating that *the initial allocation of legal entitlements does not matter from an efficiency perspective so long as they can be exchanged in a perfectly competitive market.*

This interpretation suggests that ensuring the efficiency of law is a matter of ensuring the existence of perfectly competitive markets for legal entitlements. The conditions of perfect competition include the existence of many buyers and sellers, the absence of external effects, full information about price and quality by the participants in the market and no transaction costs.

The three interpretations can be illustrated by an historical example which Coase made famous. Wood and coal-burning locomotives emit sparks that set fire to farmers' fields from time to time. Each of the parties can take precautions to reduce the damage caused by fires. To illustrate, the farmers can avoid planting and storing crops along the margins of the railroad tracks, and the railroad can install spark arresters or run fewer trains.

Upon first inspection, it seems that the law controls the incentives for precaution by the parties, and, consequently, determines the amount of damage from fires. To illustrate, injunction is the conventional remedy in property law for a nuisance. If the farmers have a right to enjoin the railroad and shut it down until it stops emitting sparks, it seems that there will be little or no damage from sparks. Conversely, if the railroad has the right to operate trains with impunity, it seems that there will be a lot of damage. According to the Coase Theorem, these appearances are misleading, because while the law creates the initial allocation of entitlements, the market determines the final allocation. To illustrate, if farmers have a right to enjoin the railroad, then can sell this right. Specifically, the railroad could pay a sum of money to the farmers in exchange for a legally binding promise not to enjoin the railroad. Conversely, if the railroad has the right to emit sparks with impunity, it can sell this right. Specifically, farmers could pay a sum of money to the railroad in exchange for a legally binding promise to reduce spark emissions.

Whatever the initial allocation of rights, the farmers and the railroad have an incentive to continue trading entitlements so long as there are potential gains from trade. As with ordinary goods, the gains from trading legal entitlements are not exhausted until each entitlement is held by the party who values it the most. To illustrate, if, say, farmers have a right to be free from sparks, and if the entitlement to emit sparks is worth more to the railroad than the right to be free from sparks is worth to farmers, both parties will benefit from the farmers selling their rights to the railroad. The potential gains from trade are exhausted when entitlements are allocated efficiently. Thus, when the market works, the equilibrium allocation of legal entitlements will be efficient.

The three interpretations of the Coase Theorem give different accounts of the conditions that must be satisfied in order for this market to work. According to the 'free exchange' interpretation, the equilibrium allocation of entitlements will be efficient if entitlements are clearly defined and contracts for their exchange are enforceable. In the example, the conditions of the 'free exchange' interpretation are apparently met when the farmers have the right to enjoin the nuisance, or when the railroad has the right to emit sparks with impunity. Thus, according to the free exchange interpretation of the Coase Theorem, it does not matter from an efficiency perspective whether farmers have the right to enjoin the railroad or the railroad has the right to pollute with impunity.

The conclusion about efficiency is different under the 'transaction cost' interpretation. If there are many farmers, the cost of negotiating and enforcing an agreement among them would be high, especially since individual farmers might hold out for a larger share of the surplus, so inefficiencies in the initial allocation of entitlements would probably persist in spite of opportunities for private agreements. On the other hand, if there are just a few farmers, the cost of negotiating and enforcing an agreement between them and the railroad would be low, so the theorem predicts that the equilibrium allocation of entitlements would be efficient.

Turning to the third version, according to the 'perfect competition' interpretation, the equilibrium allocation of entitlements will be efficient if the conditions of perfect competition are satisfied in the market for legal entitlements. In the example of the railroad and the farmers, there is only one railroad, so the market is characterized by monopoly rather than perfect competition. Furthermore, there may be other types of failure in the conditions of perfect competition. For example, farmers may have more information than the railroad about the harm caused by sparks, whereas the railroad may have more information than the farmers about the technology for reducing spark emissions. In view of these facts, the exchange of legal entitlements between the farmers and the railroad would depart far from the conditions of perfect competition, so the market might fail to cure inefficiencies in the initial allocation of legal entitlements.

Of course, the initial allocation of rights always matters from the perspective of income distribution. To illustrate, if efficiency requires the railroad to be free from injunction, granting the farmers the right to injunctive relief will motivate the railroad to try to buy this right. The purchase is a cost to the railroad and income to the farmers. Conversely, granting impunity to the railroad will save it the cost of purchasing the right and deprive farmers of the income from selling it. Like scarce resources, scarce legal rights are valuable.

IS THE COASE THEOREM TRUE OR FALSE? In economics, a 'proof' is a derivation from generally accepted behavioural assumptions. As I will show, attempts to formulate the Coase Theorem in any of its three interpretations encounter obstacles which suggests that it is probably false or a mere tautology.

The weakest form of the theorem asserts that legal entitlements will be allocated efficiently under perfect competition. When Arrow (1969) examined externalities similar to those discussed by Coase, he showed that the efficiency conditions can be interpreted as the equilibrium conditions in a competitive market for the exchange of externality rights. But, as indicated by Arrow and others (Starrett, 1972), this formal demonstration has little practical value because externalities by their nature have characteristics which prevent the formation of competitive markets.

To illustrate, suppose that pollution is forbidden except by holders of resaleable pollution coupons issued by the government. Each pollutee who holds a coupon thereby prevents pollution from occurring, whereas each polluter who acquires a coupon uses it to increase the amount of pollution. Obviously, the social benefits of an individual pollutee retaining a coupon exceed his private benefits, so pollutees will sell too many of them. Equivalently, the social cost of a polluter acquiring a coupon exceeds his private cost, so polluters will acquire too many of them. This divergence between private and social costs is itself an externality. So the attempt to eliminate externalities by setting up a market for pollution coupons just gives rise to a new type of externality (for details, see Cooter, 1982). In reality, there are no perfectly competitive markets for externalities of the type discussed by Coase, and it seems impossible for them to arise spontaneously by private agreement. There might be some way for the government to create a pseudo-market (e.g. Groves, 1976), but none has been implemented.

Turning from the perfectly competitive market interpretation to the transaction cost interpretation of the Coase Theorem, observe that a private solution is likely to be efficient in cases affecting only a few parties, as, say, when contiguous land owners negotiate concerning a nuisance caused by one of them. If only a few parties are involved, the prices of entitlements will be negotiated instead of the parties acting as price-takers, which violates an assumption of perfect competition, but such negotiations often succeed anyway. According to the transaction cost interpretation of the Coase Theorem, externality problems affecting small numbers of people should have efficient solutions.

Although accurate as a rule of thumb, the transaction cost interpretation is not strictly true. It rests upon the proposition that bargaining reaches an efficient conclusion when the costs of negotiating and enforcing agreements is nil (Regan, 1972). In reality, bargaining among small numbers of people sometimes breaks down – unions strike, hijackers kill hostages, realtors lose sales because of disagreements over the price, disputes go to trial, and so forth. The essential obstacle, which has nothing to do with the cost of communicating or enforcing agreements, is the strategic character of bargaining. By definition, a bargaining situation has the characteristic that a surplus can be achieved by agreement, but there is no settled way for dividing it up among the beneficiaries. A self-interested negotiator will press his claim to a share of the surplus as far as he dares without destroying the basis for cooperation. In economic jargon, the rational negotiator demands an additional dollar so long as the resulting increase in the probability of noncooperation creates an expected loss of less than a dollar. When negotiators underestimate an opponent's resolve, they press too hard and the negotiations fail to reach an agreement. Thus bargaining situations are inherently unstable.

Seen in this light, the transaction cost interpretation of the Coase Theorem errs in the direction of optimism by assuming that cooperation will always occur when bargaining is costless. The polar opposite viewpoint, which has been called the 'Hobbes Theorem' (Cooter, 1982), errs in the direction of pessimism by assuming that the problem of dividing the surplus can only be solved by coercive force, not by cooperation. Reality lies in between the poles of optimism and pessimism, because strategic behaviour causes bargaining to fail in some cases, but not in every case.

The challenge to theory and empirical research raised by this interpretation of the Coase Theorem is to predict when legal entitlements will be allocated efficiently by private agreements. To advance this debate, broad labels such as 'transaction costs' and 'free exchange' must yield to substantive, detailed descriptions of the conditions under which private bargaining about legal entitlements succeeds. Fortunately, a more satisfactory bargaining theory has begun to emerge in recent years which adheres more closely to reality. According to this account, bargaining will break down for strategic reasons in a percentage of cases, but in equilibrium no one is surprised by the frequency with which breakdowns occur. (The key concept is the Bayesian Nash equilibrium; see Harsanyi, 1968, and Cooter and Marks, 1982.)

In economics, an 'empirical test' is a comparison between a prediction and facts. Recently, attempts have been made to test the Coase Theorem, for example, by determining the conditions under which bargaining in small groups reaches an efficient conclusion (Spitzer, 1982). The new developments in game theory, combined with the associated empirical research, hold the promise of finally establishing a scientific account of the conditions under which inefficient allocations of legal entitlements will be cured by private agreements.

WHAT IS THE SIGNIFICANCE OF THE COASE THEOREM? Pigou used economics to defend the common law principle that a party who causes a nuisance should be enjoined or required to pay damages. According to Pigou, the common law rules tend to promote economic efficiency by internalizing social costs. In some cases, he found gaps in the common law which require supplementary legislation, such as imposing a tax upon polluters equal to the social cost of pollution.

Coase's paper was framed as an attack upon Pigou's analysis of the law of nuisance. Coase disagreed with the conclusion that government action, through nuisance law or taxation, is typically required to achieve efficiency. The Coase Theorem suggests that the externalities represented by nuisances will sometimes, or perhaps usually, be self-correcting. I have argued that the forms of market failure are too diverse to be subsumed under a reasonably circumspect concept of transaction costs, and, consequently, the transaction cost interpretation of the Coase Theorem should be regarded as false or as a tautology whose truth is achieved by inflating the definition of transaction costs. Although the obstacles to spontaneous, private solutions of externalities are broader than suggested by the Coase Theorem, the role of government in lubricating private agreements, rather than issuing commands, is much favoured in the contemporary economic understanding of regulation.

In the event that government action is required to correct a nuisance, Coase denied Pigou's claim that the common law concept of causality is a useful guide to assigning responsibility. In Coase's view, the fact that someone 'causes' a nuisance, as judged by common law principles, does not imply that holding him liable or enjoining him is efficient. For Coase, the question of efficiency is to be decided by a balancing of cost and benefits in which the role of causality is not decisive. Coase's suggestion that causality should have little bearing upon legal responsibility contradicts countless court decisions and appears to have had little impact upon the practice or theory of law.

Whatever the merits of his arguments, Coase offered a challenge to widely accepted views in public finance. Before his article appeared, not much attention was paid to the possibility that externalities could be cured by private bargains. Thus Coase's claim went to the heart of a major debate in economics. Furthermore, the publication of Coase's article can be regarded as a breakthrough for the subject which has acquired the name of 'law and economics'. Before publication of Coase's article, economic *analysis* (as opposed to economic thought) had received little application to the common law, which is at the core of legal theory and method as taught in law schools. By analysing cases from property law in a lawyerly style, yet drawing upon microeconomics to guide the analysis, Coase demonstrated the fruitfulness of the economic analysis of the common law. He inspired a generation of scholars who pioneered the economic analysis of law, although he did not use the mathematical tools which have come to characterize the subject twenty years later.

BIBLIOGRAPHY

Arrow, K. 1969. The organization of economic activity: issues pertinent to the choice of market versus non-market allocation. In *The Analysis and Evaluation of Public Expenditure: the PPB System.* US Congress, Joint Economic Committee, Washington, DC: GPO. Reprinted in *Public Expenditure and Policy Analysis*, ed. R. Haveman and J. Margolis, Chicago: Rand McNally, 1977.

Coase, R. 1960. The problem of social cost. *Journal of Law and Economics* 3(1), October, 1–44.

Cooter, R. 1980. How the law circumvents Starrett's nonconvexity. *Journal of Economic Theory* 22(3), June, 145–9.

Cooter, R. 1982. The cost of Coase. *Journal of Legal Studies* 11(1), January, 1–34.

Cooter, R. and Marks, S. 1982. Bargaining in the shadow of the law; a testable model of strategic behavior. *Journal of Legal Studies* 11(2), 225–52.

Groves, T. 1976. Information, incentives, and the internalization of production externalities. In *Theory and Measurement of Economic Externalities*, ed. A.Y. Steven, London and New York: Academic Press.

Harsanyi, J.C. 1967–8. Games with incomplete information played by 'Bayesian' players, I–III. *Management Science*, Part I, 14(3), November 1967, 159–82; Part II, 14(5), January 1968, 320–34; Part III, 14(7), March 1968, 486–502.

Pigou, A.C. 1920. *The Economics of Welfare.* London: Macmillan. 4th edn, 1932; New York: St. Martin's Press, 1952.

Regan, D. 1972. The problem of social cost revisited. *Journal of Law and Economics* 15(2), October, 427–37.

Schultze, C. 1977. *The Public Use of Private Interest.* Washington, DC: Brookings.

Spitzer, M. 1982. The Coase Theorem: some experimental tests. *Journal of Law and Economics* 25(1), 73–98.

Starrett, D. 1972. Fundamental non-convexities in the theory of externalities. *Journal of Economic Theory* 4(2), April, 180–99.

Decentralization

E. MALINVAUD

The main question to be answered by the theory of resource allocation, or by the theory of economic organization, concerns the performances of alternative systems characterized by different degrees of centralization of decision taking. A fully centralized system runs the risk of being inefficient because it does not create proper economic incentives and the centre is poorly informed. A pure market system with its high degree of decentralization runs the risk of bringing inequitable results and being inefficient because markets can never be complete, externalities exist and public wants tend to be neglected. Can these risks be avoided within the two opposite extremes of pure centralization or full decentralization? Can intermediate systems better resolve the difficulties? And if so, how?

Basic to the discussion rate are two features: the nature of the *information* held by various agents, and the *incentives* that should lead them to behave in conformity with collective requirements. These features and the issue of decentralization do not only appear for full economic systems, which this essay will consider, but also for the internal organization of firms or communities. They are stylized in the principal–agent problem: which rules should determine how to share the proceeds of an activity between the principal owner and his better-informed agent? (Ross, 1973; Grossman and Hart, 1983).

For the clarification of the complex issues involved, theory starts from a model of the conditions of economic activity. It makes assumptions such that, independently of economic organization, there exists a best outcome, or at least a set of 'optimal' outcomes. It then asks how well alternative forms of organization succeed in finding, implementing or at least approaching this best outcome or set of optimal outcomes.

By so doing, the theory discussed here neglects two related questions: how to determine what should be considered as 'the best' outcome in a society with many individuals, and which non-economic considerations interfere with the issue of decentralization? The theory of social choice shows the fundamental difficulty of the first question (Arrow, 1951), which is avoided when optimality is identified with Pareto efficiency. As for the second, philosophers may find in human nature or in the aims pursued by human societies reasons that favour some organization, beyond its economic performance; in particular, the right of individuals to autonomy appears fundamental in Western culture and is an important justification of decentralization, and even of the market system for such economists as Hayek (1944).

FORMAL CONCEPTS AND PRELIMINARIES. The following conceptual apparatus, although not yet common, is well suited to the purpose (see Hurwicz, 1960; Mount and Reiter, 1974).

An *economic environment* is defined by a set of commodities and their possible uses, by a list of agents and their characteristics (technology, endowments, preferences etc.), and by an initial information structure (what each agent knows). The feasible set of economic environments defines 'the economy'.

An important property of an economy is its higher or lower degree of *decomposability*, which concerns agents' characteristics and the information structure. The highest decomposability is assumed in competitive equilibrium theory, where all consumption is private, no external effect exists and a *private information structure* prevails (each agent perfectly knows its own characteristics and the situation on all markets, but nothing else). But models with public goods, for instance, usually admit some decomposability, which matters for the validity of the results.

An *optimality correspondence* $P: E \rightarrow A$ defines which vectors of actions simultaneously taken by the various agents are optimal when the economic environment is e, i.e. optimal vectors belong to $P(e)$ (clearly, E is the set of feasible e, i.e. 'the economy', while A is the set of feasible vectors a, each one of them defining the actions taken by all the agents). For instance $P(e)$ may be the set of Pareto efficient vectors. But in the theory discussed here, it is often more narrowly defined so as to take equity considerations into account: a social utility function may have to be maximized or a rule on the consumers 'income distribution' satisfied.

A *resource allocation mechanism* $f: E \rightarrow A$ should select one $a = f(e)$ for each environment e (in some cases f may be multivalued, i.e. become a correspondence). The best formalized mechanism is the competitive equilibrium of a 'private ownership economy'. A study of decentralization requires a careful specification of the mechanism, which is typically viewed as operating in two stages: first, an iterative exchange of messages, usually between the agents and a centre, resulting in a message correspondence $g: E \rightarrow M$ (the message $m = g(e)$ specifies what information about e has been collected at the centre), second an outcome function $h: M \rightarrow A$. For instance, the competitive mechanism is often specified as resulting from the tâtonnement process, in which an auctioneer learns which demands and supplies are announced at various proposed vectors of prices, and searches for the equilibrium prices; once these price are found, the outcome function gives the equilibrium exchanges, hence productions and consumptions.

The performances of alternative mechanisms of course concern the final result: one must know whether the outcome $f(e)$ belongs to the optimal set $P(e)$ for all environments in E, or at least for a precise subset of E, and how close it is to $P(e)$ otherwise. But interesting performances also concern intermediate features of the mechanism, which usually is iterative. At step t the previously collected message m_{t-1} is enriched according to $m_t = g_t(m_{t-1}, e)$ and, if necessary, the process could end by $a = h_t(m_t)$. In a *finite* procedure it does end at T with $m = m_T$ and $h(m) = h_T(m_T)$; but most mechanisms assume an infinite sequence of m_t for $t = 1, 2, \ldots$ ad infinitum. One must then know whether and how $h_t(m_t)$ approaches $P(e)$, monotonically or otherwise. Since the transmission of information is costly, the nature and size of the message space M_t to which m_t belongs are also important characteristics (Mount and Reiter, 1974).

THE PLANNING PROBLEM. Early in this century many economists objected to socialist planning programmes that could not be implemented, because they unrealistically assumed that a central administration could have the knowledge and computing power required for an efficient control of economic activity. The leading figure was L. von Mises (1920 in particular); but Hayek (1935) was first to emphasize the problems raised by the decentralization of information. Socialist economists answered that decentralized mechanisms could operate, either mimicking the market system while being free of its deficiencies (Lange, 1936) or using different well conceived modes of information gathering (Taylor, 1929). The debate was, in the interwar years, the subject of the '*economic theory of socialism*'. (For a well-documented survey, see Bergson, 1948.)

The problem was again taken up during the 1960s, in particular because the logic of efficient planning was discussed in Eastern and Western Europe (Arrow and Hurwicz, 1960; Kornai, 1967; Malinvaud, 1967; Heal, 1973). Many planning procedures were rigorously studied as resource allocation mechanisms. Their definition implied an iterative exchange of information between a Central Planning Board and firms, sometimes also representative consumers. The additional messages provided by the function g_t at step t then consisted of *prospective indices* announced by the Board, for instance prices for the various commodities, and replies called *proposals* sent to the Board by firms and other agents, for instance preferred techniques of production and their input requirements, or supplies and demands.

In this discussion it is common to distinguish between price-guided procedures, in which the Board announces price vectors, and other procedures, in which quantity indices or targets worked out at the centre play a more or less important role. The nature and properties of the environment are then found to be crucial for the determination of the relative performances of alternative procedures, in particular of price-guided against quantity-guided procedures (Weitzman, 1974).

The analytical study of various procedures usually assumes that decentralized agents exactly follow specified rules for the determination of their proposals and so faithfully reveal part of their private information. Some procedures are then found to be efficient and to permit achievement of distributive objectives. But efficiency is typically easier precisely in those environments that are also favourable to the efficiency of free competition. Besides the possibility of incorrect reporting, the main difficulty concerning the relevance of this literature is to know whether its models provide an approximate representation of procedures that are actually used, or at least administratively feasible. Manove (1976) has made this claim for his representation of Soviet planning.

THE PUBLIC GOOD PROBLEM. The most relevant field of application may very well be the theory of public goods. Decisions concerning the provision of public services and their financing cannot be fully decentralized; but the knowledge required is dispersed and must be gathered in a proper way. Hence even the positive theory of public goods was often formulated along lines that look like those of planning procedures (Malinvaud, 1971). The same remark applies to decisions concerning public projects with large fixed costs, even if their output is privately consumed.

Considered as a planning procedure, the search for the best decision is often viewed as involving 'prospective indices' that define amounts of service to be provided, ask for corresponding individual marginal utilities and look whether the sum of the latter would cover the cost of additional service. This is compatible with the dual arrangement for private goods, prices being announced, supplies and demands being the replies. The procedure is then quantity-guided for public goods and price-guided for private goods (Drèze and Vallée Poussin, 1971).

The collective consumption of many types of public goods is not really national but limited to local communities (primary education, city transports etc.). Administrative science sees the decentralization issue as being to know at which level decisions should be taken: at the national level, so as to distribute fairly these services among communities, or at the local level, so as to permit better adaptation to local needs and wishes. Economists do not seem to have contributed to this issue; their discussion of local public goods assumes full administrative decentralization (Tiebout, 1956).

INCENTIVE COMPATIBILITY. The study of a decentralized system has to consider whether the actual reports and behaviour of individual agents do not deviate from what they are supposed to report and do; in case of deviations, how are the performances of the system affected? The problem is serious: once the rules of organization and decisions are known, individual agents may benefit from misreporting their private information or from behaving in a way that, although deviant, does not clearly appear to be so. In other words, they may act as players in a game, rather than as members of a team, and this may be more or less detrimental for the optimality of the final result.

The problem has long been known for organizations in which some agents do not individually benefit from what is achieved and therefore lack the incentive to do their best. Monopolistic or other non-competitive behaviour is often interpreted as a breach of the normal rules of resource allocation. In the theory of public good the 'free rider problem' occurs as soon as some individuals, having a high marginal utility for the public good, would benefit from hiding this fact so as to contribute little to the financing of the good.

Study of the problem has been active during the past two decades (Green and Laffont, 1979). The fundamental difficulty has been exhibited by such results as the following one: in the classical model of an exchange economy with a finite number of consumers, no procedure can be found that would necessarily lead to a Pareto efficient result in which individuals, acting as players in a non-cooperative game, would faithfully report (Hurwicz, 1972). However, misreporting may not prevent a procedure from eventually leading to an optimum, as was proved in a number of cases.

Experiments moreover show that the game-theoretic approach to the incentive problem may be misleading because it neglects non-economic motivations that individuals may find for accepting a team-like behaviour and therefore for faithfully reporting (Smith, 1980).

BIBLIOGRAPHY

Arrow, K. 1951. *Social Choice and Individual Values.* New York: Wiley.

Arrow, K. and Hurwicz, L. 1960. Decentralization and computation in resource allocation. In *Essays in Economics and Econometrics in Honour of Harold Hotelling*, ed. R. Pfouts, Chapel Hill: University of North Carolina Press.

Bergson, A. 1948. Socialist economics. In *A Survey of Contemporary Economics*, ed. H. Ellis, Philadelphia: Blakiston.

Drèze, J. and Vallée Poussin, D. de la. 1971. A tâtonnement process for public goods. *Review of Economic Studies* 38, 133–50.

Green, J. and Laffont, J.-J. 1979. *Incentives in Public Decision-Making.* Amsterdam: North-Holland.

Grossman, S. and Hart, O. 1983. An analysis of the principal–agent problem. *Econometrica* 51(1), January, 7–45.

Hayek, F. 1935. Socialist calculation: the state of the debate. In *Collectivist Economic Planning*, ed. F. Hayek, London: G. Routledge & Sons; New York: A.M. Kelley, 1967.

Hayek, F. 1944. *The Road to Serfdom.* Chicago: University of Chicago Press.

Heal, G. 1973. *The Theory of Economic Planning.* Amsterdam: North-Holland.

Hurwicz, L. 1960. Optimality and information efficiency in resource allocation processes. In *Mathematical Methods in the Social Sciences*, ed. K.J. Arrow, S. Karlin and P. Suppes, Stanford: Stanford University Press.

Hurwicz, L. 1972. On informationally decentralized systems. In *Decision and Organization*, ed. R. Radner and C. McGuire, Amsterdam: North-Holland.

Kornai, J. 1967. *Mathematical Planning of Structural Decisions.* Amsterdam: North-Holland.

Lange, O. 1936. On the economic theory of socialism. *Review of Economic Studies* 4, 53–71, 123–42.

Malinvaud, E. 1967. Decentralized procedures for planning. In Malinvaud, E. and Bacharach, M., *Activity Analysis in the Theory of Growth and Planning*, Macmillan: London; New York: St. Martin's Press.

Malinvaud, E. 1971. A planning approach to the public good problem. *Swedish Journal of Economics*, 11, 96–112.

Manove, M. 1976. Soviet pricing, profit and technological choice. *Review of Economic Studies* 43(3), October, 413–21.

Mises, L. von 1920. Economic calculation in the socialist commonwealth. First published in German in *Archiv für Sozialwissenschaft*, April; English translation in *Collectivist Economic Planning*, ed. F. Hayek, London: G. Routledge & Sons, 1935; New York: A.M. Kelley, 1967.

Mount, K. and Reiter, S. 1974. The informational size of message spaces. *Journal of Economic Theory* 8(2), June, 161–92.

Ross, S. 1973. The economic theory of agency: the principal's problem. *American Economic Review* 63(2), May, 134–9.

Smith, V. 1980. Experiments with a decentralized mechanism for public good decisions. *American Economic Review* 70(4), September, 584–99.

Taylor, F.M. 1929. The guidance of production in a socialist state. *American Economic Review* 19, March, 1–8.

Tiebout, C.M. 1956. A pure theory of local expenditures. *Journal of Political Economy* 64, October, 416–24.

Weitzman, M. 1974. Prices versus quantities. *Review of Economic Studies* 41(4), October, 477–91.

Economic Organization and Transaction Costs

STEVEN N.S. CHEUNG

One important extension of the Coase Theorem states that, if all costs of transactions are zero, the use of resources will be similar, no matter how production and exchange activities are arranged. This implies that in the absence of transaction costs, alternative institutional or organizational arrangements would provide no basis for choice and hence could not be interpreted by economic theory. Not only would economic organization be randomly determined; there actually would not be any organization to speak of: production and exchange activities would simply be guided by the invisible hand of the market.

But organizations or various institutional arrangements do exist, and to interpret both their presence and their variation, they must be treated as the results of choice, subject to the constraints of transaction costs.

In the broadest sense transaction costs encompass all those costs that cannot be conceived to exist in a Robinson Crusoe economy where neither property rights, nor transactions, nor any kind of economic organization can be found. This breadth of definition is necessary because it is often impossible to separate the different types of cost. So defined, transaction costs may then be viewed as a spectrum of institutional costs including those of information, of negotiation, of drawing up and enforcing contracts, of delineating and policing property rights, of monitoring performance, and of changing institutional arrangements. In short, they comprise all those costs not directly incurred in the physical process of production. Apparently these costs are weighty indeed, and to term them 'transaction costs' may be misleading because they may loom large even in an economy where market transactions are suppressed, as in a communist state.

By definition, an organization requires someone to organize it. In the broadest sense, all production and exchange activities not guided by the invisible hand of the market are organized activities. Thus, any arrangement that requires the use of a manager, a director, a supervisor, a clerk, an enforcer, a lawyer, a judge, an agent, or even a middleman implies the presence of an organization. These professions would not exist in the Crusoe economy, and payments for their employment are transaction costs.

When transaction costs are defined to include all costs not found in a Crusoe economy, and economic organizations are defined equally broadly to include any arrangement requiring the service of a visible hand, a corollary appears: all organization costs are transaction costs, and vice versa. That is why during the past two decades economists have striven to interpret the various forms of organizational arrangements in terms of the varying costs of transactions.

Some obvious examples will illustrate the point. A worker in a factory (an organization) may be paid by a piece rate or by a wage rate. If the costs of measuring and enforcing performance (one type of transaction cost) are zero, then either arrangement will yield the same result. But if these costs are positive, the piece-rate contract will more likely prevail if the costs of measuring outputs are relatively low, whereas the wage contract will more likely be chosen if the costs of measuring hours and enforcing performance are low relative to the costs of measuring outputs. As another example, some restaurants (again an organization) measure the quantity of food sold; others serve buffet dinners, allowing customers to eat as much as they please at a fixed price per head. The cost of metering and quantifying food consumption relative to the basic cost of the food will determine which arrangement is chosen. In the total absence of transaction costs, the factory or the restaurant would not exist in the first place, because customers would buy directly from the input owners who produce the goods and services.

As early as 1937, R.H. Coase interpreted the emergence of the firm (an organization) in light of the costs of determining market prices (transaction costs). When these costs are substantial because of the difficulties of measuring separate contributions by workers and of negotiating prices for separate components of a product, a worker may choose to work in a factory (a firm); he surrenders the right to use his labour by contract and voluntarily submits to direction by a visible hand, instead of personally selling his services or contributions to customers through the invisible hand of the market. The firm is therefore said to supersede the market. As the supersession progresses, the saving in the costs of determining prices will be countered by the rising costs of supervision and of management in the firm. Equilibrium is reached when, at the margin, the cost saving in the former equals the rising cost in the latter.

The firm superseding the market may be regarded as a factor market superseding a product market. If all costs of transactions were zero, the two markets would be inseparable in that a payment made by a customer to the owner of a factor of production would be the same as payment made to a product seller. In such a world it would be a fallacy to speak of the factor market and the product market as coexisting entities.

The presence of transaction costs is a prelude to the separation of the factor market from the product market. However, in some arrangements, such as the use of certain piece rates, it may become impossible to separate the one market from the other. Therefore, instead of viewing the firm as superseding the market, or the factor market as superseding the product market, it is more correct to view the organizational choice as one type of contract superseding another type. In these terms, the choice of organizational arrangements is actually the choice of contractual arrangements.

When organizational choices are viewed as contractual choices, it becomes evident that it is often impossible to draw a clear dividing line separating one organization from another. Take the firm, for example. It is often the case that the entrepreneur who holds employment contracts (and it is not clear whether it is the entrepreneur who employs the workers or the workers who employ the entrepreneur) may contract with other firms; a contractor may subcontract; a subcontractor may sub-subcontract further; and a worker may contract with a number of 'employers' or 'firms'. If the chain of contracts were allowed to spread, the 'firm' might encompass the whole economy. With this approach the size of the firm becomes indeterminate and unimportant. What are important are the choice of contracts and the costs of transactions that determine this choice.

Traditional economic analysis has been confined to resource allocation and income distribution. Contractual arrangements as a class of observations have been slighted in that tradition. In a world complicated by transaction costs, this neglect not only leaves numerous interesting observations unexplained, but actually obscures the understanding of resource allocation and income distribution. The economics of an organization or institution or, for that matter, the workings of various economic systems, were never placed in the proper perspectives under the traditional approach. For generations students were told that various kinds of 'imperfections' were the cause of seemingly mysterious observations: policies were 'misguided', or antitrust specialists were barking up the wrong trees.

The costs of introducing new and more valid ideas must have been enormous. Even today textbooks still discuss marginal productivity theory only with reference to fixed wage and rental payments. Yet economists have known all along that (for labour alone) payments may be in the peripheral forms of piece rates, bonuses, tips, commissions, or various sharing arrangements; moreover, even wage rates may assume a number of forms. Each type of contract implies different costs of supervision, of measurement, and of negotiation, and the form of economic organization, along with the function of the visible hand, changes whenever a different contractual arrangement is chosen.

The choice of contractual arrangements is not, of course, confined to the factor markets. In the product markets, pricing arrangements such as tie-in sales, full-line forcing, or membership fees associated with clubs, may similarly be interpreted in light of transaction costs. Further, business organizations in mergers, franchises and various forms of integration are now beginning to be viewed as transaction-cost phenomena. Indeed, close inspection of department stores and shopping centres reveals pricing and contractual arrangements between a central agent and individual sellers, as well as among the sellers themselves, which could not be explained by textbook economics.

Transaction costs are often difficult to measure and, as noted earlier, difficult to separate by type. However, the measurement problem can be avoided if only we are able to specify how these costs vary under different observable circumstances, and their different types are separable if viewed in terms of changes at the margin. These two conditions are requisite in the derivation of testable implications for the interpretation of organizational behaviour.

The use of transaction costs to analyse institutional (organizational) choice is superior to three other approaches. One approach would focus on incentives. However, incentives are not in principle observable, and we will do better in deriving testable propositions if the same problem is viewed in terms of the costs of enforcing performance. A second approach adopts risk. However, it is difficult to ascertain how risk is altered under different circumstances. Many risk problems, such as the uncertainty of whether an agreement will be honoured, are also problems of transaction costs, and it is easier to deal directly with those. Finally, some recent advances in transaction-cost analysis have called attention to the costs embodied in dishonesty, cheating, shirking and opportunistic behaviour. Yet these are loose terms and, whatever they describe, to some extent are always to be found. To the degree that we can identify the particular costs of transactions that promote dishonesty, that shadowy explanation is no longer needed. After all, in what sense can we say a person is 'increasingly dishonest' or 'increasingly opportunistic'?

The transaction-cost approach to analysis of economic organizations can be extended upward from a few participants to the 'government' or even the nation itself. At the lower level, the owners of condominium units almost as a rule form associations with specific by-laws and elect committees to act on matters of common concern, the decisions being determined by majority vote. The transaction costs of ballot voting are less than those of using prices and dollar votes in certain circumstances, and trivial matters may even be delegated to a 'dictatorial' manager to further reduce the cost of voting. Similarly, residents in a particular location may choose to incorporate into a city, selecting their own mayor, with a committee setting up the building codes, hiring firemen and policemen, and deciding other matters of common concern.

Private property rights offer the unique advantage of allowing individual property owners the option of *not* joining an organization. This choice is an effective restraint against the adoption of an organization with higher transaction costs. It is true that a home-owner in a given region may, by majority vote, lose his option of not joining in a city corporation (unlike a worker who, in a free enterprise economy, always has the option of not joining a 'firm'). But with private property rights the majority vote aims at cost saving, and a reluctant resident may exercise his own judgement by selling his house and moving elsewhere.

Private property rights further reduce transaction costs under competition. An entrepreneur or agent who wants to recruit other resource owners to join his organization must, under competition, offer attractive terms, and this can be achieved only if his organization can effectively reduce transaction costs. On the other hand, the resource owner competing to join an organization will be more inclined to deliver a good performance when at risk of losing his job.

The option of not joining an organization and the cost-reducing function of competition are, of course, restrained when an organization is extended to encompass an entire nation. When citizenship is dictated by birth, the option of not joining is restrained, and competition among nations to recruit members is decidedly less than among organizations within a nation. This relative lack of cost-reducing mechanisms is all the more evident in a communist state, where a citizen does not have the option of choosing an organization within that state.

A communist state may be regarded as a 'superfirm' in which comrades lack the option of not joining. Each worker is assigned to a particular job supervised and directed by the visible hands of comrade officials of varying ranks. In this aspect the communist state is remarkably similar to what Coase calls a 'firm', where workers are told what to do instead of being directed by market prices. But the lack of market prices in the communist state is not due to the costs of determining prices; rather, in the absence of private property rights market prices simply do not exist, and visible supervision by a hierarchy ranking becomes the remaining alternative to chaos.

The transaction costs of operating an organization are necessarily higher in a communist state than in a free enterprise economy, due to the lack of option of not joining and the lack of competition both to recruit members among organizations and to induce members to perform well.

If the transaction costs of operating organization were zero, resource allocation and income distribution would be the same in a communist state as in a free enterprise state: consumer preferences would be revealed without cost; auctioneers and monitors would provide freely all the services of gathering and collating information; workers and other factors of production would be directed free of cost to produce in perfect accord with consumer preference; each consumer would receive goods and services in conformity with his preferences; and the total income received by each worker, as determined costlessly by an arbitrator, would equal his marginal productivity plus a share of the rents of all resources other than labour, according to any of a number of criteria costlessly agreed upon. But such an ideal situation is obviously not to be found.

We therefore conclude that the poor economic performance of a communist state is attributable to the high transaction costs of operating that organization. Under the postulate of constrained maximization, the communist state survives for the same reason that any 'inefficient' organization survives: namely, the transaction costs of *changing* an organizational (institutional) arrangement are prohibitive. Such costs include those of obtaining information about the workings of alternative institutions, and of using persuasive or coercive power to alter the status of the privileged groups whose incomes might be adversely affected by the institution of a different form of economic organization.

BIBLIOGRAPHY

Alchian, A.A. and Demsetz, H. 1972. Production, information costs, and economic organization. *American Economic Review* 62, 777–95.

Barzel, Y. 1982. Measurement costs and the organization of markets. *Journal of Law and Economics* 25, 27–48.

Cheung, S.N.S. 1969. Transaction costs, risk aversion, and the choice of contractual arrangements. *Journal of Law and Economics* 12, 23–42.

Cheung, S.N.S. 1982. *Will China Go 'Capitalist'?* Hobart Paper 94, London: International Economic Association.

Cheung, S.N.S. 1983. The contractual nature of the firm. *Journal of Law and Economics* 26, 1–21.

Coase, R.H. 1937. The nature of the firm. *Economica* 4, 386–405.

Jensen, M.C. and Meckling, W.H. 1976. Theory of the firm: managerial behavior, agency costs and ownership structure. *Journal of Financial Economics* 3, 305–60.

Klein, B., Crawford, R.G. and Alchian, A.A. 1978. Vertical integration, appropriable rents, and the competitive contracting process. *Journal of Law and Economics* 21, 297–326.

Knight, F.H. 1921. *Risk Uncertainty and Profit*. Boston: Houghton Mifflin.

McManus, J.C. 1975. The costs of alternative economic organizations. *Canadian Journal of Economics* 8, 334.

Williamson, O.E. 1975. *Markets and Hierarchies: Analysis and Anti-Trust Implications.* Glencoe, Ill.: Free Press.

Exchange

ROBERT WILSON

The accepted purview of economics is the allocation of scarce resources. Allocation comprises production and exchange, according to a division between processes that transform commodities and those that transfer control. For production or consumption, exchange is essential to efficient use of resources. It allows decentralization and specialization in production; and for consumption, agents with diverse endowments or preferences require exchange to obtain maximal benefits. If two agents have differing marginal rates of substitution then there exists a trade benefiting both. The advantages of barter extend widely, e.g. to trade among nations and among legislators ('vote trading'), but it suffices here to emphasize markets with enforceable contracts for trading private property unaffected by externalities. In such markets, voluntary exchange involves trading bundles of commodities or obligations to the mutual advantage of all parties to the transaction.

In a market economy using money or credit, terms of trade are usually specified by prices. Besides purchases at prices posted by producers and distributors, exchange occurs in bargaining, auctions, and other contexts with repeated or competitive offers. In institutionalized 'exchanges' for trading commodities, brokers offer bid and ask prices; and for trading financial instruments, specialists cross orders and maintain markets continually by trading for their own accounts.

Records of transaction prices and quantities are the raw data of many empirical studies of economic activity, and explanation of these data is a major purpose of economic theory. Theories of exchange attempt to predict the terms of trade and the resulting transactions, depending on the market structure and the agents' attributes, including such features as each agent's endowment, productive opportunities, preferences and information. Also relevant are the markets accessible, the trading rules used and the contracts available; these may depend on property rights, search or transaction costs and on events observable or verifiable to enforce contracts. If a particular trading rule is used, it specifies the actions allowed each agent in each contingency, and the trades resulting from each combination of the agents' actions. These features are the ingredients of experimental designs to test theories, and they motivate models used for empirical estimates of market behaviour. Normative considerations are also relevant, and welfare analyses emphasize the distributional consequences of alternative trading procedures and contracts.

Most theories hypothesize that each agent acts purposefully to maximize (the expected utility of) gains from trade. Some behaviour may be erratic, customary, or reflect dependency on a *status quo*, but experimental and empirical evidence substantially affirms the hypothesis of 'rational' behaviour, at least in the aggregate. Although more general theories are available, the main features are explained by preferences that are quite regular, as assumed here: monotone, convex, as smooth as necessary, and possibly allowing risk aversion.

Typically there are many efficient allocations of a fixed endowment: any allocation that equates all agents' marginal rates of substitution is efficient. In the case of risk sharing, for example, an allocation is efficient if all agents achieve the same marginal rates of substitution between income in every two states. The distribution of endowments among agents evidently matters, however, and a major accomplishment has been the identification of a small set of salient efficient allocations. Named for Léon Walras, this set is a focus of nearly all theories, in the sense that other allocations are explained by departures from the Walrasian model. A major theme is to elaborate the special role of the Walrasian allocations.

An allocation is Walrasian if it is obtainable by trading at prices such that it would cost each agent more to obtain a preferable allocation. That is, items are bought at uniform prices available to all, and each agent chooses a preferred trade within a budget constraint imposed by the value of goods sold. A Walrasian allocation is necessarily efficient to the extent that markets are complete; for another allocation preferred by every agent would cost each agent more at the current prices and therefore more in total, which cannot be true if the preferred allocation is a redistribution of the present one. Conversely, each efficient allocation is Walrasian without further trade, since the agents' common marginal rates of substitution serve as the price ratios. The basic formulation considers trade for delivery in all future contingencies, but refined formulations elaborate the realistic case that markets reopen continually and trade is confined to a limited variety of contracts for spot and contingent future delivery.

Sufficient conditions for Walrasian allocations to exist have been established. Mainly these require that agents' preferences be convex and insatiable, and that each agent has an endowment sufficient to obtain a positive income. For 'most' economies the number of Walrasian allocations is finite; strong assumptions on substitution and income effects are required to ensure uniqueness.

Walrasian allocations and prices for specified models can be computed by solving a fixed-point problem and general methods have been divised. The task is complex (e.g. linear models with integer data can yield irrational prices) but an important simplifying feature is that the Walrasian prices depend only on the distribution of agents' attributes, and in particular only on the aggregate excess demand function. Essentially, any continuous function satisfying Walras's Law and homogeneity in prices is the excess demand for some economy.

The key requirement for a Walrasian allocation is that each agent's benefit be maximized within the budget imposed by the assigned prices, and that markets clear at those prices. Complete exploitation of all gains from trade may be precluded, however, by incomplete markets, pecuniary externalities (such as absence of necessary complementary goods), or insufficient contracts; or by strategic behaviour. If producers with monopoly power restrain output to elevate prices, or practise any of the myriad forms of price discrimination, then the resulting allocation is not Walrasian. Much discrimination segments markets via quality differentiation or bundling, but equally common is discriminatory pricing of the various conditions of delivery (e.g. spatial, temporal, service priority) or nonlinear pricing of quantities (e.g. two-part and block declining tariffs) if purchases can be monitored and resale markets are absent.

The Walrasian model of exchange is substantially defined by the absence of such practices affecting prices. It also relies on a fixed specification of agents, products, markets and contracts. The theory of economies with large firms having power to influence prices and to choose product designs is significantly incomplete. The deficiencies derive partly from inadequate formulations, and partly from technical considerations: characterizations and even the existence of equilibria (in non-randomized strategies) depend on special structural features. For example, the simplest models positing simultaneous choices of qualities and prices by several firms lack equilibria; models with sequential choices encounter similar obstacles but to lesser degrees. In addition, if firms have fixed costs and must avoid losses then efficiency may require nonlinear pricing and other discriminatory practices if lump-sum assessments imposed on customers are precluded.

Market clearing is also essential to the Walrasian model and prices are determined entirely by the required equality of demand and supply. In contrast, successive markets with overlapping generations of traders need not clear 'at infinity'. Such markets can exhibit complicated dynamics even if the underlying data of the economy are stationary. Similarly, continually repeated markets, where buyers and sellers arrive at the same rate that others depart after completing transactions, admit non-Walrasian prices or may have persistent excess on one side of the market if search or dispersed bargaining prevents immediate clearing.

When it is that among the feasible allocations the best prediction might be one of the Walrasian allocations, has been answered in several ways.

Competition is the first answer. On the supply side, for instance, with many sellers each one's incentive to defect from collusive pricing arrangements is increased. Absent collusion, if prices reflect supplies offered on the market and each seller chooses an optimal supply in response to anticipations of other sellers' supplies, then each seller's optimal percentage profit margin declines inversely with the number of sellers offering substitutes. Price discrimination, such as nonlinear pricing, is inhibited if there are many sellers, resale markets are available, or customers' purchases are difficult to monitor. Without capacity limitations, direct price competition among close or perfect substitutes erodes profits since undercutting is attractive. Although these conclusions are weakened to the extent that buyers incur search or switching costs, easy entry incurring no sunk costs remains important to ensure that markets are contestable and monopoly rents are eliminated. Monopoly rents are often substantially dissipated in entry deterrence, price wars and other competitive battles to retain or capture monopoly positions. This is true both when entrants bring perfect substitutes and more generally, since entrants tend to fill in the spectra of quality attributes and conditions of delivery.

Arbitrage is important in commodity markets with standardized qualities, and especially in financial markets; to the extent that the contingent returns from one asset replicate those from a bundle of other assets, or from some trading strategy, its price is linked to the latter. Also, repeated opportunities to trade contingent on events enable a few securities to substitute for a much wider variety of absent contingent contracts.

One form of the competitive hypothesis emphasizes the option that each subset of the traders has to redistribute their endowments among themselves. For example, a seller and those who purchase from him are a coalition redistributing their resources among themselves. A core allocation is one such that no coalition can redistribute its endowments to the greater advantage of each member. The core allocations include the Walrasian allocations. A basic result first explored by F.Y. Edgeworth establishes that as the economy is enlarged by adding replicates of the original traders, the set of core allocations shrinks to the set of Walrasian allocations.

Another form emphasizes the view that in an economy so large that each agent's behaviour has an insignificant effect on the terms of trade, every trader's best option is to maximize the gains from trade at the prevailing prices. For example, any one trader's potential gain from behaviour that influences the terms of trade becomes insignificant (generically) as the set of traders expands, providing the limit distribution is 'atomless'. Similar results obtain for various models of markets with explicit price formation via auctions. Generally, an efficient allocation is necessarily Walrasian if each agent is unnecessary to attainment of others' gains from trade. An idealized formulation considers an atomless measure space of agents in which only measurable sets of agents matter and the behaviour of each single agent is inconsequential. In this case the Walrasian allocations are the only core allocations. Similarly, the allocation obtained from the Shapley value, in which each agent shares in proportion to his expected marginal contribution to a randomly formed coalition, is a Walrasian allocation.

Structural features of trading processes suggest an alternative hypothesis. Matching problems (e.g. workers seeking jobs) admit procedural rules that with optimal play yield core allocations, and for a general exchange economy an appropriately designed auction yields a core allocation. Other games have been devised for which optimal play by the agents produces a Walrasian allocation. Continual bilateral bargaining among dispersed agents (with sufficiently diverse preferences), in which agents are repeatedly matched randomly and one designated to offer some trade to the other, also results in a Walrasian allocation with optimal play. In a related vein, several methods of selecting allocations create incentives for agents to falsify reports of their preferences, and if they do this optimally then a Walrasian allocation results. Quite generally, any process that is fair in the sense that all agents enjoy the same opportunities for net trades yields essentially a Walrasian allocation. In one axiomization, some 'signal' is announced publicly and then based on his preferences each agent responds with a message that affects the resulting trades: if a core allocation is required, and each signal could be the right signal for some larger economy, then the signal must be essentially equivalent to the announcement of a Walrasian price to which each agent responds with his preferred trade within his budget specified by the price.

Traders' impatience can also affect the terms of trade. In the simplest form of impatience, agents discount delayed gains from trade. Dynamic play is assumed to be sequentially rational in the sense that a strategy must specify an optimal continuation from each contingency; this is a strong requirement and severely restricts the admissible equilibria. For example, if a seller and a buyer alternate proposing prices for trading an item, then in the *unique* equilibrium, trade occurs immediately at a price dependent on their discount rates. As the interval between offers shrinks the seller's share of the gains from trade becomes proportional to the relative magnitude of the buyer's discount rate; for example, equal rates yield equal division. Extensions to multilateral contexts produce analogous results. A monopolist with an unlimited supply selling to a continuum of buyers might plausibly extract favourable terms, but actually in any equilibrium in which the buyers' strategies are stationary, as the interval between offers shrinks the seller's profit disappears and all trade occurs immediately at a Walrasian price. Similarly, a durable-good manufacturer lacking control of resale or rental markets has an incentive to increase the output rate as the production period shrinks; or, to pre-commit to limited capacity. This emphasizes that monopoly power depends substantially on powers of commitment stemming from increasing marginal costs, capacity limitations, or other sources.

Impatience and sequential rationality can, however, produce inefficiencies in product design, as in the case of a manufacturer's choice of durability, or in market structure, as in a preference to rent rather than sell durable goods.

Complete information is a major factor justifying predictions of Walrasian prices. With complete information and symmetric trading opportunities among agents, many models predict a Walrasian outcome, but incomplete information often produces departures from the Walrasian norm.

Although information may be productively useful, in an exchange economy the arrival of information may be disadvantageous to the extent that risk-averse agents forgo insurance against its consequences. A basic result considers an exchange economy that has reached an efficient allocation before some agents receive further private information, and this fact is common knowledge: the predicted response is no further trade, though prices may change.

Each efficient allocation has 'efficiency prices' that reflect the marginal rates of substitution prevailing; in the Walrasian case all trades are made at these prices. They summarize a wealth of information about technology, endowments and preferences. Prices (and other endogenous observables) are therefore not only sufficient instruments for decentralization but also carriers of information. If information is dispersed among agents then Walrasian prices are signals, possibly noisy, that can inform an agent's trading. Models of 'temporary equilibrium' envision a succession of markets, in each of which prices convey information about future trading opportunites. 'Rational expectations' models assume that each agent maximizes an expected utility conditioned on both his private information and the informational content of prices. In simple cases, prices are sufficient statistics that swamp an agent's private information, whereas in complex real economies the informational content of prices may be elusive; nevertheless, markets are affected by inferences from prices (e.g. indices of stock and wholesale prices) and various models attempt to include these features realistically. Conversely, responses of prices to events and disclosures by firms are studied empirically.

The privacy of each agent's information about his preferences and endowment affects the realized gains and terms of trade. Many procedures require that the relative prices of 'qualities' provide incentives for self-selection. An example is a product line comprised of imperfect substitutes, in which price increments for successive quality increments induce customers to select according to their preferences. Several forms of discrimination in which prices depend on the quality (e.g. the time, location, priority or other circumstances of delivery) or, if resale is prevented, the quantity purchased, operate similarly.

Absence of the relevant contingent contracts is implicitly a prime source of inefficiencies and distributional effects. Trading may fail if adverse selection precludes effective signalling about product quality: absent quality assurance or warranties, each price at which some quality can be supplied attracts sellers offering lesser qualities. Investments in signals, possibly unproductive ones, that are more costly for sellers supplying inferior qualities induce signal-dependent schedules in which the price paid depends on the signal offered. For example, to signal his ability a worker may over-invest in education or work in a job for which he would be underqualified on efficiency grounds. If buyers make repeat purchases based on the quality experienced from trying a product, then the initial price itself, or even dissipative expenditures such as uninformative advertising, can be signals used by the seller to induce initial purchases.

Principal–agent relationships in which a risk-averse agent has superior information and his actions cannot be monitored completely by the principal require complex contracts. For example, in a repeated context with perfect capital markets and imperfect insurance, the optimal contract provides the agent with a different reward for each measurable output, and the total remuneration is the accumulated sum of these rewards. Contracting is generally affected severely by limited observation of contingencies (either events or actions relevant to incentives) and in asymmetric relationships nonlinear pricing is often optimal.

Insurance premiums may vary with coverage, for example, to counter the effects of adverse selection or moral hazard.

Labour markets are replete with complex incentives and forms of contracting, partly because workers cannot contract to sell labour forward and partly because labour contracts substitute for imperfect loan markets and missing insurance markets (e.g. against the risk of declining productivity). Workers may have superior information about their abilities, technical data, or effort and actions taken; and firms may have superior information about conditions affecting the marginal product of labour. Incentives for immediate productivity may be affected by conditioning estimates of ability on current output, or by procedures selecting workers for promotion to jobs where the impact of ability is multiplied by greater responsibilities. The complexity of the resulting incentives and contracts reflects the multiple effects of incomplete markets and imperfect monitoring.

In the context of trading rules that specify price determination explicitly, analyses of agents' strategic behaviour emphasize the role of private information. The trading rule and typically the probability distribution of agents' privately known attributes are assumed to be common knowledge; consequently, formulations pose games of incomplete information. An example is a sealed-bid auction in which the seller awards an item to the bidder submitting the highest price: suppose that each bidder observes a sample, independently and identically distributed (i.i.d.) conditional on the unknown value of the item. With equilibrium bidding strategies, as the number of bidders increases the maximal bid converges in probability, to the expectation of the value conditional on knowing the maximum of all the samples; for the common distributions this implies convergence to the underlying value. Alternative auction rules are preferred by the seller according to the extent that the procedures dilute the informational advantages of bidders (e.g. progressive oral bidding has this effect), and exploit any risk aversion. Rules can be constructed that maximize the seller's expected revenue: if bidders' valuations are i.i.d., then for the common distributions awarding the item to the highest bidder at the first or second highest price is optimal, subject to an optimal reservation price set by the seller. In such a second-price or oral progressive auction with no reservation price, bidders offer their valuations, so the price is Walrasian.

Another example is a double auction, used in the London gold and Japanese stock markets, in which multiple buyers and sellers submit bid and ask prices and then a clearing price is selected from the interval obtained by intersecting the resulting demand and supply schedules. For a restricted class of models, requiring sufficiently many buyers and sellers with i.i.d. valuations, a double auction is incentive efficient, in the sense that there is no other trading rule that is sure to be preferred by every agent; also, as the numbers increase the clearing price converges to a Walrasian price.

The effects of privileged information held by some traders have been studied in the context of markets mediated by brokers and specialists, as in most stock markets. The results show that specialists' strategies impose all expected losses from adverse selection on uninformed traders. On the other hand, specialists may profit from knowledge of the order book and immediate access to trading opportunities.

Private information severely affects bargaining. With alternating offers even the simplest examples have many equilibria, plausible criteria can select different equilibria, and a variety of allocations are possible. In most equilibria, delay in making a serious offer (one that has some chance of acceptance) is a signal that a seller's valuation is not low or a buyer's is not high; or the offers made limit the inferences the other party can make about one's valuation. When both valuations are privately known, signalling must occur in some form to establish that gains from trade exist. Typically all gains from trade are realized eventually, but significant delay costs are incurred.

In a special case, a seller with a commonly known valuation repeatedly offers prices to a buyer with a privately known valuation: assume that the buyer's strategy is a stationary one that accepts the first offer less than a reservation price, depending on his valuation. As mentioned previously for the monopoly context, as the period between offers shrinks the seller's offers decline to a price no more than the least possible buyer's valuation and trade occurs quickly: the buyer captures most of the gains. Even with alternating offers, the buyer avoids serious offers if his valuation is high and the periods short. Thus, impatience, frequent offers, and asymmetric information combine to skew the terms of trade in favour of the informed party.

The premier instance of exchange is the commodity trading 'pit' in which traders around a ring call out bid and ask prices or accept others' offers. These markets operate essentially as multilateral versions of bargaining but with endogenous matching of buyers and sellers: delay in making or accepting a serious offer can again be a signal about a trader's valuation, but with the added feature that 'competitive pressure' is a source of impatience. That is, a trader who delays incurs a risk that a favourable opportunity is usurped by a competing trader. These markets have been studied experimentally with striking results: typically most gains from trade are realized, at prices eventually approximating a Walrasian clearing price, especially if the subjects bring experience from prior replications. However, if 'rational expectations' features are added, subjects may fail to make the required inferences from information revealed by offers and transactions.

Trading rules can be designed to maximize the expected realized gains from trade, using the 'revelation principle'. Each trading rule and associated equilibrium strategies induce a 'direct revelation game' whose trading rule is a composition of the original trading rule and its strategies; in equilibrium each agent has an incentive to report accurately his privately known valuation. In the case that a buyer and a seller have valuations drawn independently according to a uniform distribution, the optimal revelation rule is equivalent to a double auction in which trade occurs if the buyer's bid exceeds the seller's offer, and the price used is halfway between these. More generally, with many buyers and sellers and an optimal rule, the expected unrealized gains from trade declines quickly as the numbers of buyers and sellers increase. Such static models depend, however, on the presumption that subsequent trading opportunities are excluded.

Enforceable contracts facilitate exchange, and most theories depend on them, but they are not entirely essential. Important in practice are 'implicit contracts' that are not enforceable except via threats of discontinuing the relationship after the first betrayal. Similarly, in an infinitely repeated situation, if a seller chooses a product's quality (say, high or lower) and price before sale, and a buyer observes the quality only after purchasing, then the buyer's strategy of being willing to pay currently only the price associated with the previously supplied quality suffices to induce continual high quality.

Studies of exchange without enforceable contracts focus on the Prisoners' Dilemma game: both parties can gain from exchange but each has an incentive to defect from his half of the agreement. In any finite repetition of this game with complete information the equilibrium strategies predict no agreements, since each expects the other to defect. Infinite repetitions can sustain agreements enforced by threats of refusal to cooperate later. With incomplete information, reputational effects can sustain agreements until near the end. For example, if one party thinks the other might automatically reciprocate cooperation, then he has an incentive to cooperate until first betrayed, and the other has an incentive to reciprocate until defection becomes attractive near the end. Reputations are important also in competitive battles among firms with private cost information: wars of attrition select the efficient survivors.

Continuing studies of exchange are likely to rely on game-theoretic methods. This approach is useful to study strategic behaviour in dynamic contexts; to elaborate the roles of private information, impatience, risk aversion and other features of agents' preferences and endowments; to describe the consequences of incomplete markets and contracting limited by monitoring and enforcement costs; and to establish the efficiency properties of the common trading rules. It also integrates theories of exchange with theories of product differentiation, discriminatory pricing and other strategic behaviour by producers. Technically, the game-theoretic approach enables a transition from theories of a large economy with a specified distribution of agents' attributes, to theories of an economy with few agents having private information but commonly known probability assessments; further realism may depend on reducing the assumed common knowledge and developing better formulations of competition among large firms. Grand theories of general economic equilibrium incorporating all these realistic aspects are unlikely until the foundations are established.

In sum, the Walrasian model remains a paradigm for efficient exchange under 'perfect' competition in which equality of demand and supply is the primary determinant of the terms of trade. Further analysis of agents' strategic behaviour with private information and market power elaborates the causes of incomplete or imperfectly competitive markets that impede efficiency, and it delineates the fine details of endogenous product differentiation, contracting and price formation essential to the application of the Walrasian model.

BIBLIOGRAPHY

Arrow, K.J. and Debreu, G. 1954. Existence of an equilibrium for a competitive economy. *Econometrica* 22, 265–90.

Arrow, K.J. and Hahn, F.H. 1971. *General Competitive Analysis.* San Francisco: Holden-Day.

Aumann, R.J. 1964. Markets with a continuum of traders. *Econometrica* 32, 39–50.

Debreu, G. 1959. *Theory of Value.* New York: John Wiley & Sons.

Debreu, G. 1970. Economies with a finite set of equilibria. *Econometrica* 38, 387–92.

Debreu, G. and Scarf, H. 1963. A limit theorem on the core of an economy. *International Economic Review* 4, 235–46.

Gresik, T. and Satterthwaite, M.A. 1984. The rate at which a simple market becomes efficient as the number of traders increases: an asymptotic result for optimal trading mechanisms. Discussion Paper 641, Northwestern University; *Journal of Economic Theory* (1987).

Grossman, S.J. and Perry, M. 1986. Sequential bargaining under asymmetric information. *Journal of Economic Theory* 39, 120–54.

Gul, F., Sonnenschein, H. and Wilson, R.B. 1986. Foundations of dynamic monopoly and the Coase conjecture. *Journal of Economic Theory* 39, 155–90.

Hildenbrand, W. 1974. *Core and Equilibria of a Large Economy.* Princeton: Princeton University Press.

Hölmstrom, B.R. and Milgrom, P.R. 1986. Aggregation and linearity in the provision of intertemporal incentives. Report Series D, No. 5, School of Organization and Management, Yale University.

Hölmstrom, B.R. and Myerson, R.B. 1983. Efficient and durable decision rules with incomplete information. *Econometrica* 51, 1799–820.

Kreps, D.M., Milgrom, P.R., Roberts, D.J. and Wilson, R.B. 1982. Rational cooperation in the finitely repeated prisoners' dilemma. *Journal of Economic Theory* 27, 245–52.

McKenzie, L. 1959. On the existence of general equilibrium for a competitive market. *Econometrica* 27, 54–71.

Milgrom, P.R. 1979. A convergence theorem for competitive bidding with differential information. *Econometrica* 47, 679–88.

Milgrom, P.R. 1985. The economics of competitive bidding: a selective survey. In *Social Goals and Social Organization*, ed. L. Hurwicz, D. Schmeidler and H. Sonnenschein, Cambridge: Cambridge University Press.

Milgrom, P.R. and Stokey, N. 1982. Information, trade, and common knowledge. *Journal of Economic Theory* 26, 17–27.

Myerson, R.B. and Satterthwaite, M.A. 1983. Efficient mechanisms for bilateral trading. *Journal of Economic Theory* 29, 265–81.

Radner, R. 1972. Existence of equilibrium of plans, prices and price expectations in a sequence of markets. *Econometrica* 40, 289–303.

Roberts, D.J. and Postlewaite, A. 1976. The incentives for price-taking behaviour in large exchange economies. *Econometrica* 44, 115–28.

Roberts, D.J. and Sonnenschein, H. 1976. The incentives for price-taking behaviour in large competition. *Econometrica* 45, 101–13.

Rubinstein, A. 1982. Perfect equilibrium in a bargaining model. *Econometrica* 50, 97–109.

Scarf, H. (with T. Hansen.) 1973. *The Computation of Economic Equilibria.* New Haven: Yale University Press.

Schmeidler, D. 1980. Walrasian analysis via strategic outcome functions. *Econometrica* 48, 1585–93.

Schmeidler, D. and Vind, K. 1972. Fair net trades. *Econometrica* 40, 637–42.
Smith, V. 1982. Microeconomic systems as experimental science. *American Economic Review* 72, 923–55.
Sonnenschein, H. 1972. Market excess demand functions. *Econometrica* 40, 549–63.
Sonnenschein, H. 1974. An axiomatic characterization of the price mechanism. *Econometrica* 42, 425–34.
Spence, A.M. 1973. *Market Signalling: Information Transfer in Hiring and Related Processes.* Cambridge, Mass.: Harvard University Press.
Wilson, R.B. 1985. Incentive efficiency of double auctions. *Econometrica* 53, 1101–16.

Experimental Methods in Economics

VERNON L. SMITH

Historically, the method and subject matter of economics have presupposed that it was a non-experimental (or 'field observational') science more like astronomy or meteorology than physics or chemistry. Based on general, introspectively 'plausible', assumptions about human preferences, and about the cost and technology-based supply response of producers, economists have sought to understand the functioning of economies, using observations generated by economic outcomes realized over time. The data of the astronomer is of this same type, but it would be wrong to conclude that astronomy and economics are methodologically equivalent. There are two important differences between astronomy and economics which help to illuminate some of the methodological problems of economics. First, based upon parallelism (the maintained hypothesis that the same physical laws hold everywhere), astronomy draws on all the relevant theory from classical mechanics and particle physics – theory which has evolved under rigorous laboratory tests. Traditionally, economists have not had an analogous body of tested behavioural principles that have survived controlled experimental tests, and which can be assumed to apply with insignificant error to the microeconomic behaviour that underpins the observable operations of the economy. Analogously, one might have supposed that there would have arisen an important area of common interest between economics and, say, experimental psychology, similar to that between astronomy and physics, but this has only started to develop in recent years.

Second, the data of astronomy are painstakingly gathered by professional observational astronomers for scientific purposes, and these data are taken seriously (if not always non-controversially) by astrophysicists and cosmologists. Most of the data of economics has been collected by government or private agencies for non-scientific purposes. Hence astronomers are directly responsible for the scientific credibility of their data in a way that economists have not been. In economics, when things appear not to turn out as expected the quality of the data is more likely to be questioned than the relevance and quality of the abstract reasoning. Old theories fade away, not from the weight of falsifying evidence that catalyses theoretical creativity into developing better theory, but from lack of interest, as intellectual energy is attracted to the development of new techniques and to the solution of new puzzles that remain untested.

At approximately the mid-20th century, professional economics began to change with the introduction of the laboratory experiment into economic method. In this embryonic research programme economists (and a psychologist, Sidney Siegel) became directly involved in the design and conduct of experiments to examine propositions implied by economic theories of markets. For the first time this made it possible to introduce *demonstrable* knowledge into the economist's attempt to understand markets.

This laboratory approach to economics also brought to the economist direct responsibility for an important source of scientific data generated by controlled processes that can be replicated by other experimentalists. This development invited economic theorists to submit to a new discipline, but also brought an important new discipline and new standards of rigour to the data gathering process itself.

An untested theory is simply a hypothesis. As such it is part of our *self*-knowledge. Science seeks to expand our knowledge of *things* by a process of testing this type of self-knowledge. Much of economic theory can be called, appropriately, 'ecclesiastical theory'; it is accepted (or rejected) on the basis of authority, tradition, or opinion about assumptions, rather than on the basis of having survived a rigorous falsification process that can be replicated.

Interest in the replicability of scientific research stems from a desire to answer the question 'Do you see what I see?' Replication and control are the two primary means by which we attempt to reduce the error in our common knowledge of economic processes. However, the question 'Do you see what I see?' contains three component questions, recognition of which helps to identify three different senses in which a research study may fail to be replicable:

(1) *Do you observe what I observe?* Since economics has traditionally been confined to the analysis of non-experimental data, the answer to this question has been trivially, 'yes'. We observe the same thing because we use the same data. This non-replicability of our traditional data sources has helped to motivate some to turn increasingly to experimental methods. We can say that you have replicated my experiments if you are unable to reject the hypothesis that your experimental data came from the same population as mine. This means that the experimenter, his/her subjects, and/or procedures are not significant treatment variables.

(2) *Do you interpret what we observe as I interpret it?* Given that we both observe the same, or replicable data, do we put the same interpretation on these data? The interpretation of observations requires theory (either formal or informal), or at least an empirical interpretation of the theory in the context that

generated the data. Theory usually requires empirical interpretation either because (i) the theory is not developed directly in terms of what can be observed (e.g. the theory may assume risk aversion which is not directly observable), or (ii) the data were not collected for the purpose of testing, or estimating the parameters of a theory. Consequently, failure to replicate may be due to differences in interpretation which result from different meanings being ascribed to the theory. Thus two researchers may apply different transformations to raw field data (e.g. different adjustments for the effect of taxes), so that the results are not replicable because their theoretical interpretations differ.

(3) *Do you conclude what I conclude from our interpretation?* The conclusions reached in two different research studies may be different even though the data and their interpretation are the same. In economics this is most often due to different model specifications. This problem is inherent in non-experimental methodologies in which, at best, one usually can estimate only the parameters of a prespecified model and cannot credibly test one model or theory against another. An example is the question of whether the Phillips' curve constitutes a behavioural trade-off between the rates of inflation and unemployment, or represents an equilibrium association without causal significance.

I. MARKETS AND MARKET EXPERIMENTS. Markets and how they function constitute the core of any economic system, whether it is highly decentralized – popularly, a 'capitalistic' system – or highly centralized – popularly, a 'planned' system. This is true for the decentralized economy because markets are the spontaneous institutions of exchange that use prices to guide resource allocation and human economic action. It is true for the centralized economy because in such economies markets always exist or arise in legal form (private agriculture in Russia) and clandestine or illegal form (barter, bribery, the trading of favours and underground exchange in Russia, Poland and elsewhere). Markets arise spontaneously in all cultures in response to the human desire for betterment (to 'profit') through exchange. Where the commodity or service is illegal (prostitution, gambling, the sale of liquor under Prohibition or of marijuana, cocaine, etc.) the result is not to prevent exchange, but to raise the risk and therefore the costs of exchange. This is because enforcement is itself costly, and it is never economical for the authorities (whether Soviet or American) even to approximate perfect enforcement. The spontaneity with which markets arise is perhaps no better illustrated than when (1979–80) US airlines for promotional purposes issued travel vouchers to their passengers. One of these vouchers could be redeemed by the bearer as a cash substitute in the purchase of new airline tickets. Consequently vouchers were of value to future passengers. Furthermore, since (as Hayek would say) the 'circumstances of time and place' for the potential redemption of vouchers were different for different individuals, there existed the preconditions for the active voucher market that was soon observed in all busy airports. Current passengers with vouchers who were unlikely to be travelling again soon held an asset worth less to themselves than to others who were more certain of their future or impending travel plans. The resulting market established prices that were discounts from the redemption or 'face' value of vouchers. Sellers who were unlikely to be able to redeem their vouchers preferred to sell them at a discount for cash. Buyers who were reasonably sure of their travel plans could save money by purchasing vouchers at a discount. Thus the welfare of every active buyer and seller increased via this market. Without a market, many – perhaps most – vouchers would not have been exercised and would thus have been 'wasted'.

The previous paragraph illustrates a fundamental hypothesis (theorem) of economics: the ('competitive') market process yields welfare improving (and, under certain limiting ideal conditions, welfare maximizing) outcomes. But is the hypothesis 'true', or at least very probably true? (Lakatos (1978) would correctly ask 'Has it led to an empirically progressive research programme?') I think it is 'true', but how do I know this? Do you see what I see? A Marxist does not see what I see in the above interpretation of a market. The young student studying economics does not see what I see, although if they continue to study economics eventually they (predictably) come to see what I see (or, at least, they say they do). Is this because we have inadvertently brainwashed them? The gasoline consumer does not see what I see. They see themselves in a *zero* sum game with an oil company: any increase in price merely redistributes wealth from the consumer to the company, which is not 'fair' since the company is richer. What I see in a market is a *positive* sum game yielding gains from exchange, which constitutes the fundamental mechanism for creating, not merely redistributing wealth. The traditional method by which the economist gets others to see this 'true' function of markets is by logical arguments (suppose it were not true, then...), examples and 'observations', such as are contained in my description of the voucher market, in which what is 'observed' is hortatively described and interpreted in terms of the hypothesis itself. But if this knowledge of the function of markets is 'true', can it be demonstrated? Experimentalists claim that laboratory experiments can provide a uniquely important technique of demonstration for supplementing the theoretical interpretation of field observations.

I conducted my first experiment in the spring of 1956. Since then hundreds of similar, as well as environmentally richer experiments have been conducted by myself and by others. In 1956, my introductory economics class consisted of 22 science and engineering students, and although this might not have been the 'large number' traditionally thought to have been necessary to yield a competitive market, I thought it was large enough for a practice run to initiate a research programme capable of falsifying the standard theory. I conducted the experiment before lecturing on the theory and 'behaviour' of markets in class so as not to 'contaminate' the sample. The 22 subjects were each assigned one card from a well-shuffled deck of 11 white and 11 yellow cards. The white cards identified the sellers, and the yellow cards identified the buyers. Each white card carried a price, known only to that seller, which represented that seller's minimum selling price for one unit, and each yellow card identified a price, known only to that buyer, representing that buyer's maximum buying price for one unit. On the left of Figure 1 is listed these so-called 'limit' prices, identified by buyer, B1, B2 etc. (in descending order, D) and by seller, S1, S2 etc. (in ascending order, S). To

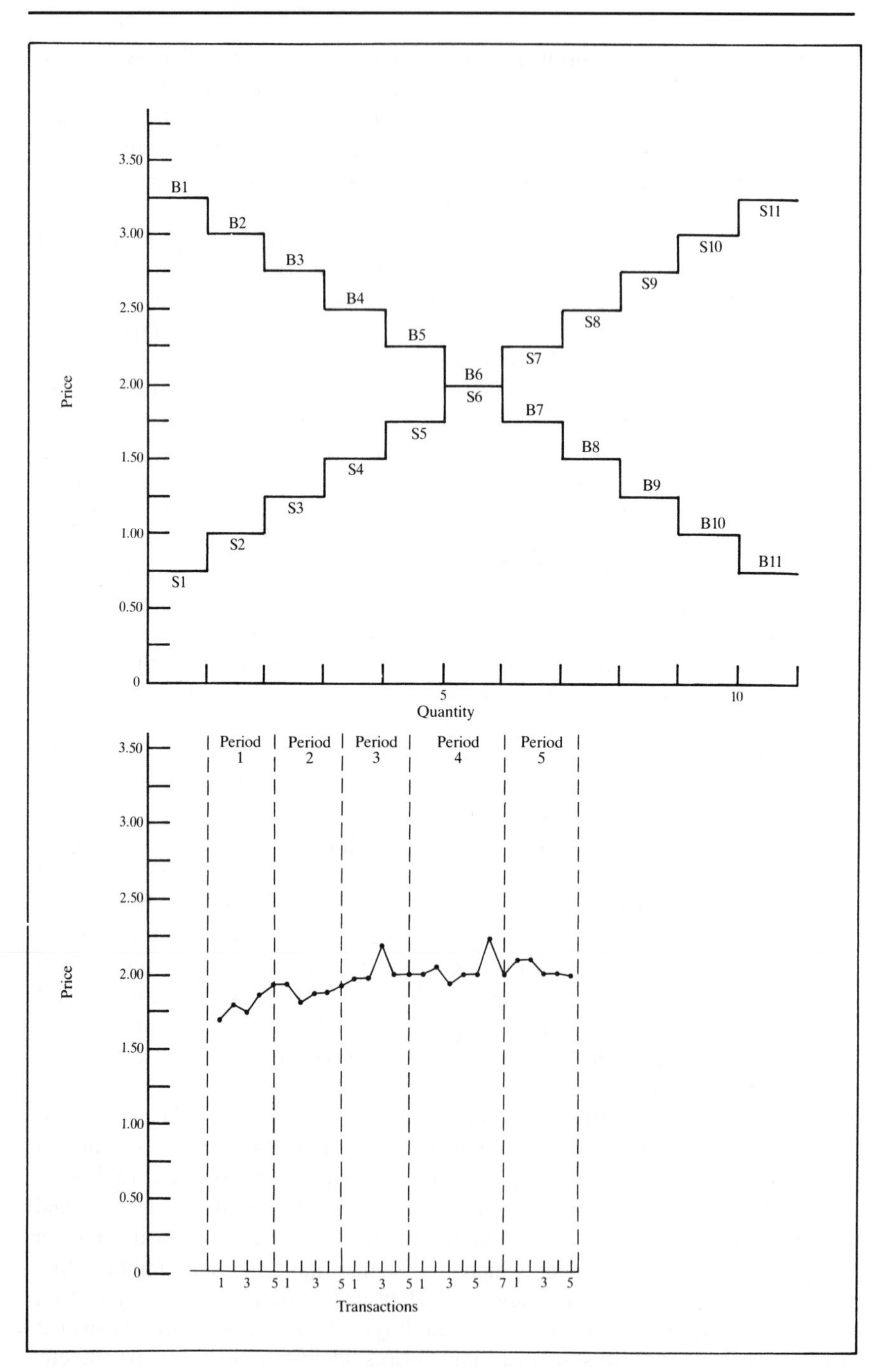
Price
Quantity
B1
B2
B3
B4
B5
B6
S6
B7
B8
B9
B10
B11
S1
S2
S3
S4
S5
S7
S8
S9
S10
S11
Period 1
Period 2
Period 3
Period 4
Period 5
Price
Transactions

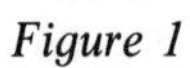
Figure 1

keep things simple and well controlled each buyer (seller) was informed that he/she was a buyer (seller) of at most one unit of the item in each of several trading periods. Thus demand, D (supply, S) was 'renewed' in each trading period as a steady state flow, with no carry-over in unsatisfied demand (or unsold stock), from one period to the next. In the airline voucher example, imagine the vouchers being issued, followed by trading; the vouchers then expire, new vouchers are issued, traded and so on. In the experiment, suppose real motivation is provided by promising to pay (in cash) to each buyer the difference between that buyer's assigned limit buying price and the price actually paid in each period that a unit is purchased in the market. Thus suppose seller 5 sells the unit to buyer 2 at the price 2.25. Then buyer 2 earns a 'profit' of $0.75 from this exchange. In this way we induce on each buyer a value (or hypothesized willingness-to-pay) equal to the assigned limit buy price. Similarly, suppose each seller is paid the difference between that seller's actual sales price and assigned limit price ('cost', or willingness-to-sell) in each trading period that a unit is sold. Thus in the previous exchange example, seller 5 earns $0.50 from the transaction.

This experimental procedure operationalizes the market preconditions that (1) 'the circumstances of time and place' for each economic agent are dispersed and known only to that agent (as in the above voucher market) and (2) agents have a secure property right in the objects of trade and the private gains ('profits') from trade (an airline travel voucher was transferable and redeemable by any bearer). The reader should note that 'profit' is identified as much with the act of buying as with that of selling. This is because 'profit' is the surplus earned by a buyer who buys for less than his willingness-to-pay, just as a seller's 'profit' is the surplus earned when an item is sold for more than the amount for which they are willing to sell. Willingness-to-sell need not have, and usually does not have anything to do with accounting 'cost', or production 'cost', from which one computes accounting profit. Willingness-to-sell, like willingness-to-buy, is determined by the immediate circumstances of each agent. Hence, a passenger might be prepared to pay the regular full fare premium on a first-class ticket for an emergency trip to visit a sick relative. The accountant's concept of profit cannot be applied to the passenger's decision any more than it can be applied to that of a passenger willing to sell a voucher at a deep discount. In what follows I will use the term 'buyer's surplus' or 'seller's surplus' instead of 'profit' to refer to the gains from exchange enjoyed by buyers or sellers because the term 'profit' is so strongly, exclusively and misleadingly associated with selling activities.

Now let us interpret the previously cited fundamental theorem of economics in the context of the experimental design contained in Figure 1. We note first that the ordered set of seller (buyer) limit prices defines a supply (demand) function (Figure 1). A supply (demand) function provides a list of the total quantities that sellers (buyers) would be willing to sell (buy) at corresponding hypothetical fixed prices. Neither of these functions is capable of being observed, scientifically, in the field. This is because the postulated limit prices are inherently private and not publicly observable. We could poll every potential seller (buyer) of vouchers in Chicago's O'Hare airport on 20 December 1979 to get each person's reported limit price, but we would have no way of validating the 'observations' thus obtained. Referring to Figure 1, we see that in my 1956 experiment, sellers (hypothetically) were just willing to sell three units at price 1.25, nine units at 2.75 and so on. Similarly buyers (hypothetically) were just willing to buy four units at 2.50, seven units at 1.75 and so on. If seller 3 is indifferent between selling and not selling at 1.25, and if every seller (buyer) is likewise indifferent at his/her limit price, then any particular unit may not be sold (purchased) at this limit price. One means of dealing with this problem in laboratory markets is to promise to pay a small 'commission', say 5 cents, to each buyer and seller for each unit bought or sold. Thus seller 3 has a small inducement to sell at 1.25 if he can do no better, and buyer 6 has a small inducement to buy at 2.00 if she can do no better.

Economic theory defines the competitive equilibrium as the price and corresponding quantity that clears the market; that is, it sets the quantity that sellers are willing to sell equal to the quantity that buyers are willing to buy. This assumes that the subjective cost of transacting is zero; otherwise any units with limit prices equal to the competitive equilibrium price will not exchange. In Figure 1 this competitive equilibrium price is 2.00. If the 5 cent 'commission' paid to each trading buyer and seller is sufficient to compensate for any subjective cost of transacting, then buyer 6 and seller 6 will each trade and the competitive equilibrium quantity exchanged will be 6 units. At the competitive equilibrium price, buyer 1 earns a surplus of $3.25 - 2.00 = 1.25$ (plus commission) per period and so on. Total surplus, which measures the maximum possible gains from exchange, or maximum wealth *created* by the existence of the market institution, is 7.50 per period, at the competitive equilibrium.

If by some miracle the competitive equilibrium price and exchange quantity were to prevail in this market, sellers 1–6 would sell, buyers 1–6 would buy, while sellers 7–11 would make no sales and buyers 7–11 would make no purchases. It might be thought that this is unfair – the market should permit some or all of the 'submarginal' buyers (sellers) 7–11 to trade – or that more wealth would be created if there were more than six exchanges. But these interpretations are wrong. By definition, buyer 10 is not willing to pay more than 1.00. Consequently, it is a peculiar notion of fairness to argue that buyer 10 should have as much priority as buyer 1 in obtaining a unit. In the airline voucher example, this would mean that a buyer who is unlikely to redeem a voucher should have the same priority as a buyer who is likely to redeem a voucher. One can imagine a market in which, say, buyer 1 is paired with seller 9 at price 3.00, buyer 2 with seller 8 at price 2.75, and so on with nine units traded. If this were to occur it would mean buyers 7–9, who are less likely to use vouchers, have purchased them, and sellers 7–9, who initially held vouchers, and were more likely to use them than buyers 7–9, have sold their vouchers. Furthermore this allocation yields additional possible gains from exchange, and is thus *not sustainable*, even if it were thought to be desirable. That is, buyer 9, who bought from seller 1 at price 1.00, could resell the unit to seller 9 (who sold her unit to buyer 2), at price (say) 2.00. Why? Because, by definition a voucher is worth 2.75 to seller 9 and only

1.25 to buyer 9. Similar additional trades can be made by buyers (sellers) 7 and 8. The end result would be that buyers 1–6 and sellers 7–11 would be the terminal holders of vouchers, just as if the competitive equilibrium had been reached initially.

Hence, either the competitive equilibrium prevails, or if inefficient trades occur at dispersed prices, then further 'speculative' gains can be made by some buyers and sellers. If these gains are fully captured the end result is the same allocation as would occur at the competitive equilibrium price and quantity.

Having specified the environment (individual private values) of our experimental market, what remains is to specify an exchange institution. In my 1956 experiment I elected to use trading rules similar to those that characterize trading on the organized stock and commodity exchanges. These markets use the 'double oral auction' procedure. In this institution as soon as the market 'opens' any buyer is free to announce a bid to buy and any seller is free to announce an offer to sell. In the experimental version each bid (offer) is for a single unit. Thus a buyer might say 'buy, 1.00', while a seller might say 'sell, 5.00', and it is understood that the buyer bids 1.00 for a unit and the seller offers to sell one unit for 5.00. Bids and offers are freely announced and can be modified. A contract occurs if any seller accepts the bid of any buyer, or any buyer accepts the offer of any seller. In the simple experimental market, since each participant is a buyer or seller of at most one unit per trading period, the contracting buyer and seller drop out of the market for the remainder of the trading period, but return to the market when a new trading 'day' begins. The experimenter announces the close of each trading period and the opening of the subsequent period, with each trading period timed to extend, say, five minutes. Each contract price is plotted on the right of Figure 1 for the five trading periods of the experiment. This result was not as expected. The conventional view among economists was that a competitive equilibrium was like a frictionless ideal state which could not be conceived as actually occurring, even approximately. It could be conceived of occurring only in the presence of an abstract 'institution' such as a Walrasian *tâtonnement* or an Edgeworth recontracting procedure. It was for teaching, not believing.

From Figure 1 it is evident that in the strict sense the competitive equilibrium was not attained in any period, but the accuracy of the competitive equilibrium theory is easily comparable to that of countless physical processes. Certainly, the data clearly do not support the monopoly, or seller collusion model. The total return to sellers is maximized when four units are sold at price 2.50. Similarly, the monopsony, or buyer collusion model requires four units to exchange at price 1.50.

Since 1956, several hundred experiments using different supply and demand conditions, experienced as well as inexperienced subjects, buyers and sellers with multiple unit trading capacity, a great variation in the numbers of buyers and sellers, and different trading institutions, have established the replicability and robustness of these results. For many years at the University of Arizona and Indiana University we have been using various computerized (the PLATO system) versions of the double 'oral' auction, developed by Arlington Williams, in which participating subjects trade with each other through computer terminals. These experiments establish that the 1956 results are robust with respect to substantial reductions in the number of buyers and sellers. Most such experiments use only four buyers and four sellers, each capable of trading several units. Some have used only two sellers, yet the competitive equilibrium model performs very well under double auction rules. Figure 2 shows the supply and demand design and the market results for a typical experiment in which subjects trade through PLATO computer terminals under computer-monitored double auction rules.

In addition to its antiquarian value, Figure 1 illustrates the problem of monitoring the rules of a 'manual' experiment. Observe that in period 4 there were seven contracts which are recorded as occurring in the price range between $1.90 and $2.25. This is not possible since there are only six buyers with limit buy prices above $1.90. Either a buyer violated his budget constraint, or the experimenter erred in recording a price in his first experiment. In Figure 2 there is plotted each contract (an accepted bid if the contract line passes through a 'dot'; an accepted offer if the line passes through a 'circle') and the bids ('dots') and offers ('circles') that preceded each accepted bid or offer. One of the several advantages of computerized experimental markets is that the complete data of the market (all bids, offers and contracts at their time of execution) are recorded accurately and non-invasively, and all experimental rules are enforced perfectly. In particular the violation of a budget constraint revealed in Figure 1, which is a perpetual problem with manually executed experiments, is not a problem when trading is perfectly computer monitored.

The rapid convergence shown in Figures 1 and 2 has not always extended to trading institutions other than the double auction. For example, the 'posted offer' pricing mechanism (associated with most retail markets), in which sellers post take it or leave it non-negotiable prices at the beginning of each period, yields higher prices and less efficient allocations than the double auction. This difference in performance becomes smaller with experienced subjects and with longer trading sequences in a given experiment (Ketcham et al., 1984). Similarly, a comparison of double auction with a sealed bid-offer auction finds the latter to be less efficient and to deviate more from the competitive equilibrium predictions (Smith et al., 1982). Thus, institutions have been demonstrated to make a difference in what we observe. The data and analysis strongly suggest that institutions make a difference because the rules (legal environment) make a difference, and the rules make a difference because they affect individual incentives.

II. BRIEF INTERPRETIVE HISTORY OF THE DEVELOPMENT OF EXPERIMENTAL ECONOMICS.

The two most influential early experimental studies represent the two primary poles of experimental economics: the study of individual preference (choice) under uncertainty (Mosteller and Nogee, 1951) and of market behaviour (Chamberlin, 1948). The investigation of uncertainty and preference has focused on the testing of von Neumann–Morgenstern–Savage subjective expected utility theory. Battalio, Kagel and others have pioneered in the testing of the Slutsky–Hicks commodity

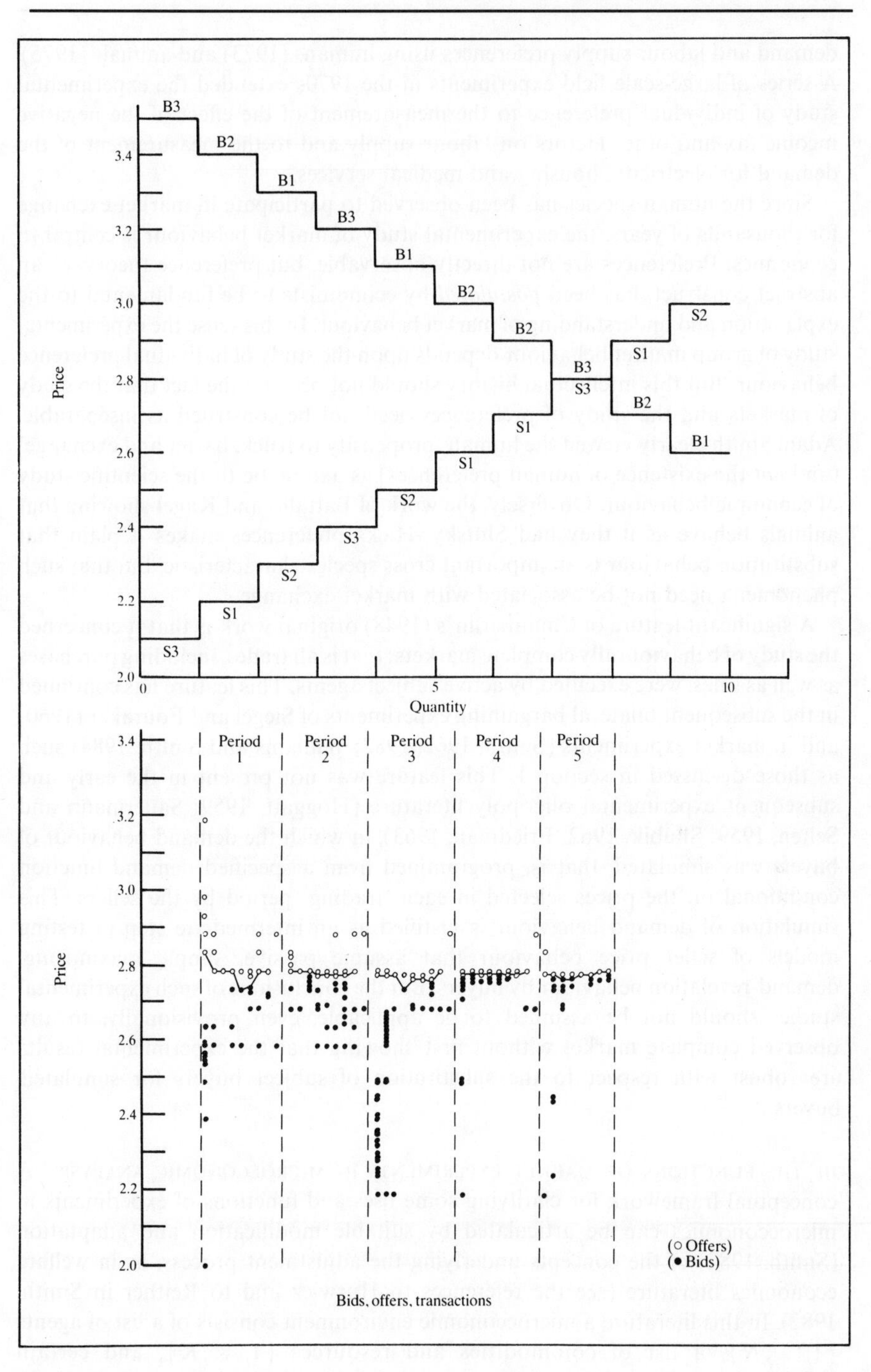
B3
B2
B1
B3
B1
B2
B2
B3
S3
B2
B1
S2
S1
S1
S1
S2
S3
S2
S1
S3
Price
3.4
3.2
3.0
2.8
2.6
2.4
2.2
2.0
0
5
10
Quantity
Period 1
Period 2
Period 3
Period 4
Period 5
(○ Offers)
(• Bids)
Bids, offers, transactions

Figure 2

demand and labour supply preferences using humans (1973) and animals (1975). A series of large-scale field experiments in the 1970s extended the experimental study of individual preference to the measurement of the effect of the negative income tax and other factors on labour supply and to the measurement of the demand for electricity, housing and medical services.

Since the human species has been observed to participate in market exchange for thousands of years, the experimental study of market behaviour is central to economics. Preferences are not directly observable, but preference theory, as an abstract construct, has been *postulated* by economists to be fundamental to the explanation and understanding of market behaviour. In this sense the experimental study of group market behaviour depends upon the study of individual preference behaviour. But this intellectual history should not obscure the fact that the study of markets and the study of preferences need not be construed as inseparable. Adam Smith clearly viewed the human 'propensity to truck, barter and exchange' (and *not* the existence of human preferences) as axiomatic to the scientific study of economic behaviour. Obversely, the work of Battalio and Kagel showing that animals behave as if they had Slutsky–Hicks preferences makes it plain that substitution behaviour is an important cross species characteristic, but that such phenomena need not be associated with market exchange.

A significant feature of Chamberlin's (1948) original work is that it concerned the study of behaviourally complete markets; that is all trades, including purchases as well as sales, were executed by active subject agents. This feature has continued in the subsequent bilateral bargaining experiments of Siegel and Fouraker (1960) and in market experiments (Smith, 1962, 1982; Williams and Smith, 1984) such as those discussed in section I. This feature was not present in the early and subsequent experimental oligopoly literature (Hoggatt, 1959; Sauermann and Selten, 1959; Shubik, 1962; Friedman, 1963), in which the demand behaviour of buyers was simulated, that is, programmed from a specified demand function conditional on the prices selected in each 'trading' period by the sellers. This simulation of demand behaviour is justified as an intermediate step in testing models of seller price behaviour that assume passive, simple maximizing, demand-revelation behaviour by buyers. But the conclusions of such experimental studies should not be assumed to be applicable, even provisionally, to any observed complete market without first showing that the experimental results are robust with respect to the substitution of subject buyers for simulated buyers.

III. THE FUNCTIONS OF MARKET EXPERIMENTS IN MICROECONOMIC ANALYSIS. A conceptual framework for clarifying some uses and functions of experiments in microeconomics can be articulated by suitable modification and adaptation (Smith, 1982) of the concepts underlying the adjustment process, as in welfare economics literature (see the references to Hurwicz and to Reither in Smith, 1982). In this literature a microeconomic environment consists of a list of agents $\{1, \ldots, N\}$, a list of commodities and resources $\{1, \ldots, K\}$, and certain characteristics of each agent i, such as the agent's preferences (utility) u_i, technological (knowledge) endowment T^i, and commodity endowment w_i. Thus agent i is defined by the triplet of characteristics $E^i = (u^i, T^i, w^i)$ defined on the K-dimensional commodity space. A microeconomic *environment* is defined by the collection $E = (E^1, \ldots, E^N)$ of these characteristics. This collection represents a set of primitive circumstances that condition agents' interaction through institutions. The superscript i, besides identifying a particular agent, also means that these primitive circumstances are in their *nature* private: it is the individual who likes, works, knows and makes.

There can be no such thing as a credible institution-free economics. Institutions define the property right rules by which agents communicate and exchange or transform commodities within the limits and opportunities inherent in the environment, E. Since markets require communication to effect exchange, property rights in messages are as important as property rights in goods and ideas. An institution specifies a language, $M = (M^1, \ldots, M^N)$, consisting of message elements $m = (m^1, \ldots, m^N)$, where M^i is the set of messages that can be sent by agent i (for example, the range of bids that can be sent by a buyer). An institution also defines a set of allocation rules $h = (h^1(m), \ldots, h^N(m))$ and a set of cost imputation rules $c = (c^1(m), \ldots, c^N(m))$, where $h^i(m)$ is the commodity allocation to agent i and $c^i(m)$ is the payment to be made by i, each as a function of the messages sent by all agents. Finally, the institution defines a set of adjustment process rules (assumed to be common to all agents), $g(t_0, t, T)$, consisting of a starting rule, $g(t_0, \cdot, \cdot)$, a transition rule $g(\cdot, t, \cdot)$, governing the sequencing of messages and a stopping rule, $g(\cdot, \cdot, T)$, which terminates the exchange of messages and triggers the allocation and cost imputation rules. Each agent's property rights in communication and exchange is thus defined by $I^i = (M^i, h^i(m), c^i(m), g(t_0, t, T))$. A microeconomic *institution* is defined by the collection of these individual property right characteristics, $I = (I^1, \ldots, I^N)$.

A microeconomic *system* is defined by the conjunction of an environment and an institution, $S = (E, I)$. To illustrate a microeconomic system, consider an auction for a single indivisible object such as a painting or an antique vase. Let each of N agents place an independent, certain, monetary value on the item $v_1, \ldots, v_N$, with agent i knowing his own value, v_i, but have only uncertain (probability distribution) information on the values of others. Thus $E^i = (v_i; P(v), N)$. If the exchange institution is the 'first price' sealed-bid auction, the rules are that all N bidders each submit a single bid any time between the announcement of the auction offering at t_0, and the closing of bids, at T. The item is then awarded to the maker of the highest bid at a price equal to the amount bid. Thus, if the agents are numbered in descending order of the bids, the first price auction institution $I_1 = (I_1^1 = [h^1(m) = 1, c^1(m) = b_1]$ and $I_1^i = [h^i(m) = 0, c^i(m) = 0]$, $i > 1$, where $m = (b_1, \ldots, b_N)$ consists of all bids tendered. That is, the item is awarded to the high bidder, $i = 1$, who pays b_1, and all others receive and pay nothing. This contrasts with the 'second price' sealed-bid auction $I_2 = (I_2^1, \ldots, I_2^N)$ in which $I_2^1 = [h^1(m) = 1, c^1(m) = b_2]$ and $I_2^2 = [h^i(m) = 0, c^i(m) = 0]$, $i > 1$; that is, the highest bidder receives the allocation but pays a price equal to the second highest bid submitted.

Another example is the English or progressive oral auction, whose rules are discussed in the article on AUCTIONS. It should be noted that the 'double oral' auction, used extensively in stock and commodity trading and in the two experimental markets discussed in section I, is a two-sided generalization of the English auction.

A microeconomic system is activated by the behavioural choices of agents in the set M. In the static, or final outcome, description of an economy, agent *behaviour* can be defined as a function (or correspondence) $m^i = \beta^i(E^i|I)$ carrying the characteristics E^i of agent i into a message m^i, conditional upon the property right specifications of the operant institution I. If all exchange-relevant agent characteristics are included in E^i, then $\beta \equiv \beta^i$ for all i. Given the message-sending behaviour of each agent, $\beta(E|I)$, the institution determines the outcomes

$$h^i(m) = h^i[\beta(E^1|I), \ldots, \beta(E^N|I)]$$

and

$$c^i(m) = c^i[\beta(E^1|I), \ldots, \beta(E^N|I)].$$

Within this framework we see that agents do not choose allocations directly; agents choose messages with institutions determining allocations under the rules that carry messages into allocations. (You cannot choose to 'buy' an auctioned item; you can only choose to raise the standing bid at an English auction or submit a particular bid in a sealed bid auction.) However, the allocation and cost imputation rules may have important incentive effects on behaviour, and therefore messages will in general depend on these rules. Hence, market outcomes will result from the conjunction of institutions' and agents' behaviour.

A proper theory of agents' behaviour allows one to deduce a particular β function based on assumptions about the agent's environment and the institution, and his motivation to act. Auction theory is perhaps the only part of economic theory that is fully institution specific. For example, in the second price sealed bid auction it is a dominant strategy for each agent simply to bid his or her value; that is

$$b_i = \beta(E^i|I_2) = \beta(v_i|I_2) = v_i, \qquad i = 1, \ldots, N.$$

The resulting outcome is that $b_1 = v_1$ is the winning bid and agent 1 pays the price v_2. Similarly, in the English auction, agent 1 will eventually exclude agent 2 by raising the standing bid to v_2 (or somewhat above), and obtain the item at this price. In the first price auction Vickrey proved that if each agent maximizes expected surplus $(v_1 - b_1)$ in an environment with $P(v) = v$ (the v_i are drawn from a constant density on $[0, 1]$), then we can deduce the noncooperative equilibrium bid function, $b_i = \beta(E^i|I_1) = \beta[v_i; P(v), N|I_1] = (N-1)v_i|N$ (see the article on AUCTIONS for a more complete discussion).

With the above framework it is possible to explicate the roles of theory and experiment, and their relationship, in a progressive research programme (Lakatos, 1978) of economic analysis. But to do this we must first ask two questions:

(1) 'Which of the elements of a microeconomic system are not observable?' The nonobservable elements are (i) preferences, (ii) knowledge endowments and (iii) agent message behaviour, $\beta(E^i|I)$. Even if the messages are available and recorded, we still cannot observe message behaviour functions because we cannot observe, or vary, preferences. The best we can do with field observations of outcomes is to interpret them in terms of models based on assumptions about preferences (Cobb–Douglas, constant elasticity of substitution, homothetic), knowledge (complete, incomplete, common), and behaviour (cooperative, noncooperative). Any 'tests' of such models must necessarily be joint tests of all of these unobservable elements. More often the econometric exercise is parameter estimation, which is conditional upon these same elements.

(2) 'What would we like to know?' We would like to know enough about how agents' behaviour is affected by alternative environments and institutions so that we can classify them according to the mapping they provide into outcomes. Do some institutions yield Pareto optimal outcomes and/or stable prices, and if, so are the results robust with respect to alternative environments?

These two questions together tell us what we want to know is inaccessible in natural experiments (field data) because key elements of the equation are unobservable and/or cannot be controlled. If laboratory experiments are to help us learn what we want to know, certain precepts that constitute proposed sufficient conditions for a valid controlled microeconomic experiment must be satisfied:

(1) *Non-satiation* (or monotonicity of reward). Subject agents strictly prefer any increase in the reward medium, π; that is $U_i(\pi_i)$ is monotone increasing for all i.

(2) *Saliency*. Agents have the unqualified right to claim rewards that increase (decrease) in the good (bad) outcomes, x_i, in an experiment; the institution of an experiment renders these rewards salient by defining outcomes in terms of the message choices of agents.

In both the field and the laboratory it is the institution that induces value on messages, given each agent's (subjective) value of commodity outcomes. In the laboratory we use a monetary reward function to induce utility value on the abstract accounting outcomes ('commodities') of an experiment. Thus, agent i is given a concave schedule, $V_i(x_i)$, defining the 'redemption value' in dollars for x_i units purchased in an experimental market, and is assured of receiving a net payment equal to $V_i(x_i)$ less the purchase prices of the x_i units in the market. If the x_i units are all purchased at price p (which is the assumption used to derive a hypothetical demand schedule) the agent is paid $\pi_i = V_i(x_i) - px_i$, with utility $u^i(x_i) = U_i(\pi_i(x_i))$. In defining demand it is assumed that the agent directly chooses x_i (that is $x_i = m_i$). Therefore, if i maximizes $u^i(x_i) = U_i[V(x_i) - px_i]$, then at a maximum we have $U_i' \cdot [V_i'(x_i) - p] = 0$, giving the demand function $x_i = V_i'^{(-1)}(p)$ if $U_i' > 0$, where $V_i'^{(-1)}$ is the inverse of i's marginal redemption value of x_i units. (The same procedure for a seller using a cost function $C_j(x_j)$ and paying $px_j - C_j(x_j)$ allows one to induce a marginal cost supply of j.) This illustration generalizes easily: if the joint redemption value is $V_i(x_i, y_i)$ for two abstract commodities (x_i, y_i), $u^i = U_i[V^i(x_i, y_i)]$ induces an indifference map given by the level curves of $V^i(x_i, y_i)$, on (x_i, y_i), with marginal rate of substitution $U'_i V^i_x | U'_i V^i_y = V^i_x | V^i_y$, if $U'_i > 0$. If $V^i(x_i, X)$ is the reward function, with x_i a private and X a common (public) outcome good, we are able to control preferences in the study of public good allocation mechanisms, or if

$$X = \sum_{i=1}^{N} x_i$$

we are poised to study allocation with an 'atmospheric' externality (Coursey and Smith, 1985).

The first two precepts are sufficient to allow us to assert that we have created a microeconomic system $S = (E, I)$ in the laboratory. But to assure that we have created a controlled microeconomy, we need two additional precepts:

(3) *Dominance.* Own rewards dominate any subjective costs of transacting (or other motivation) in the experimental market.

As with any person, subject agents may have variables other than money in their utility functions. In particular, if there is congnitive and kinesthetic (observe the traders on a Stock Exchange floor) disutility associated with the message-transaction process of the institution, then utility might be better written $U_i(\pi_i, m^i)$. To the extent that this is so we induce a smaller demand on i with the payoff $V_i(x_i)$ than was computed above, and we lose control over preferences. As a practical matter experimentalists think the problem can usually be finessed by using rewards that are large relative to the complexity of the task, and by adopting experimental procedures that reduce complexity (e.g. using the computer to record decisions, perform needed calculations, provide perfect recall, etc.). Another approach, as noted in Section I, is to pay a small commission for each trade to compensate for the subjective transaction costs.

(4) *Privacy.* The subjects in an experiment each receive information only on his/her own reward schedule.

This precept is used to provide control over interpersonal utilities (payoff externalities). Real people may experience negative or positive utilities from the rewards of others, and to the extent that this occurs we lose control over induced demand, supply and preference functions. Remember that the reward functions have the same role in an experiment that preference functions have in the economy, and the latter preferences are private and non-observable.

If our interest is confined to testing hypotheses from theory, we are done. Precepts (1)–(4) are sufficient to provide rigorous tests of the theorist's ability to model individual and market behaviour. But one naturally asks is replicable results from the laboratory are transferable to field environments. This requires.

(5) *Parallelism.* Propositions about behaviour and/or the performance of institutions that have been tested in one microeconomy (laboratory or field) apply also to other microeconomies (laboratory or field) where similar *ceteris paribus* conditions hold.

Astronomy, meteorology, biology and other sciences use the maintained hypothesis that the same physical laws hold everywhere. Economics postulates that when the environment and institution are the same, behaviour will be the same; that is, behaviour is determined by a relatively austere subset of life's parameters. Whether this is 'true' is an empirical question. Hence, when one experimentalist studies variations on the treatment variables of another it is customary to replicate the earlier work to check parallelism. Similarly, one must design field experiments, or devise econometric models using non-experimental field data, that provide tests of the transferability of experimental results to any particular market in the field. Only in this way can questions of parallelism be answered. They are not answered with speculations about alleged differences between the experimental subject's behaviour and (undefined) 'real world' behaviour. The experimental laboratory *is* a real world, with real people, real institutions, real payoffs and commodities just as real as stock certificates and airline travel vouchers, both of which have utility because of the claim rights they legally bestow on the bearer.

IV. CLASSIFYING THE APPLICATION OF EXPERIMENTAL METHODS. There are many types of experiments and many fields of economic study to which experimental methods have been applied.

The experimental study of auctions makes the most extensive use of models of individual behaviour based explicitly on the message requirements of the different institutions. This literature provides test comparisons of predicted behaviour, $m^i = \beta(E^i|I)$, with observations on individual choice, $\hat{m}_i = \beta(\hat{E}_i|I)$ for given realizations, $\hat{E}_i$ (such as values, $\hat{v}_i$, where they are assigned at random). The large literature on experimental double auctions makes no such individual comparisons, because the theoretical literature had not yielded tractable models of individual bid-offer behaviour (but recent contributions by Friedman (1984), and Wilson (1984) are providing such models). Here as in most other areas of experimental research the comparisons are between the predicted price–quantity outcomes of static theory (such as competitive, monopoly and Cournot models), and observed outcomes. But double auctions have been studied (see references in Smith, 1982) in a variety of environments; for example, the effect of price floors and ceilings have been examined (see references in Plott, 1982). In all cases these studies are making comparisons. In *nomotheoretical* experiments one compares theory and observation, whereas in *nomoempirical* experiments one compares the effect of different institutions and/or environments as a means of documenting replicable empirical 'laws' that may stimulate modelling energy in new directions. The idea that formal theory must precede meaningful observation does not account for most of the historical development of science. *Heuristic* or exploratory experiments that provide empirical probes of new topics and new experimental methods should not be discouraged.

In industrial organization, and antitrust economics, experimental methods have been applied to examine the effects of monopoly, conspiracy and alleged anticompetitive practices, and to study the concept of natural monopoly and its relation to scale economics, entry cost and the contestable markets hypothesis (see references in Plott, 1982; Smith, 1982; Coursey et al., 1984).

An important development in the experimental study of allocation processes has been the extension of experimental market methods to majority rule (and other) committee processes, and to market-like group processes for the provision of goods which have public or common outcome characteristics (loosely, public goods). These studies have examined public good allocation under majority (and Roberts') rules for committee including the effect of the agenda (see the references to Fiorina and Plott, and Levine and Plott in Smith, 1982), and under compensated unanimity processes suggested by theorists (see the references in Coursey and Smith, 1985). Generally, this literature reports substantial experimental support for the theory of majority rule outcomes, the theory of agenda processes (the sequencing of issues for voting decisions) and for incentive compatible models of the provision of public goods.

BIBLIOGRAPHY

Battalio, R., Kagel, J., Winkler, R., Fisher, E., Basmann, R. and Krasner, L. 1973. A test of consumer demand theory using observations of individual consumer purchases. *Western Economic Journal* 11(4), December, 411–28.

Chamberlin, E. 1948. An experimental imperfect market. *Journal of Political Economy* 56, April, 95–108.

Coursey, D., Isaac, M., Luke, M. and Smith, V. 1984. Market contestability in the presence of sunk (entry) costs. *Rand Journal of Economics* 15(1), Spring, 69–84.

Coursey, D. and Smith, V. 1985. Experimental tests of an allocation mechanism for private, public or externality goods. *Scandinavian Journal of Economics* 86(4), 468–84.

Friedman, D. 1984. On the efficiency of experimental double auction markets. *American Economic Review* 74(1), March, 60–72.

Friedman, J. 1963. Individual behavior in oligopolistic markets: an experimental study. *Yale Economic Essays* 3(2), 359–417.

Hoggatt, A. 1959. An experimental business game. *Behavioral Science* 4(3), July, 192–203.

Kagel, J., Battalio, R., Rachlin, H., Green, L., Basmann, R. and Klemm, W. 1975. Experimental studies of consumer behaviour using laboratory animals. *Economic Inquiry* 13(1), March, 22–38.

Ketchman, J., Smith, V. and Williams, A. 1984. A comparison of posted-offer and double-auction pricing institutions. *Review of Economic Studies* 51(4), October, 595–614.

Lakatos, I. 1978. *The Methodology of Scientific Research Programmes, Philosophical Papers*, Vol. 1. Ed. J. Worrall and G. Currie, Cambridge: Cambridge University Press.

Mosteller, F. and Nogee, P. 1951. An experimental measurement of utility. *Journal of Political Economy* 59, October, 371–404.

Plott, C. 1982. Industrial organization theory and experimental economics. *Journal of Economic Literature* 20(4), December, 1485–527.

Sauermann, H. and Selten, R. 1959. Ein Oligopolexperiment. *Zeitschrift für die Gesamte Staatswissenschaft* 115(3), 427–71.

Shubik, M. 1962. Some experimental non zero sum games with lack of information about the rules. *Management Science* 81(2), January, 215–34.

Siegel, S. and Fouraker, L. 1960. *Bargaining and Group Decision Making*. New York: McGraw-Hill.

Smith, V. 1962. An experimental study of competitive market behavior. *Journal of Political Economy* 70, April, 111–37.

Smith, V. 1982. Microeconomic systems as experimental science. *American Economic Review* 72(5), December, 923–55.

Smith, V., Williams, A., Bratton, K. and Vannoni, M. 1982. Competitive market institutions: double auctions versus sealed bid-offer auctions. *American Economic Review* 72(1), March, 58–77.

Williams, A. and Smith, V. 1984. Cyclical double-auction markets with and without speculators. *Journal of Business* 57(1) Pt 1, January, 1–33.

Wilson, R. 1984. Multilateral exchange. Working Paper No. 7, Stanford University, August.

Externalities

J.-J. LAFFONT

Competitive equilibria are Pareto optimal when they exist if preferences are locally non-satiated and if externalities are not present in the economy. Why externalities upset the first fundamental theorem of welfare economics and which economic policies can remedy this failure are the major questions addressed below.

TECHNOLOGICAL EXTERNALITIES. Let us call technological externality, the indirect effect of a consumption activity or a production activity on the consumption set of a consumer, the utility function of a consumer or the production function of a producer. By indirect, we mean that the effect concerns an agent other than the one exerting this economic activity and that this effect does not work through the price system.

Externalities may be positive or negative and are quite diverse. Major examples include pollution activities (air pollution, water pollution, noise pollution...), malevolence and benevolence, positive interaction of production activities. From a practical point of view the most significant are negative pollution activities, so that we can say that the theory of technological externalities is essentially the foundation of environmental economics.

The formalization of technological externalities is achieved in microeconomics by making production sets, utility functions and production sets (or functions) affected by externalities functionally dependent on the activities of the other agents creating these indirect effects.

For example, the utility function of a consumer is made dependent on the level of production of a firm polluting the air breathed by the consumer. This modelling option that we will implicitly adopt here is right as long as the link between production and air pollution is not alterable.

If de-polluting activities are possible the link between the level of pollution and the economic activities generating them must be made explicit. An important difficulty in analysing these activities is due to the non-convexities which they usually introduce.

PECUNIARY EXTERNALITIES. During the 1930s, a confused debate occurred between economists on the relevance of pecuniary externalities, i.e. on externalities which work through the price system. A quite general consensus was that pecuniary externalities are irrelevant for welfare economics: the fact that by increasing my consumption of whisky I affect your welfare through the consequent increase in price does not jeopardize the Pareto optimality of competitive equilibria.

This is true when all the assumptions required for the competitive equilibria to be Pareto optimal are satisfied. In such a framework, prices only equate supply and demand and pecuniary externalities do not matter. As soon as we move away from this set of assumptions, prices generally play additional roles. For example, in economies with incomplete contingent markets, prices span the subspace in which consumption plans can be chosen. In economies with asymmetric information, prices transmit information. When agents affect prices, they affect the welfare of the other agents by altering their feasible consumption sets or their information structures. Pecuniary externalities matter for welfare economics.

In what follows we focus only on technological externalities.

COMPETITIVE EQUILIBRIUM WITH EXTERNALITIES. How is the characterization of Pareto optima in convex economies affected by externalities? Very simply, as Pigou early understood. The classical equality of marginal rates of substitution and marginal rates of transformation must now be expressed using *social* marginal rates and not only *private* marginal rates as in an economy without externalities. Social marginal rates must be computed taking into account direct *and* indirect effects of economic activities. For example, the marginal cost of a polluting activity must include not only the direct marginal cost of production, but also the marginal cost imposed on the environment.

Note that Pareto optima do not exclude polluting activities, but set them at levels such that their social marginal benefit equates their social marginal cost well computed.

It is now easy to understand that in a private competitive economy, equilibria will not be in general Pareto optimal since the private decentralized optimizations of economic agents lead them to the equalization of *private and not social* marginal rates through the price system.

MARKETS FOR POLLUTION RIGHTS. Consider for concreteness a firm polluting a consumer. One potential solution is to create a market for this externality. Before producing, the firm must buy from the consumer the right to pollute. If both actors were behaving competitively with respect to the price of this right, the competitive equilibrium in the economy with an extended price system would be Pareto optimal, since there is no externality left.

A number of difficulties exist with this approach. In general we cannot expect agents to behave competitively unless we are in the special case of impersonal externalities. Then, there is a fundamental non-convexity in the case of negative externalities since as a negative externality increases the production set shrinks, but there is a limit to this effect which is the zero production level. Competitive equilibria cannot then exist unless bounds are set on supplies of pollution rights. (For a positive price, a firm would like to offer an infinite amount of pollution rights and close down.)

In the above set-up, the implicit status quo was the absence of externalities. The initial rights are a clean environment: 'Polluters must pay.' We can instead give to the polluting firm the right to pollute and then ask the consumer to buy from the firm a decrease of his pollution. This different allocation of initial rights does not upset the Pareto optimality of the competitive equilibrium, but of course has distributional effects.

TAXATION OF EXTERNALITIES. The likely strategic behaviour by agents on markets of pollution rights makes taxation of externalities the most common policy tool. The polluter must then pay for each unit of a polluting activity a tax which equals the marginal cost imposed by this activity on the other agents. The polluter than internalizes the externality and Pareto optimality is restored. If the externality is positive he must be similarly subsidized.

Note that nothing is said about the amount of taxes so obtained by the Government. There is no presumption that it is given to the polluters. In fact, the implicit assumption is that it is redistributed through lump sum transfers which do not affect agents' behaviours (in the sense of their first order conditions). From the point of view of Pareto optimality, the important goal is to modify polluters' behaviours.

If lump sum transfers are not available, the budget of the Government must be balanced and then goods different from the polluting activities must be taxed or subsidized to solve the ensuing second best problem.

The major difficulty with this solution is informational.

IMPERFECT INFORMATION. The traditional theory of externalities has proceeded as if the regulators had complete knowledge of the economy and were therefore able to compute optimal taxes, or as if agents were not behaving strategically with respect to their private information. Very often this is not the case and the problem is to elicit this private information and use it to compute taxes, a more difficult problem.

Intuitively, the solution of what is now a second best problem is to have taxes which depend nonlinearly on polluting activities. This nonlinearity may sometimes take the extreme form of a zero tax up to a given amount and a very large tax above, a mechanism which is equivalent to a quota.

PLANNING AND EXTERNALITIES. Externalities are not only a problem of market economies with an insufficient number of markets. One way to suppress an externality between two agents is to have them integrate into a single agent. All externalities would be internalized if the whole economy was integrated.

Leaving aside imperfect information and the associated strategic behaviours, the planning problem of these integrated agents is more complicated than if externalities were not present. Planning procedures appropriated to externalities have been provided.

EXTERNALITIES AND COOPERATIVE GAME THEORY. Suppose we attempt to represent the outcome of cooperation in an economy with externalities by the core. The core is the set of allocations which are not blocked by any coalition. A coalition blocks an allocation if it can do better for all its members than this allocation.

Externalities introduce a difficulty in the definition of a blocking coalition. When a group of agents envision forming a coalition they must conjecture what will be the behaviour of the complementary coalition since it is affected by the externalities of this complementary coalition.

Two extreme notions have been proposed. In the α-core a coalition is said to block an allocation if it can do better, whatever the actions of the complementary coalition. This is extremely prudent. In the β-core a coalition is said to block an allocation if, for any action of the complementary coalition, it can do better. The β-core is of course included in the α-core.

Results depend a lot on these conjectures about the actions of the complementary coalition, an unsatisfactory feature. One lesson, however, is that the core may be empty, i.e. that externalities introduce an element of instability in economic games.

HISTORICAL NOTE. Following the pioneering work by Sidgwick (1887) and Marshall (1890), Pigou (1920) has provided the basic theory of static technological externalities. Coase (1960) has explained how initial rights could be assigned in various ways. Arrow (1969) has explained how externalities could be internalized by the creation of additional markets. Starrett (1972) has pointed out the associated problem of nonconvexity. The first theorem of existence of an equilibrium with externalities has been provided by McKenzie (1955). Shapley and Shubik (1969) studied the core with externalities. A large number of authors have studied various second best problems associated with externalities (Buchanan, 1969; Plott, 1966; Diamond, 1973; Sandmo, 1975).

BIBLIOGRAPHY

Arrow, K. 1969. The organization of economic activity: issues pertinent to the choice of market versus non-market allocation. In Joint Economic Committee, *The Analysis and Evaluation of Public Expenditures: the PPB System*, Washington, DC: Government Printing Office, 47–64.

Buchanan, J.M. 1969. External diseconomies, corrective taxes and market structure. *American Economic Review* 59, 174–6.

Coase, R.H. 1960. The problem of social cost. *Journal of Law and Economics* 3, 1–44.

Diamond, P. 1973. Consumption of externalities and imperfect corrective pricing. *Bell Journal of Economics and Management*, Autumn, 526–38.

McKenzie, L. 1955. Competitive equilibrium with dependent consumer preferences. In *Proceedings of the Second Symposium in Linear Programming*, ed. H.A. Antosiewicz, Washington, DC.

Marshall, A. 1890. *Principles of Economics.* London: Macmillan; 8th edn, New York: Macmillan Co., 1948.
Pigou, A.C. 1920. *The Economics of Welfare.* London: Macmillan; New York: St. Martin's Press, 1952.
Plott, C.R. 1966. Externalities and corrective taxes. *Economica* 33, 84–7.
Sandmo, A. 1975. Optimal taxation in the presence of externalities. *Swedish Journal of Economics* 77, 96–8.
Shapley, L. and Shubik, M. 1969. On the core of an economic system with externalities. *American Economic Review* 59, 687–9.
Sidgwick, H. 1887. *Principles of Political Economy.* 2nd edn, London and New York: Macmillan.
Starrett, D. 1972. Fundamental non-convexities in the theory of externalities. *Journal of Economic Theory* 4, 180–99.

Fraud

EDI KARNI

An agent is said to have committed fraud when he misrepresents the information he has at his disposal so as to persuade another individual (principal) to choose a course of action he would not have chosen had he been properly informed. The essential element of this phenomenon is the presence of two individuals both of whom have something to gain from co-operating with each other but who have conflicting interests and differential information. More specifically, it is critical that the agent be both better informed than the principal and in a position to use his superior knowledge to affect the principal's actions so as to increase his own share of the total benefit at the principal's expense. As the choice of terminology indicates, fraud is a special case of a more general class of economic phenomena known as agency relationships. (For a more elaborate discussion and citations see Arrow, 1985.)

Fraud may assume different forms. To focus our discussion, however, we consider the provision by a producer (agent) of misinformation so as to induce customers (principals) to purchase goods or services which, if adequately informed, they would not buy. Our discussion draws heavily upon Darby and Karni (1973), which was the first and so far the most elaborate attempt at an economic analysis of the phenomenon of fraud.

THE PREVALENCE OF FRAUD. Fraud is as prevalent and as persistent as the asymmetrical information necessary to support it. Thus fraud may occur whenever the cost of verification of the producer's claims prior to the actual purchase of the good or service is prohibitively high. For some goods the producer's claims are easily verifiable through their use, for example, the performance of a car, the effectiveness of a painkiller. In these cases, if the population participating in the market is sufficiently stable, the scope for fraud by established firms is limited by the need to maintain their reputations. In such markets fraud may nevertheless be practised by transient firms and fly-by-night operators.

Fraudulent practices of a more persistent nature may occur in service industries where the separation of the diagnosis from provision of the service itself is impractical and where, moreover, the assessment of the quality of service is difficult if not impossible. This is the case when the ultimate performance of the good being serviced depends on several inputs and/or the relation between the service input and the ultimate performance is stochastic. To grasp the point consider a patient who complains of stomach pain. Suppose that the patient is treated with two different medications and undergoes surgery. Should the pain disappear the patient would be unable to determine which, if any, of the possible remedies was responsible for his cure.

THE ECONOMIC CONSEQUENCES OF FRAUD. The opportunities for fraud manifest themselves in voluntary arrangements that define the principal–agent relation, whose purpose is to inhibit the actual perpetration of fraud, and in resource misallocation.

Voluntary arrangements and institutions such as formal warranties and service contracts may be regarded as insurance schemes. However, by placing responsibility for the cost of maintenance on the supplier these contracts eliminate the supplier's incentive to defraud his customers. Thus, in the absence of direct means of verification, extended warranties and service contracts may be regarded as means by which producers authenticate their claims (see Hirshleifer, 1973, for a discussion of authentication as an information-induced behavioural mode). The scope for formal service contracts and warranties is limited by the usual 'moral hazard' problem in other words, the adverse effect on the owner's incentive to take the necessary care in using the good may undermine these institutions.

A less formal arrangement is the 'client relationship'. This form of principal–agent relation is an implicit agreement that the customer will continue to patronize the service shop as long as he has no reason to suspect fraud. Lacking the means necessary for a direct assessment of the service provided, customers may exploit the opportunity afforded by repeated relations to detect whether a supplier performs at the desired level by using statistical methods. Recognizing this and the need to cultivate a clientele discourages the supplier from defrauding regular customers. This personal relationship replaces the anonymity typical of markets in which information is symmetrically endowed. Obviously this consideration does not apply to transient clientele. Indeed, large parts of the folklore surrounding the tourist industry consist of accounts of flagrant fraudulent practices. (For a more detailed discussion of the client relationship, see Darby and Karni, 1973; Glazer, 1984.)

The profit opportunities made possible by fraud attract resources to industries where such opportunities exist. When barriers to entry do not exist excessive profits are eliminated. The resulting resource allocation, however, is distorted as scarce resources are employed in the provision of unnecessary services.

THE DETERRENCE OF FRAUD. Successful detection and prosecution of fraud have a deterrent effect that benefits society. Thus, a case can be made for social intervention. This may take the form of awarding multiple damages to successful prosecution of fraud that would reflect the full social benefit from its deterrence. Such a policy would have the effect of increasing private vigilance in dealing with fraudulent practices and, with appropriate penalties on the practitioners, reduce the amount of fraud to a socially desirable level. Alternatively, adherence to non-fraudulent practices may be enforced by the law enforcement agencies of the government. (For a detailed discussion, see Darby and Karni, 1973.)

Since the provision of misinformation may just as well be the result of sheer incompetence as of intentional deception, successful fraud-deterring policy will also increase the competence level of the suppliers of services. Unlike the elimination of intentional misrepresentation of information, however, increasing the level of competence involves investment of scarce resources on the part of the suppliers. Therefore, in setting the goals for a policy whose aim is to reduce fraud, the additional gains from the associated increase in the level of competence must be weighed against the corresponding resource cost. The optimal level of fraud may not be zero.

BIBLIOGRAPHY

Arrow, K.J. 1985. The economics of agency. In *Principals and Agents: The Structure of Business*, ed. J.N. Pratt and R. Zeckhauser, Cambridge, Mass.: Harvard Business School Press.

Darby, M.R. and Karni, E. 1973. Free competition and the optimal amount of fraud. *Journal of Law and Economics* 16(1), April, 67–88.

Glazer, A. 1984. The client relationship and a 'just' price. *American Economic Review* 74(5), December, 1089–95.

Hirshleifer, J. 1973. Where are we in the theory of information? *American Economic Review* 63(2), May, 31–9.

Hidden Actions, Moral Hazard and Contract Theory

ROGER GUESNERIE

'Moral hazard' in the literal sense refers to the adverse effects, from the insurance company's point of view, that insurance may have on the insuree's behaviour. As an extreme but standard example, a fire insurance holder may burn the property in order to obtain the insured sums. Although the expression can be found in earlier literature, its extensive use in economics can be dated from Arrow's *Essays in the Theory of Risk-bearing* (1971), which had a decisive influence in popularizing the term as well as in stimulating a systematic study both of the subject itself and of related phenomena. Arrow stresses that the complete set of markets required for first best efficiency often cannot be organized. The (so-called) Arrow–Debreu contracts which are needed would have to be contingent on states of nature. This term, 'states of nature', has to be taken in its meaning in decision theory where it refers to random events whose realization reflects an exogenous choice by 'Nature', and not an endogenous choice by agents. However, states of nature may not be observable either directly or indirectly, so that real contracts have to rely upon imperfect proxies. Take the overly simple fire insurance example. Arrow–Debreu contingent contracts would make indemnification conditional only on the occurrence of those natural events that can cause fire, such as thunderstorms, whereas actual real-world contracts make it dependent upon the occurrence of fire itself, whether due to an unusual exogenous event, or to a more normal exogenous event coupled with insufficient care.

Following Arrow, modern economic terminology has come to use 'moral hazard' to mean the unobservability of contingencies, about which information is needed in order to design first-best efficient contracts. Consider now a general framework of contracts, it is normally the case that the relevant contractual information can be obtained through observation of actions and outcomes, the latter themselves dependent on states of nature. Assuming that outcomes are always observed, moral hazard is therefore restricted to mean that some actions of one or more of the parties are not publicly observable (i.e. by all parties to the contract). With the more suggestive terminology of Arrow, moral hazard is thus associated with the existence of *hidden actions* in a contractual relationship.

This definition deserves three comments.

(i) 'Moral hazard' has unfortunate ethical connotations. Given that parties to contracts are usually modelled as standard maximizers of utility, it seems preferable to employ the term *hidden actions*.

(ii) Recent literature on contracts distinguishes between the observability and the verifiability of actions. A variable can be observable by all the parties to a contract, but not to outsiders to the contract. In particular, it may provide no evidence for a court of law. It is then said to be non-verifiable. Then *hidden actions* conveys the right idea but not the right nuance, and we should rather speak of *unverifiable actions*.

(iii) Difficulties in organizing a contractual relationship arise not only from actions that some parties can hide but also from the limited accessibility of the information that some parties use before taking actions. This may be private information of one party about itself (an agent usually knows his own characteristics better than do his partners in the contract), or information on some relevant states of nature which can influence the outcome of the relationship. Such difficulties are thus due to *hidden knowledge* as well as to hidden actions. Consider again an example drawn from insurance. Insurance companies (life insurance, car insurance) face both good risks and bad risks, i.e. agents who for a given level of care or prevention have to be assigned different probabilities of injury. This distinction thus refers to privately known characteristics of the insurees themselves rather than to the actions they take. Hidden knowledge generates opportunism. Faced with a set of contracts, high risk and low risk people will select different contracts; this is self-selection or, from the company's point of view, adverse selection. The distinction between hidden actions and hidden knowledge seems more suggestive than the more usual distinction in contract theory between moral hazard and adverse selection. Although we will examine some problems in which hidden actions and hidden knowledge are mixed, the main subject of this article is the analysis of contractual problems raised by hidden actions. Attention will be focused primarily on an abstract hidden action model, rather on the subject-specific discussions which generated the main building blocks of that model.

I. THE BASIC HIDDEN ACTION MODEL OF A BILATERAL RELATIONSHIP

The prototype model considered in this section owes much to the pioneering work of Ross (1973), Mirrlees (1974 and 1976) and Holmstrom (1979), and its presentation here draws heavily on the syntheses of Grossman and Hart (1983a). It is a principal–agent model with one principal and one agent. The agent chooses from among available actions one which together with random events (states of nature) determines a measurable result, which most of the time is a money payment to the principal. The principal is interested in the results as well as in the money remuneration he gives to the agent. The agent has a utility function depending upon the action taken and on the money transfer he receives from the principal. Some actions are more costly or involve higher 'effort'. Indeed, in many specific models the action variable is a loosely defined effort level: effort of the manager when the principal consists of shareholders, effort of firms when the principal is a bank.

In the simpler version of the model considered here, each utility function is separable, and risk-neutrality vis-à-vis income obtains, with a utility linear in income. It is assumed that the agents' actions are not observable but that the results are verifiable. A contract between the principal and the agent then consists of a reward schedule which associates a money transfer to any possible result. Analytically an optimal contract for the principal is a solution (if any) to a programme which maximizes over the set of all reward schedules, under a constraint of individual rationality for the agent.

The solution just sketched calls for preliminary comments:

(i) In the degenerate case where there is no choice of action, the principal–agent problem reduces to a pure risk-sharing question, whose solution depends on the risk-aversion of the parties concerned. In particular, a risk-neutral agent bears all income fluctuations and provides full insurance to his risk-averse partners. An optimal contract between a risk-neutral firm and risk-averse workers leads to utility profiles of workers constant across states of nature and a constant wage in states where workers are employed. This latter remark is at the core of the theory of implicit contracts initiated by Azariadis (1975), Bailey (1974) and Gordon (1974).

(ii) With a non-degenerate set of actions, but with an observability assumption, the optimal contract trades off between efficiency and risk-sharing considerations. Following the usual terminology, the corresponding contract is referred to as first best. When actions are not observable, the reward scheme has to be based on results only. It is generally impossible to reward actions indirectly in a way which mimics the first best contract. We then have to determine a second best contract.

First insights into the model are obtained when the reward schedule is restricted to be an affine function of the money outcome. Then, when the principal is risk-neutral and the agent is risk-averse, the optimal contract trades off between incentives and risk-sharing requirements in a way which confirms intuition. A positive fixed fee has to be combined with a linear schedule the slope of which is, however, smaller than the marginal value of the performance for the principal.

The derivation of the optimal non-linear second best contract leads to a serious analytical difficulty, which has been of primary concern to analysts. In the context of moral hazard this difficulty was initially stressed by Mirrlees (1975), and was independently discovered and analysed in the context of a general equilibrium second best problem by Guesnerie and Laffont (1978). It can be described as follows: For a given reward schedule, the agent's utility as an indirect function of actions is not generally quasi-concave. Hence, when the parameters of the reward schedule are modified the optimal response of the agent may jump. Although this jump only occurs for exceptional values of the parameters, it may still be the case that the optimal contract systematically selects such exceptional values (this is really the essence of the point made by Mirrlees and Guesnerie–Laffont). Then the local description of the agent's local behaviour from the first order conditions of utility maximization – which is analytically very convenient – becomes invalid. This failure of the so-called 'first-order approach' has generated contributions which are decisive for a rigorous analysis of the problem (see e.g. Rogerson, 1985).

The research has led us to a much more thorough understanding of an optimal schedule. In particular, it has made clear that the reward associated to a given result reflects the Bayesian statistical inference made by the principal from this result, although this convenient interpretation should not hide the fact that the principal does not ignore the agent's action! However, the results on the shape of the optimal schedule are somewhat deceptive. As the statistical inference argument suggests, few restrictions on it can be deduced from general theory. Even monotonicity – higher rewards for higher results – cannot be guaranteed, without strong assumptions on the distribution of results conditional on actions. For example, monotonicity obtains with the monotone likelihood ratio property introduced in this problem by Milgrom (1981) and the concavity of distribution function condition (see Grossman and Hart, 1983a). Non-monotonicity is hardly surprising; imagine that the most desirable actions from the principal's point of view give rise to high results and to low results with smaller probability but never to intermediate results. Conceivably, intermediate results will thus be less rewarded than low results.

In this rather disappointing picture, a result of general relevance does emerge. Although weak, it is remarkably robust. All variables that are correlated with the noise carry useful information for the design of optimal contracts. New information is redundant only when existing variables are sufficient statistics (see Holmstrom, 1979; Gjesdal, 1982).

To complete the picture, cases where the first best is implementable have to be stressed.

(i) If the agent is risk-neutral, a reward schedule which gives him the money result up to some constant provides correct incentives (such a reward schedule is reminiscent of the Groves scheme in an adverse selection problem). The agent then acts as a residual claimant and chooses the first best action.

(ii) Suppose that one result signals for sure that some non-optimal action has been chosen (i.e. this result has probability zero when the optimal action is taken). Then, if a high penalty is associated with this result, the agent will be deterred from choosing any action for which this result can occur with non-zero probability. It follows that the first-best action will be chosen if there is a subset of highly penalized results that are reached with probability zero when the optimal action is taken, and with positive probability when any non-optimal action is taken. In particular, if the result is a noisy estimate of the action, the first best is implementable when the noise is additive and has compact support. The power of high penalties, at least in some contexts, is a striking feature of moral hazard problems. We will come back to this point later.

II. FURTHER GENERAL CONSIDERATIONS ON HIDDEN ACTION MODELS

We will examine briefly four directions of development for the basic hidden action model described in section I.

II.1 The complexity of the optimal reward schedule. The results described in the previous section suggest contractual arrangements which are more complex than those observed in real situations. Several explanations have been suggested: for example, bounded rationality of the parties is a plausible argument for the use of unsophisticated reward schemes. Another possible explanation might be found in the inadequacy of the modelling options described in section I. This is a subject of current research and an interesting point has recently been made by Holmstrom and Milgrom (1985). They modify the basic model by assuming that the agent has progressive information on the occurrence of the outcome so that he can continuously adapt his action (here, his effort) in the time interval where the relationship takes place. They show that the optimal reward schedule, which in the standard version of these problems is highly non-linear, becomes linear. Although this conclusion relies on special assumptions concerning the agent's utility and the noise, it suggests that the enrichment of the action space of the agent leads to simpler reward schedules.

II.2 Mixing adverse selection and moral hazard. It has been argued above that hidden action and hidden knowledge determine two polar cases in the theory of contracts – in fact many contract problems involve both hidden action and hidden knowledge. In the mixed case the non-linear reward scheme thus has three different roles. It should provide correct incentives by limiting the distortion between the value of outcome for the principal and the agent's reward, and should induce adequate risk-sharing; these two functions are already central to the hidden action model. In addition, it should keep control of the self-selection process by inducing satisfactory choices of agents of different characteristics. The determination of the optimal contract in the mixed case then assimilates the analytical difficulties of each of the polar cases (each of these polar cases is reasonably well understood, and for a synthesis on an adverse selection principal–agent problem, in a spirit similar to Grossman and Hart's article on moral hazard, see Guesnerie and Laffont (1984)). The understanding of the intricacies of the general case requires further investigation. The analysis of an intermediate case provides a useful benchmark. It is presented now.

Consider a pure hidden knowledge problem when actions of the agent are observable although characteristics are not. Let us introduce the moral hazard ingredient that actions are no longer perfectly observable. Their observation is affected by noise. The new problem calls for two immediate remarks: first, if the parties are risk-averse, the introduction of noise will reduce social welfare (when compared to its pure adverse selection maximum level); second, if the adverse selection problem is degenerate, i.e. the agent's characteristics are known, there is no welfare loss when agents are risk-neutral. This absence of welfare loss can be shown to extend to a non-degenerate hidden knowledge model. For a large class of noises, with risk-neutral agents, the maximum adverse selection welfare, can be at least approximately reached when the observation of actions becomes noisy. In other words, the second best adverse selection welfare can still be implemented with noisy observations. This (quasi) implementation obtains either by using a family of quadratic schedules (see Picard, 1987) or by using a single schedule, different from the adverse selection optimal schedule, but obtained from it as the solution of a convolution equation when the noise is additive (see Caillaud, Guesnerie and Rey, 1986) or a Fredholm equation for non-additive noise (see Melumad and Reichelstein, 1986). Furthermore, when one of the action variables can be observed, a family of linear schedules may serve for implementation whatever the distribution of noise (it is then a universal family of schedules) or a family of truncated linear schedules may serve for implementation when the noise is small. However, these appealing properties are likely to hold in circumstances which are rather special (see Laffont and Tirole (1986) for one of these special cases, and Caillaud, Guesnerie and Rey (1986) for a comprehensive analysis of this problem).

II.3 Monitoring devices and high penalties. We have provided an interpretation of the basic hidden action model where 'results' are an intrinsic and unavoidable outcome of the relationship. There are cases, however, where the principal is only interested in the actions taken by the agents and where the inference on the action is made from observations which are obtained from a special device: examples of such monitoring devices which allow more precise interference of the behaviour of an agent are audits.

If the basic frame is easily adapted to the study of such a situation when the monitoring device is given, or even if there are several possible monitoring devices, a basic difficulty occurs when the frequency of use of such a monitoring device is not fixed. The nature of the difficulty is the following: the use of the monitoring device being costly, the principal can economize on expected costs by writing a contract which stipulates that the control device will only be used with probability smaller than one, rather than for sure. But whatever the probability chosen, it is often the case that the principal can reduce it further and modify penalties and rewards accordingly in such a way that the choice of action is unchanged. This argument was made in particular by Polinsky and Shavell (1979; see also Rubinstein, 1979) who were considering the substitutability between the probability and the magnitude of legal fines. The fact is that the expected value of the fine may be held constant when the probability of control is decreased and the magnitude of the fine is increased. This argument has proved to be remarkably robust (for extensions, see Nalebuff and Scharfstein, 1985). In particular, it does not depend upon the risk-aversion of agents, at least in a bilateral relationship. In our framework, it suggests that the optimal contract, when the use of monitoring devices is costly, may be stochastic and may involve a low probability of control, together with (possibly) high penalties and rewards. Again, real contractual arrangements do suggest neither the use of high penalties, nor the substitution of penalties to control frequencies, at least to the extent predicted by the above theory. A more careful analysis of the problems suggests at least three reasons for the first noted discrepancies (and at the same time three directions of improvements for the basic model).

(i) Our argument holds in the special case of a hidden action relationship in which all the elements of the problem are in the language of the theory, 'common knowledge'. For example, it assumes that the agent's risk-aversion is exactly known by the principal or that the distribution functions of the random variables is common knowledge. Giving up one of these assumptions amounts to introducing hidden knowledge into the relationship. The efficiency of high penalties does not seem to be robust to the introduction of these considerations.

(ii) The credibility of the principal's commitment to some probability of control is problematic. It would require the implementation of some kind of public lottery.

(iii) The outcome of control via a monitoring device should be verifiable. If not, the principal would have an incentive to announce results which highly penalize the agent. Some neutral third party is required. But the danger of collusion between this third party and another party increases with the amount of penalties (or reward). (For an analysis of collusion in a three parties relationship, see Tirole, 1986.)

II.4 The dynamics of moral hazard contracts. Assume that the basic principal–agent relationship is repeated. The one-period game described above is extended to a large number of periods (assuming for simplicity separability between periods). It is intuitively clear from the law of large numbers that time filters out uncertainty and allows a more and more accurate knowledge of the mean action taken by the agent. Repetition should thus alleviate moral hazard problems. The formal analysis confirms and makes precise these findings, at least when parties to the contract put enough weight on the future. If agents are interested only in the average pay-off over an infinity of periods or if both have a (common) discount rate close enough to one, there exist dynamic contracts which allow one to approximate the first best welfare level (see Radner, 1981, 1985). It would, however, be premature to conclude from this neat result that moral hazard problems disappear within a long enough relationship. Let us make clear the limits of this result.

(i) The result only holds for discount rates close to one. Even then, it does not provide a characterization of the truly optimal policy (it uses an a priori policy which is shown to be quasi-optimal). *A fortiori*, the characteristics of the optimal policy for lower values of the discount rates are not well understood. The study of simple cases such as the one considered by Henriet and Rochet (1984) suggests that the present reward at any period should put more weight on observed performances which are more recent. This is in sharp contrast with what happens in an adverse selection problem, where the observation serves to estimate the value of unobservable characteristics, a case in which the Henriet–Rochet model leads one to base the reward on the mean of observation before the present period.

(ii) The model supposes both that the principal can commit himself to the announced strategy and that the agent is locked-in in the relationship, but is not necessarily needed for the conclusion. In addition, the principal's policy relies on the threat of high penalties, a feature of contracts the adequacy of which has been questioned in the previous subsection. The commitment assumption is subject to the usual objections. The lock-in assumption for the agent is also much debatable. The agent should at least be allowed to smooth his income through time by access to financial markets. Exit of the agent via financial markets is a subject of present research.

(iii) As in the static case, many interesting dynamic problems mix hidden action and hidden knowledge. This leads to more intricate phenomena as demonstrated by the models of Holmstrom (1982b) or Harris and Holmstrom (1982). Assume as in these models, the output of a worker is the product of an unobservable characteristic (say skill) and of an action (say effort). The firms' inference from the sequence of outputs aims at determining both effort and skill. In their turn, workers are induced to over-invest in effort in the first periods to signal high skill and to under-invest when their position has been established. This has some resemblance to real academic life rather than to a pure hidden action dynamic model.

II.5 Tournaments and moral hazard in a group. The so-called tournament model focuses attention on a relationship involving one principal and several agents. With several agents, the contracts are not necessarily independent: the reward of one agent can be based not only upon his performance but also upon the performance of the other. One polar case of interdependent contract is the contract associated with a rank-order tournament where actual outputs are ranked and the reward jumps with the rank. With two agents the winner has the highest prize (R & D competition for patents induces a similar structure of rewards: see Guesnerie and Tirole, 1985). Let us briefly mention the main direction explored by the tournament literature.

(i) Lazear and Rosen (1981), in a two-agent model, compare the rank-order tournament with special independent contracts, i.e. linear contracts, and discuss the relative merits of both.

(ii) Independent non-linear contracts are dominated by dependent contracts only when the principal can infer more information on the variables faced by the agent (before his decision was made) from the whole set of outcomes than he can infer from any single outcome. In such circumstances Green and Stokey (1983), Holmstrom (1982a) and Nalebuff and Stiglitz (1983), focus attention on situations in which the mean of outcomes is a sufficient statistic for the variables unknown to the principal. Thus, the optimal contract is only dependent upon the mean of outcomes and the individual outcome.

(iii) First best can be approximately implemented from rank order tournaments with high penalties when the number of participants is large enough (see

Holmstrom, 1982; Nalebuff and Stiglitz, 1983). In the different but related context of moral hazard in teams, Holmstrom (1982) has stressed that a team can behave poorly in the solution of moral hazard problems when no agent in the group can act as residual claimant. The group thus cannot commit itself credibly to use a sharing rule which induces efficient effort. The existence of a residual claimant is essential for making credible the threat of destruction.

CONCLUSION

One of the two obvious omissions in the present review has already been stressed. Applications of the basic ideas to different subjects have not been reviewed. The 'horizontal' presentation adopted here should be complemented by 'vertical' readings which describe the implications of the basic ideas in different fields. The second omission is the fact that the work reviewed is only of partial equilibrium nature. However, the hidden action model is part of the contractual approach to economics which has developed since the 1970s from a recognition of the failure of the impersonal market hypothesis to explain certain phenomena. The corresponding literature had the more or less explicit ambition of assessing the aggregate implications of the existence of contractual arrangements at the micro level. In particular, the study of the general equilibrium implications of moral hazard is an important topic. It has not been presented here, partly from lack of space, and partly because a coherent presentation of existing work is more difficult.

In conclusion, let us briefly mention a number of directions of present research.

First, the nature of competition is affected by the presence of moral hazard at the micro level. Helpman and Laffont (1975), Arnott and Stiglitz (1985) and Hellwig (1987) analyse this problem.

Second, normative economics should take into account the specification of contractual relationships. In particular, one can expect that the contractual approach will favour a better assessment of the informational constraints faced by government action. Also, moral hazard at the micro level is responsible for externalities, the particular features of which are analysed in the case of the labour market by Arnott and Stiglitz (1985).

Finally, the examination of the aggregate consequences of contractual arrangements in the labour market is a subject of intensive research – Shapiro and Stiglitz (1984) argue that in the absence of direct penalties (for reasons discussed above) for breach of labour contracts, unemployment serves as a 'discipline device'. Other work on the general equilibrium consequences of the contractual labour conditions – in case of hidden action – include Malcomson and MacLeod (1986).

BIBLIOGRAPHY

Arnott, R. and Stiglitz, J. 1985. Labour turnover, wage structures, and moral hazard: the inefficiency of competitive markets. *Journal of Labor Economics* 3, 434–62.

Arrow, K.J. 1964. *Essays in the Theory of Risk-Bearing*. Chicago: Aldine.

Arrow, K.J. 1985. The Economics of Agency. In *Principals and Agents: The Structure of Business* ed. J. Pratt and R. Zeckhauser, Boston: Harvard Business School Press, 37–51.
Azariadis, C. 1975. Implicit contracts and underemployment equilibria. *Journal of Political Economy* 83, 1183–202.
Bailey, M. 1974. Wages and employment under uncertain demand. *Review of Economic Studies* 41, 37–50.
Bester, H. 1985. Screening versus rationing in credit markets with imperfect information. *American Economic Review* 75(4), 850–55.
Bhattacharya, S. 1983. Tournaments and incentives: heterogeneity and essentiality. Research Paper no. 695, Graduate School of Business, Stanford University.
Caillaud, B., Guesnerie, R. and Rey, P. 1986. Contracts with adverse selection and moral hazard: the case of risk neutral partners. Mimeo.
Calvo, G. and Wellicz, S. 1978. Supervision, loss of control and the optimal size of the firm. *Journal of Political Economy* 86(5), 943–52.
Diamond, D. 1984. Financial intermediation and delegated monitoring. *Review of Economic Studies* 51(3), 393–414.
Fama, E. 1980. Agency problems and the theory of the firm. *Journal of Political Economy* 88, 268–307.
Gibbons, R. 1985. Essays on labor markets and internal organization. Unpublished dissertation, Stanford University, July.
Gjesdal, F. 1982. Information and incentives: the agency information problem. *Review of Economic Studies* 49, 373–90.
Gordon, D. 1974. A neo-classical theory of Keynesian unemployment. *Economic Inquiry* 12, 431–59.
Green, J. and Stokey, N. 1983. A comparison of tournaments and contracts. *Journal of Political Economy* 91, 349–64.
Grossman, S. and Hart, O. 1983a. An analysis of the principal–agent problem. *Econometrica* 51, 7–45.
Grossman, S. and Hart, O. 1983b. Implicit contracts under asymmetric information. *Quarterly Journal of Economics*, Supplement, 71, 123–57.
Guesnerie, R. and Laffont, J.J. 1978. Taxing price makers. *Journal of Economic Theory* 19(2), 423–55.
Guesnerie, R. and Laffont, J.J. 1984. A complete solution to a class of principal–agent problem with an application to a self managed firm. *Journal of Public Economics* 25(3) 329–69.
Guesnerie, R. and Tirole, J. 1985. L'économie de la recherche développement. *Revue économique* 5, 843–71.
Harris, M. and Holmstrom, B. 1982. A theory of wage dynamics. *Review of Economic Studies* 49, 315–33.
Hellwig, M. 1987. Some recent developments in the theory of competition in markets with adverse selection. *European Economic Review* 31(1/2), 319–25.
Helpman, E. and Laffont, J.J. 1975. On moral hazard in general equilibrium theory. *Journal of Economic Theory* 10(1), 8–23.
Henriet, D. and Rochet, J.C. 1984. The logic of bonus-penalty systems in automobile insurance. Working Paper No. A273 0784, Ecole Polytechnique.
Holmstrom, B. 1979. Moral hazard and observability. *Bell Journal of Economics* 10, 74–91.
Holmstrom, B. 1982a. Moral hazard in teams. *Bell Journal of Economics* 13, 324–40.
Holmstrom, B. 1982b. Managerial incentive problems – a dynamic perspective. In *Essays in Economics and Management in Honor of Lars Wahlbeck*, Helsinki: Swedish School of

Economics.
Holmstrom, B. and Milgrom, P. 1985. Aggregation and linearity in the provision of intertemporal incentives. Cowles Discussion Paper no. 742, April.
Holmstrom, B. and Ricart-Costa, J. 1984. Managerial incentives and capital management. Cowles Discussion Paper no. 729, November.
Holmstrom, B. 1983. Equilibrium long-term contracts. *Quarterly Journal of Economics*, Supplement, 98, 23–54.
Joskow, P. 1985. Vertical integration and long-term contracts. *Journal of Law, Economics and Organization* 1, Spring, 33–80.
Laffont, J.J. and Tirole, J. 1986. Using cost observation to regulate firms. *Journal of Political Economy* 94(3), Pt I, 614–41.
Lambert, R. 1986. Executive effort and selection of Risky projects. *Rand Journal of Economics* 16, 77–88.
Lazear, E. and Rosen, S. 1981. Rank order tournaments on optimum labour contracts. *Journal of Political Economy* 89(5), 841–64.
Malcomson, J. 1984. Work incentives, hierarchy, and internal labor markets. *Journal of Political Economy* 92(3), 486–507.
Melumad, N. and Reichelstein, S. 1985. Value of communication in agencies. Mimeo.
Milgrom, P. 1981. Good news and bad news: representation theorems and applications. *Bell Journal of Economics* 12, 380–91.
Mirrlees, J. 1974. Notes on welfare economics, information, and uncertainty. In *Essays in Economic Behavior Under Uncertainty*, ed. M. Balch, D. McFadden and S. Wu, Amsterdam: North-Holland, 243–258.
Mirrlees, J. 1975. The theory of moral hazard and unobservable behavior – Part I. Mimeo, Nuffield College, Oxford.
Mirrlees, J. 1976. The optimal structure of authority and incentives within an organization. *Bell Journal of Economics* 7, 105–31.
Mookherjee, D. 1984. Optimal incentives schemes with many agents. *Review of Economic Studies* 51(3), 433–46.
Nalebuff, B. and Stiglitz, J. 1983. Prizes and incentives: towards a general theory of compensation and competition. *Bell Journal of Economics* 13, 21–43.
Newbery, D. and Stiglitz, J. 1983. Wage rigidity, implicit contracts and economic efficiency: are market wages too flexible? Economic Theory Discussion Paper 68, Cambridge University.
Picard, P. 1987. On the design of incentives schemes under moral hazard and adverse selection. *Journal of Public Economics.*
Polinsky, A. and Shavell, S. 1979. The optimal tradeoff between the probability and the magnitude of fines. *American Economic Review* 69(5), 880–89.
Radner, R. 1981. Monitoring cooperative agreements in a repeated principal–agent relationship. *Econometrica* 49, September, 1127–48.
Radner, R. 1985. Repeated principal–agent games with discounting. *Econometrica* 53, 1173–98.
Rogerson, W. 1985. 'The first-order approach to principal–agent problems', *Econometrica*, 53, 1357–68.
Ross, S. 1973. The economic theory of agency: the principal's problem. *American Economic Review* 63, 134–9.
Rubinstein, A. 1979. Offenses that may have been committed by accident – an optimal policy of retribution. In *Applied Game Theory*, ed. S. Brahms, A. Shotter and G. Schwödiauer, Würtzburg: Physica-Verlag, 406–413.

Shapiro, C. and Stiglitz, J. 1984. Equilibrium unemployment as a worker incentive device. *American Economic Review* 74, 433–44.
Shavell, S. 1979. Risk sharing and incentives in the principal and agent relationship. *Bell Journal of Economics* 10, 55–73.
Stiglitz, J. and Weiss, A. 1985. Credit rationing in markets with imperfect information. *American Economic Review* 71(3), 393–410.
Stiglitz, J. 1974. Incentives and risk sharing in sharecropping. *Review of Economic Studies* 41(2), 219–55.
Tirole, J. 1986. Hierarchies and bureaucracies: on the role of collusion in organizations. *Journal of Law Economics and Organization* 2(2), 181–214.
Williamson, O. 1985. *The Economic Institutions of Capitalism.* New York: Free Press.
Yaari, M. 1976. A law of large numbers in the theory of consumer's choice under uncertainty. *Journal of Economic Theory* 12, April, 202–17.

Implicit Contracts

COSTAS AZARIADIS

An implicit contract is a theoretical construct meant to describe complex agreements, written and tacit, between employers and employees, which govern the exchange of labour services when various types of job-specific investments inhibit labour mobility, and opportunities to shed risk are limited by imperfectly developed markets for contingent claims. This construct differs from the more familiar one of a neoclassical labour exchange in emphasizing a trading process, frequently over a long period of time, between two *specific* economic units (say a worker and a firm, union and management, etc.) rather than the impersonal, and often instantaneous, market process in which wages decentralize and coordinate the actions of labour suppliers and labour demanders.

Adam Smith's exposition of occupational wage differentials (1776, book I, ch. 10) recognized very early the idiosyncratic nature of the labour market and, in particular, that employment risk affected wages in various occupations. Since then economists have accumulated many facts, raw or stylized, which are best understood if one abandons the traditional view that the shadow price of labour is simply the wage rate. Prominent among explananda are the widespread use of temporary layoffs as a means of regulating the volume of employment (Feldstein, 1975); the continuity of jobs by many primary wage earners (Hall, 1982); the collective bargaining tradition of leaving the volume of employment at the discretion of management while predetermining money wage rates two or three years in advance.

To these, one must add certain 'impressions' or softer facts about the labour market which arise from the central role labour services possess in macroeconomic models. There is, indeed, among macroeconomists a shared impression (Hall, 1980) that, over a typical business cycle, average real compensation per hour fluctuates considerably less than does the marginal revenue-product of labour or, for that matter, the total volume of employment.

One consequence is that wage and price rigidity, are among the key assumptions of Keynesian macroeconomics, both in the Hicksian IS/LM framework and in the concept of quantity-constrained equilibrium originally developed by Clower (1965) and formalized by Bénassy (1975) and Drèze (1975). Another is the overwhelming importance of words like 'jobs' and 'unemployment', both in our colloquial vocabulary and in the specialized lexicon of economics. In particular, 'involuntary unemployment' is for many academic economists the *sine qua non* of modern macroeconomics.

The technically minded reader will find many of these issues surveyed in a number of specialized papers of which the most recent are Hart (1983) and Rosen (1985).

WAGES AND EMPLOYMENT. The earliest literature on implicit contracts exploits an insight of Frank Knight (1921), who argued that inherently 'confident and venturesome' entrepreneurs will offer to relieve their employees of some market risks in return for the right to make allocative decisions. The formal development of this idea began with three independently written papers by Baily (1974), Gordon (1974) and Azariadis (1975), motivated by the seeming puzzle of layoffs. In an unusual coincidence, all three authors took the employment relation not simply as a sequential spot exchange of labour services for money, but as a more complicated long-term attachment; labour services are traded in part for an insurance contract that protects workers from random, publicly observed fluctuations in their marginal revenue-product. The idea was that workers could purchase insurance only from their employers, not from third parties.

Risk-averse workers deal with risk-neutral entrepreneurs who head firms consisting of three departments: a production department that purchases labour services and credits each worker with his marginal revenue-product of labour (MRPL); an insurance department that sells actuarially fair policies and, depending on the state of nature, credits the worker with a net insurance indemnity (NII) or debits him with a net insurance premium; and an accounting department that pays each employed worker a wage, w, with the property that w = MRPL + NII in every state of nature.

Favourable states of nature are associated with high values of MRPL; in these the net indemnity is negative and wages fall short of the MRPL. Adverse states of nature correspond to low values of MRPL, to positive net insurance indemnities and to wages in excess of MRPL. An implicit contract is then a complete description, made before the state of nature becomes known, of the labour services to be rendered unto the firm in each state of nature, and of the corresponding payments to be delivered to the worker. The contract is implementable if we assume the state of nature is as easily verifiable as events are in a normal insurance contract.

An immediate consequence of this framework is that wages are disengaged from the marginal revenue-product of labour. In fact, if the amount of labour performed by employed workers per unit time is fixed institutionally, then each worker's consumption is proportional to the wage rate; an actuarially fair insurance policy should make this consumption independent of the MRPL by stabilizing the purchasing power of wages over states of nature. Therefore, the real wage rate is rigid.

In traditional macroeconomic models, of course, wage rigidity by itself is insufficient to cause unemployment: if wages do not adjust for some reason, then neither does the demand for labour. The argument does not carry over to implicit contracts because of the very separation between wages and the marginal revenue product of labour. A complete theory of unemployment must explain why layoffs are preferred to work-sharing in adverse states of nature, and why laid-off workers are worse off than their employed colleagues.

This is not a simple task if one thinks of implicit contracts as ordinary explicit timeless insurance contracts between risk-averse workers and risk-neutral entrepreneurs. All contracts of this type would share a basic property of optimum insurance schemes; namely, keeping the worker's marginal utility of consumption independent of all random, publicly observed events – including such events as 'employment' or 'unemployment'.

To explain layoff unemployment, we need to distort or complicate the insurance contract in some significant way. A distortion that was noted early in the implicit contract literature is the dole. In an extremely adverse state of nature, the flow of insurance indemnities to workers can become a substantial drain on profit; one way to staunch losses is to place the burden of insurance on an outside party, the dole.

The practice of layoffs is simply the administrative counterpart of this insurance-shifting manoeuvre; workers consent in advance that some of them may be separated from their jobs in order to become eligible for unemployment insurance (UI) payments from an outside public agency. Furthermore, no worker will contract his labour unless the expected value (utility) of the total package, taken over all possible states of nature, exceeds the value of being on the dole in every state. This means, in turn, that employed workers receive a wage in excess of UI payments and are therefore to be envied by their laid-off colleagues – a situation that many economists would call 'involuntary unemployment'.

The fact that laid-off workers would gladly exchange places with their employed colleagues is not in itself sufficient to establish a misallocation of resources. After all, accident victims may very well envy more fortunate individuals without any implication that the insurance industry works poorly. Layoffs, by themselves, could be no more than the luck of the draw unless we can demonstrate that they constitute, in some sense, socially inefficient underemployment. This is clearly impossible within the Walras–Arrow–Debreu model; and it is for this reason that the early literature on contracts turned to institutions like the dole in order to explain layoff unemployment.

PRIVATE INFORMATION. One fundamental departure from the Walrasian paradigm that received much attention in the early 1980s was a weakening of the information assumptions: information becomes 'private' or 'asymmetric', which simply means that not everyone is equally informed about the relevant state of nature. This is a perfectly sensible observation, for what justifies the trading of implicit contracts in the first place is that third parties simply are not as well informed about someone's income or employment status as is his employer; the employer, in turn, may be less informed about an employee's non-labour income and job opportunites than is the worker himself.

The thread was picked up by a number of authors who studied the properties of wages and employment for two main cases: in the first, entrepreneurs possess superior information about labour demand (Hall and Lilien, 1979; Grossman and Hart, 1981; Azariadis, 1983; Farmer, 1984); in the second case, workers possess superior information about labour supply, as in Cooper (1983). Suppose, for instance, that wages and employment do not depend on the unobservable true state of nature but on what the better informed contractant (say, the employer) *announces* that state to be. The question now becomes how to design contracts that reward entrepreneurs who tell the truth and punish those who lie.

One desirable property of contracts is that the truth should be the value-maximizing strategy for firms: truth-telling ought to be consistent with equality between the marginal cost and the marginal revenue-product of labour. Furthermore, entrepreneurs who misrepresent actual conditions should be punished, say, for knowingly under-reporting demand.

Under-reporting demand does turn out to be a problem in contracts that permit employers to slash both workforce and the wage bill when demand is slack, and do it in such a manner as to reduce cost more than revenue. To avoid this temptation, a properly designed contract specifies a highly variable pattern of employment over states of nature; that is, one in which employment is below what is socially optimal and the marginal product of labour is correspondingly above the marginal rate of substitution between consumption and leisure. It is in this sense that asymmetric information is said to result in socially inefficient underemployment or unemployment.

What relation is there between the layoffs we all know and the inefficient underemployment of a model economy that suffers from asymmetric information? To go from the latter to the former, one must understand first why layoffs are a more common means of reducing employment than is work-sharing. Second, a general equilibrium picture of underemployment would require an explanation of why underemployed (or unemployed) individuals are not hired by other employers. Third, and most important, the unemployment found in this private-information story is a response to private, firm-specific risk; most economists, however, consider the unemployment observed in market economies to be a reaction to social risks, especially to business cycles set in motion by aggregate demand disturbances. Unless one intends to make the far-fetched claim that the general public is unaware of, or cannot observe, whatever disturbances set off business cycles (e.g. changes in government consumption, money supply or consumer confidence), does it not appear that information-based unemployment simply describes the behaviour of an isolated firm?

The answer is not obvious. Note, however, that in order to have an inefficient volume of equilibrium employment, it is sufficient that *some but not all* information be private. In fact, it is not difficult to imagine general equilibrium extensions of the work we are discussing that would include both public and private information. Such extensions will be useful, especially if they manage to establish a firm link between inefficient underemployment and extreme values of some publicly observed aggregate disturbance.

EMPIRICAL IMPLICATIONS. Whether information is publicly shared or in the private domain, wages in implicit contracts do not merely reflect the marginal product of labour or the workers' marginal rate of substitution between consumption and leisure, as they might in more conventional theories. The empirical implications of this insight are just being worked out, and they seem to be quite considerable. At the most aggregative level, one can make sense of the oft-verified fact (Neftci, 1978) that hourly wages in manufacturing show little cyclical variability and are best described as a random walk.

In fact, it seems preferable to have empirical investigations of this sort at a less aggregated level. Aggregate studies are victims of selection bias: they fail to capture changes in the composition of output or of the labour force, which are themselves sufficient to induce substantial cyclical movement in economy-wide wages even if the business cycle does not affect the real wage of any skill grade in any industry.

Consider, for instance, a fictitious economy with homogeneous labour in which almost all industries experience little cyclical fluctuation except one, the quad industry, which is thoroughly buffeted by the business cycle. If labour mobility is good across industries, quad workers will suffer more layoffs and enjoy a wage higher than elsewhere whenever they are employed. The economy-wide average wage will vary procyclically.

Another phenomenon accounted for naturally by implicit contracts is the behaviour of occupational wage differentials (i.e. of the unskilled-to-skilled wage ratio). These have shown a definite countercyclical tendency, widening in contractions and narrowing in booms, both in the US and in the UK.

To see why, suppose that we drop the postulate of labour homogeneity in the economy just described and admit two skill grades. For simplicity, assume that the cycle is of such amplitude that there is no unemployment outside the quad industry, while unemployment in the quad industry falls solely on common labourers. These workers are thus the only group in the economy to suffer layoffs; in return they receive a wage above that of common workers outside the quad industry and below that of skilled workers – in the quad industry or out. As the cycle unfolds, then, the economy-wide wage average for craftsmen remains unaltered, the one for labourers changes procyclically, and occupational wage differentials follow a countercyclical pattern.

Intertemporal labour supply models of the type pioneered by Lucas and Rapping (1969) are another area that may in the future make fruitful use of implicit contracts. Econometric work on intertemporal labour substitution identifies the preferences of a 'typical' working household from time-series data on wages and salaries. The outcome is invariably an estimate of the wage-elasticity of labour supply that is so low as to be inconsistent with time-series data on employment

(Kydland and Prescott, 1982). In other words, someone who believes that the wage rate represents an important conditioning factor for labour supply and demand will find that wage rates do not vary sufficiently over the business cycle to account for observed fluctuations in employment.

Employment in an implicit contract, however, reflects the underlying value of labour's marginal revenue-product, whereas wages are smoothed averages of the MRPL over time or states of nature. Small fluctuations in contract wages are in principle consistent with substantial variations in contract employment; whether these are mutually consistent *in practice* remains to be seen from empirical work.

MACROECONOMIC ASPECTS. From empirical labour economics we turn to the macroeconomic issues that provided the original impetus for the development of implicit contracts. Unemployment, says this theory, is the result of differential information: a credible signal from employers to employees that product demand is slackening, or one from employees to employers that job opportunities are really better elsewhere.

Newer ideas that seem to be building on this basic piece of intuition are outlined later in this article. But whatever progress we have made towards understanding fluctuations in employment has not dispelled the dense fog that still shrouds the issue for wage rigidity. All we have to go on is the early result of Martin Baily that insurance makes the wage rate less variable than it otherwise might be. This stickiness, however, is a property of the *real* rather than the nominal wage rate, and it is the latter that is assumed to be right in Keynesian macroeconomics.

Rigidity, of course, does not necessarily imply complete time-invariance, nor does it require money wages to change less frequently than other prices; it is simply an information-processing failure. The standard procedure in collective bargains, for instance, is to predetermine money wages several years in advance; more often than not those wages are invariant to any information that may accumulate over the duration of the contract. Only in exceptional circumstances are money wages in the United States allowed to reflect *any* contemporaneous developments in the cost of living (indexation) or in the profitability of the employer (bankruptcy).

The mystery of wage rigidity is then the failure of contracts to set money wages as *functions* of publicly available information that is obviously relevant to the welfare of all parties. Why does the wage-setting process choose to ignore this information? One answer is transaction costs and/or bounded rationality: contracts are cheaper to evaluate and implement when they are defined by a few simple numbers rather than by complicated rules that condition employment or wages on contingent events. Another possibility is to exploit the great multiplicity of equilibria that is typical of economies with missing securities markets (Azariadis and Cooper, 1985). One of these equilibria features predetermined prices and wages, while employment and other quantity variables adjust fully to short-term disturbances. Wage rigidity here is like a Nash equilibrium: it is the best response of a firm in a labour market in which the wages paid by all other firms fail to reflect new information instantaneously.

IMPLEMENTATION. An implicit contract is formally defined as a collection of schedules describing how the terms of employment for one person or group of persons change in response to unexpected changes in the economic environment. What brings contractants together? How detailed are their agreements? And what mechanisms are there to enforce such agreements once they are reached? After an initial stage of fairly rapid development, research is returning to these elementary questions as if trying to clarify the axiomatic basis of the underlying theory.

What brings potential contractants together is the opportunity jointly to reap substantial returns on investments peculiar to their relationship. The idea is apparent in Becker's theory of specific human capital (1964) and in Williamson's hypothesis (1979) of physical assets that are specific to a given supplier–customer pair. To reap any returns, contractants must wed themselves to one partner, forsaking all others, for some period of time. Maintaining such a special relationship involves the transactions costs of creating an idiosyncratic asset, as well as an implicit contract; that is, a number of rules that define how the partners have decided to share the returns in various possible future circumstances.

There are, of course, circumstances that are not explicitly covered, either because they are not observable at reasonable cost or because contractants think of them as unlikely or unworthy of note. Irrespective of the possible events that are covered and of the prior rules that govern the distribution of returns to shared investments, all contractants are required to bear risk and to subordinate their short-term interest to longer-term considerations.

Workers, for instance, suffer layoffs in recessions while firms hoard labour in order to preserve a long-term relationship. What mechanisms keep constraints together in adverse circumstances?

One mechanism – studied extensively by Radner (1981), Townsend (1982) and others – is reputation: if somebody deviates from the terms of the contract, the deviation becomes widely known, and the deviant finds it diffcult to locate trading partners in the future. That works well if the time horizon is fairly long or the future is fairly important relative to the present; reputations are likely to be important for firms, less so for workers.

Another method of enforcement is by a third party: a monitor, arbitrator or court of law. In order for a third party to enforce a contract, it has to be able to observe all the prices and all the quantities specified in it – the employment status, hours worked and wage rate of every worker. That is an unreasonably large informational burden to place on someone who is outside the special relationship called a contract. Outsiders can be expected to observe at low cost only certain aggregates or averages, but not very much in the way of idiosyncratic detail.

How does one design and enforce contracts when outsiders are poorly informed about the trades among contractants? According to Hölmstrom (1983) and Bull (1986), self-interest will enforce contracts that third parties are not sufficiently informed to implement.

In particular, workers will put in the required amount of effort on the job, not because effort can be ascertained easily by an outside arbitrator but rather because they know that their wages and speed of promotions depend on performance. And employers will be careful not to break even the most implicit of their commitments if doing so will compromise their ability to attract workers in the future. As of this writing, the design of self-enforcing contracts seems to be the central theoretical problem in the field of implicit contracts.

BIBLIOGRAPHY

Azariadis, C. 1975. Implicit contracts and underemployment equilibria. *Journal of Political Economy* 83, 1183–202.

Azariadis, C. 1983. Employment with asymmetric information. *Quarterly Journal of Economics* 98, Supplement, 157–72.

Azariadis, C. and Cooper, R. 1985. Nominal wage-price rigidity as a rational expectations equilibrium. *American Economic Review, Papers and Proceedings* 75, 31–5.

Baily, M. 1974. Wages and employment under uncertain demand. *Review of Economic Studies* 41, 37–50.

Becker, G. 1964. *Human Capital.* New York: Columbia University Press.

Bénassy, J.-P. 1975. Neo-Keynesian disequilibrium in a monetary economy. *Review of Economic Studies* 42, 502–23.

Bull, C. 1986. The existence of self-enforcing implicit contracts. *Quarterly Journal of Economics.*

Clower, R. 1965. The Keynesian counter-revolution: a theoretical appraisal. In *The Theory of Interest Rates*, ed. F. Hahn and F. Brechling, London: Macmillan; New York, St. Martin's Press, 1965.

Cooper, R. 1983. A note on overemployment/underemployment in labor contracts under asymmetric information. *Economics Letters* 12, 81–7.

Drèze, J. 1975. Existence of an equilibrium under price rigidity and quantity rationing. *International Economic Review* 16, 301–20.

Farmer, R. 1984. A new theory of aggregate supply. *American Economic Review* 74, 920–30.

Feldstein, M. 1975. The importance of temporary layoffs: an empirical analysis. *Brookings Papers on Economic Activity* 3, 725–44.

Gordon, D.F. 1974. A neoclassical theory of Keynesian unemployment. *Economic Inquiry* 12, 431–49.

Grossman, S. and Hart, O. 1981. Implicit contracts, moral hazard, and unemployment. *American Economic Review, Papers and Proceedings* 71, 301–7.

Hall, R. 1980. Employment fluctuations and wage rigidity. *Brookings Papers on Economic Activity* 8, 91–124.

Hall, R. 1982. The importance of lifetime jobs in the US economy. *American Economic Review, Papers and Proceedings* 72, 716–24.

Hall, R. and Lilien, D. 1979. Efficient wage bargains under uncertain supply and demand. *American Economic Review* 69, 868–79.

Hart, O. 1983. Optimal labour contracts under asymmetric information: an introduction. *Review of Economic Studies* 50, 3–35.

Hölmstrom, B. 1983. Equilibrium long-term labor contracts. *Quarterly Journal of Economics* 98, Supplement, 23–54.

Knight, F. 1921. *Risk, Uncertainty and Profit*. Boston: Houghton Mifflin.

Kydland, F. and Prescott, E. 1982. Time to build and aggregate fluctuations. *Econometrica* 50, 1345–70.

Lucas, R. and Rapping, L. 1969. Real wages, employment and inflation. *Journal of Political Economy* 77, 721–54.

Neftci, S. 1978. A time-series analysis of the real wages–employment relationship. *Journal of Political Economy* 86, 281–91.

Radner, R. 1981. Monitoring cooperative agreements in a repeated principal–agent relationship. *Econometrica* 49, 1127–48.

Rosen, S. 1985. Implicit contracts: a survey. *Journal of Economic Literature* 23, 1144–75.

Smith, A. 1776. *An Inquiry into the Nature and Causes of the Wealth of Nations.* London: Pelican Books, 1970.

Townsend, R. 1982. Optimal multiperiod contracts and the gain from enduring relationships under private information. *Journal of Political Economy* 90, 1166–86.

Williamson, O. 1979. Transaction-cost economics: the governance of contractual relations. *Journal of Law and Economics* 22(2), October, 233–61.

Incentive Compatibility

JOHN O. LEDYARD

Allocation mechanisms, organizations, voting procedures, regulatory bodies and many other institutions are designed to accomplish certain ends such as the Pareto-efficient allocation of resources or the equitable resolution of disputes. In many situations it is relatively easy to conceive of feasible processes; processes which will accomplish the goals if all participants follow the rules and are capable of handling the informational requirements. Examples of such mechanisms include marginal cost pricing, designed to attain efficiency, and equal division, designed to attain equity. Of course once a feasible mechanism is found, the important question then becomes whether such a mechanism is also informationally feasible and compatible with 'natural' incentives of the participants. Incentive compatibility is the concept introduced by Hurwicz (1972, p. 320) to characterize those mechanisms for which participants in the process would not find it advantageous to violate the rules of the process.

The historical roots of the idea of incentive compatibility are many and deep. As was pointed out in one of a number of recent surveys,

> the concept of incentive compatibility may be traced to the 'invisible hand' of Adam Smith who claimed that in following individual self-interest the interests of society might be served. Related issues were a central concern in the 'Socialist Controversy' which arose over the viability of a decentralized socialist society. It was argued by some that such societies would have to rely on individuals to follow the rules of the system. Some believed this reliance was naive; others did not. (Goves and Ledyard, 1986, p. 1).

Further, the same issues have arisen in the design of voting procedures. Concepts and problems related to incentives were already identified and documented in the 18th century in dicsussions of proposals by Borda to provide alternatives to majority rule committee decisions.

Incentive compatibility is both desirable and elusive. The desirability of incentive compatibility can be easily illustrated by considering public goods, goods such that one consumer's consumption of them does not detract from another consumer's simultaneous consumption of that good. The existence of these collective consumption commodities creates a classic situation of *market failure*; the inability of markets to arrive at a Pareto-optimal allocation. It was commonly believed, prior to Groves and Ledyard (1977), that in economies with public goods it would be impossible to devise a decentralized process that would allocate resources efficiently since agents would have an incentive to 'free ride' on others' provision of those goods in order to reduce their own share of providing them. Of course, Lindahl (1919) had proposed a feasible process which mimicked markets by creating a separate price for each individual's consumption of the public good. This designed process was, however, rejected as unrealistic by those who recognized that these 'synthetic markets' would be shallow (essentially monopsonistic) and therefore buyers would have no incentive to treat prices as fixed and invariant to their demands. The classic quotation is '...it is in the selfish interest of each person to give *false* signals, to pretend to have less interest in a given collective consumption activity than he really has...' (Samuelson, 1954, pp. 388–9). Allocating public goods efficiently through Lindahl pricing would be feasible and successful if consumers followed the rules; but, it would not be successful since the mechanism is not incentive compatible. If buyers do not follow the rules, efficient resource allocation will not be achieved and the goals of the design will be subverted because of the motivations of the participants. Any institution or rule, designed to accomplish group goals, must be incentive compatible if it is to perform as desired.

The elusiveness of incentive compatibility can be most easily illustrated by considering a situation with only private goods. Economists generally model behaviour in private goods markets by assuming that buyers and sellers 'follow the rules' and take prices as given. It is now known, however, that as long as the number of agents is finite then any one of them can still gain by misbehaving and, furthermore, can do so in a way which cannot be detected by anyone else. The explanation is provided in two steps. First, if there are a finite number of traders, and none have a perfectly elastic offer curve (which will be true if preferences are non-linear) then one trader can gain by being able to control prices. For example, a buyer would want to set prices where his marginal benefit equalled his marginal outlay and thereby gain monopsonistic benefits. Of course, if the others know that buyer's demand curve (either directly or through inferences based on revealed preference), then they would know that the buyer was not 'taking prices as given' and could respond with a suitable punishment against him. This brings us to our second step. Even though others can monitor and prohibit price setting behaviour, our benefit-seeking monopsonist has another strategy which can circumvent this supervision. He calculates a (false) demand curve which, when added to the others' offer curves, produces an equilibrium price equal to that which he would have set if he had direct control. He then calculates a set of preferences which yields that demand curve and participates in the process *as if he had these (false) preferences.* Usually this involves simply acting as if one has a slightly lower demand curve than one really does. Since preferences are not able to be observed by others, he can follow this behaviour which looks like it is price-taking, and therefore 'legal', and can do individually better. The unfortunate implication of such concealed misbehaviour is that the mechanism performs other than as intended. In this case, resources are artificially limited and too little is traded to attain efficiency.

In 1972 Hurwicz established the validity of the above intuition. His theorem can be precisely stated after the introduction of some notation and a framework for further discussion.

THE IMPOSSIBILITY THEOREM. The key concepts include economic environments, allocation mechanisms, incentive compatibility, the no-trade option and Pareto-efficiency. We take up each in turn.

An *economic environment*, those features of an economy which are to be taken as given throughout the analysis, includes a description of the agents, the feasible allocations they have available and their preferences for those allocations. While many variations are possible, I concentrate here on a simple model. Agents (consumers, producers, politicians, etc.) are indexed by $i = 1, \ldots, n$. X is the set of feasible allocations where $x = (x^i, \ldots, x^n)$ is a typical element of X. (An exchange environment is one in which X is the set of all $x = (x^1, \ldots, x^n)$ such that $x^i \geqslant 0$ and $\Sigma x^i = \Sigma w^i$, where w^i is i's initial endowment of commodities.) Each agent has a selfish utility function $u^i(x^i)$. The environment is $e = [I, X, u^1, \ldots, u^n]$. A crucial fact is that initially *information is dispersed* since i, and only i, knows u^i. We identify the specific knowledge i initially has as i's *characteristic*, e^i. In our model, $e^i = u^i$.

Although there are many variations in models of allocation mechanisms, I begin with the one introduced by Hurwicz (1960). An *allocation mechanism* requests information from the agents and then computes a feasible allocation. It requests information in the form of messages m^i from agent i through a *response function* $f^i(m^i, \ldots, m^n)$. Agent i is told to report $f^i(m, e^i)$ if others have reported m and i's characteristic is e^i. An equilibrium of these response rules, for the environment e, is a joint message m such that $m^i = f^i(m, e^i)$ for all i. Let $\mu(e, f)$ be the set of equilibrium messages for the response functions f in the environment e. The allocation mechanism computes a feasible allocation x by using an *outcome function* $g(m)$ on equilibrium messages. The net result of all of this in the environment e is the allocation $g[\mu(e, f)] = x$ *if all i follow the rules*, f. Thus, for example, the *competitive mechanism* requests agents to send their demands as a function of prices which are in turn computed on the basis of the aggregate demands reported by the consumers. In equilibrium, each agent is simply allocated their stated demand. (An alternative mechanism, yielding exactly the same allocation in one iteration, would request the demand *function* and then compute the equilibrium price and allocation for the reported demand functions.) It is well known, for exchange economies with only private goods, that if agents report their true demands then the allocations computed by the competitive mechanism will be Pareto-optimal.

It is obviously important to be able to identify those mechanisms, those rules of communication, that have the property that they are self-enforcing. We do that by focusing on a class of mechanisms in which each agent gains nothing, and perhaps even loses, by misbehaving. While a multitude of misbehaviours could be considered it is sufficient for our purposes to consider a slightly restricted range. In particular we can concentrate on undetectable behaviour, behaviour which no outside agent can distinguish from that prescribed by the mechanism. We model this limitation on behaviour by requiring the agent to restrict his misrepresentations to those which are consistent with some characteristic he might have. An allocation mechanism is said to be *incentive compatible* for all environments in the class E if there is no agent i and no environment e in E and no characteristic e^{*i} such that (e/e^{*i}) is in E (where (e/e^{*i}) is the environment derived from e by replacing e^i with e^{*i}) and such that

$$u^i\{g[\mu(e,f)],e^i\} > u^i\{g[\mu(e/e^{*i},f],e^i\}$$

where $u^i(x^*,e^i)$ is i's utility function in the environment e. That is, no agent can manipulate the mechanism by pretending to have a characteristic different from the true one and do better than acting according to the truth. The agent has an incentive to follow the rules and the rules are compatible with his motivations.

Incentive compatibility is at the foundation of the modern *theory of implementation.* In that theory, one tries to identify conditions under which a particular social choice rule or performance standard, $P: E \rightarrow X$, can be recreated by an allocation mechanism under the hypothesis that individuals will follow their self-interest when they participate in the implementation process. In our language, the rule P is implementable if and only if there is an incentive compatible mechanism (f,g) such that $g[\mu(e,f)] = P(e)$ for all e in E. The theory of implementation seeks to answer the question 'which P are implementable?' We will see some of the answers below for P which select from the set of Pareto-efficient allocations. Those interested in more general goals and performance standards should consult Dasgupta, Hammond and Maskin (1979) or Postlewaite and Schmeidler (1986).

An allocation mechanism is said to have the *no trade-option* if there is an allocation θ at which each participant may remain. In exchange environments the initial endowment is usually such an allocation. Mechanisms with a no-trade option are non-coercive in a limited sense. If an allocation mechanism possesses the no-trade option then the allocation it computes for an environment e, if agents follow the rules, must leave everyone at least as well off, using the utility functions for e, as they are at θ. That is, for all i and all e in E

$$u^i\{g[\mu(e,f)],e^i\} > u^i(\theta,e^i).$$

An allocation mechanism is said to be *Pareto-efficient* in E if the allocations selected by the mechanism, when agents follow the rules, are Pareto-optimal in e. That is, for each e in E there is no allocation x^* in X such that, for all i,

$$u^i(x^*,e^i) \geqslant u^i\{g[\mu(e,f)],e^i\}$$

with strict inequality for some i.

With this language and notation, Hurwicz's theorem on the elusive nature of incentive compatibility in private markets, subsequently expanded by Ledyard and Roberts (1974) to include public goods environments, can now be easily stated.

Theorem: In classical (public or private) economic environments with a finite number of agents, there is no incentive compatible allocation mechanism which possesses the no-trade option and is Pareto-efficient. (Classical environments include pure exchange environments with Cobb–Douglas utility functions.)

A more general version of this theorem, in the context of social choice theory, has been proven by Gibbard (1973) and Satterthwaite (1975) with the concept of a 'non-dictatorial social choice function' replacing that of a 'mechanism with the no-trade option'.

There are a variety of possible reactions to this theorem. One is simply to give up the search for solutions to market failure since the theorem seems to imply that one should not waste any effort trying to create institutions to allocate resources efficiently. A second is to notice that, at least in private markets, if there are a very large number of individuals in each market then efficiency is 'almost' attainable (see Roberts and Postlewaite, 1976). A third is to recognize that the behaviour of individuals will generally be different from that implicitly assumed in the definition of incentive compatibility. A fourth is to accept the inevitable, lower one's sights, and look for the 'most efficient' mechanism among those which are incentive compatible and satisfy a voluntary participation constraint. We consider the last two options in more detail.

OTHER BEHAVIOUR: NASH EQUILIBRIUM. If a mechanism is incentive compatible, then each agent knows that his best strategy is to follow the rules according to his true characteristic, *no matter what the other agents will do.* Such a strategic structure is referred to as a dominant strategy game and has the property that no agent need know or predict anything about the others' behaviour. In mechanisms which are not incentive compatible, each agent must predict what others are going to do in order to decide what is best. In this situation agents' behaviour will not be as assumed in the definition of incentive compatibility. What it will be continues to be an active research topic and many models have been proposed. Since most of these are covered in Groves and Ledyard (1986), I will concentrate on the two which seem most sensible. Both rely on game-theoretic analyses of the strategic possibilities. The first concentrates on the outcome rule, g, and postulates that agents will not choose messages to follow the specifications of the response functions but to do the best they can against the messages sent by others. Implicitly this assumes that there is some type of iterative process (embodied in the response rules) which allows revision of one's message in light of the responses of others. We can formalize this presumed strategic behaviour in a new concept of incentive compatibility. An allocation mechanism (f, g) is called *Nash incentive compatible* for all environments in E if there is no environment e, no agent i, and no message m^{*i} which i can send such that

$$u^i(g[\mu(e,f)/m^{*i}, e^i]) > u^i(g[\mu(e,f), e^i])$$

where $\mu(e,f)$ is the 'equilibrium' message of the response rules f in the environment e, $g(m)$ is the outcome rule and $[m/m^{*i}]$ is the vector m where m^{*i} replaces m^i. In effect this requires the equilibrium messages of the response rules to be Nash equilibria in the game in which messages are strategies and payoffs are given by $u[g(m)]$. It was shown in a sequence of papers written in the late 1970s, including those by Groves and Ledyard (1977), Hurwicz (1979), Schmeidler (1980) and Walker (1981), that Nash incentive compatibility is not elusive. The effective output of that work was to establish the following.

Theorem: In classical (public or private) economic environments with a finite number of agents, there are many Nash incentive compatible mechanisms which possess the no-trade option and are Pareto-efficient.

With a change in the predicted behaviour of the participants in the mechanism, in recognition of the fact that in the absence of dominant strategies agents must follow some other self-interested strategies, the pessimism of the Hurwicz theorem is replaced by the optimistic prediction of a plethora of possibilities. (See Dasgupta, Hammond and Maskin (1979), Postlewaite and Schmeidler (1986) and Groves and Ledyard (1986) for comprehensive surveys of these results including many for more general social choice environments.) Although it remains an unsettled empirical question whether participants will indeed behave this way, there is a growing body of experimental evidence that seems to me to support the behavioural hypotheses underpinning Nash incentive compatibility, especially in iterative tâtonnement processes.

OTHER BEHAVIOUR: BAYES' EQUILIBRIUM. The second approach to modelling strategic behaviour of agents in mechanisms, when dominant strategies are not available, is based on Bayesian decision theory. These models, called *games of incomplete information* (see Myerson, 1985) concentrate on the beliefs of the players about the situation in which they find themselves. In the simplest form, it is postulated that there is a common knowledge (everyone knows that everyone knows that ...) probability function, $\pi(e)$, which describes everyone's prior beliefs. Each agent is then assumed to choose that message which is best against the expected behaviour of the other agents. The expected behaviour of the other agents is also constrained to be 'rational' in the sense that it should be best against the behaviour of others. This presumed strategic behaviour is embodied in a third type of incentive compatibility. (It could be argued that the concept of incentive compatibility remains the same, based on non-cooperative behaviour in the game induced by the mechanism, while only the presumed information structure and sequence of moves required to implement the allocation mechanism are changed. Such a view is not inconsistent with that which follows.) An allocation mechanism (f, g) is called *Bayes incentive compatible* for all environments in E, given π on E, if there is no environment e^*, no agent i and no message m^{*i}

which i can send such that

$$\int u^i\{g[\mu(e,f)/m^{*i}], e^{*i}\}\, d\pi(e|e^{*i}) > \int u^i\{g[\mu(e,f), e^{*i}]\, d\pi(e|e^{*i})\}$$

where, as before, μ is the equilibrium message vector and g is the outcome rule. Further, $\pi(e|e^{*i})$ is the conditional probability measure on e given e^{*i}, and u^i is a von Neumann–Morgenstern utility function. In effect, this requires the equilibrium messages of the response rules to be Bayes equilibrium outcomes of the incomplete information game with messages as strategies, payoffs $u[g(m)]$ and common knowledge prior π.

There are two types of results which deal with the possibilities for Bayes incentive compatible design of allocation mechanisms, neither of which is particularly encouraging. The first type deals with the possibilities for incentive compatible design which is independent of the beliefs. The typical theorem is illustrated by the following result proven by Ledyard (1978).

Theorem: In classical economic environments with a finite number of agents, there is no Bayes incentive compatible mechanism which possesses the no-trade option and is Pareto-efficient *for all π on E.*

Understanding this result is easy when one realizes that any mechanism (f, g) is Bayes incentive compatible for all π for all e in E if and only if it is (Hurwicz) incentive compatible for all e in E. Thus the Hurwicz impossibility theorem again applies.

The second type of result is directed towards the possibilities for a specific prior π; that is, towards what can be done if the mechanism can depend on the common knowledge beliefs. The most general characterizations of the possibilities for Bayes incentive compatible design can be found in Palfrey and Srivastava (1987) and Postlewaite and Schmeidler (1986). They have shown that two conditions, called monotonicity and self-selection, are necessary and sufficient for a social choice correspondence to be implementable in the sense that there is a Bayes incentive compatible mechanism that reproduces that correspondence. The details of these conditions are not important. What is important is that many correspondences do not satisfy them. In particular, there appear to be many priors π and many sets of environments E for which there is no mechanism which is Bayes incentive compatible, provides a no-trade option and is Pareto-efficient. Thus, impossibility still usually occurs even if one allows the mechanism to depend on the prior.

One recent avenue of research which promises some optimistic counterweight to these negative results can be found by Palfrey and Srivastava (1987). In much the same way that the natural move from Hurwicz incentive compatibility to Nash incentive compatibility created opportunities for incentive compatible design, these authors have shown that a move back towards dominant strategies may also open up possibilities. Refinements arise by varying the equilibrium concept in a way that reduces the number of (Bayes or Nash) equilibria for a given e or π. More and Repullo use subgame perfect Nash equilibria. Palfrey and Srivastava eliminate weakly dominated strategies from the set of Nash equilibria. They have discovered that, in pure exchange environments, virtually all performance correspondences are implementable if behaviour satisfies these refinements. In particular, any selection from the Pareto-correspondence is implementable for these refinements, and so there are many refined-Nash incentive compatible mechanisms which are Pareto-efficient and allow a no-trade option. It is believed that these results will transfer naturally to refinements of Bayes equilibria, but the research remains to be done.

INCENTIVE COMPATIBILITY AS A CONSTRAINT. Another of the reactions to the Hurwicz impossibility result is to accept the inevitable, to view incentive compatibility as a constraint, and to design mechanisms to attain the best level of efficiency one can. If full efficiency is possible, it will occur as the solution. If not, then one will at least find the second-best allocation mechanism. Examples of this rapidly expanding research literature include work on optimal auctions (Harris and Raviv, 1981; Matthes, 1983; Myerson, 1981), the design of optimal contracts for the principal–agent problem and the theory of optimal regulation (Baron and Myerson, 1982). As originally posed by Hurwicz (1972, pp. 299–301), the idea is to adopt a social welfare function $W(x, e)$, a measure of the social welfare attained from the allocation x if the environment is e, and then to choose the mechanism (f, g) to maximize the (expected) value of W subject to the 'incentive compatibility constraints', the constraint that the rules (f, g) be consistent with the motivations of the participants. One chooses (f, g) to

$$\text{maximize} \int W\{g[\mu(e, f)], e\}\, \mathrm{d}\pi(e)$$

subject to, for every i, every e and every e^{*i},

$$\int u^i\{g[\mu(e/e^{*i}, f)], e^i\}\, \mathrm{d}\pi(e|e^i) \leqslant \int u^i(g[\mu(e, f), e^i])\, \mathrm{d}\pi(e|e^i).$$

As formalized here the incentive compatibility constraints embody the concept of Bayes incentive compatibility. Of course, other behavioural models could be substituted as appropriate.

Sometimes a voluntary participation constraint, related to the no-trade option of Hurwicz, is added to the optimal design problem. One form of this constraint requires that (f, g) also satisfy, for every i and every e,

$$\int u^i\{g[\mu(e)], e^i\}\, \mathrm{d}\pi(e|e^i) \geqslant \int u^i(\theta[e], e^i)\, \mathrm{d}\pi(e|e^i).$$

In practice, this optimization can be a difficult problem since there are a large number of possible mechanisms (f, g). However, an insight due to Gibbard (1973) can be employed to reduce the range of alternatives and simplify the analysis. Now called the *revelation principle*, the observation he made was that, to find the maximum, it is sufficient to consider only mechanisms, called direct revelation mechanisms, in which agents are asked to report their own characteristics. The reason is easy to see. Suppose that (f^*, g^*) solves the maximum problem. Let (F^*, G^*) be a new (direct revelation) mechanism defined by $F^{*i}(m, e^i) = e^i$ and $G^*(m) = g[\mu(m, f)]$. Each i is told to report his characteristic and then G^* computes the allocation by computing that which would have been chosen if the original mechanism (f, G^*) had been used honestly in the reported environment. (F^*, G^*) yields the same allocation as (f^*, g^*), *if each agent reports the truth.* But the incentive compatibility constraints, which (f^*, g^*) satisfied, ensure that each agent will want to report truthfully. Thus, whatever can be done, by any arbitrary mechanism subject to the Bayes incentive compatibility constraints, can be done with direct revelation mechanisms subject to the constraint that each agent wants to report their true characteristic. One need only choose a function $G: E \rightarrow X$ to

$$\text{maximize} \int W[G(e), e]\, \mathrm{d}\pi(e)$$

subject to, for every i, e and e^i,

$$\int u^i[G(e/e^{*i}), e^i]\, \mathrm{d}\pi(e|e^i) \leqslant \int u^i[G(e), e^i]\, \mathrm{d}\pi(e|e^i),$$

and

$$\int u^i[G(e), e^i]\, \mathrm{d}\pi(e|e) \geqslant \int u^i(\theta[e], e^i)\, \mathrm{d}\pi(e|e^i).$$

There are at least two problems with this approach to organizational design. The first is that the choice of mechanism depends crucially on the prior beliefs, π. This is a direct result of the use of Bayes incentive compatibility in the constraints. Since the debate is still open let me simply summarize some of the arguments. One is that if the mechanism chosen for a given situation does not depend on common knowledge beliefs then we would not be using all the information at our disposal to pursue the desired goals and would do less than is possible. Further, since the beliefs are common knowledge we can all agree as to their validity (misrepresentation is not an issue) and therefore to their legitimate inclusion in the calculations. An argument is made against this on the practical grounds that one need only consider actual situations, such as the introduction of new technology by a regulated utility or the acquisition of a major new weapons system by the government, to understand the difficulties involved in arriving at agreements about the particulars of common knowledge. Another argument against is based on the feeling that mechanisms should be robust. A 'good' mechanism should be able to be described in terms of its mechanics and, while it probably should have the capacity to incorporate the common knowledge relevant to the current situation, it should be capable of being used in many situations. How to capture these criteria in the constraints or the objective function of the designer remains an open research question.

The second problem with the optimal auction approach to organizational design is the reliance on the revelation principle. Restricting attention to direct revelation mechanisms, in which an agent reports his entire characteristic, is an efficient way to prove theorems, but it provides little guidance for those interested in actual organization design. For example it completely ignores the informational requirements of the process and limitations, if any, in the information processing capabilities of the agents or the mechanism. Writing down one's preferences for all possible consumption patterns is probably harder than writing down one's entire demand surface which is certainly harder than simply reacting to a single price vector and reporting only the quantities demanded at that price. A failure to recognize the information processing constraints in the optimization problem is undoubtedly one of the reasons why there has been limited success in using the theory of optimal auctions to explain the existence of pervasive institutions, such as the first-price sealed-bid auction used in competitive contracting or the posted price institution used in retailing.

SUMMARY. Incentive compatibility captures the fundamental positivist notion of self-interested behaviour that underlies almost all economic theory and application. It has proven to be an organizing principle of great scope and power. Combined with the modern theory of mechanism design, it provides a framework in which to analyse such diverse topics as auctions, central planning, regulation of monopoly, transfer pricing, capital budgeting and public enterprise management. Incentive compatibility provides a basic constraint on the possibilities for normative analysis. As such it serves as the fundamental interface between what is desirable and what is possible in a theory of organizations.

BIBLIOGRAPHY

Baron, D. and Myerson, R. 1982. Regulating a monopolist with unknown costs. *Econometrica* 50, 911–30.

Dasgupta, P., Hammond, P. and Maskin, E. 1979. The implementation of social choice rules: some general results on incentive compatibility. *Review of Economic Studies* 46, 185–216.

Gibbard, A. 1973. Manipulation of voting schemes: a general result. *Econometrica* 41, 587–602.

Groves, T. and Ledyard, J. 1977. Optimal allocation of public goods: a solution to the 'free rider' problem. *Econometrica* 45, 783–809.

Groves, T. and Ledyard, J. 1986. Incentive compatibility ten years later. In *Information, Incentives, and Economic Mechanisms*, ed. T. Groves, R. Radner and S. Reiter. Minneapolis: University of Minnesota Press.

Harris, M. and Raviv, A. 1981. Allocation mechanisms and the design of auctions. *Econometrica* 49, 1477–99.

Hurwicz, L. 1960. Optimality and informational efficiency in resource allocation processes. In *Mathematical Methods in the Social Sciences*, ed. K. Arrow, S. Karlin and P. Suppes, Stanford: Stanford University Press, 27–46.

Hurwicz, L. 1972. On informationally decentralized systems. In *Decision and Organization: A Volume in Honor of Jacob Marschak*, ed. R. Radner and C.B. McGuire, Amsterdam: North-Holland, 297–336.

Hurwicz, L. 1979. Outcome functions yielding Walrasian and Lindahl allocations at Nash equilibrium points. *Review of Economic Studies* 46, 217–25.

Ledyard, J. 1978. Incomplete information and incentive compatibility. *Journal of Economic Theory* 18, 171–89.

Ledyard, J. and Roberts, J. 1974. On the incentive problem with public goods. Discussion Paper No. 116, Center for Mathematical Studies in Economics and Management Science, Northwestern University.

Lindahl, E. 1919. *Die Gerechtigkeit der Besteuerung.* Lund. Partial translation in *Classics in the Theory of Public Finance*, ed. R.A. Musgrave and A.T. Peacock, London and New York: Macmillan, 1958.

Matthews, S. 1983. Selling to risk averse buyers with unobservable tastes. *Journal of Economic Theory* 30, 370–400.

Moore, J. and Repullo, R. 1986. Subgame perfect implementation. London School of Economics, Working Paper.

Myerson, R.B. 1981. Optimal auction design. *Mathematics of Operations Research* 6, 58–73.

Myerson, R.B. 1985. Bayesian equilibrium and incentive compatibility: an introduction. In *Social Goals and Social Organization: Essays in Memory of Elisha Pazner*, ed. L. Hurwicz, D. Schmeidler and H. Sonnenschein, Cambridge: Cambridge University Press.

Palfrey, T. and Srivastava, S. 1986. Implementation in exchange economies using refinements of Nash equilibrium. Graduate School of Industrial Administration, Carnegie-Mellon University, July 1986.

Palfrey, T. and Srivastava, S. 1987. On Bayesian implementable allocations. *Review of Economic Studies* 54(2), 193–208.

Postlewaite, A. and Schmeidler, D. 1986. Implementation in differential information economics. *Journal of Economic Theory* 39(1), June, 14–33.

Roberts, J. and Postlewaite, A. 1976. The incentives for price-taking behavior in large economies. *Econometrica* 44, 115–28.

Samuelson, P. 1954. The pure theory of public expenditure. *Review of Economics and Statistics* 36, 387–9.

Satterthwaite, M. 1975. Strategy-proofness and Arrow's conditions: existence and correspondence theorems for voting procedures and social welfare functions. *Journal of Economic Theory* 10, 187–217.

Schmeidler, D. 1980. Walrasian analysis via strategic outcome functions. *Econometrica* 48, 1585–93.

Walker, M. 1981. A simple incentive compatible scheme for attaining Lindahl allocations. *Econometrica* 49, 65–71.

Incentive Contracts

EDWARD P. LAZEAR

Incentives are the essence of economics. The most basic concept, demand, considers how to induce a consumer to buy more of a particular good; that is, how to give him an incentive to purchase. Similarly, supply relationships are descriptions of how agents respond with more output or labour to additional compensation.

Incentive contracts arise because individuals love leisure. In order to induce them to forego some leisure, or put alternatively, to put forth effort, some form of compensation must be offered. The theme of this essay is that different forms of incentive contracts deal with some aspects of the problems better than others. The strength of one type of contract is the weakness of another. The labour market trades off these strengths and weaknesses and thereby selects a set of institutions. In what follows, the development of the literature on incentive contracts is briefly discussed. The emphasis is on concepts rather than specific papers or authors, so the bibliography is far from exhaustive.

To discuss incentive contracts, the most general concepts must be narrowed. This essay does that in two ways. First, attention here is restricted to the labour market. At a more general level, incentive contracts can relate to other areas as well. For example, the government may want to have a space satellite built at the lowest possible cost. To do so, incentives must be set appropriately or the producer may charge too much or fail to meet desired quality standards. This problem is analogous to those that arise in the labour context, but for the most part they are ignored, except when isomorphic with the labour market paradigm. Similarly, the law and economics literature is another area where incentive problems are studied, usually in the context of accident liability (see, for example, Green, 1976; Polinsky, 1980; Shavell, 1980). These specific questions are ignored as well, except as they border on the labour market context. Second, the focus is on observability problems. Standard labour supply functions, where hours of work can be observed and paid, are incentive contracts. However, standard labour supply issues are eliminated from consideration since they are dealt with in other essays in *The New Palgrave*.

GENERAL FRAMEWORK

An employer in a competitive environment must induce a worker to perform at the efficient level of effort or face extinction. The reason is simple: if one employer can, through clever use of an incentive contract, get a worker to perform at a more efficient level, that firm's cost will be lower. Lower costs imply that higher wages can be paid to workers and all workers will be stolen from inefficient firms. As a result, the objective function that is taken as standard for the firm is:

$$\operatorname*{Max}_{F} F(Q, E) - C(E), \tag{1}$$

where Q is output and E is worker effort. Thus $F(Q, E)$ is the compensation schedule that the firm announces to the worker; $C(E)$ is the worker's cost of effort function, to be thought of as the dollar cost associated with supplying effort level E.

The competitive nature of the firm in factor and product markets implies that the firm must maximize worker net wealth as in (1) subject to the zero profit constraint:

$$Q = F(Q, E). \tag{2}$$

Output is defined so that each unit sells for \$1 (the numeraire). Thus (2) merely says that output, Q, must be paid entirely to the worker otherwise another firm could steal the worker away by paying more.

The incentive problem arises because the worker takes the compensation scheme $F(Q, E)$ as given and chooses effort to maximize expected utility. Once the worker has accepted the job, his problem is:

$$\operatorname*{Max}_{E} F(Q, E) - C(E). \tag{3}$$

The worker's effort supply functions comes from solving the first-order condition associated with (3) or

$$C'(E) = \frac{\partial F}{\partial Q} \cdot \frac{\partial Q}{\partial E} + \frac{\partial F}{\partial E}, \tag{4}$$

which says that the worker sets the marginal cost of effort equal to its marginal return to him. The transformation of effort into output, (i.e. $\partial Q/\partial E$) depends on the production function. A convenient specification is

$$Q = E + v, \tag{5}$$

so that output is the sum of effort, E, and luck, v.

An incentive contract selects $F(Q, E)$ subject to the zero-profit constraint,

(2), taking into account that the worker behaves according to (4). There are an infinite variety of incentive contracts that are subsumed by $F(Q, E)$. To make things clear, we consider two polar extremes – the salary and the piece rate (for a more detailed treatment, see Lazear, 1986).

Let us define a salary as compensation that depends only on input so that $F(Q, E)$ takes the form $S(E)$. An hourly wage is an example. Irrespective of the amount that is produced during the hour, the worker receives a fixed amount that depends only on the fact that he supplies E of effort for the hour. (Of course, difficulty in measuring E may be a compelling reason to avoid this form of incentive contract.) At the other extreme is a piece rate where compensation depends only on output so that $F(Q, E)$ takes the form of $R(Q)$. There, no matter how much or how little effort the worker exerts, his compensation depends only on the number of units produced. Both salaries and piece rates are incentive contracts; the first provides incentives by paying workers on the basis of input. The second provides incentives by paying on the basis of output. More sophisticated incentive contracts, which blend the two or use multiperiod approaches are discussed later.

THE PRINCIPAL–AGENT PROBLEM

At the centre of the incentive contract literature is the 'principal–agent' problem. The principal, say, an employer, wants to induce its agent, say, a worker, to behave in a way that is beneficial to the employer. The problem is that the principal's knowledge is imperfect; either he cannot see what the agent does (as in the case of a taxi driver who can sleep on the job) or he cannot interpret the actions (as in the case of an auto mechanic who replaces a number of parts to correct a perhaps simple malfunction). The incentive contracts that can be used to address the problem were discussed early by Ross (1973), Mirrlees, (1976), Calvo and Wellisz (1978) and by Becker and Stigler (1974). The last, in particular, uses a sampling approach. For example, a politician can be required to post a large bond on taking office. If he is caught engaging in some malfeasant behaviour, he forfeits the bond. This contract is based on output, which is observed infrequently or imperfectly. Other kinds of incentive contracts are discussed in the following sections.

PAYMENT BY OUTPUT

Sharecropping. One of the earliest examples of incentive contracts that is based on output is sharecropping. In sharecropping, the owner contracts to split the output of the land in some proportion with the individual who farms and lives on it. It was also one of the first incentive schemes that was clearly analysed (see Johnson, 1950, and later Cheung, 1969 and Stiglitz, 1974). The original problem as formulated in sharecropping can be seen as follows.

Payment is conditional only on Q and by some fixed proportion so that the worker receives γQ. Using (4) and (5), compensation of this sort implies that the worker's first-order condition is

$$C'(E) = \gamma,$$

so that the worker sets the marginal cost of effort equal to γ. But (5) implies that the marginal value of effort is \$1, which exceeds γ so that the worker puts forth too little effort. This is inefficient. Additionally, if the farmer can obtain land without limit, he pushes his sharecropping acreage to the point where the next unit of land has zero marginal product. This is clearly inefficient but can be remedied if landowners can select sharecroppers and terms according to the amount of land each works. Both the owner and worker could be made better off if the worker could be induced, by another incentive contract, to produce where $C'(E) = 1$.

Renting the land to the farmer and allowing the farmer to keep all of the output accomplishes this. Under rental, the worker's compensation is [Q-Rent]. By (4) and (5), the worker is induced to set $C'(E) = 1$; the marginal cost and marginal value of output are equated. Of course, rental does not solve all of the problems. Absent in the production function in (5) is that maintenance may be required. For example, if the farmer does not fertilize the land, it may not produce as well in the future. A renter, who can move on to the next plot after the soil is drained of minerals, has little incentive to put resources into the land. Thus the solution is to sell the land to the farmer. Then the individual who works the land has the correct incentives, either because he will continue to use it in the future or because the sale price will reflect the quality of the land. But sale of the land begs most of the questions. The sale may not come about because of the farmer's capital constraints, because of his lack of entrepreneurial skill, or because of his distaste for risk. (Note that risk is shifted from owners to farmers even in sharecropping and renting. Only labour contracts based exclusively on effort shift the risk entirely to the owner.)

The sharecropping paradigm applies to industrial production as well. Profit-sharing arrangements are, in many respects, like sharecropping. This is especially true when there is only one worker. Partnerships are similar. The same incentive problems arise. A worker who can quit and move on to another firm without penalty does not have the same desire to maintain the equipment as the firm's owner. Again the solution is to sell the capital to the worker, but this simply redefines the owner. Then there is no principal–agent problem because there is no agent. This can be considered in more detail in the next section.

Piece rates. Piece-rate compensation is not much different from sharecropping, the latter being a special case of the former (see Stiglitz, 1975). The owner allows the worker (or farmer) to use his capital (or land) and pays the worker according to some function of output. In the simplest scheme, a linear piece rate is used and the worker is paid rate R per unit Q so that compensation is RQ. The worker's maximization problem (3) and (4) implies that the worker sets $C'(E) = R$. The firm's zero-profit constraint in (2) implies that $Q = RQ$ or that

$R=1$. Thus the piece rate is efficient because the worker sets the marginal cost of effort equal to its marginal social value, \$1.

The issue is only slightly more complicated if capital is involved. A linear piece rate with an intercept (i.e. compensation equal to $A+RQ$) will do the job. This incentive contract achieves first-best efficiency. The worker's first-order condition, (4), still guarantees that he sets $C'(E)=R$. The intercept drops out. But the zero-profit constraint now becomes:

$$Q - \text{rental cost of capital} = A + RQ.$$

The firm must 'charge' the worker for the cost of using the capital, but how should this be done? R can be reduced below 1 or A can be set to a negative number. The answer is that $A = -$(rental cost of capital) and $R=1$. Since (4) does not contain A, the worker does not respond to changes in A. However, reducing R below 1 causes the worker to reduce effort. Thus the efficient incentive contract, which also maximizes worker wealth subject to the firm's zero-profit constraint requires that $R=1$. Zero profit requires that $A = -$(rental cost of capital).

A major advantage to the use of piece rates as an incentive contract is that it tolerates heterogeneity of worker ability. More able – that is, lower effort cost – workers choose higher levels of effort but are paid more. There is no inefficiency involved in having workers of both types in the firm. Of course, if capital is important so that the worker is 'charged' A for the right to work on a machine, only workers above some threshold ability level will choose to work. But workers self-sort. There is no need for the firm to do anything other than pay the efficient piece rate, in this case $R=1$.

Linear piece rates are no longer appropriate incentive contracts if workers are risk-averse. In general, a non-linear scheme will do better but will fail to achieve first-best solutions. As long as asymmetric information exists, so that individual actions cannot be observed and contracted upon, Pareto optimal risk-sharing is precluded (see Hölmstrom, 1979; Harris and Raviv, 1979.)

Payment of relative output. The study of relative compensation has become increasingly important. There are two approaches in this literature. The first, from Lazear and Rosen (1981), characterizes the labour market as a tournament, where one worker is pitted against another. The one with the highest level of output receives the winning prize (i.e. the high-wage job) while the other gets the losing prize (i.e. the low-wage job). By increasing the spread between the winning and losing prizes, incentives are provided to work hard. The optimum spread induces workers to move to the point where the marginal cost of effort exactly equals the marginal (social) return to it. The major advantages to payment by tournament method are twofold. First, tournaments require only that relative comparisons be made. It may be cheaper to observe that one worker produces more than another than to determine the actual amount that each produces. Second, compensation by rank 'differences out' common noise. For example, sales may be low because the economy is in a slump, which has nothing to do with worker effort. Risk aversion operates against penalizing or rewarding workers for factors over which they have no control. But since the slump affects both workers equally, relative comparisons are unaffected. The best worker still produces more, even though both produce small amounts.

Tournament-type incentive contracts induce workers to behave efficiently if they are risk neutral. They are easy to use but carry one major disadvantage. Workers increase the probability of winning, not only by doing well themselves but also by causing the opponent to do poorly. Thus tournaments discourage cooperation. This results in wage compression, which works to discourage the aggressive behaviour of workers who are competing for the same job. Other work in the area of tournament-type incentive contracts includes Nalebuff and Stiglitz (1983), Green and Stokey (1983) and Carmichael (1983).

The second approach, from Hölmstrom (1982), suggests that if levels of output can be observed, then payments can be based, at least in part, on a term average. As Hölmstrom points out, a tournament is not a sufficient statistic, so that using a team average allows the firm better to address risk aversion. This incentive device also takes out common noise. A peer average picks up disturbances that are common to the industry and allows the firm to cater to the tastes of risk-averse workers.

PAYMENT BY INPUT

Observability of effort. It is commonly alleged that payment of a salary or hourly wage does not provide workers with the appropriate incentives. Whether or not this is true depends on the connection between the measurement of time and measurement of effort. To see this, suppose that effort can be observed perfectly, but that output cannot be observed at all. For example, suppose that it is easy to measure the number of calories burned up by a worker during his work day, but it is impossible to separate his output from that of his peers. Payment by effort is a first-best incentive contract. The compensation scheme that pays the worker $1 per unit of effort exerted induces him to set $C'(E) = 1$, which, as we have seen, is first best. Note further that this is first best even for risk-averse workers since compensation does not vary with random productivity shocks, v (see Hall and Lilien, 1979).

The allegation that effort pay does not provide incentives is based on the difference between hours of work and effort. If hours were a perfect proxy for effort, then payment of an hourly wage would be an optimal incentive contract. But because workers can vary work per hour, the connection breaks down. Payment per hour provides appropriate incentives for choice of the number of hours, but does not deal with what is done within the hour.

Payment by effort and worker sorting. Piece rates induce workers to sort appropriately. Above, it was argued that workers who cannot produce a sufficiently high level of output will not come to a firm that 'charges' for use of capital. Salaries (or hourly wages) that pay on the basis of an imperfect measure of effort encourage the lower-quality workers to come to the firm. Lazear (1986) demonstrates that a separating equilibrium (see, e.g., Rothschild and Stiglitz, 1976; Salop and Salop, 1976) exists where high-quality workers choose to work at firms that pay piece rates and low-quality ones choose salaries. The difference in quality across firms might lead one to conclude that movement to output-based incentive contracts increases total output. In fact, the reverse may well be true. In the same sense that screening in Spence (1973) is socially unproductive, forcing salary firms to adopt piece-rate incentive contracts wastes resources on a potentially useless signal.

Incentive contracts and product quality. Sometimes quantity is easier to observe than quality. The problem with incentive contracts that are based on output quantity is that they induce the worker to go for speed and to ignore quality. If quality can be observed, then the worker can be compensated appropriately for quantity and quality. The appropriate compensation function is essentially the consumer's demand for the product as it varies with quality and quantity. But if quality cannot be observed, payment by input 'solves' the quantity/quality problem. If the worker is paid, say, by hour, and is merely instructed to produce goods of a given quality, he has no incentive to deviate from that instruction. Compensation is based only on input, so there is no desire to rush the job. Of course, this requires a method of monitoring effort cheaply (see Lazear, 1986, for a full discussion of the trade-offs).

OTHER ISSUES IN INCENTIVE CONTRACTING

Efficient separation and long-term investments. A properly structured incentive contract must induce the correct amount of long-term investment. The problem is most clearly seen in the context of specific human capital, as in Becker (1962, 1975). Specific human capital is only valuable when the worker is employed at the current firm. As such, workers are reluctant to invest in specific capital because the firm may capriciously fire the worker, in which case the investment is lost. Similarly, firms are reluctant to invest because the worker may capriciously quit. The incentive contract that Becker suggests is a sharing of investment costs and returns by both workers and firms (Hashimoto and Yu, 1980, model this more precisely). Kennan (1979) points out that a particular kind of severance pay solves the investment problem. It is akin to the liability rules that are efficient in auto accident problems. But as Hall and Lazear (1984) argue, these rules may actually induce too much investment. Since a worker is compensated for the full investment whether work occurs or not, he has no incentive to account for situations that make a separation optimal. For example, if it were optimal to sever the work relationship 25 per cent of the time, the worker should behave as if a specific investment that yields $1 return only yields $0.75. A full-reimbursement severance pay arrangement ensures a full $1, irrespectively of the status of work, and induces too much investment.

More general issues of efficient separation arise in the labour market context, and incentive contracts must be structured to deal with these problems. Hall and Lazear (1984) consider a variety of different incentive contracts and conclude that none generally achieves first best. One that comes close to doing so is Vickrey's (1961) bilateral auction approach. There, compensation and work are separated so that the worker and firm have incentives to reveal the true relevant values. Another scheme is coordinated severance pay, suggested by d'Aspremont and Gerard-Varet (1979). Sufficiently high penalties on the firm associated with a worker's refusal to work induces the firm to behave in a manner that is apparently first best.

Intertemporal incentive contracts. Sometimes, the fact that workers live for more than one period allows contracts to be structured in a way that solves incentive problems. This is the subject of Lazear (1979, 1981). The problem is that as a worker approaches the end of his career, he has an incentive to shirk because the costs, even of being fired, are reduced as his retirement date draws near. A way to discourage shirking is to tilt the age-earnings profile and couple it with a contingent pension. Young workers are paid less than their marginal products: old workers are paid more. In equilibrium, shirking is discouraged and workers receive exactly their lifetime marginal products. The distortion in the timing of the payments implies that workers do not voluntarily choose to work the correct number of hours. Thus hours constraints are required, an extreme form of which is mandatory retirement. Other work that has refined or provided empirical support for that concept is Kuhn (1986), and Hutchens (1986a, b).

There are other papers that focus on the intertemporal aspects of incentive contracts. The first, Fama (1980) argues that the market provides a discipline on workers. In a spot market, the wage that another firm is willing to offer a worker next period depends on how well he did last period. Fama shows that this can act as a perfect incentive device. Of course, no end-game problems are addressed by this mechanism, but it does demonstrate the possibility of incentive provision even without explicit or implicit contracts. The second idea is attributable to Rogerson (1985). The emphasis here is on risk-sharing, but the work has some features in common with Fama (1980). In particular, memory plays a strong role in these incentive contracts, so that an outcome that affects the current wage also affects the future wage.

Intertemporal strategic behaviour by firms. Once intertemporal contracts are considered, it is necessary to examine the issue of opportunistic behaviour by firms. It may be that a firm does not know a worker's cost of effort function, $C(E)$. Actions that the worker takes may reveal information about that function. The firm can use that information in subsequent periods against the worker. As a result, the worker attempts to disguise $C(E)$, leading to inefficiencies. Such is the case of salesmen, whose next period quota depends on this period's performance. In Lazear (1986), it is shown that a properly structured contract in a competitive labour market can undo the effects of this kind of strategic behaviour. This is a specific example of the general theorem on revelation presented in Harris and Townsend (1981). It is also related to the literature on planned economies, since bureaucrats tend to make things look worse than they are to lessen next period's requirements or to increase next period's budget allocation (see, e.g., Weitzman, 1976, 1980; Fan, 1975).

Insurance. Finally, there is a closely related literature that examines insurance contracts. That literature focuses, for the most part, on the trade-off between insurance and inefficiency in the labour market. Some of the more important papers in that literature include Harris and Hölmstrom (1982), Grossman and Hart (1983) and Green and Kahn (1983).

CONCLUSION

Although incentive problems are pervasive, the market has found a number of solutions. These involve payment by output of the piece rate or sharecropping variety; payment by relative output, exemplified by labour market tournaments; payment by measured input, such as hours of work; and multi-period incentive contracts. The contracts do not always achieve the first best, especially when risk aversion is an issue. Still, the rick variety of institutions that address incentive problems and the large amount of literature devoted to study attest to the problem's importance in the labour market context.

BIBLIOGRAPHY

Becker, G.S. 1962. Investment in human capital: a theoretical analysis. *Journal of Political Economy* 70, October, 9–49.

Becker, G.S. 1975. *Human Capital: A Theoretical and Empirical Analysis, with Special Reference to Education.* 2nd edn, New York: Columbia University Press for the National Bureau of Economic Research.

Becker, G.S. and Stigler, G.J. 1974. Law enforcement, malfeasance, and compensation of enforcers. *Journal of Legal Studies* 3, January, 1–18.

Calvo, G. and Wellisz, S. 1978. Supervision, loss of control and optimum size of the firm. *Journal of Political Economy* 86, October, 943–52.

Carmichael, H.L. 1983. The agent–agents problem: payment by relative output. *Journal of Labor Economics* 1, January, 50–65.

Cheung, S.N.S. 1969. *The Theory of Share Tenancy: With Special Application to Asian Agriculture and the First Phase of Taiwan Land Reform.* Chicago: University of Chicago Press.

d'Aspremont, C. and Gerard-Varet, L.A. 1979. Incentives and incomplete information. *Journal of Public Economics* 11, February, 25–45.

Fama, E. 1980. Agency problems and the theory of the firm. *Journal of Political Economy* 88, April, 288–307.

Fan, L.-S. 1975. On the reward system. *American Economic Review* 65, March, 226–9.

Green, J.R. 1976. On the optimal structure of liability laws. *Bell Journal of Economics* 7, Autumn, 553–74.

Green, J.R. and Kahn, C. 1983. Wage employment contracts. *Quarterly Journal of Economics* 98, 173–88.

Green, J.R. and Stokey, N.L. 1983. A comparison of tournaments and contracts. *Journal*

of Political Economy 91, June, 349–64.
Grossman, S. and Hart, O. 1983. Implicit contracts under asymmetric information. *Quarterly Journal of Economics* 71, 123–57.
Hall, R.E. and Lazear, E.P. 1984. The excess sensitivity of layoffs and quits to demand. *Journal of Labor Economics* 2, April, 233–58.
Hall, R.E. and Lilien, D. 1979. Efficient wage bargains under uncertain supply and demand. *American Economic Review* 69, December, 868–79.
Harris, M. and Hölmstrom, B. 1982. A theory of wage dynamics. *Review of Economic Studies* 49, July, 315–33.
Harris, M. and Raviv, A. 1979. Optimal incentive contracts with imperfect information. *Journal of Economic Theory* 20(2), April, 231–59.
Harris, M. and Townsend, R. 1981. Resource allocation under asymmetric information. *Econometrica* 49, January, 33–64.
Hashimoto, M. and Yu, B. 1980. Specific capital, employment contracts, and wage rigidity. *Bell Journal of Economics*, Autumn, 536–49.
Hölmstrom, B. 1979. Moral hazard and observability. *Bell Journal of Economics* 10, Spring, 74–91.
Hölmstrom, B. 1982. Moral hazard in teams. *Bell Journal of Economics* 13, Autumn, 324–40.
Hutchens, R. 1986a. Delayed payment contracts and a firm's propensity to hire older workers. *Journal of Labor Economics* 4(4), October, 439–57.
Hutchens, R. 1986b. An empirical test of Lazear's theory of delayed payment contracts. Working paper, Cornell University Institute for Labor and Industrial Relations.
Johnson, D.G. 1950. Resource allocation under share contracts. *Journal of Political Economy* 58, 111–23.
Kennan, J. 1979. Bonding and the enforcement of labor contracts. *Economic Letters* 3, 61–6.
Kuhn, P.J. 1986. Wages, effort, and incentive compatibility in life-cycle employment contracts. *Journal of Labor Economics* 4, January 28–49.
Lazear, E.P. 1979. Why is there mandatory retirement? *Journal of Political Economy* 87, December, 1261–84.
Lazear, E.P. 1981. Agency, earnings profiles, productivity and hours restrictions. *American Economic Review* 71, September, 606–20.
Lazear, E.P. 1986. Salaries and piece rates. *Journal of Business* 59(3), July, 405–31.
Lazear, E.P. and Rosen, S. 1981. Rank order tournaments as optimum labor contracts. *Journal of Political Economy* 89, 841–64.
Mirrlees, J.A. 1976. The optimal structure of incentives with authority within an organization. *Bell Journal of Economics* 7, Spring, 105–31.
Nalebuff, B.J. and Stiglitz, J.E. 1983. Prizes and incentives: toward a general theory of compensation and competition. *Bell Journal of Economics* 14, Spring, 21–43.
Polinsky, A.M. 1980. Strict liability vs. negligence in a market setting. *American Economic Review* 70(2), May, 363–7.
Rogerson, W.P. 1985. Repeated moral hazard. *Econometrica* 53, January, 69–76.
Ross, S.A. 1973. The economic theory of agency: the principal's problem. *American Economic Review* 63, May, 134–9.
Rothschild, M. and Stiglitz, J.E. 1976. Equilibrium in competitive insurance markets: an essay on the economics of imperfect information. *Quarterly Journal of Economics* 90, November, 629–49.
Salop, J. and Salop, S. 1976. Self-selection and turnover in the labor market. *Quarterly Journal of Economics* 90, November, 619–27.
Shavell, S. 1980. Strict liability versus negligence. *Journal of Legal Studies*, January, 1–25.

Spence, A.M. 1973. Job market signalling. *Quarterly Journal of Economics* 87, August, 355–74.

Stiglitz, J.E. 1974. Incentive and risk sharing in sharecropping. *Review of Economic Studies* 41, April, 219–55.

Stiglitz, J.E. 1975. Incentives, risk, and information: notes toward a theory of hierarchy. *Bell Journal of Economics and Management Science* 6, Autumn, 552–79.

Vickrey, W. 1961. Counterspeculation, auctions, and competitive sealed tenders. *Journal of Finance* 16, 8–37.

Weitzman, M. 1976. The new Soviet incentive model. *Bell Journal of Economics* 7(1), Spring, 251–7.

Weitzman, M. 1980. The 'Ratchet Principle' and performance incentives. *Bell Journal of Economics* 11(1), Spring, 302–8.

Incomplete Contracts

OLIVER HART

The past decade has witnessed a growing interest in contract theories of various kinds. This development is partly a reaction to our rather thorough understanding of the standard theory of perfect competition under complete markets, but more importantly to the resulting realization that this paradigm is insufficient to accommodate a number of important economic phenomena. Studying in more detail the process of contracting – particularly its hazards and imperfections – is a natural way to enrich and amend the idealized competitive model in an attempt to fit the evidence better.

In one sense, contracts provide the foundation for a large part of economic analysis. Any trade – as a quid pro quo – must be mediated by some form of contract, whether it be explicit or implicit. In the case of spot trades, however, where the two sides of the transaction occur almost simultaneously, the contractual element is usually down-played, presumably because it is regarded as trivial (although we will argue below that this need not be the case). In recent years, economists have become much more interested in long-term relationships. where a considerable amount of time may elapse between the quid and the quo. In these circumstances, a contract becomes an essential part of the trading relationship.

Research on contracts has progressed along several different lines. Two prominent areas of work are principal–agent theory and implicit labour contract theory. In these literatures, the focus is on risk-sharing or income-smoothing as the motivation for a contract; that is, on the gains the parties receive from transferring income from one state of the world or one period to another. For example, in implicit contract theory, it is supposed that workers are constrained in their ability to get insurance or to borrow on the open market and that employers therefore offer these services as part of an employment contract.

While 'income-smoothing' is undoubtedly important, there are arguably more fundamental factors underlying the existence of long-term contracts. A basic reason for long-term relationships is the existence of investments which are to some extent party specific; that is, once made, they have a higher value inside the relationship than outside. Given this 'lock-in' effect, each party will have some monopoly power ex-post, althouth there may be plenty of competition ex-ante, before investments are sunk. Since the parties cannot rely on the market once their relationship is underway, a long-term contract is an important way for them to regulate, and divide up the gains from, their trade. This will be the case even if the parties are risk neutral and have access to perfect capital markets, that is, even if the income-smoothing role is completely inessential. Moreover, in the case, say, of supply contracts involving large firms, risk neutrality and perfect capital markets may be reasonable approximations in view of the many outside insurance and borrowing/lending opportunities available to such parties.

In spite of their importance, contracts whose *raison d'être* is the regulation of specific relationships have been the subject of little analysis. A notable early reference is Becker's (1964) analysis of worker training. More recently, Williamson (1985) and Klein et al. (1978) have emphasized the difficulty of writing contracts which induce efficient relationship-specific investments as an important factor in explaining vertical integration.

In this essay I will try to summarize what is known theoretically about contracts of this type. I will focus particularly on the problems which arise when the parties write a contract which is incomplete in some respects. Given the rudimentary state of our knowledge of the area, the essay is inevitably quite speculative in nature. The reader who is interested in an elaboration of some of the ideas presented here, and how they fit into the rest of contract theory, might want to consult Hart and Hölmstrom (1987).

1. THE BENEFITS OF WRITING LONG-TERM CONTRACTS GIVEN RELATIONSHIP-SPECIFIC INVESTMENTS. The role of a long-term contract when there are relationship-specific investments can be seen from the following example (based on Grout, 1984). Let B, S be, respectively, the buyer and seller of (one unit of) an input. Suppose that in order to realize the benefits of the input, B must make an investment, a, which is specific to S; for example, B might have to build a plant next to S. Assume that there are just two periods; the investment is made at date 0, while the input is supplied and the benefits are received at date 1. S's supply cost at date 1 is c, while B's benefit function is $b(a)$ (all costs and benefits are measured in date 1 dollars).

If no long-term contract is written at date 0, the parties will determine the terms of trade from scratch at date 1. If we assume that neither party has alternative trading partners at date 1, there is, given B's sunk investment cost a, a surplus of $b(a)-c$ to be divided up. A simple assumption to make is that the parties split this 50:50 (this is the Nash bargaining solution). That is, the input price p will satisfy $b(a)-p=p-c$. This means that the buyer's overall payoff, net of his investment cost, is

$$b(a)-p-a=\frac{b(a)-c}{2}-a. \tag{1}$$

The buyer, anticipating this payoff, will choose a to maximize (1), i.e. to maximize $1/2\, b(a) - a$.

This is to be contrasted with the efficient outcome, where a is chosen to maximize total surplus, $b(a) - c - a$. Maximizing (1) will lead to underinvestment; in fact, in extreme cases, a will equal zero and trade will not occur at all. The inefficiency arises because the buyer does not receive the full return from his investment – some of this return is appropriated by the seller in the date 1 bargaining. Note that an upfront payment from S to B at date 0 (to compensate for the share of the surplus S will later receive) will not help here, since it will only change B's objective function by a constant (it is like a lump-sum transfer). That is, it redistributes income without affecting real decisions.

Efficiency can be achieved if a long-term contract is written at date 0 specifying the input price p^* in advance. Then B will maximize $b(a) - p^* - a$, yielding the efficient investment level, a^*. An alternative method is to specify that the buyer must choose $a = a^*$ (if not he pays large damages to S) – the choice of p can then be left until date 1, with an upfront payment by S being used to compensate B for his investment. The second method presupposes that investment decisions are publicly observable, and so in practice may be more complicated than the first (see below).

We see then that a long-term contract can be useful in encouraging relationship-specific investments. The word 'investment' should be interpreted broadly here; the same factors will apply whenever one party is forced to pass up an opportunity as a result of a relationship with another party (e.g. A's 'investment' in the relationship with B may be not to lock into C). That is, the crucial element is a sunk cost (direct or opportunity) of some sort (an effort decision is one example of a sunk cost). Note that the income-transfer motive for a long-term contract is completely absent here; there is no uncertainty and everything is in present value terms.

Given the advantages of long-term contracts in specific relationships, the question that obviously arises is why we do not see more of them, and why those we do see seem often to be limited in scope. To this question we now turn.

2. THE COSTS OF WRITING LONG-TERM CONTRACTS. Contract theory is sometimes dismissed because 'we don't see the long-term contingent contracts that the theory predicts'. In fact, there is no shortage of complex long-term contracts in the world. Joskow (1985), for example, in his recent study of transactions between electricity generating plants and minemouth coal suppliers finds that some contracts between the parties extend for fifty years, and a large majority for over ten years. The contractual terms include quality provisions, formulae linking coal prices to costs and prices of substitutes, indexation clauses and so on. The contracts are both complicated and sophisticated. Similar findings are contained in Goldberg and Erickson's (1982) study of petroleum coke.

At a much more basic level, a typical contract for personal insurance with its many conditions and exemption clauses, is not exactly a simple document. Nor for that matter is a typical house rental agreement. On the other hand, labour contracts are often surprisingly rudimentary, at least in certain respects (for example, there is little indexation of wages to retail prices or to firm employment or sales; layoff pay is limited, etc.).

Given that complex long-term contracts are found in some situations but not others, it is natural to explain any observed contract as an outcome of an optimization process in which the relative benefits and costs of additional length and complexity are traded off at the margin. In the last section, we indicated some of the benefits of a long-term contract. (The example considered was sufficiently straightforward that the ideal long-term contract was a simple noncontingent one; however, with the inclusion of such factors as uncertainty about payoffs and variable quality of the input, the optimal contract would be a (possibly much more complex) contingent one.) But what about the costs? These are much harder to pin down since they fall under the general heading of 'transaction costs', a notoriously vague and slippery category. Of these, the following seem to be important: (1) the cost to each party of anticipating the various eventualities that may occur during the life of the relationship; (2) the cost of deciding, and reaching an agreement about, how to deal with such eventualities; (3) the cost of writing the contract in a sufficiently clear and unambiguous way that the terms of the contract can be enforced; and (4) the legal cost of enforcement.

One point to note is that *all* these costs are present also in the case of *short-term* contracts, although presumably they are usually smaller. In particular, since the short-term future is more predictable, the first cost is likely to be much reduced, and so possibly is the third. However, it certainly is not the case that there is a sharp division between short-term contracts and long-term contracts, with, as is sometimes supposed, the former being costless and the latter being infinitely costly.

It is also worth emphasizing that, when we talk about the cost of a long-term contract, we are presumably referring to the cost of a 'good' long-term contract. There is rarely significant cost or difficulty in writing *some* long-term contract. For example, the parties to an input supply contract could agree on a fixed price and level of supply for the next fifty years. They do not presumably because such a rigid arrangement would be very inefficient. (In some cases the courts will not enforce such an agreement, taking the point of view that the parties could not really have intended it to apply unchanged for such a long time. A clause to the effect that the parties really do mean what they say should be enough to overcome this difficulty, however. In other cases, it may be impossible to write a binding long-term contract because the identities of some of the parties involved may change. For example, one party may be a government that is in office for a fixed period, and it may be impossible for it to bind its successors. This latter idea underlies the work of Kydland and Prescott (1977) and Freixas et al. (1985).)

Due to the presence of transaction costs, the contracts people write will be *incomplete* in important respects. The parties will quite rationally leave out many contingencies, taking the point of view that it is better to 'wait and see what happens' than to try to cover a large number of individually unlikely eventualities. Less rationally, the parties will leave out other contingencies that they simply do not anticipate. Instead of writing very long-term contracts the parties will write limited-term contracts, with the intention of renegotiating these when they come to an end. (A paper which explores the implications of this is Crawford, 1986.) Contracts will often contain clauses which are vague or ambiguous, sometimes fatally so.

Anyone familiar with the legal literature on contracts will be aware that almost every contractual dispute that comes before the courts concerns a matter of incompleteness. In fact, incompleteness is probably at least as important empirically as asymmetric information as an explanation for departures from 'ideal' Arrow–Debreu contingent contracts. In spite of this, relatively little work has been done on this topic, the reason presumably being that an analysis of transaction costs is so complicated. One problem is that the first two transaction costs referred to above are intimately connected to the idea of bounded rationality (as in Simon, 1982), a successful formalization of which does not yet exist. As a result, perhaps, the few attempts that have been made to analyse incompleteness have concentrated on the third cost, the cost of writing the contract.

One approach, due to Dye (1985), can be described as follows. Suppose that the amount of input, q, traded between a buyer and seller should be a function of the product price, p, faced by the buyer: $q = f(p)$. Writing down this function is likely to be costly. Dye measures the costs in terms of how many different values q takes on as p varies; in particular, if $\#\{q \mid q = f(p) \text{ for some } p\} = n$, the cost of the contract is $(n-1)c$, where $c > 0$. This means that a noncontingent statement '$q = 5$ for all p' has zero cost, the statement '$q = 5$ for $p \leqslant 8$, $q = 10$ for $p > 8$' has cost c, and so on.

The costs Dye is trying to capture are real enough, but the measure used has some drawbacks. It implies for example, that the statement '$q = p^{1/2}$ for all p' has infinite cost if p has infinite domain, and does not distinguish between the cost of a simple function like this and the cost of a much more complicated function. As another example, a simple indexation clause to the effect that the real wage should be constant (i.e. the money wage $= \lambda p$ for some λ) would never be observed since, according to Dye's measure, it too has infinite cost. In addition, the approach does not tell us how to assess the cost of indirect ways of making q contingent; for example, the contract could specify that the buyer, having observed p, can choose any amount of input q he likes, subject to paying the seller σ for each unit.

There is another way of getting at the cost of including contingent statements. This is to suppose that what is costly is describing the state of the world ω rather than writing a statement per se. That is, suppose that ω cannot be represented simply by a product price, but is very complex and of high dimension – e.g., it includes the state of demand, what other firms in the industry are doing, the state of technology, etc. Many of these components may be quite nebulous. To describe the state ex-ante in sufficient detail that an outsider, e.g. the courts, can verify whether a particular state $\omega = \hat{\omega}$ has occurred, and so enforce the contract, may be prohibitively costly. Under these conditions, the contract will have to omit some (in extreme cases, all) references to the underlying state.

Similar to this is the case where what is costly is describing the *characteristics* of what is traded or the *actions* (e.g. investments) the parties must take. For example, suppose that there is only one state of the world, but that q now represents the quality of the item traded rather than the quantity. An ideal contract would give a precise description of q. However, quality may be multidimensional and very difficult to describe unambiguously (and vague statements to the effect that quality should be 'good' may be almost meaningless). The result may be that the contract will have to be silent on many aspects of quality and/or actions.

Models of this sort of incompleteness have been investigated by Grossman and Hart (1987) and Hart and Moore (1985) for the case where the state of the world cannot be described and by Bull (1985) and Grossman and Hart (1986, 1987) for the case where quality and/or actions cannot be specified. These models do not rely on any asymmetry of information between the parties. Both parties may recognize that the state of the world is such that the buyer's benefit is high or the seller's cost is low, or that the quality of an item is good or bad or that an investment decision is appropriate or not. The difficulty is conveying this information to others. *That is, it is the asymmetry of information between the parties on the one hand, and outsiders, such as the courts, on the other, which is the root of the problem.*

To use the jargon, incompleteness arises because states of the world, quality and actions are *observable* (to the contractual parties) but not *verifiable* (to outsiders).

We describe an example of an incomplete contract along these lines in the next section.

3. INCOMPLETE CONTRACTS: AN EXAMPLE. We will give an example of an incomplete contract for the case where it is prohibitively costly to specify the quality characteristics of the item to be exchanged or the parties' investment decisions. Similar problems arise when the state of the world cannot be described. The example is a variant of the models in Grossman and Hart (1986, 1987), Hart and Moore (1985).

Consider a buyer B who wishes to purchase a unit of input from a seller S. B and S each make a (simultaneous) specific investment at date 0 and trade occurs at date 1. Let I_B, I_S denote, respectively, the investments of B and S, and to simplify assume that each can take on only two values, H or L (high or low). These investments are observable to B and S, but are not verifiable (they are complex and multidimensional, or represent effort decisions) and hence are noncontractible. We assume that at date 1 the seller can supply either 'satisfactory' input or 'unsatisfactory' input. 'Unsatisfactory' input has a zero benefit for the buyer and zero cost for the seller (so it is like not supplying at all). 'Satisfactory' input yields benefits and costs which depends on ex-ante investments. These are indicated in Figure 1.

The first component refers to the buyer's benefit, v, and the second to the seller's cost, c. So when $I_S = H, I_B = H, v = 10$ and $c = 6$ (if input is 'satisfactory').

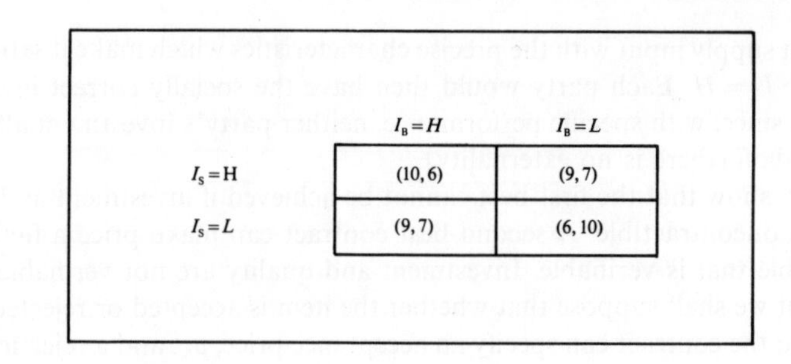

	$I_B = H$	$I_B = L$
$I_S = H$	(10, 6)	(9, 7)
$I_S = L$	(9, 7)	(6, 10)

Figure 1

From these gross benefits and costs must be subtracted investment costs, which we assume to be 1.9 if investment is high and zero if it is low (for each party). (All benefits and costs are in date 1 dollars.) Note that there is no uncertainty and so attitudes to risk are irrelevant.

Our assumption is that the characteristics of the input (e.g. whether it is 'satisfactory') are observable to both parties, but are too complicated to be specified in a contract. The fact that they are observable means that the buyer can be given the option to reject the input at date 1 if he does not like it. This will be important in what follows.

An important feature of the example is that the seller's investment affects not only the seller's costs but also the buyer's benefit, and the buyer's investment affects not only the buyer's benefit but also the seller's costs. The idea here is that a better investment by the seller increases the quality of 'satisfactory' input; and a better investment by the buyer reduces the cost of producing 'satisfactory' input, that is input that can be used by the buyer.

For instance, one can imagine that B is an electricity generating plant and S is a coal mine that the plant is sited next to. I_B might refer to the type of coal-burning boiler that the plant installs and I_S to the way the coal supplier develops the mine. By investing in a better boiler, the power plant may be able to burn lower quality coal, thus reducing the seller's costs, while still increasing its gross (of investment) profit. On the other hand, by developing a good seam, the coal supplier may raise the quality of coal supplied while reducing its variable cost.

The first-best has $I_B = I_S = H$, with total surplus equal to $(10–6) - 3.8 = 0.2$ (if $I_B = H$ and $I_S = L$, or vice versa, surplus $= 0.1$ and if $I_B = I_S = L$, no trade occurs and surplus is zero). This could be achieved if *either* investment *or* quality were contractible as follows. If investment is contractible, an optimal contract would specify that the buyer must set $I_B = H$ and the seller $I_S = H$ and give the buyer the right to accept the input at date 1 at price p_1 or reject it at price p_0. If $10 > p_1 - p_0 > 6$, the seller will be induced to supply satisfactory input (the gain, $p_1 - p_0$, from having the input accepted exceeds the seller's supply cost) and the buyer to accept it (the buyer's benefit exceeds the increment price $p_1 - p_0$). If, on the other hand, quality is contractible, the contract could specify that the seller must supply input with the precise characteristics which make it satisfactory when $I_B = I_S = H$. Each party would then have the socially correct investment incentives since, with specific performance, neither party's investment affects the other's payoff (there is no externality).

We now show that the first-best cannot be achieved if investment and quality are both noncontractible. A second-best contract can make price a function of any variable that is verifiable. Investment and quality are not verifiable (nor is v or c), but we shall suppose that whether the item is accepted or rejected by the buyer is, so the contract can specify an acceptance price, p_1, and a rejection price, p_0. In fact, p_0, p_1 can also be made functions of (verifiable) messages that the buyer and seller send each other, reflecting the investment decisions that both have made (as in Hart and Moore, 1985). The following argument is unaffected by such messages and so, for simplicity, we ignore them (the interested reader is referred to Hart and Holmstrom, 1987).

Can we sustain the first-best by an appropriate choice of p_0, p_1? The seller always has the option of choosing $I_S = L$ and producing an item of unsatisfactory quality, which yields him a net payoff of p_0. In order to induce him not to do this, we must have

$$p_1 - 6 - 1.9 \geqslant p_0, \text{ i.e. } p_1 - p_0 \geqslant 7.9. \tag{2}$$

Similarly the buyer's net payoff must be no less than $-p_0$ since he always has the option of choosing $I_B = L$ and rejecting the input. That is,

$$10 - p_1 - 1.9 \geqslant -p_0, \text{ i.e. } p_1 - p_0 \leqslant 8.1. \tag{3}$$

So $(p - p_0)$ must lie between 7.9 and 8.1.

Now the seller has an additional option. If he expects the buyer to set $I_B = H$, he can choose $I_S = L$ and, given that $8.1 \geqslant p_1 - p_0 \geqslant 7.9$, still be confident that trade of 'satisfactory' input will occur under the original contract at date 1 (the buyer will accept satisfactory input since $v = 9 > p_1 - p_0$, while the seller will supply it since $p_1 - p_0 > 7 = c$). But if the seller deviates, his payoff rises from $p_1 - 6 - 1.9$ to $p_1 - 7$. (The example is symmetric and so a similar deviation is also profitable for the buyer.) Hence the $I_B = I_S = H$ equilibrium will be disrupted.

We see, then, that the first-best cannot be sustained if investment and quality are both uncontractible. The reason is that it will be in the interest of the seller (or the buyer) to reduce investment since, although this reduces social benefit by lowering the buyer's (or seller's) benefit, it increases the seller's (or buyer's) own profit. The optimal second-best contract will instead have $I_B = H$, $I_S = L$ (or vice versa), which will be sustained by a pair of prices p_0, p_1 such that $9 > p_1 - p_0 > 7$. Total surplus will be 0.1 instead of the first-best level of 0.2. (Note the importance of the assumption that both the buyer and seller can choose $I = H$ or L. If only the buyer (or the seller) can choose $i = L$, the first-best can be achieved by choosing $p_1 - p_0$ between 6 and 7 (or 9 and 10): any deviation by the buyer (or the seller) will then be unprofitable since it will lead to no trade.)

The conclusion is that inefficiencies can arise in incomplete contracts even though the parties have common information (both observe investments and both observe quality). The particular inefficiency that occurs in the model analysed is in ex-ante investments. Ex-post trade is always efficient relative to these investments since p_1, p_0 can and will be chosen such that $v > p_1 - p_0 > c$, i.e. the seller wants to supply and the buyer to receive satisfactory input. The example can be regarded as formalizing the intuition of Williamson (1985) and Klein et al. (1978) that relationship-specific investments will be distorted due to the impossibility of writing complete contingent contracts – note that this result is achieved without imposing arbitrary restrictions on the form of the permissible contract (e.g. we have not ruled out the existence of long-term contracts from the start). (There is one exception to this statement – we have excluded the participation of a third party to the contract; for a discussion and justification of this, see Hart and Holmstrom, 1987.)

The example may be used to illustrate a theory of ownership presented in Grossman and Hart (1986, 1987). It is sometimes suggested that when transaction costs prevent the writing of a complete contract, there may be a reason for firm integration (see Williamson, 1985). Consider the payoffs of Figure 1 and suppose that B takes over S. The control that B thereby gains over S's assets may allow B to affect S's costs in various ways, and this may reduce the possibility of opportunistic behaviour by S. To take a very simple (and contrived) example, suppose that if S chooses $I_S = L$, B can take some action, α with respect to S's assets at date 1 so as to make S's cost of supplying either satisfactory or unsatisfactory input equal to 9 (in the coal–electricity example, α might refer to the part of the mine's seam the coal is taken out of; note that we now drop the assumption that the cost of supplying unsatisfactory input is zero). Imagine furthermore that this action increases B's benefit, so that B will indeed take it at date 1 if S chooses L. Then with this extra degree of freedom, the first-best can be achieved. In particular, if $p_1 = p_0 + 6.1$, $I_S = I_L = H$ is a Nash equilibrium since, by the above reasoning, any deviation by the seller will be punished, while if the buyer deviates, the seller will supply unsatisfactory input given that $p_1 < p_0 + 7$.

Note that if action α could be specified in the initial contract, there would be no need for integration: the initial contract would simply say that B has the right to choose α at date 1. Ownership becomes important, however, if (i) α is too complicated to be specified in the date 0 contract and therefore qualifies as a residual right of control; and (ii) residual rights of control over an asset are in the hands of whomever owns that asset. The point is that under incompleteness the allocation of residual decision rights matters since the contract cannot specify precisely what each party's obligations are in every state of the world. To the extent that ownership of an asset guarantees residual rights of control over that asset, vertical and lateral integration can be seen as ways of ensuring particular – and presumably efficient – allocations of residual decision rights. (While in the above example, integration increases efficiency, this is in no way a general conclusion. In Grossman and Hart (1986, 1987), examples are presented where integration reduces efficiency.)

Before concluding this section, we should emphasize that for reasons of tractability we have confined our attention to incompleteness due to a very particular sort of transaction cost. In practice, some of the other transactions costs we have alluded to are likely to be at least as important, if not more so. For example, in the type of model we have analysed, although the parties cannot describe the state of the world or quality characteristics, they are still supposed to be able to write a contract which is unambiguous and which anticipates all eventualities. This is very unrealistic. In practice, a contract might, say, have B agreeing to rent S's concert hall for a particular price. But suppose S's hall then burns down. The contract will usually be silent about what is meant to happen under these conditions (there is no hall to rent, but should S pay B damages and if so how much?), and so, in the event of a dispute, the courts will have to fill in the 'missing provision'. (A situation where it becomes impossible or extremely costly to supply a contracted for good is known as one of 'impossibility' or 'frustration' in the legal literature.) An analysis of this sort of incompleteness, although extremely hard, is a very important topic for future research. It is likely to yield a much richer and more realistic view of the way contracts are written and throw light on how courts should assess damages (this latter issue has begun to be analysed in the law and economics literature; see e.g., Shavell, 1980).

4. SELF-ENFORCING CONTRACTS. The previous discussion has been concerned with explicit binding contracts that are enforced by outsiders, such as the courts. Even the most casual empiricism tells us that many agreements are not of this type. Although the courts may be there as a last resort (the shadow of the law may therefore be important), these agreements are enforced on a day to day basis by custom, good faith, reputation, etc. Even in the case of a serious dispute, the parties may take great pains to resolve matters themselves rather than go to court. This leads to the notion of a self-enforcing or implicit contract (the importance of informal arrangements like this in business has been stressed by Macaulay (1963) and Ben-Porath (1980) among others).

People often by-pass the legal process presumably because of the transaction costs of using it. The costs of writing a 'good' long-term contract discussed in Section 2 are relevant here. So also is the skill with which the courts resolve contractual disputes. If contracts are incomplete and contain missing provisions as well as vague and ambiguous statements, appropriate enforcement may require abilities and knowledge (what was in the parties' minds?) that many judges and juries do not possess. This means that going to court may be a considerable gamble – and an expensive one at that. (This is an example of the fourth transaction cost noted in Section 2.)

Although the notion of implicit or self-enforcing contracts is often invoked, a formal study of such agreements has begun only recently (see, e.g. Bull, 1985), with a considerable stimulus coming from the theory of repeated games. This literature has stressed the role of *reputation* in 'completing' a contract. That is, the idea is that a party may behave 'reasonably' even if he is not obliged to do so, in order to develop a reputation as a decent and reliable trader. In some instances such reputational effects will operate only within the group of contractual parties – this is sometimes called *internal* enforcement of the contract – while in others the effects will be more pervasive. The latter will be the case when some outsiders to the contract, for example other firms in the industry or potential workers for a firm, observe unreasonable behaviour by one party, and as a result are more reluctant to deal with it in the future. In this case the enforcement is said to be *external* or *market-based*. Note that there may be a tension between this external enforcement and the reasons for the absence of a legally binding contract in the first place – the more people can observe the behaviour, the more likely it is to be verifiable.

The distinction between an incomplete contract and a standard asymmetric information contract should be emphasized here. It is the former that allows reputation to operate since the parties have the same information and can observe whether reasonable behaviour is being maintained. In the latter case, it is unclear how reputation can overcome the asymmetry of information between the parties that is the reason for the departure from an Arrow–Debreu contract.

The role of reputation in sustaining a contract can be illustrated using the following model (based on Bull (1985) and Kreps (1984); this is an even simpler model of incomplete contracts than that of the last section). Assume that a buyer, B, and a seller, S, wish to trade an item at date 1 which has value v to the buyer and cost c to the seller, where $v > c$. There are no ex-ante investments and the good is homogeneous, so quality is not an issue. Suppose, however, that it is not verifiable whether trade actually occurs. Then a legally binding contract which specifies that the seller must deliver the item and the buyer must pay p, where $v > p > c$, cannot be enforced. The reason is that, assuming (as we shall) that simultaneous delivery and payment are not feasible, if the seller has to deliver first, the buyer can always deny that delivery occurred and refuse payment, while if the buyer has to pay first, the seller can always claim later that he did deliver even though he did not. As a result, if the parties must rely on the courts, a gainful trading opportunity will be missed.

The idea that not even the level of trade is verifiable is extreme, and Bull (1985) in fact makes the more defensible assumption that it is the quality of the good that cannot be verified (in Bull's model, S is a worker and quality refers to his performance). Bull supposes that quality is observable to the buyer only with a lag, so that take it or leave it offers of the type considered in the last section are not feasible. As a result the seller always has an incentive to produce minimum quality (which corresponds in the above model to zero output). Making quantity nonverifiable is a cruder but simpler way of capturing the same idea (this is the approach taken in Kreps, 1984).

Note that in the above model incompleteness of the contract arises entirely from transaction cost (3), the difficulty of writing and enforcing the contract.

To introduce reputational effects one supposes that this trading relationship is repeated. Bull (1985) and Kreps (1984) follow the supergame literature and assume infinite repetition in order to avoid unravelling problems. This approach, as is well known, suffers from a number of difficulties. First, the assumption of infinite (or in some versions, *potentially* infinite) life is hard to swallow. Secondly, 'reasonable' behaviour, i.e. trade, is sustained by the threat that if one party behaves unreasonably so will the other party from then on. While this threat is 'credible' (more precisely, subgame perfect), it is unclear why the parties could not decide to continue to trade after a deviation, i.e. to 'let bygones be bygones' (see Farrell, 1984).

It would seem that a preferable approach is to assume that the relationship has finite length, but introduce asymmetric information, as in Kreps and Wilson (1982) and Milgrom and Roberts (1982). The following is based on some very preliminary work that Bengt Holmstrom and I have undertaken along these lines.

Suppose that there are two types of buyers in the population, honest and dishonest. Honest buyers will always honour any agreement or promise that they have made, while dishonest ones will do so only if this is profitable. A buyer knows his own type, but others do not. It is common knowledge that the fraction of honest buyers in the population is π, $0 < \pi < 1$. In contrast, all sellers are known to be dishonest. All agents are risk neutral.

Assume for simplicity that a single buyer and seller are matched at date 0 with neither having any alternative trading partners at this date or in the future. Consider first the one-period case. Then a date 0 agreement can be represented as follows.

The interpretation is that the buyer promises to pay the seller p_1 before date 1 (stage I); in return, the seller promises to supply the item at date 1 (stage II); and in return for this, the buyer promises to make a further payment of p_2 (stage III).

We should mention one further assumption. Honest buyers, although they never breach an agreement first, are supposed to feel under no obligation to fulfil the terms of an agreement that has already been broken by a seller (interestingly, althouth this is a theory of buyer psychology, it has parallels in the common law). Note that if a buyer ever breaks an agreement first, he reveals himself to be dishonest, with the consequence that no further self-enforcing agreement with the seller is possible and hence trade ceases.

What is an optimal agreement? Consider Figure 2. The seller knows that he will receive p_2 only with probability π since a dishonest buyer will default at the last stage. Since the seller is himself dishonest, he will supply at Stage II only if it is profitable for him to do so, i.e. only if

$$\pi p_2 - c \geqslant 0. \tag{4}$$

Assume for simplicity that the seller has all the bargaining power at date 0

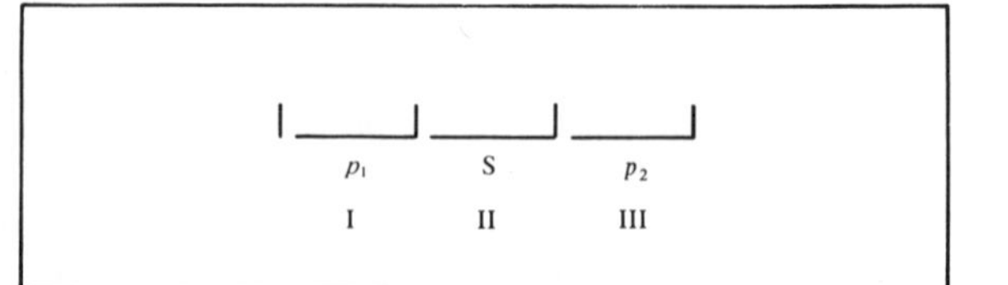

Figure 2

(nothing that follows depends on this). Then the seller will wish to maximize his overall payoff

$$p_1 + \pi p_2 - c, \tag{5}$$

subject to (4) which makes it credible that he will supply at stage II and also the constraint that he does not discourage an honest buyer from participating in the agreement at date 0. Since with (4) satisfied, buyers know that they will receive the item for sure, this last condition is

$$v - p_1 - p_2 \geqslant 0. \tag{6}$$

Note that a dishonest buyer's payoff $v - p_1$ is always higher than an honest buyer's payoff given in (6), so there is no way to screen out dishonest buyers. In the language of asymmetric information models, the equilibrium is a pooling one.

Since the seller's payoff is increasing in p_1, (6) will hold with equality (the buyer gets no surplus). (More generally, changes in p_1 simply redistribute surplus between the two parties without changing either's incentive to breach.) If we substitute for p_1 in (5), the seller's payoff becomes $v - p_2(1-\pi) - c$, which, when maximized subject to (4), yields the solution $p_2 = c/\pi$. The maximized net payoff is

$$v - c/\pi, \tag{7}$$

which is less than the first-best level, $v - c$.

We see then that the conditions for trade are more stringent in the absence of a binding contract. If $c/(\pi) > v > c$, there are gains from trade which would not be realized in a one-period relationship.

Suppose now that the relationship is repeated. Consider a two-period version of the above and assume no discounting. Now the diagram shown in Figure 3 applies. That is, the agreement says that the buyer pays, the seller supplies the first time, the buyer pays more, the seller supplies a second time and the buyer makes a final payment. Rather than solving for the optimal arrangement, we shall simply show that the seller can do better than in the one period case. Let $p_3 = c/\pi$, $p_2 = c$ and $p_1 = 2v - c - (c)/\pi$. Then (i) the seller will supply at Stage IV (if matters have got that far), knowing that he will receive p_3 with probability π; (ii) both honest and dishonest buyers will pay p_2 at Stage III, the latter because, at a cost of c, they thereby ensure supply worth $v > c$ at Stage IV; (iii) the seller will supply at stage II because this gives him a net payoff of

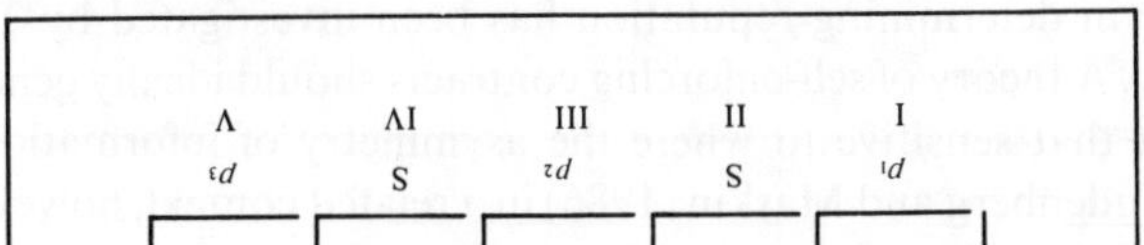

V IV III II I
p_3 S p_2 S p_1

Figure 3

$p_2 + \pi p_3 - 2c \geqslant 0$, while if he does not the arrangement is over and his payoff is zero; (iv) an honest buyer is prepared to participate since his surplus is non-negative (actually zero).

The seller's overall expected net payoff is

$$p_1 + \pi_2 + \pi p_3 - 2c = 2v - c - \frac{c}{\pi}, \tag{8}$$

which *exceeds* twice the one-period payoff. Hence trade is more likely to take place in a two-period relationship than in a one-period one. In fact it can be shown that the above is an *optimal* two-period agreement.

Repetition improves things by allowing the honest buyer to pay less second time round (Stage III) than third time round (Stage V). That is, the arrangement *back-loads* payments. This is acceptable to the seller because he knows that even a dishonest buyer will not default at Stage III since he has a large stake in the arrangement continuing. To put it another way, the dihonest buyer does not want to reveal his dishonesty at too early a stage.

The same arrangement can be used when there are more than two periods; the buyer promises to pay c at every stage except the last, when he pays (c/π). In fact the per period surplus of the seller from such an arrangement converges to the first-best level $(v - c)$ as the number of periods tends to ∞ (assuming no discounting, of course).

Although the above analysis is extremely provisional and sketchy, we can draw some tentative conclusions about the role of reputation and indicate some directions for further research. First, the notion of a psychic cost of breaking an agreement seems to be a useful – as well as a not unrealistic – basis for a theory of self-enforcing contracts. It is obviously desirable to drop the assumption that some agents are completely honest and others completely dishonest, and assume instead that the typical trader has a finite psychic cost of breaking an agreement, where this cost is distributed in the population in a known way. In other words, everybody 'has their price', but this price varies. Preliminary work along these lines suggests that the above results generalize; in particular, repetition makes it easier to sustain a self-enforcing agreement.

Of course, asymmetries of information about psychic costs are not the only possible basis for a theory of reputation. For example, the buyer and seller could have private information about v and c, and might choose their trading strategies to influence perceptions about the values of these variables (the role of uncertainty about v and c in determining reputation has been investigated by Thomas and Worrall, 1984). A theory of self-enforcing contracts should ideally generate results which are not that sensitive to where the asymmetry of information is placed. The work of Fudenberg and Maskin (1986) in a related context, however, suggests that this may be a difficult goal to achieve.

There are a number of other natural directions in which to take the model. One is to introduce trade with other parties. For example, the seller may trade with a succession of buyers rather than a single one. The extent to which repetition increases per period surplus in this case depends on whether new buyers observe the past broken promises of the seller. (This determines the degree to which external enforcement operates: more generally, a new buyer may observe that default occurred in the past, but be unsure about who was responsible for it.) If new buyers do not observe past broken promises, repetition achieves nothing, which gives a very strong prediction of the possible benefits of a long-term relationship between a fixed buyer and seller. Even if past broken promises are observed perfectly, it appears that, *ceteris paribus*, a single long-term agreement may be superior to a succession of short-term ones. The reason is that in the latter case the constraint is imposed that each party must receive non-negative surplus over *their* term of the relationship, whereas in the former case there is only the single constraint that surplus must be non-negative over the whole term (see Bull, 1985; Kreps, 1984).

Probably the most important extension is to introduce incompleteness due to other sorts of transaction costs, e.g. the 'bounded rationality' costs (1) and (2) discussed in Section 2. The problem is that the same factors which make it difficult to anticipate and plan for eventualities in a formal contract apply also to informal arrangements. That is, an informal arrangement is also likely to contain many 'missing provisions'. But then the question arises, what constitutes 'reasonable' or 'desirable' behaviour (in terms of building a reputation) with regard to states or actions that were not discussed ex-ante? Custom, among other things, is likely to be important under these conditions: behaviour will be 'reasonable' or 'desirable' to the extent that it is generally regarded as such (for a good discussion of this, see Kreps, 1984). This raises many new and interesting (as well as extremely difficult) questions.

5. SUMMARY AND CONCLUSIONS. The vast majority of the theoretical work on contracts to date has been concerned with what might be called 'complete' contracts. In this context, a complete contract means one that specifies each party's obligations in every conceivable eventuality, rather than a contract that is fully contingent in the Arrow–Debreu sense. In particular, according to this terminology, the typical asymmetric information contract found in the principal–agent or implicit contract literatures (see Hart and Holmstrom, 1987) is complete.

In reality it is usually impossible to lay down each party's obligations completely and unambiguously in advance, and so most actual contracts are seriously incomplete. In this essay, we have tried to indicate some of the implications of such incompleteness. Among other things, we have seen that incompleteness can lead to departures from the first-best even when there are no asymmetries of information among the contracting parties (and, moreover, the parties are risk neutral).

More important perhaps than this is the fact that incompleteness raises new and difficult questions about how the behaviour of the contracting parties is determined. To the extent that incomplete contracts do not specify the parties' actions fully, i.e. they contain 'gaps', additional theories are required to tell us how these gaps are filled in. Among other things, outside influences such as custom or reputation may become important under these conditions. In addition, outsiders, such as the courts (or arbitrators), may have a role to play in filling in missing provisions of the contract and resolving ambiguities rather than in simply enforcing an existing agreement. Incompleteness can also throw light on the importance of the allocation of decision rights or rights of control. If it is too costly to state precisely how a particular asset is to be used in every state of the world, it may be efficient simply to give one party 'control' of the asset, in the sense that he is entitled to do what he likes with it, subject perhaps to some explicit (contractible) limitations.

While the importance of incompleteness is very well recognized by lawyers, as well as by those working in law and economics, it is only beginning to be appreciated by economic theorists. It is to be hoped that work in the next few years will lead to significant advances in our formal understanding of this phenomenon. Unfortunately, progress is unlikely to be easy since many aspects of incompleteness are intimately connected to the notion of bounded rationality, a satisfactory formalization of which does not yet exist.

As a final illustration of the importance of incompleteness, consider the following question. Why do parties frequently write a limited term contract, with the intention of renegotiating this when it comes to an end, rather than writing a single contract that extends over the whole length of their relationship? In a complete contract framework such behaviour cannot be advantageous, since the parties could just as well calculate what will happen when the contract expires and include this as part of the original contract. It is to be hoped that future work on incomplete contracts will allow this very basic question to be answered.

BIBLIOGRAPHY

Becker, G. 1964. *Human Capital.* New York: Columbia University Press.

Ben-Porath, Y. 1980. The F-connection: families, friends, and firms and the organizing of exchange. *Population and Development Review* 6, March, 1–30.

Bull, C. 1985. The existence of self-enforcing implicit contracts. C.V. Starr Center, New York University.

Crawford, V. 1986. Long-term relationships governed by short-term contracts. Princeton University.

Dye, R. 1985. Costly contract contingencies. *International Economic Review* 26, 1, 233–50.

Freixas, X., Guesnerie, R. and Tirole, J. 1985. Planning under incomplete information and the ratchet effect. *Review of Economic Studies* 52(2), 169, 173–92.

Fudenberg, D. and Maskin, E. 1986. The Folk Theorem in repeated games with discounting and with incomplete information. *Econometrica* 54(3), 533–54.

Goldberg, V. and Erickson, J. 1982. Long-term contracts for petroleum coke. Department of Economics Working Paper Series No. 206, University of California, Davis, September.

Grossman, S. and Hart O. 1986. The costs and benefits of ownership: a theory of vertical and lateral integration. *Journal of Political Economy* 94(4), August, 691–76.

Grossman, S. and Hart, O. 1987. Vertical integration and the distribution of property rights. In *Economic Policy in Theory and Practice*, Sapir Conference Volume, London: Macmillan Press.

Grout, P. 1984. Investment and wages in the absence of binding contracts: a Nash bargaining approach. *Econometrica* 52(2), March, 449–60.

Hart, O. and Hölmstrom, B. 1987. The theory of contracts. In *Advances in Economic Theory, Fifth World Congress*, ed. T. Bewley, Cambridge: Cambridge University Press.

Hart, O. and Moore, J. 1985. Incomplete contracts and renegotiation. London School of Economics, Working Paper.

Joskow, P. 1985. Vertical integration and long-term contracts. *Journal of Law, Economics and Organization* 1, Spring.

Klein, B., Crawford, R. and Alchian, A. 1978. Vertical integration, appropriate rents and the competitive contracting process. *Journal of Law and Economics* 21, 297–326.

Kreps, D. 1984. Corporate culture and economic theory. Mimeo, Stanford University, May.

Kreps, D. and Wilson, R. 1982. Reputation and imperfect information. *Journal of Economic Theory* 27, 253–79.

Kydland, F. and Prescott, E. 1977. Rules rather than discretion: the inconsistency of optimal plans. *Journal of Political Economy* 85(3), 473–92.

Macaulay, S. 1963. Non-contractual relations in business: a preliminary study. *American Sociological Review* 28, February, 55–67.

Milgrom, P. and Roberts, D.J. 1982. Predation, reputation and entry deterrence. *Journal of Economic Theory* 27, 280–312.

Shavell, S. 1980. Damage measures for breach of contract. *Bell Journal of Economics* 11(2), Autumn, 466–90.

Simon, H. 1982. *Models of Bounded Rationality.* Cambridge, Mass.: MIT Press.

Thomas, J. and Worrall, T. 1984. Self-enforcing wage contracts. Mimeo, University of Cambridge.

Williamson, O. 1985. *The Economic Institutions of Capitalism.* New York: Free Press.

Incomplete Markets

CHARLES WILSON

Markets are complete when every agent is able to exchange every good either directly or indirectly with every other agent. When markets are not complete, two fundamental properties of a competitive equilibrium with complete markets may no longer be satisfied. First, stockholders may not agree on the optimal production plan for a firm. Secondly, even in a model of pure exchange, a competitive allocation may not be Pareto optimal even when we restrict attention to allocations which are 'consistent' with the market structure. It is with the failure of this optimality property that this essay will be concerned.

Most of the literature on incomplete markets has been motivated by the analysis of competitive markets in the context of uncertainty. A good starting point for a discussion of this literature is the work of Arrow (1971). He demonstrated that extending the static analysis of competitive markets under certainty to the case of uncertainty requires the introduction of a contingent claims market for each good for every possible state of the world. He went on to examine the extent to which the same result could be achieved with a smaller number of markets. He showed that if spot markets are complete and their prices are perfectly forecast, then a complete set of markets can be attained with only one contingent claim (security) for each state. Before the state is realized, agents trade the state contingent securities. Once the state realized, a spot market opens and the consumer adjusts his consumption bundle, taking into account any transfers of purchasing power resulting from his earlier exchange of state contingent securities. This market structure reduces the number of securities required to achieve any Arrow–Debreu allocation by a factor equal to the number of goods in each state.

Arrow's argument can be generalized to allow for an arbitrary set of securities. In general, a typical security may specify a different payment of goods in any number of states of the world. Nevertheless, if the set of securities is to duplicate the effect of Arrow's state contingent securities for every possible price vector, the number of securities must always be at least as large as the number of states (see e.g. Townsend, 1978). A moment of reflection is enough to convince almost anyone that this is still an unreasonably large number. It is probably impossible even to list all of the contingencies one can imagine, much less set up an explicit market for each one. Evidently, a realistic analysis of competitive markets under uncertainty must allow for markets which are incomplete.

Once we consider incomplete markets, the efficiency properties of the competitive allocation must be reexamined. If, for instance, we use the Pareto criteria and ignore any limitations on the feasible allocations implied by the market structure, then we should generally not expect a competitive allocation to be Pareto optimal. The reason is that, when markets are incomplete, there is no guarantee that any Pareto optimal allocations can be attained simply by reallocating available securities and then letting agents trade on the spot market.

To illustrate the point with the simplest possible example, consider a pure exchange economy consisting of two agents and two states of nature with a single good in each state. Without a securities market to allow the transfer of purchasing power between states, no trade between the agents is possible. In this example, therefore, the competitive allocation is Pareto optimal if and only if the initial endowment is Pareto optimal.

If the model is to provide the foundation for the analysis of the effect of government intervention, however, the unrestricted Pareto criterion may be of little use. A more appropriate welfare criterion should compare the market allocation to the set of allocations which can be achieved by a feasible institution. If the absence of certain security markets reflects some fundamental technological constraints, then those same constraints need to be reflected in the analysis of the performance of any other institution. On the other hand, one of the instruments that an institution might use is the assignment of ownership rights to existing securities. At the very least, therefore, we should test the efficiency of the market allocation relative to the set of allocations which can be implemented simply by redistributing the existing set of securities.

In order to formulate such a definition we must be precise about what we mean by the set of allocations which are consistent with a given allocation of securities. Once a state is realized, there must be a restriction on the allocations which can be implemented for any given distribution of securities. Otherwise, a mechanism in the spot markets can be introduced to undo any restrictions imposed by the allocation of securities. One possibility is to suppose that final allocations must be attainable as competitive equilibria in the spot markets, given the distribution of income implied the allocation of securities. This approach leads to the following definition suggested by Hart (1975). An allocation x is *constrained Pareto optimal* for a set of securities Q if (i) it is a competitive equilibrium for some allocation of securities in Q, and (ii) there is no Pareto superior allocation $\hat{x}$ which is a competitive equilibrium allocation for some other allocation of securities in Q. (This is a slight restatement of Hart's definition. It corresponds to the definition of *constrained Pareto suboptimal* allocation given by Geanakoplos and Polemarchakis, 1985.)

With a complete set of securities, the first welfare theorem implies that any competitive equilibrium is constrained Pareto optimal. (It is also an implication of the second welfare theorem that the set of constrained Pareto optimal allocations corresponds to the set of unconstrained Pareto optima.) A similar result can be established as long as we restrict ourselves to pure exchange economies with only one good in each state. For these economies, the allocation of securities determines the final allocation of goods in each state independently of the preferences of the individual agents. Consequently, the economy is equivalent to an economy in which preferences are defined directly on the allocation of securities. It then follows again from the first welfare theorem that any competitive allocation is constrained Pareto optimal.

Once we allow for more than one good in each state, however, this conclusion changes. The reason is that a redistribution of the ownership of securities may lead to a change in the spot market prices which in turn implies redistribution of real income which cannot be duplicated by the exchange of securities at the existing prices. (In contrast, when markets are complete, any allocation of real income can be achieved by redistributing securities.) Consequently, it is possible to increase the welfare of every agent in the economy by increasing the purchasing power of some agents at the expense of others through a redistribution of the ownership of securities. The idea can be illustrated with a simple example.

Consider an economy with three agents, *a*, *b* and *c*, and two states of the world, 1, 2. In each state *i* there are two goods, labelled X and Y (Table 1). Suppose the preferences and endowments of the agents are given by the following table where x_i^α and y_i^α is the consumption of goods X and Y respectively by agent α in state *i*.

TABLE 1

Agent	Endowments		Utility
	(X_1, Y_1)	(X_2, Y_2)	
a	(0, 2)	(2, 0)	$x_1^a + \varepsilon \min\{x_2^a, y_2^a\}$
b	(2, 0)	(0, 2)	$\varepsilon \min\{x_1^b, y_1^b\} + x_2^b$
c	(1, 1)	(1, 1)	$y_1^c + y_2^c$

In this economy, agent *a* is endowed with two units of good Y in state 1 and two units of good X in state 2. He consumes only good X in state 1 and always consumes an equal amount of both goods in state 2. For each pair of units of the two goods he consumes in state 2 he is willing to give up ε units of his consumption of good X in state 1. The endowment and preferences of agent *b* are the same except that the role of the two states is reversed. Agent *c* is endowed with one unit of good X in both states but consumes only good Y. His marginal rate of substitution between consumption in the two states is unity.

Suppose there is a single security which promises to deliver one unit of good X in each state. Since there is nothing for which to exchange this security, the equilibrium income and spot prices in each state will be determined solely by the endowments of the agents in that state. It is easy to check that the relative price of the two goods is unity in both states. Agent *a* consumes two units of good X in state 1 and one unit of each good in state 2. Agent *b* consumes one unit of each good in state 1 and two units of good X in state 2. Agent *c* consumes two units of good Y in both states.

Even though the security will never be traded in the market, it can be used by the government to redistribute purchasing power in the two states and thereby change the spot prices. Suppose, for instance, that agents *a* and *b* must each supply agent *c* with two units of the security. Then the effect is the same as if the endowments were changed as shown in Table 2.

TABLE 2

Agent	Endowments	
	(X_1, Y_1)	(X_2, Y_2)
a	$(-2, 2)$	$(0, 0)$
b	$(0, 0)$	$(-2, 2)$
c	$(5, 1)$	$(5, 1)$

For this economy the equilibrium price of good Y in terms of good X in each state is $5/2$. Agent *a* consumes the three units of good X in state 1 and nothing in state 2. Agent *b* consumes nothing in state 1 and all three units of good X in state 2. Agent *c* consumes the three units of good Y in both states.

Now compare the welfare of the two agents in the two economies. Without the transfer payments, agents *a* and *b* attain an expected utility of $2+\varepsilon$ while agent *c* attains an expected utility of 4. With the transfer payments, agents *a* and *b* both attain an expected utility of 3 while agent *c* attains a utility of 6. Consequently, for $0<\varepsilon<1$, the equilibrium with transfer payments Pareto dominates the equilibrium without transfer payments. By transferring purchasing power to agent *c* in both states, the economy has made the price of the goods demanded by agents *a* and *b* cheaper in those states where they value their increased welfare the most. Notice that with a complete set of markets, this Pareto superior allocation would also have been achieved without any transfer payments. In this case, the equilibrium price of good Y in terms of good X is $1/2$ in each state with a unitary relative price of the goods across states.

The possibility that securities can be reallocated to attain a Pareto superior allocation when markets are incomplete was first illustrated by Hart (1975). He provided an example in which removing securities and hence decreasing the possibilities for trade actually resulted in a Pareto superior allocation. The intuition is similar to that provided in the example above. If markets are not complete, the introduction of a new security may change the spot market prices in such a way that utility of agents decreases unless they can make trades which are not available with the existing set of securities.

Hart also provided an example to illustrate another important point. If a typical security promises to pay (or receive) goods in more than one state, then the set of trades spanned by the market may depend on the spot prices. He used this insight to construct an example in which there are two competitive equilibria, one of which Pareto dominates the other. Hart's work has been generalized in a number of directions by Geanakoplos and Polemarchakis (1985). They have established that when markets are incomplete and there are at least two goods in each state, then the allocation is 'generically' constrained suboptimal; this implies in particular that Hart's example of Pareto dominance is not generic.

Recently, Cass (1985) and Geanakoplos and Mas-Colell (1985) have investigated the implications for equilibrium when some of the assets are 'nominal', i.e. assets in which the returns in any state are denominated in some unit of account. Subject to a few qualifications, they have demonstrated that, so long as markets are incomplete, the dimension of indeterminancy is generally equal to the number of states minus one.

To understand the logic of this result, suppose that the prices in each spot market $s \in \{1, \ldots, S\}$, are normalized so that they sum to q_s. Then for each vector, $q = (q_1, \ldots, q_s)$, any given nominal asset corresponds to a unique real asset which pays q_s units of each good in each state s. Since markets are incomplete, any nonproportional change in q will generically change the set of (state contingent) commodity bundles spanned by the set of securities (together with the spot markets). Consequently, the equilibrium allocation associated with any two (non-proportional) vectors q will generally be different. We conclude that generically the dimension of equilibrium allocations should be $S - 1$.

BIBLIOGRAPHY

Arrow, K. 1953. The role of securities in the optimal allocation of risk-bearing. Reprinted in *Essays in the Theory of Risk-Bearing*, Chicago: Markham Publishing Co., 1973.

Cass, D. 1985. On the 'number' of equilibrium allocations with incomplete financial markets. CARESS Working Paper No. 85–16, University of Pennsylvania.

Geanakoplos, J. and Mas-Colell, A. 1985. Real indeterminacy with financial assets. Yale University, October.

Geanakoplos, J. and Polemarchakis, H. 1985. Existence, regularity, and constrained suboptimality of competitive portfolio allocations when the asset market is incomplete. Yale University, October.

Hart, O. 1975. On the optimality of equilibrium when the market structure is incomplete. *Journal of Economic Theory* 11(3), December, 418–43.

Townsend, R. 1978. On the optimality of forward markets. *American Economic Review* 68(1), March, 54–66.

Market Failure

JOHN O. LEDYARD

The best way to understand market failure is first to understand market success, the ability of a collection of idealized competitive markets to achieve an equilibrium allocation of resources which is Pareto optimal. This characteristic of markets, which was loosely conjectured by Adam Smith, has received its clearest expression in the theorems of modern welfare economics. For our purposes, the first of these, named the First Fundamental Theorem of welfare economics, is of most interest. Simply stated it reads: (1) if there are enough markets, (2) if all consumers and producers behave competitively, and (3) if an equilibrium exists, then the allocation of resources in that equilibrium will be Pareto optimal. (See Arrow, 1951, or Debreu, 1959.) Market failure is said to occur when the conclusion of this theorem is false; that is, when the allocations achieved with markets are not efficient.

Market failure is often the justification for political intervention in the marketplace (for one view, see Bator, 1958, section V). The standard argument is that if market allocations are inefficient, everyone can and should be made better off. To understand the feasibility and desirability of such Pareto-improving interventions, we must achieve a deeper understanding of the sources of market failure. Since each must be due to the failure of at least one of the three conditions of the First Theorem, we will consider those conditions one at a time.

The first condition requires there to be enough markets. Although there are no definitive guidelines as to what constitutes 'enough', the general principle is that if any actor in the economy cares about something that also involves an interaction with at least one other actor, then there should be a market for that something; it should have a price (Arrow, 1969). This is true whether the something is consumption of bread, consumption of the smoke from a factory, or the amount of national defence. The first of these examples is a standard private good, the second is an externality and the third is a public good. All need to be priced if we are to achieve a Pareto-optimal allocation of resources; without these markets, actors may be unable to inform others about mutually beneficial trades which can leave both better off.

The informational role of markets is clearly highlighted by a classic example of market failure analysed by Scitovsky (1954). In this example, a steel industry, which must decide now whether to operate, will be profitable if and only if a railroad industry will begin operations within five years. The railroad industry will be profitable if and only if the steel industry is operating when the railroad industry begins its own operations. Clearly each cares about the other and it is efficient for each to operate; the steel industry begins today and the railroad industry begins later. Nevertheless, if there are only spot markets for steel, the railroad industry cannot easily inform the steel industry of its interests through the marketplace. This inability to communicate desirable interactions and to coordinate timing is an example of market failure and has been used as a justification for public involvement in development efforts; a justification for national planning. However, if we correctly recognize that there are simply too few markets, we can easily find another solution by creating a futures market for steel. If the railroad industry is able to pay today for delivery of steel at some specified date in the future then both steel and railroad industries are able to make the other aware of their interests through the marketplace. It is easy to show that as long as agents behave competitively and equilibrium exists the addition of futures markets will solve this type of market failure.

A completely different example of the informational role of markets arises when actors in the marketplace are asymmetrically informed about the true state of an uncertain world. The classic example involves securities markets where insiders may know something that outsiders do not. Even if it is important and potentially profitable for the uninformed actor to know the information held by the informed actor, there may not be enough markets to generate an efficient allocation of resources. To see this most clearly, suppose there are only two possible states of the world. Further suppose there are two consumers, one of whom knows the true state and one of whom thinks each state is equally likely. If the only markets that exist are markets for physical commodities then the equilibrium allocation will not in general be Pareto optimal. One solution is to create a contingent claims market. An 'insurance' contract can be created in which delivery and acceptance of a specified amount of the commodity is contingent on the true state of the world. Assuming both parties can, ex post, mutually verify which is indeed the true state of the world, if both behave competitively and an equilibrium allocation exists, it will be Pareto optimal, given the information structure. A more general and precise version of this theorem can be found in Radner (1968).

Analysing this example further, we note that in equilibrium the prices of commodities in the state which is not true will be close to or equal to zero, since at positive prices the informed actor will always be willing to supply an infinite amount contingent on the false state, knowing delivery will be unnecessary. If the uninformed actor is clever and realizes that prices will behave this way in equilibrium then he can become informed simply by observing which contingency prices are zero. If he then uses this information which has been freely provided by the market, the equilibrium will be Pareto optimal under full information. In a very simple form, this is the idea behind rational expectations (see Muth, 1961). With clever competitive actors, it may not be necessary to create all markets in order to achieve a Pareto-efficient equilibrium allocation.

Completing markets seems to be an easy technique to correct market failure. The suggestions that taxes and subsidies (Pigou, 1932) or property rights reassignments (Coase, 1960) can cure market failure follow directly from this observation. However, an unintended consequence can sometimes occur after the creation of these markets. In some cases, adding more markets may cause conditions (2) and (3) of the First Theorem to be false. Curing one form of market failure can lead to another. To understand how this happens and how the second condition requiring competitive behaviour can be affected, consider the informed consumer in our previous example. If he realizes that the uninformed consumer is going to make inferences based indirectly on his actions, then he should not behave competitively because he could do better by pretending to be uninformed. He can, by strategically limiting the supply of information of which he is the monopoly holder, do better than if he behaved competitively. It is only his willingness to supply infinite amounts of the commodity in the false state that gives away his knowledge. Supplying only a little commodity contingent on that (false) state in return for a small payment today would not allow the uninformed agent to infer anything, and would allow the informed agent to make a profit from his monopoly position. This is not very different from the standard example of a violation of condition (2), monopoly supply of a commodity.

A different example of this phenomenon of unintended outcomes arises when markets are created to allocate public goods. It is now well known that the introduction of personal, Lindahl prices to price individual demands for a public good does indeed lead to Pareto-optimal allocations if consumers behave competitively (see Foley, 1970). However, under this scheme, each agent becomes a monopsonist in one of the created markets and, therefore, has an incentive to understate demand and not to take prices as given. This is the phenomenon of 'free riding', often alluded to as the reason why the creation of markets may not be a viable solution to market failure. To understand why, let us now examine the second condition of the First Theorem in more detail.

The second condition of the First Theorem about market success is that all actors in the marketplace behave competitively. This means that each must act as if they cannot affect prices and, given prices, as if they follow optimizing behaviour. Consumers maximize preferences subject to budget constraints and producers maximize profits, each taking prices as fixed parameters. This condition will be violated when actors can affect the values that equilibrium prices take and in so doing be better off. The standard example of market failure due to a violation of this condition is monopoly in which one actor is the sole supplier of an output. By artificially restricting supply, this actor can cause higher prices and make himself better off even though the resulting equilibrium allocation will be inefficient.

Can we correct market failure due to non-competitive behaviour? To find an answer let us first isolate those conditions under which agents find it in their interests to follow competitive behaviour. The work of Roberts and Postlewaite (1976) has established that if each agent holds only a small amount of resources relative to the aggregate available, then they will usually be unable to manipulate prices in any significant way and will act as price takers. It is the depth of the market that is important. This is also true when the commodity is information. If each agent is informationally small, in the sense that he either knows very little or what he does know is of little importance to others, then he loses little by behaving competitively (see Postlewaite and Schmeidler, 1986). On the other hand, if he is informationally important, as in the earlier example, he may have an incentive to behave non-competitively. The key is the size of the agent's resources, both real and informational, relative to the market.

The solution to market failure from non-competitive behaviour then seems to be to ensure that all agents are both resource and informationally small. Of course this must be accomplished through direct intervention, as in the anti-trust laws and the securities market regulations of the United States, and may not be feasible. For example, it may not be possible to correct this type of market failure by simply telling agents to behave competitively. In such an attempt, one would try to enforce a public policy that all firms must charge prices equal to the marginal cost of output. But, unless the costs and production technology of the firm can be directly monitored, a monopolist can easily act as if he were setting price equal to marginal cost while using a false cost curve. It would be impossible for an outside observer to distinguish this non-competitive behaviour from competitive behaviour without directly monitoring the cost curve. If the monopolist were a consumer whose preferences were unobservable, then even monitoring would not help. In general, market failure from non-competitive behaviour is difficult to correct while still retaining markets. We will hint at some alternatives below.

Expansion of the number of markets can also lead to violations of the third condition of the First Theorem. For illustration we consider three examples. The first and simplest of these is the case of increasing returns to scale in production. The classic case is a product which requires a fixed set-up cost and a constant marginal cost to produce. (More generally we could consider non-convex production possibilities sets.) If the firm acts competitively in this industry and if the price is above marginal cost, the firm will supply an infinite amount. If the price is at or below marginal cost the firm will produce nothing. If the consumers' quantity demand is positive and finite at a price equal to marginal cost, then there is no price such that supply equals demand. Equilibrium does not exist. The real implication of this situation is not that markets do not equilibrate or that trade does not take place; it is that a natural monopoly exists. There is room for at most one efficient firm in this industry. Again it is the assumption of competitive behaviour which is ultimately violated.

The next example, due to Starrett (1972), involves an external diseconomy. Suppose there is an upstream firm that pollutes the water and a downstream firm that requires clean water as an input into its production process. It is easy to show that if such a diseconomy exists and if the downstream firm always has the option of inaction (i.e. it can use no inputs to produce no outputs at zero cost), then the aggregate production possibilities set of the economy when expanded to allow enough markets cannot be convex. (See Ledyard, 1976 for a formal proof.) If the production possibilities set of the economy is non-convex then, as in the last example, it is possible that a competitive equilibrium will not exist. Expansion of the number of markets to solve the inefficiencies due to external diseconomies can lead to a situation in which there is no competitive equilibrium.

The last example, first observed by Green (1977) and Kreps (1977), arises in situations of asymmetric information. Recall the earlier example in which one agent was fully informed about the state of the world while the other thought each state was equally likely. Suppose preferences and endowments in each state are such that if both know the state then the equilibrium prices in each state are the same. Further, suppose that if the uninformed agent makes no inferences about the state from the other's behaviour then there will be different prices in each state. Then no (rational expectations) equilibrium will exist. If the informed agent tries to make inferences the prices will not inform him, and if the uninformed agent does not try to make inferences the prices will inform him. Further, it is fairly easy to show that if a market for information could be created (ignoring incentives to hide information) the resulting possibilities set is in general non-convex. In either case there is no equilibrium.

Most examples of non-existence of equilibrium seem to lead inevitably to non-competitive behaviour. In our example of non-existence due to informational asymmetries, it is natural for the informed agent to behave as a monopolist with respect to that information. In the example of the diseconomy, if a market is created between the upstream and the downstream firm, each becomes a monopoly. If there is a single polluter and many pollutees, the polluter holds a position similar to a monopsony. The non-existence problem due to the fundamental non-convexity caused by the use of markets to eliminate external diseconomies is simply finessed by one or more of the participants assuming non-competitive behaviour. An outcome occurs but it is not competitive and, therefore, not efficient.

Market failure, the inefficient allocation of resources with markets, can occur if there are too few markets, non-competitive behaviour, or non-existence problems. Many suggested solutions for market failure, such as tax-subsidy schemes, property rights assignments and special pricing arrangements are simply devices for the creation of more markets. If this can be done in a way that avoids non-convexities and ensures depth of participation, then the remedy can be beneficial and the new allocation should be efficient. On the other hand, if the addition of markets creates either non-convexities or shallow participation, then attempts to cure market failure from too few markets will simply lead to market failure from monopolistic behaviour. Market failure in this latter situation is fundamental. Examples are natural monopolies, external diseconomies, public goods and informational monopolies. If one wants to achieve efficient allocations of resources in the presence of such fundamental failures, one must accept self-interested behaviour and explore non-market alternatives. A literature using this approach, sometimes called implementation theory and sometimes called mechanism design theory, was initiated by Hurwicz (1972) and is surveyed in Groves and Ledyard (1986).

BIBLIOGRAPHY

Arrow, K. 1951. An extension of the basic theorems of classical welfare economics. In *Proceedings of the Second Berkeley Symposium on Mathematical Statistics and Probability*, ed. J. Neyman, Berkeley: University of California Press.

Arrow, K. 1969. The organization of economic activity: issues pertinent to the choice of market versus non-market allocation. In Joint Economic Committee. *The Analysis and Evaluation of Public Expenditures: The PPB System*, Washington, DC: Government Printing Office, 47–64.

Bator, F. 1958. The anatomy of market failure. *Quarterly Journal of Economics*, 351–79.

Coase, R. 1960. The problem of social cost. *Journal of Law and Economics* 3, 1–44.

Debreu, G. 1959. *Theory of Value: an axiomatic analysis of economic equilibrium.* Cowles Foundation Monograph No. 17. New York: Wiley.

Foley, D. 1970. Lindahl's solution and the core of an economy with public goods. *Econometrica* 38, 66–72.

Green, J. 1977. The nonexistence of informational equilibria. *Review of Economic Studies* 44, 451–63.

Groves, T. and Ledyard, J. 1986. Incentive compatibility ten years later. In *Information, Incentives, and Economic Mechanisms*, ed. T. Groves, R. Radner and S. Reiter, Minneapolis: University of Minnesota Press.

Hurwicz, L. 1972. On informationally decentralized systems. In *Decision and Organization*, ed. C.B. McGuire and R. Radner, Amsterdam: North-Holland.

Kreps, D. 1977. A note on 'fulfilled expectations' equilibria. *Journal of Economic Theory* 14, 32–43.

Ledyard, J. 1976. Discussion of 'On the Nature of Externalities'. In *Theory and Measurement of Economic Externalities*, ed. S. Lin, New York: Academic Press.

Muth, J. 1961. Rational expectations and the theory of price movements. *Econometrica* 29, 315–35.

Pigou, A. 1932. *The Economics of Welfare*. 4th edn, New York: Macmillan; New York: St. Martin's Press, 1952.

Postlewaite, A. and Schmeidler, D. 1986. Differential information and strategic behaviour in economic environments: a general equilibrium approach. In *Information, Incentives, and Economic Mechanisms*, ed. T. Groves, R. Radner and S. Reiter, Minneapolis: University of Minnesota Press.

Radner, R. 1968. Competitive equilibrium under uncertainty. *Econometrica* 36, 31–58.

Roberts, J. and Postlewaite, A. 1976. The incentives for price-taking behavior in large exchange economies. *Econometrica* 44, 115–27.

Scitovsky, T. 1954. Two concepts of external economies. *Journal of Political Economy* 62, 70–82.

Starrett, D. 1972. Fundamental non-convexities in the theory of externalities. *Journal of Economic Theory* 4, 180–99.

Mechanism Design

ROGER B. MYERSON

1. OVERVIEW. A mechanism is a specification of how economic decisions are determined as a function of the information that is known by the individuals in the economy. In this sense, almost any kind of market institution or economic organization can be viewed, in principle, as a mechanism. Thus mechanism theory can offer a unifying conceptual structure in which a wide range of institutions can be compared, and optimal institutions can be identified.

The basic insight of mechanism theory is that *incentive constraints* should be considered coequally with *resource constraints* in the formulation of the economic problem. In situations where individuals' private information and actions are difficult to monitor, the need to give people an incentive to share information and exert efforts may impose constraints on economic systems just as much as the limited availability of raw materials. The theory of mechanism design is the fundamental mathematical methodology for analysing these constraints.

The study of mechanisms begins with a special class of mechanisms called *direct-revelation* mechanisms, which operate as follows. There is assumed to be a mediator who can communicate separately and confidentially with every individual in the economy. This mediator may be thought of as a trustworthy person, or as a computer tied into a telephone network. At each stage of the economic process, each individual is asked to report all of his private information (that is, everything that he knows that other individuals in the economy might not know) to the mediator. After receiving these reports confidentially from every individual, the mediator may then confidentially recommend some action or move to each individual. A direct-revelation mechanism is any rule for specifying how the mediator's recommendations are determined, as a function of the reports received.

A direct-revelation mechanism is said to be *incentive compatible* if, when each individual expects that the others will be honest and obedient to the mediator, then no individual could ever expect to do better (given the information available to him) by reporting dishonestly to the mediator or by disobeying the mediator's recommendations. That is, if honesty and obedience is an equilibrium (in the game-theoretic sense) then the mechanism is incentive compatible.

The analysis of such incentive-compatible direct-revelation mechanisms might at first seem to be of rather narrow interest, because such fully centralized mediation of economic systems is rare, and incentives for dishonesty and disobedience are commonly observed in real economic institutions. The importance of studying such mechanisms is derived from two key insights: (i) for any equilibrium of any general mechanism, there is an incentive-compatible direct-revelation mechanism that is essentially equivalent; and (ii) the set of incentive-compatible direct-revelation mechanisms has simple mathematical properties that often make it easy to characterize, because it can be defined by a set of linear inequalities. Thus, by analysing incentive-compatible direct-revelation mechanisms, we can characterize what can be accomplished in all possible equilibria of all possible mechanisms, for a given economic situation.

Insight (i) above is known as the *revelation principle*. It was first recognized by Gibbard (1973), but for a somewhat narrower solution concept (dominant strategies, instead of Bayesian equilibrium) and for the case where only informational honesty is problematic (no moral hazard). The formulation of the revelation principle for the broader solution concept of Bayesian equilibrium, but still in the case of purely informational problems, was recognized independently by many authors around 1978 (see Dasgupta, Hammond, and Maskin, 1979; Harris and Townsend, 1981; Holmstrom, 1977; Myerson, 1979; and Rosenthal, 1978). Aumann's (1974, 1987) concept of *correlated equilibrium* gave the first expression to the revelation principle in the case where only obedient choice of actions is problematic (pure moral hazard, no adverse selection). The synthesis of the revelation principle for general Bayesian games with incomplete information, where both honesty and obedience are problematic, was given by Myerson (1982). A generalization of the revelation principle to multistage games was stated by Myerson (1986).

The intuition behind the revelation principle is as follows. First, a central mediator who has collected all relevant information known by all individuals in the economy could issue recommendations to the individuals so as to simulate the outcome of any organizational or market system, centralized or decentralized. After the individuals have revealed all of their information to the mediator, he can simply tell them to do whatever they would have done in the other system. Second, the more information that an individual has, the harder it may be to prevent him from finding ways to gain by disobeying the mediator. So the incentive constraints will be least binding when the mediator reveals to each individual only the minimal information needed to identify his own recommended action, and nothing else about the reports or recommendations of other individuals. So, if we assume that the mediator is a discrete and trustworthy information-processing device, with no costs of processing information, then there is no loss of generality in assuming that each individual will confidentially reveal all of his information to the mediator (maximal revelation to the trustworthy mediator), and the mediator in return will reveal to each individual only his own recommended action (minimal revelation to the individuals whose behaviour is subject to incentive constraints).

The formal proof of the revelation principle is difficult only because it is cumbersome to develop the notation for defining, in full generality, the set of all general mechanisms, and for defining equilibrium behaviour by the individuals in any given mechanism. Once all of this notation is in place, the construction of the equivalent incentive-compatible direct-revelation mechanism is straightforward. Given any mechanism and any equilibrium of the mechanism, we simply specify that the mediator's recommended actions are those that would result in the given mechanism if everyone behaved as specified in the given equilibrium when their actual private information was as reported to the mediator. To check that this constructed direct-revelation mechanism is incentive compatible, notice that any player who could gain by disobeying the mediator could also gain by similarly disobeying his own strategy in the given equilibrium of the given mechanism, which is impossible (by definition of equilibrium).

2. MATHEMATICAL FORMULATIONS. Let us offer a precise general formulation of the proof of the revelation principle in the case where individuals have private information about which they could lie, but there is no question of disobedience of recommended actions or choices. For a general model, suppose that there are n individuals, numbered 1 to n. Let C denote the set of all possible combinations of actions or resource allocations that the individuals may choose in the economy. Each individual in the economy may have some private information about his preferences and endowments, and about his beliefs about other individuals' private information. Following Harsanyi (1967), we may refer to the state of an individual's private information as his *type*. Let T_i denote the set of possible types for any individual i, and let $T = T_1 \times \ldots \times T_n$ denote the set of all possible combinations of types for all individuals.

The preferences of each individual i may be generally described by some *payoff function* u_i: $C \times T \rightarrow \mathbb{R}$, where $u_i(c, (t_1, \ldots, t_n))$ denotes the payoff, measured in some von Neumann–Morgenstern utility scale, that individual i would get if c was the realized resource allocation in C when $(t_1, \ldots, t_n)$ denotes the actual types of the individuals $1, \ldots, n$ respectively. For short, we may write $t = (t_1, \ldots, t_n)$ to describe a combination of types for all individuals.

The beliefs of each individual i, as a function of his type, may be generally described by some function $p_i(\cdot|\cdot)$, where $p_i(t_1, \ldots, t_{i-1}, t_{i+1}, \ldots, t_n|t_i)$ denotes the probability that individual i would assign to the event that the other individuals have types as in $(t_1, \ldots, t_{i-1}, t_{i+1}, \ldots, t_n)$, when i knows that his own type is t_i. For short, we may write $t_{-i} = (t_1, \ldots, t_{i-1}, t_{i+1}, \ldots, t_n)$, to describe a combination of types for all individuals other than i. We may let $T_{-i} = T_1 \times \ldots \times T_{i-1} \times T_{i+1} \times \ldots \times T_n$ denote the set of all possible combinations of types for the individuals other than i.

The general model of an economy defined by these structures $(C, T_1, \ldots, T_n, u_i, \ldots, u_n\, p_1, \ldots, p_n)$ is called a *Bayesian collective-choice problem.*

Given a Bayesian collective-choice problem, a general *mechanism* would be any function of the form $\gamma: S_1 \times \ldots \times S_n \to C$, where, for each i, S_i is a nonempty set that denotes the set of strategies that are available for individual i in this mechanism. That is, a general mechanism specifies the strategic options that each individual may choose among, and the social choice or allocation of resources that would result from any combination of strategies that the individuals might choose. Given a mechanism, an *equilibrium* is any specification of how each individual may choose his strategy in the mechanism as a function of his type, so that no individual, given only his own information, could expect to do better by unilaterally deviating from the equilibrium. That is, $\sigma = (\sigma_1, \ldots, \sigma_n)$ is an equilibrium of the mechanism γ if, for each individual i, σ_i is a function from T_i to S_i, and, for every t_i in T_i and every s_i in S_i,

$$\Sigma_{t_{-i} \in T_{-i}} p_i(t_{-i}|t_i) u_i(\gamma(\sigma(t)), t) \geqslant \Sigma_{t_{-i} \in T_{-i}} p_i(t_{-i}|t_i) u_i(\gamma(\sigma_{-i}(t_{-i}), s_i), t).$$

(Here $\sigma(t) = (\sigma_1(t_1), \ldots, \sigma_n(t_n))$ and $(\sigma_{-i}(t_{-i}), s_i) = (\sigma_1(t_1), \ldots, \sigma_{i-1}(t_{i-1}), s_i, \sigma_{i+1}(t_{i+1}), \ldots, \sigma_n(t_n))$.) Thus, in an equilibrium σ, no individual i, knowing only his own type t_i, could increase his expected payoff by changing his strategy from $\sigma_i(t_i)$ to some other strategy s_i, when he expects all other individuals to behave as specified by the equilibrium σ. (This concept of equilibrium is sometimes often called *Bayesian equilibrium* because it respects the assumption that each player knows only his own type when he chooses his strategy in S_i. For a comparison with other concepts of equilibrium, see Dasgupta, Hammond, and Maskin (1979) and Palfrey and Srivastava (1987).)

In this context, a direct-revelation mechanism is any mechanism such that the set S_i of possible strategies for each player i is the same as his set of possible types T_i. A direct-revelation mechanism is (Bayesian) incentive-compatible iff it is an equilibrium (in the Bayesian sense defined above) for every individual always to report his true type. Thus, $\mu: T_1 \times \ldots \times T_n \to C$ is an incentive-compatible direct-revelation mechanism if, for each individual i and every pair of types t_i and r_i in T_i,

$$\Sigma_{t_{-i} \in T_{-i}} p_i(t_{-i}|t_i) u_i(\mu(t), t) \geqslant \Sigma_{t_{-i} \in T_{-i}} p_i(t_{-i}|t_i) u_i(\mu(t_{-i}, r_i), t).$$

(Here $(t_{-i}, r_i) = (t_1, \ldots, t_{i-1}, r_i, t_{i+1}, \ldots, t_n)$.) We may refer to these constraints as the *informational incentive constraints* on the direct-revelation mechanism μ. These informational incentive constraints are the formal representation of the economic problem of *adverse selection*, so they may also be called adverse-selection constraints (or self-selection constraints).

Now, to prove the revelation principle, given any general mechanism γ and any Bayesian equilibrium σ of the mechanism γ, let μ be the direct-revelation mechanism μ defined so that, for every t in T,

$$\mu(t) = \gamma(\sigma(t)).$$

Then this mechanism μ always leads to the same social choice as γ does, when the individuals behave as in the equilibrium σ. Furthermore, μ is incentive compatible because, for any individual i and any two types t_i and r_i in T_i,

$$\Sigma_{t_{-i}\in T_{-i}} p_i(t_{-i}|t_i)u_i(\mu(t),t) = \Sigma_{t_{-i}\in T_{-i}} p_i(t_{-i}|t_i)u_i(\gamma(\sigma(t)),t)$$

$$\geqslant \Sigma_{t_{-i}\in T_{-i}} p_i(t_{-i}|t_i)u_i(\gamma(\sigma_{-i}(t_{-i}),\sigma_i(r_i)),t) = \Sigma_{t_{-i}\in T_{-i}} p_i(t_{-i}|t_i)u_i(\mu(t_{-i},r_i),t).$$

Thus, μ is an incentive-compatible direct-revelation mechanism that is equivalent to the given mechanism γ with its equilibrium σ.

Notice that the revelation principle asserts that any pair consisting of a mechanism *and* an equilibrium is equivalent to an incentive-compatible direct-revelation mechanism. Thus, a general mechanism that has several equilibria may correspond to several different incentive-compatible mechanisms, depending on which equilibrium is considered.

Furthermore, the same general mechanism will generally have different equilibria in the context of different Bayesian collective-choice problems, where the structure of individuals' beliefs and payoffs are different. For example, consider a first-price sealed-bid auction where there are five potential bidders who are risk-neutral with independent private values drawn from the same distribution over \$0 to \$10. If the bidders' values are drawn from a uniform distribution over this interval then there is an equilibrium in which each bidder bids 4/5 of his value. On the other hand, if the bidders' values are drawn instead from a distribution with a probability density that is proportional to the square of the value, then there is an equilibrium in which each bidder bids 8/9 of his value. So in one situation the first-price sealed-bid auction (a general mechanism) corresponds to an incentive-compatible mechanism in which the bidder who reports the highest value gets the object for 4/5 of his reported value; but in the other situation it corresponds to an incentive-compatible mechanism in which the bidder who reports the highest value gets the object for 8/9 of his reported value. There is no incentive-compatible direct-revelation mechanism that is equivalent to the first-price sealed-bid auction in all situations, independently of the bidders' beliefs about each others' values. Thus, if we want to design a mechanism that has good properties in the context of many different Bayesian collective-choice problems, we cannot necessarily restrict out attention to incentive-compatible direct-revelation mechanisms, and so our task is correspondingly more difficult. (See Wilson (1985) for a remarkable effort at this kind of difficult question.)

Even an incentive-compatible mechanism itself may have other dishonest equilibria that correspond to different incentive-compatible mechanisms. Thus, when we talk about selecting an incentive-compatible mechanism and assume that it will then be played according to its honest equilibrium, we are implicitly making an assumption about the selection of an equilibrium as well as of a mechanism or communication structure. Thus, for example, when we say that a particular incentive-compatible mechanism maximizes a given individual's expected utility, we mean that, if you could choose any general mechanism for coordinating the individuals in the economy and if you could also (by some public statement, as a focal arbitrator, using Schelling's (1960) *focal-point effect*) designate the equilibrium that the individuals would play in your mechanism, then you could not give this given individual a higher expected utility than by choosing this incentive-compatible mechanism and its honest equilibrium.

In many situations, an individual may have a right to refuse to participate in an economic system or organization. For example, a consumer generally has the right to refuse to participate in any trading scheme and instead just consume his initial endowment. If we let $w_i(t_i)$ denote the utility payoff that individual i would get if he refused to participate when his type is t_i, and if we assume that an individual can make the choice not to participate after learning his type, then an incentive-compatible mechanism μ must also satisfy the following constraint, for every individual i and every possible type t_i:

$$\Sigma_{t_{-i} \in T_{-i}} p_i(t_{-i}|t_i) u_i(\mu(t), t) \geqslant w_i(t_1).$$

These constraints are called *participational incentive constraints*, or *individual-rationality* constraints.

In the analysis of Bayesian collective-choice problems, we have supposed that the only incentive problem was to get people to share their information, and to agree to participate in the mechanism in the first place. More generally, a social choice may be privately controlled by one or more individuals who cannot be trusted to follow some prespecified plan when it is not in their best interests. For example, suppose now that the choice in C is privately controlled by some individual (call him 'individual 0') whose choice of an action in C cannot be regulated. To simplify matters her, let us suppose that this individual 0 has no private information. Let $p_0(t)$ denote the probability that this individual would assign to the event that $t = (t_1, \ldots, t_n)$ is the profile of types for the other n individuals, and let $u_0(c, t)$ denote the utility payoff that this individual receives if he chooses action c when t is the actual profile of types. Then, to give this active individual an incentive to obey the recommendations of a mediator who is implenting the direct-revelation mechanism μ, μ must satisfy

$$\Sigma_{t \in T} p_0(t) u_0(\mu(c), t) \geqslant \Sigma_{t \in T} p_0(t) u_0(\delta(\mu(c)), t)$$

for every function $\delta: C \rightarrow C$. These constraints assert that obeying the actions recommended by the mediator is better for this individual than any disobedient strategy δ under which he would choose $\delta(c)$ if the mediator recommended c. Such constraints are called *strategic incentive constraints* or *moral-hazard constraints*, because they are the formal representation of the economic problem of moral hazard.

For a formulation of general incentive constraints that apply when individuals both have private information and control private actions, see Myerson (1982) or (1985).

3. APPLICATIONS. In general, the mechanism-theoretic approach to economic problems is to list the constraints that an incentive-compatible mechanism must satisfy, and to try to characterize the incentive-compatible mechanisms that have properties of interest.

For example, one early contribution of mechanism theory was the derivation of general *revenue equivalence* theorems in auction theory. Ortega–Reichert (1968) found that, when bidders are risk-neutral and have private values for the object being sold that are independent and drawn from the same distribution, then a remarkably diverse collection of different auction mechanisms all generate the same expected revenue to the seller, when bidders use equilibrium strategies. In all of these different mechanisms and equilibria, it turned out that the bidder whose value for the object was highest would always end up getting the object, while a bidder whose value for the object was zero would never pay anything. By analysing the incentive constraints, Harris and Raviv (1981), Myerson (1981) and Riley and Samuelson (1981) showed that all incentive-compatible mechanisms with these properties would necessarily generate the same expected revenue, in such economic situations.

Using methods of constrained optimization, the problem of finding the incentive-compatible mechanism that maximizes some given objective (one individual's expected utility, or some social welfare function) can be solved for many examples. The resulting optimal mechanisms often have remarkable qualitative properties.

For example, suppose a seller, with a single indivisible object to sell, faces 5 potential buyers or bidders, whose private values for the object are independently drawn from a uniform distribution over the interval from $0 to $10. If the objective is to maximize the sellers' expected revenue, optimal auction mechanisms exist and all have the property that the object is sold to the bidder with the highest value for it, except that the seller keeps the object in the event that the bidders' values are all less than $5. Such a result may seem surprising, because this event could occur with positive probability (1/32) and in this event the seller is getting no revenue in an 'optimal' auction, even though any bidder would almost surely be willing to pay him a positive price for the object. Nevertheless, no incentive compatible mechanism (satisfying the participational and informational incentive constraints) can offer the seller higher expected utility than these optimal auctions, and thus no equilibrium of any general auction mechanism can offer higher expected revenue either. Maximizing expected revenue requires a positive probability of seemingly wasteful allocation.

The threat of keeping the object, when all bidders report values below $5, increases the seller's expected revenue because it gives the bidders an incentive to bid higher and pay more when their values are above $5. In many other economic environments, we can similarly prove the optimality of mechanisms in which seemingly wasteful threats are carried out with positive probability. People have intuitively understood that costly threats are often made to give some individual an incentive to reveal some information or choose some action, and the analysis of incentive constraints allows us to formalize this understanding rigorously.

In some situations, incentive constraints imply that such seemingly wasteful allocations may have to occur with positive probability in all incentive-compatible mechanisms, and so also in all equilibria of all general mechanisms. For example, Myerson and Satterthwaite (1983) considered bilateral bargaining problems between a seller of some object and a potential buyer, both of whom are risk-neutral and have independent private values for the object that are drawn out of distributions that have continuous positive probability densities over some pair of intervals that have an intersection of positive length. Under these technical (but apparently quite weak) assumptions, it is impossible to satisfy the participational and informational incentive constraints with any mechanism in which the buyer gets the object whenever it is worth more to him than to the buyer. Thus, we cannot hope to guarantee the attainment of full ex-post efficiency of resource allocations in bilateral bargaining problems where the buyer and seller. Thus, we cannot hope to guarantee the attainment of full ex-post efficiency with welfare and efficiency questions, it may be more productive to try to characterize the incentive-compatible mechanisms that maximize the expected total gains from trade, or that maximize the probability that a mutually beneficial trade will occur. For example, in the bilateral bargaining problem where the seller's and buyer's private values for the object are independent random variables drawn from a uniform distribution over the interval from $0 to $10, both of these objectives are maximized subject to incentive constraints by mechanisms in which the buyer gets the object if and only if his value is greater than the seller's value by $2.50 or more. Under such a mechanism, the event that the seller will keep the object when it is actually worth more to the buyer has probability 7/32, but no equilibrium of any general mechanism can generate a lower probability of this event.

The theory of mechanism design has fundamental implications about the domain of applicability of Coase's (1960) theorem, which asserts the irrelevance of initial property rights to efficiency of final allocations. The unavoidable possibility of failure to realize mutually beneficial trades, in such bilateral trading problems with two-sided uncertainty, can be interpreted as one of the 'transactions costs' that limits the validity of Coase's theorem. Indeed, as Samuelson (1985) has emphasized, reassignment of property rights generally changes the payoffs that individuals can guarantee themselves without selling anything, which changes the right-hand sides of the participational incentive constraints, which in turn can change the maximal social welfare achievable by an optimal incentive-compatible mechanism.

For example, consider again the case where there is one object and two individuals who have private values for the object that are independent random variables drawn from a uniform distribution over the interval from $0 to $10. When we assumed above that one was the 'seller', we meant that he had the right to keep the object and pay nothing to anyone, until he agreed to some other arrangement. Now, let us suppose instead that the rights to the object are distributed equally between the two individuals. Suppose that the object is a divisible good and each individual has a right to take half of the good and pay nothing, unless he agrees to some other arrangement. (Assume that, if an individual's value for the whole good is t_i, then his value for half would be $t_i/2$.) With this symmetric assignment of property rights, we can design incentive-compatible mechanisms in which the object always ends up being owned entirely by the individual who has the higher value for it, as Cramton, Gibbons and Klemperer (1987) have shown.

For example, consider the game in which each individual independently puts money in an envelope, and then the individual who put more money in his envelope gets the object, while the other individual takes the money in both envelopes. This game has an equilibrium in which each individual puts into his envelope an amount equal to one-third of his value for the whole good. This equilibrium of this game is equivalent to an incentive-compatible direct-revelation mechanism in which the individual who reports the higher value pays one-third of his value to buy out the other individual's half-share. This mechanism would violate the participational incentive constraints if one individual had a right to the whole good (in which case, for example, if his value were $10 then he would be paying $3.33 under this mechanism for a good that he already owned). But with rights to only half of the good, no type of either individual could expect to do better (at the beginning of the game, when he knows his own value but not the other's) by keeping his half and refusing to participate in this mechanism.

More generally, redistribution of property rights tends to reduce the welfare losses caused by incentive constraints when it creates what Lewis and Sappington (1988) have called *countervailing incentives*. In games where one individual is the seller and the other is the buyer, if either individual has an incentive to lie, it is usually because the seller wants to overstate his value or the buyer wants to understate his value. In the case where either individual may buy the other's half-share, neither individual can be sure at first whether he will be the buyer or the seller (unless he has the highest or lowest possible value). Thus, a buyer-like incentive to understate values, in the event where the other's value is lower, may help to cancel out a seller-like incentive to overstate values, in the event where the other's value is higher.

The theory of mechanism design can also help us to appreciate the importance of mediation in economic relationships and transactions. There are situations in which, if the individuals were required to communicate with each other only through perfect noiseless communication channels (e.g., in face-to-face dialogue), then the set of all possible equilibria would be much smaller than the set of incentive-compatible mechanisms that are achievable with a mediator. (Of course, the revelation principle asserts that the former set cannot be larger than the latter.)

For example, consider the following 'sender-receiver game' due to J. Farrell. Player 1 has a privately known type that may be α or β, but he has no payoff-relevant action to choose. Player 2 has no private information, but he must choose an action from the set $\{x, y, z\}$. The payoffs to players 1 and 2 respectively depend on 1's type and 2's action as follows.

	x	y	z
α	2, 3	1, 2	0, 0
β	4, − 3	8, − 1	0, 0

At the beginning of the game, player 2 believes that each of 1's two possible types has probability 1/2.

Suppose that, knowing his type, player 1 is allowed to choose a message in some arbitrarily rich language, and player 2 will hear player 1's message (with no noise or distortion) before choosing his action. In every equilibrium of this game, including the randomized equilibria, player 2 must choose y with probability one, after every message that player 1 may choose in equilibrium. (See Farrell, 1988, or Myerson, 1988.) If there were some message that player 1 could use to increase the probability of player 2 choosing x (e.g.: 'I am α, so choosing x would be best for us both!'), then he would always send such a message when his type was α. (It can be shown that no message could ever induce player 2 to randomize between x and z.) So not receiving such a message would lead 2 to infer that 1's type was β, which implies that 2 would rationally choose z whenever such a message was not sent, so that both types of 1 should always send the message (any randomization between x and y is better than z for both types of 1). But a message that is always sent by player 1, no matter what his type is, would convey no information to player 2, so that 2 would rationally choose his ex-ante optimal action y.

If we now allow the players to communicate through a mediator who uses a randomized mechanism, then we can apply the revelation principle to characterize the surprisingly large set of possible incentive-compatible mechanisms. Among all direct-revelation mechanisms that satisfy the relevant informational incentive constraints for player 1 and strategic incentive constraints for player 2, the best for player 2 is as follows: if player 1 reports to the mediator that his type is α then with probability 2/3 the mediator recommends x to player 2, and with probability 1/3 the mediator recommends y to player 2; if player 1 reports to the mediator that his type is β then with probability 2/3 the mediator recommends y to player 2, and with probability 1/3 the mediator recommends z to player 2. Notice that this mechanism is also better for player 1 than the unmediated equilibria when 1's type is α, although it is worse for 1 when his type is β.

Other mechanisms that player 2 might prefer would violate the strategic incentive constraint that player 2 should not expect to gain by choosing z instead of y when y is recommended. If player 2 could precommit himself always to obey the mediator's recommendations, then better mechanisms could be designed.

4. EFFICIENCY. The concept of efficiency becomes more difficult to define in economic situations where individuals have different private information at the time when the basic decisions about production and allocation are made. A welfare economist or social planner who analyses the Pareto efficiency of an economic system must use the perspective of an outsider, so he cannot base his analysis on the individuals' private information. Otherwise, public testimony as to whether an economic mechanism or its outcome would be 'efficient' could implicitly reveal some individuals' private information to other individuals, which could in turn alter their rational behaviour and change the outcome of the mechanism! Thus, Holmstrom and Myerson (1983) argued that efficiency should be considered as a property of mechanisms, rather than of the outcome or

allocation ultimately realized by the mechanism (which will depend on the individuals' private information).

Thus, a definition of Pareto efficiency in a Bayesian collective-choice problem must look something like this: 'a mechanism is efficient if there is no other feasible mechanism that may make some other individuals better off and will certainly not make other individuals worse off.' However, this definition is ambiguous in at least two ways.

First, we must specify whether the concept of feasibility takes incentive constraints into account or not. The concept of feasibility that ignores incentive constraints may be called *classical feasibility*. In these terms, the fundamental insight of mechanism theory is that incentive constraints are just as real as resource constraints, so that incentive compatibility may be a more fruitful concept than classical feasibility for welfare economics.

Second, we must specify what information is to be considered when, in determining whether an individual is 'better off' or 'worse off'. One possibility is to say that an individual is made worse off by a change that decreases his expected utility payoff as would be computed before his own type or any other individuals' types are specified. This is called the *ex ante* welfare criterion. A second possibility is to say that an individual is made worse off by a change that decreases his conditionally expected utility, given his own type (but not given the types of any other individuals). An outside observer, who does not know any individual's type, would then say that an individual may be made worse off, in this sense, if this conditionally expected utility would be decreased for at least one possible type of the individual. This is called the *interim* welfare criterion. A third possibility is to say that an individual is made worse off by a change that decreases his conditionally expected utility given the types of all individuals. An outside observer would then say that an individual may be worse off in this sense if his conditionally expected utility would be decreased for at least one possible combination of types for all the individuals. This is called the *ex post* welfare criterion.

If each individual knows his own type at the time when economic plans and decisions are made, then the interim welfare criterion should be most relevant to a social planner. Thus, Holmstrom and Myerson (1983) argue that, for welfare analysis in a Bayesian collective-choice problem, the most appropriate concept of efficiency is that which combines the interim welfare criterion and the incentive-compatible definition of feasibility. This concept is called *incentive efficiency*, or *interim incentive efficiency*. That is, a mechanism $\mu: T \to C$ is incentive efficient if it is an incentive-compatible mechanism and there does not exist any other incentive-compatible mechanism $\gamma: T \to C$ such that for every individual i and every type t_i in T_i,

$$\Sigma_{t_{-i} \in T_{-i}} p_i(t_{-i}|t_i) u_i(\gamma(c), t) \geqslant \Sigma_{t_{-i} \in T_{-i}} p_i(t_{-i}|t_i) u_i(\mu(c), t),$$

and there is at least one type of at least one individual for which this inequality is strict. If a mechanism is incentive efficient then it cannot be common knowledge among the individuals, at the stage when each knows only his own type, that there is some other incentive-compatible mechanism that no one would consider worse (given his own information) and some might consider strictly better.

For comparison, another important concept is classical ex post efficiency, defined using the ex post welfare criterion and the classical feasibility concept. That is, a mechanism $\mu: T \to C$ is (*classically*) *ex post efficient* iff there does not exist any other mechanism $\gamma: T \to C$ (not necessarily incentive compatible) such that, for every individual i and every combination of individuals' types t in $T = T_1 \times \ldots \times T_n$,

$$u_i(\gamma(t), t) \geqslant u_i(\mu(t), t),$$

with strict inequality for at least one individual and at least one combination of individuals' types.

The appeal of ex post efficiency is that there may seem to be something unstable about a mechanism that sometimes leads to outcomes such that, if everyone could share their information, they could identify another outcome that would make them all better off. However, we have seen that bargaining situations exist where no incentive-compatible mechanisms are ex post efficient. In such situations, the incentive constraints imply that rational individuals would be unable to share their information to achieve these gains, because if everyone were expected to do so then at least one type of one individual would have an incentive to lie.

Thus, a benevolent outside social planner who is persuaded by the usual Paretian arguments should choose some incentive-efficient mechanism. To determine more specifically an 'optimal' mechanism within this set, a social welfare function is needed that defines tradeoffs, not only between the expected payoffs of different individuals but also between the expected payoffs of different types of each individual. That is, given any positive utility-weights $\lambda_i(t_i)$ for each type t_i of each individual i, one can generate an incentive-efficient mechanism by maximizing

$$\Sigma_{i=1}^{n} \Sigma_{t_i \in T_i} \lambda_i(t_i) \Sigma_{t_{-i} \in T_{-i}} p_i(t_{-i}|t_i) u_i(\mu(c), t)$$

over all $\mu: T \to C$ that satisfy the incentive constraints; but different vectors of utility weights may generate different incentive-efficient mechanisms.

5. BARGAINING OVER MECHANISMS. A positive economic theory must go beyond welfare economics and try to predict the economic institutions that may actually be chosen by the individuals in an economy. Having established that a social planner can restrict his attention to incentive-compatible direct-revelation mechanisms, which is a mathematically simple set, it is natural to assume that rational economic agents who are themselves negotiating the structure of their economic institutions should be able to bargain over the set of incentive-compatible direct-revelation mechanisms. But if we assume that individuals know their types already at the time when fundamental economic plans and decisions are made, then we need a theory of mechanism selection by individuals who have private information.

When we consider bargaining games in which individuals can bargain over mechanisms, there should be no loss of generality in restricting our attention to equilibria in which there is one incentive-compatible mechanism that is selected with probability one independently of anyone's type. This proposition, called the *inscrutability principle*, can be justified by viewing the mechanism-selection process as itself part of a more broadly defined general mechanism and applying the revelation principle. For example, suppose that there is an equilibrium of the mechanism-selection game in which some mechanism μ would be chosen if individual 1's type were α and some other mechanism ν would be chosen if 1's type were β. Then there should exist an equivalent equilibrium of the mechanism-selection game in which the individuals always select a direct-revelation mechanism that coincides with mechanism μ when individual 1 confidentially reports type α to the mediator (in the implementation of the mechanism, after it has been selected), and that coincides with mechanism ν when 1 reports type β to the mediator.

However, the inscrutability principle does not imply that the possibility of revealing information during a mechanism-selection process is irrelevant. There may be some mechanisms that we should expect not to be selected by the individuals in such a process, precisely because some individuals would choose to reveal information about their types rather than let these mechanisms be selected. For example, consider the following Bayesian collective-choice problem, due to Holmstrom and Myerson (1983). There are two individuals, 1 and 2, each of whom has two possible types, α and β, which are independent and equally likely. There are three social choice options, called x, y and z. Each individual's utility for these options depends on his type according to the following table.

Option	*1, α*	*1, β*	*2, α*	*2, β*
x	2	0	2	2
y	1	4	1	1
z	0	9	0	−8

The incentive-efficient mechanism that maximizes the ex ante expected sum of the two individuals' utilities is as follows: if 1 reports type α and 2 reports α then choose x, if 1 reports type β and 2 reports α then choose z, and if 2 reports β then choose y (regardless of 1's report). However, Holmstrom and Myerson argue that such a mechanism would not be chosen in a mechanism-selection game that is played when 1 already knows his type, because, when 1 knows that his type is α, he could do better by proposing to select the mechanism that always chooses x, and 2 would always want to accept this proposal. That is, because 1 would have no incentive to conceal his type from 2 in a mechanism-selection game if his type were α (when his interests would then have no conflict with 2's), we should not expect the individuals in a mechanism-selection game to agree inscrutably to an incentive-efficient mechanism that implicitly puts as much weight on 1's type-β payoff as the mechanism shown above.

For another example, consider again the sender-receiver game due to Farrell. Recall that y would be the only possible equilibrium outcome if the individuals could communicate only face-to-face, with no mediation or other noise in their communication channel. Suppose that the mechanism-selection process is as follows: first 2 proposes a mediator who is committed to implement some incentive-compatible mechanism; then 1 can either accept this mediator and communicate with 2 thereafter only through him, or 1 can reject this mediator and thereafter communicate with 2 only face-to-face. Suppose now that 2 proposes that they should use a mediator who will implement the incentive-compatible mediation plan that is best for 2 (recommending x with probability $2/3$ and y with probability $1/3$ if 1 reports α, recommending y with probability $2/3$ and z with probability $1/3$ if 1 reports β). We have seen that this mechanism is worse than y for 1 if his type is β. Furthermore, this mechanism would be worse than y for player 1 under the ex ante welfare criterion, when his expected payoffs for type α and type β are averaged, each with weight $1/2$. However, it is an equilibrium of this mechanism-selection game for player 1 always to accept this proposal, no matter what his type is. If 1 rejected 2's proposed mediator, then 2 might reasonably infer that 1's type was β, in which case 2's rational choice would be z instead of y, and z is the worse possible outcome for both of 1's types.

Now consider a different mechanism-selection process for this example, in which the informed player 1 can select any incentive-compatible mechanism himself, with only the restriction that 2 must know what mechanism has been selected by 1. For any incentive-compatible mechanism μ, there is an equilibrium in which 1 chooses μ for sure, no matter what his type is, and they thereafter play the honest and obedient equilibrium of this mechanism. To support such an equilibrium, it suffices to suppose that, if any mechanism other than μ were selected, then 2 would infer that 1's type was β and therefore choose z. Thus, concepts like sequential equilibrium from noncooperative game theory cannot determine the outcome of this mechanism-selection game, beyond what we already know from the revelation principle; we cannot even say that 1's selected mechanism will be incentive-efficient. To get incentive efficiency as a result of mechanism-selection games, we need some further assumptions, like those of cooperative game theory.

An attempt to extend traditional solution concepts from cooperative game theory to the problem of bargaining over mechanisms has been proposed by Myerson (1983, 1984a, 1984b). In making such an extension, one must consider not only the traditional problem of how to define reasonable compromises between the conflicting interest of different individuals, but also the problem of how to define reasonable compromises between the conflicting interest of different types of the same individual. That is, to conceal his type in the mechanism-selection process, an individual should bargain for some inscrutable compromise between what he really wants and what he would have wanted if his type had been different; and we need some formal theory to predict what a reasonable inscrutable compromise might be. In the above sender-receiver game, where only type β of player 1 should feel any incentive to conceal his type, we might expect an inscrutable compromise to be resolved in favor of type α. That is, in the mechanism-selection game where 1 selects the mechanism, we might expect both types of 1 to select the incentive-compatible mechanism that is best for type α. (In this mechanism, the mediator recommends x with probability 0.8 and y with probability 0.2 if 1 reports α; and the mediator recommends x with probability 0.4, y with probability 0.4, and z with probability 0.2 if 1 reports β.) This mechanism is the *neutral optimum* for player 1, in the sense of Myerson (1983).

BIBLIOGRAPHY

Aumann, R.J. 1974. Subjectivity and correlation in randomized strategies. *Journal of Mathematical Economics* 1, 67–96.

Aumann, R.J. 1987. Correlated equilibrium as an expression of Bayesian rationality. *Econometrica* 55, 1–18.

Coase, R. 1960. The problem of social cost. *Journal of Law and Economics* 3, 1–44.

Cramton, P., Gibbons, R. and Klemperer, P. 1987. Dissolving a partnership efficiently. *Econometrica* 55, 615–32.

Dasgupta, P., Hammond, P. and Maskin, E. 1979. The implementation of social choice rules: some general results on incentive compatibility. *Review of Economic Studies* 46, 185–216.

Farrell, J. 1988. Meaning and credibility in cheap-talk games. In *Mathematical Models in Economics*, ed. M. Dempster, Oxford: Oxford University Press.

Gibbard, A. 1973. Manipulation of voting schemes: a general result. *Econometrica* 41, 587–602.

Harris, M. and Raviv, A. 1981. Allocation mechanisms and the design of auctions. *Econometrica* 49, 1477–99.

Harris, M. and Townsend, R.M. 1981. Resource allocation under asymmetric information. *Econometrica* 49, 33–64.

Harsanyi, J.C. 1967. Games with incomplete information played by Bayesian players. *Management Science* 14, 159–82, 320–34, 481–502.

Holmstrom, B. 1977. On incentives and control in organizations. PhD dissertation, Stanford University Graduate School of Business.

Holmstrom, B. and Myerson, R.B. 1983. Efficient and durable decision rules with incomplete information. *Econometrica* 51, 1799–819.

Lewis, T.R. and Sappington, D.E.M. 1988. Countervailing incentives in agency problems. Bell Communications Research and University of California at Davis, Mimeo.

Myerson, R.B. 1979. Incentive compatibility and the bargaining problem. *Econometrica* 47, 61–74.

Myerson, R.B. 1981. Optimal auction design. *Mathematics of Operation Research* 6, 58–73.

Myerson, R.B. 1982. Optimal coordination mechanisms in generalized principal-agent problems. *Journal of Mathematical Economics* 10, 67–81.

Myerson, R.B. 1983. Mechanism design by an informed principal. *Econometrica* 51, 1767–97.

Myerson, R.B. 1984a. Two-person bargaining problems with incomplete information. *Econometrica* 52, 461–87.

Myerson, R.B. 1984b. Cooperative games with incomplete information. *International Journal of Game Theory* 13, 69–86.

Myerson, R.B. 1985. Bayesian equilibrium and incentive compatibility. In *Social Goals and Social Organization*, ed. L. Hurwicz, D. Schmeidler and H. Sonnenschein, Cambridge: Cambridge University Press, 229–59.

Myerson, R.B. 1986. Multistage games with communication. *Econometrica* 54, 323–58.

Myerson, R.B. 1988. Incentive constraints and optimal communication systems. In *Proceedings of the Second Conference on Theoretical Aspects of Reasoning about Knowledge*, ed. M.Y. Vardi, Los Altos: Morgan Kaufmann, 179–93.

Myerson, R.B. and Satterthwaite, M. 1983. Efficient mechanisms for bilateral trading. *Journal of Economic Theory* 29, 265–81.

Ortega-Reichert, A. 1968. Models for competitive bidding under uncertainty. PhD dissertation, Stanford University Department of Operations Research.

Palfrey, T. and Srivastava, S. 1986. On Bayesian implementable allocations. *Review of Economic Studies* 54, 193–208.

Riley, J.G. and Samuelson, W.F. 1981. Optimal auctions. *American Economic Review* 71, 381–92.

Rosenthal, R.W. 1978. Arbitration of two-party disputes under uncertainty. *Review of Economic Studies* 45, 595–604.

Samuelson, W. 1985. A comment on the Coase theorem. In *Game-Theoretic Models of Bargaining*, ed. A.E. Roth, Cambridge: Cambridge University Press, 321–39.

Schelling, T.C. 1960. *The Strategy of Conflict*. Cambridge, Mass.: Harvard University Press.

Wilson, R. 1985. Incentive efficiency of double auctions. *Econometrica* 53, 1101–15.

Moral Hazard

Y. KOTOWITZ

The problem of moral hazard is pervasive in economic activities. Economists have been well aware of its existence as the following quote from the *Wealth of Nations* will testify:

> The directors of such companies, however, being the managers rather of other peoples' money than of their own, it cannot well be expected, that they should watch over it with the same anxious vigilance with which the partners in a private copartnery frequently watch over their own... Negligence and profusion, therefore, must always prevail, more or less, in the management of the affairs of such a company (Smith, 1776, p. 700).

However, theoretical developments and their application to specific problems have only proceeded over the past 25 years and are still the subject of vigorous research. While we have a considerable understanding of the problem, we do not as yet understand fully market and social responses to it. In the following I shall attempt to explain the nature of the problem and selectively illustrate the flavour of current theoretical developments.

Moral hazard may be defined as actions of economic agents in maximizing their own utility to the detriment of others, in situations where they do not bear the full consequences or, equivalently, do not enjoy the full benefits of their actions *due to uncertainty and incomplete or restricted contracts* which prevent the assignment of *full* damages (benefits) to the agent responsible. It is immediately apparent that this definition includes a wide variety of externalities, and thus may lead to nonexistence of equilibria or to inefficiencies of equilibria when they exist.

It is a special form of incompleteness of contracts which creates the conflict between the agent's utility and that of others. Such incompleteness may arise due to several reasons: the coexistence of unequal information and risk aversion or joint production, costs and legal barriers to contracting and costs of contract enforcement. We shall analyse each in turn.

UNEQUAL INFORMATION. Agents may possess exclusive information. Arrow (1985) classifies such informational advantages as 'hidden action' and 'hidden information'. The first involves actions which cannot be accurately observed or inferred by others. It is therefore impossible to condition contracts on these actions. The second involves states of nature about which the agent has some, possibly incomplete, information which determines the appropriateness of the agent's actions, but which are imperfectly observable by others. Thus, even if agents' actions are costlessly observable by others, they do not know with certainty whether the actions were in their interest.

Commonly analysed examples of hidden actions are: workers' effort, which cannot be costlessly monitored by employers, precautions taken by the insured to reduce the probability of accidents or damages due to them, which cannot be costlessly monitored by insurers. Criminal activity clearly belongs in this category as well.

Examples of hidden information are expert services – such as physicians, lawyers, repairmen, managers and politicians.

Where consequences of specific agents' actions can be separated from those of others, even though the consequences may be affected by random, unobservable states of nature, the problem may be easily solved if agents are risk neutral, by simply assigning the full consequences to the agent, in exchange for a fixed fee. This is in effect a complete contract. The problem of contract incompleteness arises when agents are risk averse or where assignment of responsibility to one agent cannot be made.

When agents are risk averse, assigning full damages (benefits) to them assigns them all risk due to random states of nature. Risk averse agents would like to purchase insurance against such risks. However, it is impossible for others to separate the consequences of agents' actions from random elements which cannot be controlled by the agent. Insurance against the latter will inevitably insulate agents from the consequences of their own actions. The agent may, of course, offer to supply information about the unobserved actions or states – but such information cannot be credible.

Optimal contracts generally involve some degree of insurance and hence lead to a conflict between incentives and risk sharing. Most of the literature on moral hazard has concentrated on this case. We shall come back to it.

When precise assignment of responsibility to individual agents is impossible, full assignment of consequences to individual agents cannot be achieved. By definition, this is the case for crime, where the identity of the perpetrator is generally not known with certainty. The design of punishments and the interaction with enforcement activities to apprehend and convict criminals is treated extensively in the literature (see e.g. Becker, 1968).

Group production is another area where assignment may be impossible. Some forms of collective punishment on the group as a whole when output falls short of a specified quota, with some allocation rule when output meets or exceeds the quota may serve to elicit the desired output (Holmstrom, 1982). However, the conditions under which this is possible are quite restricted.

Similar problems arise where quality of products is difficult to ascertain because they must be used jointly with another service or product, because their performance is affected by the conditions and nature of use. For example drugs must be used in conjunction with physicians' services. Failure of the drug may result from its poor quality, from misdiagnosis by the physician (who may prescribe the wrong drug) or from failure to follow instructions by the patient. In the absence of these complications, it would be optimal for the manufacturer, who knows the quality of his product, to supply a guarantee of performance, in order to remove the incentive to supply lower quality. As well, the guarantee serves at least partly to insure risk averse consumers against random variations in the performance of the drug. Even if the manufacturer is risk averse, his risk is mitigated by the 'law of large numbers', so it is optimal for him to act as insurer.

However, under the circumstances above, such insurance creates a moral hazard problem for the physician and the patient, who may use insufficient care in diagnosis and use. Any risk sharing among the relevant parties therefore induces a moral hazard problem which cannot be avoided in the presence of private information, even if all parties are risk neutral.

BARRIERS TO CONTRACTING. Incomplete contracts may also arise in the absence of private information due to the costs of writing detailed contingent contracts. This problem is particularly severe in contracts involving complex transactions and long periods. When uncertainty about the future is great, the number and nature of eventualities to be considered is clearly very large. The cost of anticipating them and writing a contract which species or elicits desired actions may be very large. The cost of reaching agreement on the proper actions in each eventuality may well be prohibitive. If the probability of any event is small, and the cost of agreement high, it may pay to leave the contract vague and wait for the resolution of uncertainty before reaching agreement. Of course, this is precisely the case in spot market transactions. However, frequently decisions must be made prior to the resolution of uncertainty. For example, specialized investments in physical or human capital must be made by the parties before production and trading begin (Becker, 1964). The nature of the investment may well depend on the transaction price, which may in turn depend on information revealed after the investment is made. A limited agreement on investment and trading may be optimal, leaving transaction price to future negotiation. This, however, may lead to a moral hazard problem. Opportunistic behaviour in subsequent periods by one of the parties may lead to termination of trading or unfavourable contract terms for the party which invested in specialized capital. Knowing that this may occur, the incentive to invest is reduced. The resulting inefficiency may well fall short of the costs of complete contracts. Williamson (1985) argues that such problems may give rise to vertical integration.

Contracts are too costly to write when transactions are infrequent and small. Most spot market transactions between retailers and consumers fall in this category. Blanket contracts offered by sellers in the form of 'money back guarantees' or exchange privileges may be substituted for explicit contingent contracts – but they are subject to moral hazard on the consumers' side. Alternatively the state legislates fair trading laws which serve as generalized contracts.

Contracts are lacking altogether when transactions are random or involuntary. Accidental damages inflicted on one party by another as in a traffic accident are good examples. Here again, the law must form a generalized contract. It is obvious that such a law cannot possibly allow for all contingencies, so that it constitutes an incomplete contract, giving rise to moral hazard problems. The question of the design of liability rules has been extensively analysed in the law and economics literature (Posner, 1977).

Finally, contracts may be restricted by law or by the limited financial resources of agents. For example, even if managers are risk neutral, their financial resources may be insufficient to allow them to become sole proprietors, without relying on outside capital. Shareholders and bondholders must then share in the risk – raising a moral hazard problem due to the informational advantages of managers. For an extensive analysis of these problems, see Jensen and Meckling (1976).

Similarly, when punishments are limited by law, moral hazard may not be resolved even where actions can be costlessly observed ex post. Thus, for example, bankruptcy and limited liability provisions insure borrowers against extremely unfavourable states of nature without limiting the gains from extremely favourable ones. This creates a moral hazard problem, inducing borrowers to undertake riskier projects. Stiglitz and Weiss (1981) show that lenders will sometimes require collateral and ration loans in attempting to overcome these difficulties.

PROBLEMS OF ENFORCEMENT. A related barrier to complete contracting arises from costs and other limitations on enforcement. When enforcement is costly, it may be more efficient to live with the inefficiencies generated by the moral hazard, than to try to enforce the optimal contingent contract. A common way to overcome such difficulties is by way of posting a bond, which is forfeit in the event of non-performance. However, restricted financial resources generally prevent bonding.

Under conditions where enforcement is not economical, contracts must be *self-enforcing*. It is unimportant whether contracts are explicit or implicit, as they frequently are in labour markets. To be viable, contracts must make subsequent actions by contracting parties consistent with their self interest, that is they must allow for the potential exercise of moral hazard. This problem is at the heart of non-cooperative game theory, which defines moral hazard as opportunistic behaviour.

So far we have surveyed the conditions under which a moral hazard problem cannot be trivially resolved. This raises three questions which theorists have begun tackling in the past two decades: (a) the nature of optimal contracts in the presence of moral hazard; (b) market and institutional/legal response to these problems; and (c) welfare consequences.

OPTIMAL CONTRACTS. The problem has mainly been tackled by Agency theory. Following seminal work by Wilson (1969) and Ross (1973) the optimal (typically second best) reward structure for an agent is derived on the basis of observed variables, usually under 'hidden action' assumptions. Some of the main results for risk averse agents are given below. (a) Optimal contracts require risk sharing between principal and agent which creates a moral hazard problem in the form of insufficient incentives. (b) Efficient contracts should utilize all the information available, i.e. they should be constructed on the basis of statistical inference from the informational available on the hidden action of the agent (Holmstrom, 1979). Thus monitoring, which reduces inference errors, is productive. (c) The nature of the reward schedule is sensitive to the nature of the information available, the residual uncertainty and the degree of risk aversion of the agent and principal. This observation is troubling because incentive contracts observed in reality are generally simple and uniform across a variety of agents and information sets. Long-term contracts, explicit or implicit (client relations), tend to mitigate moral hazard problems, by introducing a reward for not exploiting short-term informational advantages, and because cumulative information reduces uncertainty. Hence, for example, experience rating in insurance contracts.

MARKET AND INSTITUTIONAL RESPONSES. Market responses may invalidate or reinforce the special features of contracts to mitigate the moral hazard problem. These responses depend on the nature of competition. Free entry and the existence of unobserved differences among agents create the additional problem of adverse selection. We shall therefore reflect only on market responses which are mainly a consequence of moral hazard.

As indicated above, contracts typically require some risk sharing (coinsurance) between the parties when agents are risk averse. Therefore, agents generally bear more risk than they desire. If they are able to purchase additional insurance from third parties, the moral hazard problem is aggravated, making the original contract inefficient. This requires exclusivity in contracting. Thus, for example, insurance companies do not allow insurance claims for damage due to fire, health or accident insurance from more than one company. It is obvious that any restriction on coinsurance can be circumvented if such claims are allowed. At the extreme, agents might have more than full coverage, inducing intentional damages, such as arson.

This tendency for exclusivity is reinforced by the advantages of long-term contracting. In the presence of risk aversion or limits on agents' capital which prevent effective bonding, it may be necessary to promise future rewards to mitigate short-term opportunistic behaviour. Termination of the agreement will deny these rewards and thus operates as a threat. This requires that contracts yield some rents to agents, so that their removal may constitute a punishment. Thus for example, the utility of being employed must exceed the utility of being unemployed (Shapiro and Stiglitz, 1984).

This requires rationing, which is not undone by competition. If being fired by one's employer leads to immediate employment elsewhere at the same wage, rather than to a significant period of unemployment, the threat of firing is ineffective. An equilibrium must be supported by the transaction costs of finding new employment or by a collective use of the information contained in the firing. Such information is indeed relevant for hiring decisions by other firms. Its use depends on the costs of obtaining such information. Markets develop to supply such information, thereby increasing the effectiveness of such agreements. Credit information bureaus and employment agencies are some examples. Fama (1980) argues that such 'reputation' mechanisms eliminate moral hazard problems in executive markets. However, as the information is subject to noise, it is clear that moral hazard problems cannot be entirely resolved.

Non-market institutions may develop to mitigate some of these problems. Professional licensing and certification limit the number of physicians, lawyers and many other professionals. Aside from issues of assurance of minimum quality and monopoly, these arrangements ensure rents to the professions involved and, hence, make licence removal a significant penalty (Arrow, 1963).

The consequences of moral hazard in political processes have largely been neglected by economists. Exceptions are Stigler (1971) and Peltzman (1976), who analysed the motivations of regulators, and Buchanan and Tullock (1962). The theoretical tools of agency, contract and game theory have yet to be fruitfully employed in this area. Given the expanding role of government and the evidence of widespread abuses in the political process, such application promises to yield significant dividends.

GENERAL EQUILIBRIUM AND WELFARE EFFECTS. There has been little research on the welfare implications of moral hazard. An exception is Stiglitz (see e.g. Arnott and Stiglitz, 1985), who noted that the existence of moral hazard creates second best contracts. In an economy characterized by such contracts, changes in contracts between any two parties have significant first order effects on social welfare, in contrast to the Arrow–Debreu economy, where first order effects of individual actions are zero at an optimum. As we have seen, moral hazard may lead to rationing and queues, suboptimal expenditure of hidden actions and imperfections in capital markets.

This is not surprising because moral hazard is basically a form of externality. It is well known that uninternalized externalities lead to non-concavities, possible non-existence of equilibria and inefficiencies. The existence of such inefficiencies signals a possible role for government. However, government intervention may well cause more problems than it solves. For example, attempts to supplement deficient insurance markets in the form of universal income (social security, income taxation) insurance, have run into serious moral hazard problems of work incentives, tax avoidance and evasion, etc. It is at least partly because of these moral hazard problems that such markets failed to develop. It is therefore unclear whether government supply of these services enhance welfare.

In contrast, government policies which enhance complete contracts and improve their enforcement, can be welfare enhancing. Examples are contract law, liability rules and trade regulations.

BIBLIOGRAPHY

Arnott, R. and Stiglitz, J. 1985. Labor turnover, wage structures, and moral hazard: the inefficiency of competitive markets. *Journal of Labor Economics* 3, 434–62.

Arrow, K. 1963. Uncertainty and the welfare economics of medical care. *American Economic Review* 53, 541–67.

Arrow, K. 1985. The economics of agency. In *Principals and Agents: The Structure of Business*, ed. J. Pratt and R. Zeckhauser, Boston: Harvard Business School Press, 37–51.

Becker, G. 1964. *Human Capital*. New York: Columbia University Press.

Becker, G. 1968. Crime and punishment – an economic approach. *Journal of Political Economy* 76, 169–217.

Becker, G. and Stigler, G. 1974. Law enforcement, malfeasance and compensation of enforcers. *Journal of Legal Studies* 3, 1–18.

Buchanan, J.M. and Tullock, G. 1962. *The Calculus of Consent*. Ann Arbor: University of Michigan Press.

Fama, E. 1980. Agency problems and the theory of the firm. *Journal of Political Economy* 88, 288–307.

Green, J. 1985. Differential information, the market and incentive compatibility. In *Frontiers of Economics*, ed. K.J. Arrow and S. Honkapohja, Oxford: Basil Blackwell, 178–99.

Harris, M. and Raviv, A. 1979. Optimal incentive contracts with imperfect information. *Journal of Economic Theory* 20, 231–59.

Hölmstrom, B. 1979. Moral hazard and observability. *Bell Journal of Economics* 10, 74–91.

Hölmstrom, B. 1982a. Moral hazard in teams. *Bell Journal of Economics* 13, 314–40.

Jensen, M. and Meckling, W. 1976. Theory of the firm: managerial behavior, agency costs, and capital structure. *Journal of Financial Economics* 3, 305–60.

Peltzman, S. 1976. Towards a more general theory of regulation. *Journal of Law and Economics* 19, 211–40.

Posner, R. 1977. *The Economic Analysis of Law*. 2nd edn, Boston: Little, Brown.

Ross, S. 1973. The economic theory of agency: the principal's problem. *American Economic Review* 63, 134–9.

Shapiro, C. and Stiglitz, J. 1984. Equilibrium unemployment as a worker incentive device. *American Economic Review* 74, 433–44.

Shavell, S. 1979. Risk sharing and incentives in the principal and agent relationship. *Bell Journal of Economics* 10, 55–73.

Smith, A. 1776. *An Inquiry into the Nature and the Causes of the Wealth of Nations*. Ed. E. Cannan, New York: Modern Library, 1937.

Stigler, G. 1971. The theory of economic regulation. *Bell Journal of Economics and Management Science* 2, 3–21.

Stiglitz, J. and Weiss, A. 1981. Credit rationing in markets with imperfect information. *American Economic Review* 71, 393–410.

Williamson, O. 1985. *The Economic Institutions of Capitalism*. New York: Free Press.

Wilson, R. 1969. The structure of incentives for decentralisation under uncertainty. In *La Décision*, Paris: Editions du Centre National de la Recherche Scientifique.

Natural Selection and Evolution

SIDNEY G. WINTER

Important theoretical concepts tend to resist satisfactory definition (cf. Stigler, 1957). Such concepts are in the service of the expansive ambitions of the theories in which they occur, and must accordingly respond flexibly to the changing requirements for maintaining order in a changing intellectual empire. The term 'evolution' – obviously important in biology, but also in the physical and social sciences – provides a good illustration of this principle. A prominent biologist and author of a highly expansive treatise on biological evolution had the following to offer in his glossary:

> *Evolution.* Any gradual change. Organic evolution, often referred to as evolution for short, is any genetic change in organisms from generation to generation, or more strictly, a change in gene frequencies within populations from generation to generation (Wilson, 1975).

Note the abrupt and radical reduction in the breadth of the conceptual field from the first phrase of this definition to the last. The beginning connects the term to common discourse; the reference to gene frequencies at the end clearly brands the term as belonging to biology, but does not do much to explicate it. The layman is left wondering whether this is meant to cover what happened to the dinosaurs, and perhaps puzzled also as to whether 'gradual change' adequately captures the common features of organic evolution, cultural evolution and stellar evolution.

To the extent that biology 'owns' the concept of natural selection and evolution, the meanings of these terms tend to be regarded as biology-specific. It then seems to follow that the application of evolutionary thinking in other realms falls under the rubric 'biological analogies', whence it is believed to follow, further, that the appropriateness of an evolutionary approach somehow depends on the closeness of the parallels that can be drawn between the situation in view and situations considered in biology.

The quest for close parallels is substantially impeded by the fact that a prominent feature of the biological scene, sexual reproduction, is, one might say, peculiar. Although asexual or haploid reproduction plays a significant role in biological reality, and this is suitably reflected in portions of biological theory, critics of 'biological analogies' tend to stress the question 'what is the analogue of genetic inheritance?' with sexual reproduction in mind. A persuasive case can be made that the inability to complete an analogy in this respect is not necessarily a bar to its utility. It is certainly true, nevertheless, that a great deal of biological theory cannot readily be adapted for use in non-biological arenas because the implications of sexual reproduction are so central to the analysis.

This essay puts forward a radical approach to these issues: it challenges biology's basic ownership claim to the concept of evolution by natural selection. An account of the basic framework of evolutionary analysis is set forth, and while this account attaches meanings to 'evolution' and 'selection' that are obviously strongly influenced by evolutionary biology, it adapts more readily to discussion of various types of cultural evolution than to biological evolution (at least to the extent that the latter involves sexual reproduction). Examples of the application of the evolutionary viewpoint to economics are then provided in discussions of two areas, the evolution of productive knowledge and the character of Economic Man.

THE FRAMEWORK OF EVOLUTIONARY ANALYSIS. Fundamentally, and in the most abstract terms, an evolutionary process is a process of information storage with selective retention. Consider, for illustrative purposes, the books in an undergraduate library. Such a library typically has many copies of some books. Given the hazards of loss, pilferage and wear and tear, as contrasted with the comparative constancy of much of the subject matter, the library will not infrequently order new copies of books it has long possessed.

Although each individual volume is informationally complex and in some respects unique, there are nevertheless 'types' of books, for example, volumes with the same author and title. Formally, 'same author and title as' is an equivalence relation on the set of books, and a relation of particular interest to librarians, students, professors and others. There are, however, a great many other equivalence relations: 'same publisher as', 'same Library of Congress classification as', 'same colour as' and so forth. In fact, given the complexity of the individuals (volumes) that make up the library, the possibilities for defining equivalence relations – which in effect describe alternative approaches to describing the library – are virtually endless.

Now consider the change in such a library over the course of a year – say, at successive annual inventory times when the academic year is over, no books are circulating and all those that are going to be returned have been returned. In terms of a hypothetical exhaustive description of the library, which for example would note every change in yellow highlighting and marginal question marks, the amount of change is enormous in the sense that it would take a great many bytes of information to describe it. A more practical approach to describing the change is to take one or more interesting equivalence relations and count members of equivalence classes at the two dates. For example, for each title-and-author the number of elements in that equivalence class and in the library at t could be counted and the result compared with the number in that same equivalence class and in the library at $t+1$. While a librarian might be chiefly interested in accounting for the difference in the two numbers, an evolutionary theorist is more likely to divide the latter number by the former and call the result the (observed) 'fitness' of that title-and-author. (Of course, this can only be done provided the denominator is not zero.)

Proceeding along this line, it is possible to discuss how the library evolves (at the title-and-author level) by 'natural selection'. This term refers to the action of the complex collection of processes that are involved in the introduction to and disappearance from the library of individual volumes. The word 'natural' connotes the expectation that these processes cannot be entirely explained by reference to the intent of some individual actor who is effectively in charge of the whole situation – perhaps the head librarian. (Were this expectation not held, the evolutionary approach to understanding the library might well be abandoned in favour of an attempt to fathom the intentions of the controlling actor.)

As described thus far, the evolutionary approach to understanding the library may provide a useful framework, but it is not a theory. In particular, the notion of 'fitness' provides a purely tautological 'explanation' of how the library changes over time. (It is also only a partial explanation, first because of the problem of new acquisitions (zero denominators), but more fundamentally because it treats of a small structure of equivalence relations and does not aspire to complete description.) There is no difficulty in converting this framework into a genuine theory; for example; just assume that 'title and author fitnesses' are constant over time. This theory has abundant empirical content; unfortunately, it is false. A weaker version, substituting 'approximately constant' will fare very little better. The difficulty lies not in the construction, within such an evolutionary framework, of genuine theories with empirical content, but in producing successful ones. More specifically, some non-tautological propositions about theoretical fitness must be derived and turn out to be true of observed fitness. Whether the quest for such propositions proves successful depends on the equivalence relations chosen for study.

In the library example, the choice of title-and-author as the focal equivalence relation for the theory is a masterstroke of creative insight (or would be if it were not obvious). With title and author as taxonomic criteria, a great deal of detailed information about individual volumes is succinctly captured. Also, the fact that there are printers and publishers (and copyright laws) has strong implications for the precision of the 'inheritance' mechanism in this evolutionary system, and the selection mechanism has persistent features reflecting the existence and persistence of academic departments, professors, large enrolment courses, reading lists and library budget levels.

Detailed knowledge of the actual systems governing inheritance and selection would certainly be helpful to the evolutionary scientist seeking to understand the library, but it is not essential. Once 'on to' the idea that 'same title and author' is an important relation in the larger context that affects the evolution of the library, the investigator can make progress without necessarily knowing the answers to a lot of questions about why this idea is fruitful.

So far as the formal, tautological structure of the evolutionary approach is concerned, the investigator could just as well be working with the equivalence classes induced by the relation 'same word appears as the first word on page fifteen'. The investigator can still count volumes and measure fitness, and it will still be true (*ex post*) that the fittest types come to dominate the library – or more precisely, that approximately equal fitness is a requirement for long-term coexistence in the library environment. It would be surprising, however, if interesting empirical regularities emerged from such an inquiry.

If the foregoing discussion of the evolution of the undergraduate library were an attempt at developing a biological analogy, it would be time to pull back the veil from the correspondences that have not been made explicit thus far. The equivalence classes of 'same title and author as' correspond to species. Different editions or printings of a given book correspond to genotypes because there are systematic differences among them, yet the differences are small compared to the differences between classes. Underlining, yellow highlighting, torn pages and the like are examples of phenotypic variation, which reflect the incidents and accidents encountered by an individual volume over its life cycle. The Library of Congress provides a readymade taxonomic structure to facilitate discussion of evolution above the 'species' level. Journals are apparently a different life form altogether, since the usual close association of title and author does not prevail.

One could just as well, however, take evolutionary bibliography as the prototypical evolutionary science and think of biology in terms of bibliographic analogies (setting aside, of course, the facts of history and the wide difference in degree of development of the two subjects). In this perspective, the key idea on which the power of the evolutionary approach is seen to rest is that of an equivalence class within which the elements (individuals) are close copies of each other in observable respects. The meaning of 'close' involves a contrast between small intra-class variation and large inter-class variation in the system of equivalence classes. Related fundamental ideas are the idea of counting or otherwise measuring the aggregate of elements in such an equivalence class at different points in time, plus the notion that, over time, new individuals appear in a previously existing class – implying that somewhere and somehow, the capacity to produce new individual copies exists.

Biological species that reproduce sexually represent a complex variant of this basic evolutionary paradigm. The part of the process that involves the production of the most exact copies, the replication of chromosomes in the course of gametogenesis, involves information that is a complete genetic description neither of the parent nor of the offspring. The concept of genetically identical individuals – individuals that are alike the way different copies of the same printing of a book are alike – is prominent in theoretical models, but because of the genetic complexity of individuals and the character of sexual reproduction the phenomenon is rare in the part of nature where sexual reproduction prevails. One consequence is that the concept of a 'species', which is so central to evolutionary biology, displays imperfectly resolved tensions between taxonomic criteria and reproductive (inter-breeding) criteria. This difficulty is a peculiarity associated with the phenomenon of sexual reproduction. Perhaps it is in part a reflection of the fact that the major substantive problem of the origin of species is not concusively solved, and it would be counterproductive to leave no flexibility in the definition of species while pursuing that important goal.

In any case, the contention here is that the empirical application of the framework of evolutionary analysis requires in general the development of a taxonomic system (or more formally, a system of equivalence relations on the set of individuals considered) to which generalized concepts of inheritance, fitness and selection can be applied.

EVOLUTION OF PRODUCTIVE KNOWLEDGE. Many prominent economists have endorsed some version of the idea that evolutionary principles, or biological science, provide intellectual models that economists would do well to emulate. Marshall's famous dictum that 'The Mecca of the economist lies in economic biology rather than in economiic dynamics' (Marshall, 1920, p. xiv) is an obxious and important case in point. Thomas (1983) analyses with admirable thoroughness the origin, meaning and implications of this statement in the development of Marshall's thought, emphasizing the central importance of the idea of *irreversible* evolutionary change in economic life. Somewhat less well known, perhaps is Schumpeter's statement that

> The essential point to grasp is that in dealing with capitalism we are dealing with an evolutionary process.... Capitalism, then, is by nature a form or method of economic change and not only never is but never can be stationary (Schumpeter, 1942, p. 82).

In Schumpeter's case, too, irreversible change is probably dominant among the connotations of 'evolution', a term which he employed quite frequently.

Neither Marshall nor Schumpeter presented what the above discussion argues to be the key to the development of a predictive evolutionary science – a suggestion about how to interpret economic reality in terms of a system of equivalence relations that effectively breathes empirical content into generalized notions of inheritance and selection. Such a suggestion was advanced, albeit sketchily, by Thorstein Veblen in his paper, 'Why Economics is not an Evolutionary Science' (1898, pp. 70–71, emphasis supplied):

> For the purpose of economic science the process of cumulative change that is to be accounted for is the sequence of *change in the methods of doing things* – the methods of dealing with the material means of life.

Although perhaps not as a result of direct influence from Veblen, a similar proposal (emphasizing imitation of 'rules of behaviour') figures in the classic essay on evolutionary economics by Alchian (1950). The idea is featured more prominently in Winter (1971), and more prominently still, under the rubric of 'routines', by Nelson and Winter (1982). It is the evolutionary economist's answer to an important element in the critique of 'biological analogies' offered by Penrose (1952).

Evolutionary economics thus attaches central importance to a question that is not merely unanswered, but unasked in the context of orthodox economic theory: what are the social processes by which productive knowledge is *stored*? Certainly the concepts of production sets and functions do not seriously evoke this question, and even the bulk of the theoretical literature concerned with technical change disregards the issue as it probes the causes and consequences of things becoming 'known' that were formerly 'unknown'. From an evolutionary viewpoint, abstracting from the storage process in this fashion inevitably has a crippling effect on the effort to understand the appearance of new methods of doing things and the selective pressures to which innovations and innovators are subjected. In particular, the fact may be overlooked that the role of business firms as sources of innovation is intimately related to their social role as repositories of productive knowledge.

These themes cannot be explored in detail here. By way of illustration, however, consider one example of a method of doing things – the method of producing written text that resembles print, called 'typewriting'. There is an equivalence relation 'same (alphabet) keyboard as' on the set of machines used for this purpose, and an equivalence class called 'standard (QWERTY) keyboard'. There is a related human skill called 'touch typing', and an equivalence class of skilled typists 'trained on standard keyboard'. The early evolutionary history of these familiar phenomena has been nicely analysed and described by Arthur (1984) and David (1985). It stands as a warning against simplistic ascriptions of optimality to the outcomes of evolutionary processes. As David explains, the familiar arrangement of keys on the standard keyboard originated as an adaptive response to a particular technical problem – the problem of key jamming produced by typists typing on a machine vastly different from the modern typewriter (be it mechanical, electric, electronic, or a facet of the capabilities of a computer). In particular, the text being produced was invisible to the typist, and jamming of the keys was both hard to detect and serious in its consequences. After many decades of evolution, during which the typewriter itself has been radically transformed, the QWERTY keyboard survives and still performs its intended function of slowing typists down.

David argues convincingly that a central feature of the social process that replicates QWERTY over the generations, to the exclusion of alternatives that permit faster typing, is the complementarity between typewriters and skilled typists. Absent machines with an alternative keyboard, nobody learns an alternative touch typing skill. Absent a good supply of appropriately trained typists, a shift to alternative machines does not pay.

There are some interesting facets of this situation that Arthur and David do not touch upon. One reason that the supply of typists plays the role it does is that touch typing is a tacitly known skill. Although considered with symbol production, it is not transferable from individual to individual by symbolic communication. One cannot give a lecture to a roomful of typists and thereby convert their skills from one keyboard to another. Typists do not know (in a conscious or articulable way) how they do what they do. As a matter of fact, the level of performance displayed by a highly skilled typist remains mysterious even upon scientific analysis, seemingly surpassing bounds set by known facts of human neurophysiology (Salthouse, 1984). The tacit character of typing skill implies high switching costs; the high performance levels achievable even under the QWERTY handicap presumably reduce the incentives to switch (assuming the demand for typing services is price inelastic).

The social process that maintains the QWERTY typewriting method on a large scale is a complex and multi-faceted phenomenon, involving a host of factors traditionally regarded as economic, plus others, such as tacit knowledge, that have more recently entered the disciplinary lexicon. The story of this somewhat obsessive social memory is the story of an innovation; on the hand, it is also a story of how success was precluded for a number of other innovative efforts. In both of its aspects, it has counterparts today. For them, as for QWERTY, understanding how and why methods of doing things *do not* change is fundamental to understanding how and why they *do* change.

ECONOMIC MAN: THE EVOLUTIONARY CRITIQUE. Economists are wont to regard themselves as hard-headed realists in their assessments of the world in general and of human nature in particular. The trained eye of the economist penetrates facades of pompous pretence, cunning deceit and impassioned demagoguery, discerning the rational pursuit of self-interest in martyr, merchant and murderer alike. Many such penetrating analyses contain, no doubt, an important element of truth. Arguably, the making of them is an important role played by economists and others in a free society. For the purposes of economic science, however, the model of the rational self-interested individual has serious limitations. When it is not a transparent caricature (the textbook consumer who cares only about consumption of goods and services), it is often an obscure tautology (with no definite limits set on what may affect 'utility' and hence choice).

From an evolutionary viewpoint, the key question is which, if any, of the various theoretically described subspecies of *homo economicus* might have been well adapted to the real environments that have shaped humanity. A realistic and *scientific* appraisal of human nature (and the degree and nature of the self interest manifested therein) is an appraisal supportable by reference to the biological and cultural determinants of contemporary human behaviour and the evolutionary forces that have shaped those determinants. If, in a particular instance, the implications of such an appraisal turn out to be different from those of 'hard headed' economic analysis, then economics ought to change – presuming of course, that the objective in view is the advance of economic science.

Outside of the realm of human motivation, economists routinely (but often implicitly) make use of theoretical assumptions that are plainly not 'hard headed' but the reverse. The leading case in point is the assumption that society somehow provides perfect and costless enforcement of contracts. A second case is disregard of social networks (defined by various criteria) as determinants of transacting patterns. One does not have to be imbued with an evolutionary viewpoint, but only moderately experienced in the world, to acknowledge that economic analysis based on such assumptions may yield a seriously distorted image of reality. Where an evolutionary viewpoint comes in handy is in discussing how and why the economy functions as well as it does in spite of the limitations of third party contract enforcement, and the role that non-economic social relations may play in making this possible.

To some extent, the errors introduced by excesses of hard and soft headedness tend to cancel out. Markets perform sometimes well and sometimes poorly, and economics has managed to discover a good deal about this matter in spite of the fact that it has left entirely out of account two major categories of reasons. The burdens of carrying along the two sets of errors have, nevertheless, been heavy. It is important to leave them behind.

Progress is being made in doing so. As economics breaks out of the shell formed by its first approximation assumptions, its relationships to other social sciences and to biology become both more obvious and more fruitful. The intertwined themes of the role of self interest in behaviour and the bases of social cooperation are fundamental not just in economics but in all of social science, and in much of biology as well. Jack Hirshleifer, who has repeatedly and insightfully emphasized the universality of these themes, recently proclaimed that '*there is only one social science*' (1985, p. 53). For a 'generalized economics' to serve as that one social science, economics 'will have to deal with man as he really is – self-interested or not, fully rational or not' (ibid., p. 59).

Although it is probably premature to announce a contest to provide the best name for unified social science – a contest that would no doubt evoke numerous alternatives to 'generalized economics' – it does seem that many of the elements are at hand for a move toward unification. Major contributions from a variety of directions have vastly improved understanding of how cooperative behaviour in general and exchange behaviour in particular can arise in spite of weak or nonexistent institutional support. Some of these involve explicit use of the evolutionary framework (e.g. Axelrod, 1984); some do not (e.g. Williamson, 1985). All are at least potentially adaptable to a general multi-level evolutionary scheme in which patterns reproduced by a variety of mechanisms are subjected to selective pressure. Major difficulties, and major controversies, attend the problem of characterizing the linkages between the levels. On this front too there is recent progress, particularly the work of Boyd and Richerson (1985), who study the interactions of biological and cultural evolution with the aid of a collection of 'dual inheritance' models. Such interactions have, of course, implications for the understanding of human biology as well as for the study of culture.

In sum, natural selection and evolution should not be viewed as concepts developed for the specific purposes of biology and possibly appropriable for the specific purposes of economics, but rather as elements of the framework of a new conceptual structure that biology, economics and the other social sciences can comfortably share.

BIBLIOGRAPHY

Alchian, A. 1950. Uncertainty, evolution and economic theory. *Journal of Political Economy* 58, June, 211–21.

Arthur, W.B. 1984. Competing technologies and economic prediction. *Options* (I.I.A.S.A., Laxenburg, Austria), April, 10–13.

Axelrod, R. 1984. *The Evolution of Cooperation.* New York: Basic Books.

Boyd, R. and Richerson, P. 1985. *Culture and the Evolutionary Process.* Chicago: University of Chicago Press.

David, P. 1985. CLIO and the economics of QWERTY. *American Economic Review* 75(2), May, 332–37.

Hirshleifer, J. 1985. The expanding domain of economics. *American Economic Review* 75(6), December, 53–68.

Marshall, A. 1920. *Principles of Economics*, 8th edn, London: Macmillan, 1953; New York: Macmillan, 1956.

Nelson, R. and Winter, S. 1982. *An Evolutionary Theory of Economic Change.* Cambridge, Mass.: Harvard University Press.

Penrose, E. 1952. Biological analogies in the theory of the firm. *American Economic Review* 42, December, 804–19.

Schumpeter, J. 1942. *Capitalism, Socialism and Democracy.* 3rd edn, New York: Harper, 1950.

Stigler, G. 1957. Perfect competition, historically contemplated. In G. Stigler, *Essays in the History of Economics*, Chicago: University of Chicago Press, 1965.

Salthouse, T. 1984. The skill of typing. *Scientific American* 250(2), February, 128–35.

Thomas, B. 1983. Alfred Marshall on economic biology. Paper presented to the History of Economics Society, May.

Veblen, T. 1898. Why economics is not an evolutionary science. In T. Veblen, *The Place of Science in Modern Civilization*, New York: Russell & Russell, 1961.

Williamson, O. 1985. *The Economic Institutions of Capitalism.* New York: Free Press.

Wilson, E. 1975. *Sociobiology: a New Synthesis.* Cambridge, Mass.: Harvard University Press.

Winter, S. 1971. Satisficing, selection and the innovating remnant. *Quarterly Journal of Economics* 85(2), May, 237–61.

Organization Theory

THOMAS MARSCHAK

Since all the social sciences deal with human organizations, (families, bureaucracies, tribes, corporations, armies), the term 'organization theory' appears in all of them. What has distinguished the economists' pursuit of organization theory from that of sociologists, of political scientists and of psychologists (say those psychologists working in the field called 'organizational behaviour')? First, the real organizations that have inspired the theorizing of economists are the economy, the market and the firm. Second, economists, with their customary taste for rigour, have sought to define formally and precisely the vague terms used in informal discourse about organizations, in such a way as to capture the users' intent. They have sought to test plausible propositions about organizations – either by proving that they follow from simple, reasonable and precisely stated assumptions, or (rarely) by formulating the propositions as statements about observable variables on which systematic rather than anecdotal data can be collected, and then applying the normal statistical procedures of empirical economics. (Here we shall only consider testing of the first type.) Third, much of the economists' organization theory is not descriptive but normative; it concerns not what is, but what could be. It takes the viewpoint of an organization *designer*. The organization is to respond to a changing and uncertain environment. The designer has to balance the 'benefits' of these responses against the organization's *informational costs*; good responses may be costly to obtain. In addition, the designer may require the responses to be *incentive-compatible*: each member of the organization must *want* to carry out his/her part of the total organizational response in just the way the designer intends.

The design point of view has old and deep roots in economics. Adam Smith's 'invisible hand' proposition is a statement about the achievements of markets as resource-allocating devices. If one reinterprets it as a comparative conjecture about alternative designs for a resource-allocating organization – namely, that a design using prices is superior to other possible designs – then it becomes an ancestor of the organization-design point of view. In any case, that point of view appears very clearly in Barone's 'The Ministry of Production in the collectivist state' (1908), and in the debates about 'the possibility of socialism' (i.e. of a centrally directed economy) in the 1930s and 1940s (Hayek, 1935; Lange, 1938; Dobb, 1940; Lerner, 1944).

Nearly all the debaters agreed that if the designer of resource-allocating schemes for an economy has a clean slate and can construct any scheme at all, then he must end up choosing some form of the price mechanism; for example, a scheme of the Lange–Lerner sort. Here a Centre announces successive trial prices; in response to each announcement, profit-maximizing demands are anonymously sent to the Centre by managers, and utility-maximizing demands are sent by consumers; in response to the totals of intended demands, the Centre announces new prices; the final announced prices are those which evoke zero excess demands, and the corresponding intended productions and consumptions are then carried out. The debate dealt largely with the informational virtues of such a price scheme as compared to an extreme centralized alternative scheme. The alternative scheme (never made very explicit) appears to be one wherein managers and consumers report technologies, tastes and endowments to the Centre, which thereupon computes the economy's consumptions and productions; those become commands to be followed.

In retrospect, the extreme centralized alternative seems an unimaginative straw man, since one can imagine a whole spectrum of designs lying between extreme centralization, on the one hand, and the price scheme, on the other; namely, designs in which some of the agents' private information is centrally collected (or pooled), but not all of it. In any case, the debaters agreed that the price scheme is informationally superior to the centralized alternative because (1) in the former, small computations are performed simultaneously by very many agents (though possibly many times), whereas in the latter an immense central computation is required (though required only once), and (2) the messages required in the former (prices and excess demands) are small (though sent many times) while in the latter a monstrously large information transmission is required (though only once).

Persuasive as this claim may appear, a moment's thought reveals how very many gaps need to be filled before the claim becomes provable or disprovable. If a proposed scheme is to be operated afresh at regular intervals (in response, say, to new and randomly changing tastes, technologies and endowments), then what is the designer's measure of a proposed allocation scheme's gross performance (against which a scheme's cost must be balanced)? Is it, for example, the expected value of the gross national product in the period which follows each operation of the scheme? Or is it perhaps a two-valued measure which takes the value one when the scheme's final allocation is Pareto-optimal and individually rational (i.e. every consumer ends up with a bundle at least as good as his/her endowment) and takes the value zero otherwise? When is the scheme to be determined if it comprises a sequence (possibly infinite) of steps? What interim action (resource allocation) is in force while the proposed scheme is in operation and before it yields a final action? For alternative investments in information-processing facilities, how long does the sequence's typical step take? (The longer a step takes, the longer one waits until a given terminal step is reached and the longer an unsatisfactory interim action is in force.)

Once such gaps are filled in, the claim becomes, in principle, a verifiable conjecture. Without venturing to fill them in, economists were nevertheless sufficiently intrigued by the intuitive (but quite unverified) informational appeal of the Lange–Lerner scheme so that they proceeded to construct many more schemes of a similar kind in a variety of settings, including multidivisional firms, for example, as well as planned economies with technologies less well behaved than the classic (convex) ones (see Heal, 1986). These efforts were partly stimulated by (and, in turn, stimulated) the development of algorithms for general constrained optimization, which often had a natural interpretation as schemes wherein a 'Centre' makes announcements and other 'persons' respond without directly revealing their private information. (One can so interpret, for example, certain gradient methods for constrained optimization, as well as the 'decomposed' version of the simplex algorithm for linear programming.)

If the informational appeal of schemes of the Lange–Lerner type was powerful but unverified, what of the incentive side? Here the 'possibility-of-socialism' writers were divided. A sceptic like Hayek (1935, pp. 219–20) asked why a manager would want to follow the Lange–Lerner rules. One (unsupported) reply – hinted at in various places in the debate – is that to induce a manager to follow the rules we need only pay him a reward which is some non-decreasing function of his enterprise's profit. The incentive question becomes acute when one turns to the scheme that is the analogue of the Lange–Lerner scheme if there are public goods; namely, the Lindahl scheme (Lindahl, 1919), when that is given a central-price-announcer interpretation. (The scheme was developed before the possibility-of-socialism debates but appears to have been unknown to the debaters.) For here, as Samuelson (1954) was the first to note, the prospective consumer of a public good may perceive an advantage in falsifying his demand for it; that is, in disobeying the designer's rule. (In fact, it turned out later (Hurwicz, 1972) that the same difficulty can arise without public goods; that is, in the original Lange–Lerner scheme itself.) It took about three decades after the possibility-of-socialism debate until one had the framework to study with precision the question of when incentive-compatible schemes of the price-announcer type – or indeed of any type – can be constructed for economies or for organizations i,n general.

On the informational side of the design question, a 1959 paper by Hurwicz (Hurwicz, 1960) proved to be a major step towards precise conjectures (as opposed to broadly appealing but unverifiable claims) about the informational merits of alternative resource-allocating schemes for economies, or indeed alternative designs for organizations in general. The key notion is that of an *adjustment process*, to be used by an n-person organization confronting a changing environment $e=(e_1,\ldots,e_n)$, lying always in some set E of possible environments. Here e_1 is that aspect of the environment e observed by person i. Assume that the possible values of e_i comprise a set E_1 and that $E = E_1 \times \cdots \times E_n$. If, for example, the organization is an exchange economy, then e_i is composed of l's endowment and i's preference ordering on alternative resource allocations; if $n - 2$, then E might be the set of classic Edgeworth-box economies. An adjustment process is a quadruple $\pi - (M, m_0, f, h)$, where M is a set called a *language* and is the cartesian product of n *individual languages* M_i; f is an n-tuple $(f_1, \ldots, f_n)$; f_i is a function from $M \times E_i$ to M_i; $m_0 = (m_{01}, \ldots, m_{0n})$ is an *initial* message n-tuple in M; h is a function, called the *outcome function*, from $M \times E$ to A; and A is a set of organization *actions* or *outcomes* (e.g. resource allocations). Imagine the environment to change at regular intervals. Following each new environment, person i emits the initial message m_{0i} in M_i. At step 1, person i emits the message $m_{1i} = f_i(m_0, e_i)$ in M_i, and at the typical subsequent step t, person i emits $m_{ti} = f_i(m_{t-1}, e_i)$, where $m_{ti} \in M_i$ and m_{t-1} denotes an element of M; namely $(m_{t-1,1}, \ldots, m_{t-1,n})$. At a terminal step T, the organization takes the action (or puts into effect the outcome) $h(m_T, e)$ in A which is its final response to the environment e. The process is *privacy-preserving* in the sense that e enters i's function f_i only through e_i, which is i's private knowledge. One might require a similar property for h, that is, that h be an n-tuple $(h_1, \ldots, h_n)$, where h_i is a function from $M \times E_i$ to a set A_i of possible values of i's *individual action* (thus A is the cartesian product $A_1 \times \cdots \times A_n$). In the useful special case of a 'non-parametric' outcome function, where h does not depend on e at all, such privacy-preservation for action selection holds trivially.

Note that we can endow person i with a memory. To do so, let every element m_i of the M_i be a *pair* (m_i^*, m_i^{**}), where m_i^* denotes memory and m_i^{**} denotes a message sent to (noticed by) others; specify that for $k \neq i$, f_k is insensitive to (its value does not depend on) m_i^*. By making the set in which m_i^* lies sufficiently large, we can let i remember, at every step, all that he has observed of the organization's messages thus far. We can, moreover, let i send messages always to j and to no one else by specifying that for $k \neq i$, $k \neq j$, f_k is sensitive to the ith component of m. We can let i send a message to j and to no one else *at some specific step* t^* by specifying that when all person's memories tell them that t^* has been reached, then for $k \neq i$, $k \neq j$, f_k is insensitive to the ith component of m.

The adjustment process, as the object to be chosen by the designer, is a concept sufficiently broad and flexible to accommodate all the economists' iterative resource allocation schemes for economies as well as a rich variety of designs for other organizations. All organizations, after all, respond to a changing environment of which each member observes only some aspect in which he/she is the specialist, and the environment's successive values are unknown to the designer when a design is to be chosen. If those values *were* known (e.g. if the environment were constant), then there would be no need for message exchanges at all: each member could simply be programmed once and for all to take a correct (a best) action or sequence of actions. In all organizations, moreover, members engage in dialogue that eventually yields an organizational response to the current environment (an action).

With regard to the classic claim that price schemes are informationally superior designs when the organization is an economy, the adjustment-process concept has permitted a first rigorous test. The test takes the view that we can (as a reasonable starting place) ignore the pre-equilibrium performance of a price scheme (formulated as an adjustment process), and can focus entirely on its *equilibrium* achievements. For any e in E let M^e denote the set of *equilibrium messages*; that is, every $m^e = (m_1^e, \ldots, m_n^e)$ in M^e satisfies $f_i(m^e, e) = m_i^e$ for all i. Confine attention to processes with non-parametric outcome functions h (i.e. h depends only on m, not on e) and, for the case where W is a set of exchange economies, formulate the competitive (the Walrasian) mechanism as a non-parametric process, say $\pi^* = (M^*, m_0^*, f^*, h^*)$. The typical element m of M^* comprises a vector of proposed prices and an $(n-1)$-tuple of proposed trade vectors; f_i yields i's intended trade vector – or, in an alternative version, a *set* of acceptable trade vectors – at the just-announced prices; and h is a projection function yielding the 'trade' portion of m. For the process π^* and for every e in a classical set E, all the *equilibrium outcomes for e* – that is, all those allocations (trade $(n-1)$-tuples) a satisfying $a = h^*(m)$ for all m in M^{*e} – are Pareto-optimal and individually rational. One now asks the following question: does there exist any other process $\pi = (M, m_0, f, h)$ such that (i) for all e in the same set E every equilibrium outcome is again Pareto-optimal and individually rational, and (ii) the process π is informationally 'cheaper' than π^*? A natural starting place for the assessment of informational cost is size of the language. If one confines oneself to processes π in which M is in a finite Euclidean space, then a natural measure of language size is dimension. But then the question just posed has a trivial Yes as its answer, since one can always code a message of arbitrary dimension as a one-dimensional message. To rule out such coding, one imposes 'smoothness' on the process π. For example, one considers the mapping t from A (the set of outcomes), to the subsets of E, such that for every e in $t(a)$, a is an equilibrium outcome for e, and one requires that t contain a Lipschitzian selection. It turns out that for classic sets E and for language dimension as the cost measure, no smooth process satisfying (i) and (ii) exists (Hurwicz, 1972). The result extends (for more general sorts of smoothness requirements) to processes with non-Euclidean languages and language-size measures more general than dimension (Mount and Reiter, 1974; Walker, 1977; Jordan, 1982).

These results are clearly a first step towards vindicating the classic claim that the price process is informationally superior. To go further, one would like to consider pre-equilibrium outcomes – so that the final allocation is the one attained at a fixed, but well-chosen, terminal step – and to take account of the change in the time required to reach that terminal step as one varies the investment in the information-processing facilities available for carrying out the typical step. It seems plausible that a version of the competitive process that converges rapidly to its equilibrium messages will rank high relative to other processes once this complication is added. One would like the 'smoothness' requirement to arise naturally from a model of a well-behaved information technology rather than being introduced (as at present) in an ad-hoc manner. One would like to leave the setting just sketched, wherein messages and outcomes are points of a continuum, to see whether analogous results hold when both messages and outcomes (allocations) have to be rounded off to a chosen precision. (A limited analogue of the dimensional-minimality result just sketched has in fact been obtained in such a discrete setting (Hurwicz and Marschak, 1985).)

For organizations in general, the requirements of Pareto-optimality and individual rationality are replaced by some given set of desired (and equally acceptable) responses to every possible given environment. The problem facing a designer who is unconcerned about incentive aspects can then be put as follows. Given a set E and a *desired-performance correspondence* ϕ from E to the subsets of an outcome (action) set A, find an adjustment process $\pi = (M, m_0, f, h)$ which *realizes* ϕ – that is, which satisfies $a \in \phi(e)$ if $a = h(m, e)$ and $m \in M^e$ – and whose informational costs (suitably measured) are no less than those of any other process which realizes ϕ.

Note that a far more ambitious task could be given the designer instead. Let the designer have preferences over alternative environment/outcome/cost triples and let the preferences be represented by a utility function. The ambitious task is then to find a process π, and an accompanying selection function, which chooses a unique equilibrium outcome in the set M^e for every e, so as to maximize the designer's expected utility (expectation being taken with respect to the random variable e). It seems clear that such unbounded designer's rationality is too ambitious a standard; organization theory would freeze in its tracks if it adopted such a standard. The realization of a given performance correspondence at minimum informational cost is a reasonable step towards bounded rationality, especially if the performance correspondence is not stringent. (Thus ϕ might assign to e all outcomes which are within a certain specified distance of an outcome that is 'ideal' for e – say an outcome that maximizes some pay-off function.)

The preceding bounded-rationality version of the designer's task can again be modified by allowing some 'dynamics'; that is, permitting choice of terminal step rather than focusing on equilibrium outcomes. Whether we do so or not, we now have a precise version of the general performance-versus-cost problem which we claimed at the start to be a distinctively 'economists'' contribution to organization theory. (The problem is surved in more detail in Marschak, 1986.)

When one turns to incentive issues, a certain 'contraction' of the adjustment-process concept has proven useful. The object chosen by the designer now becomes a *game form* (S, g), where $S = S_1 \times \cdots \times S_n$; S_1 is the set of person i's possible *strategies* s_i; and g is an outcome function from S to A (the set of organizational actions or outcomes). Person i's local environment e_i specifies (among other things) i's preferences over the alternative organizational outcomes. The set of Nash-equilibrium strategy n-tuples associated with the triple (S, g, e), denoted $N_{sg}(e)$, is the set of n-tuples $s = (s_1, \ldots, s_n)$ such that given $e = (e_1, \ldots, e_n)$, each person i regards the outcome $g(s)$ to be at least as good as the outcome $g(s_1, \ldots, s_{i-1}, \bar{s}_i, s_{i+1}, \ldots, s_n)$ for all $\bar{s}_i$ in S_i. Suppose the designer is again given a desired-performance correspondence ϕ from E to the subsets of A. Then the incentive problem may be put this way: find a game form (S, g) such that for every e in E and every s in $N_{sg}(e)$, the outcome $g(s)$ is contained in the set $\phi(e)$. Such a game form *Nash-implements* ϕ. We can trivially find an adjustment process (M, m_0, f, h) whose equilibrium outcomes for every e comprise exactly the set $\{a: a = g(s); s \in N_{sg}(e)\}$. (To do so, let $M = M_1 \times \cdots \times M_n = S_1 \times \cdots \times S_n$; let f_i satisfy $f_i((s_1, \ldots, s_n), e_i) = s_i$ if and only if, given e_i, i regards the outcome $g(s)$ to be at least as good as the outcome $g(s_1, \ldots, s_{i-1}, \bar{s}_i, s_{i+1}, \ldots, s_n)$ for all $\bar{s}_i$ in S_i; and let $h(s) = g(s)$.) Much has now been learned about what sorts of performance functions ϕ (including economically interesting ones) can be implemented and what sorts cannot (for a survey, see Hurwicz, 1986). We again have the 'dynamic' shortcoming noted before: if, for every e, an outcome in the set $\{a \in N_{sg}(e): s \in S\}$ is indeed to be reached by operating an adjustment process (as in the economists' allocation mechanisms), then the behaviour of the process prior to equilibrium must be studied. Doing so may, moreover, introduce quite new strategic considerations, since a fresh incentive problem may arise at each step of the process: at each step a member may ask whether carrying out the designer's instructions (applying f_i) is what he/she really wants to do.

Thus both on the informational and the incentive sides, a very large research agenda stretches before the economic organization theorist. Moreover, the abstract theorizing we have sketched is very far indeed from making good contact with the institutional facts about real organizations. One may take the design point of view, but even a designer is constrained by those facts.

In particular, the notion of *hierarchy* (the 'organization chart'), which appears so often in popular discourse, is very hard indeed to pin down in the adjustment-process framework. To define 'hierarchy', we first have to define 'authority'. When does an adjustment process have the property that person 1 is in authority over person 2? Probably the best one can hope for (Hurwicz, 1971) is this: person 1 is in authority over person 2 if (1) at the terminal step T, m_{T2} depends only on $m_{T-1,1}$; and (2) $m_{T-1,1}$ is sensitive to e_1. If we did not add requirement (2), then person 1's apparent terminal instruction to person 2 (embodied in the pre-terminal message $m_{t-1,1}$) might in fact be a robot-like repetition (perhaps in recorded form) of a 'command' that 2 gave to 1 at step $T-2$. On the other hand, we might satisfy the sensitivity required by (2) in such a trivial way that we have not really succeeded in ruling out person 2 as the 'true' (though somewhat disguised) commander. Authority is, in short, a very fragile concept from a formal point of view.

Yet it is a central concept in influential writings like those of Williamson (1975). His book is a rich source of institutionally motivated conjectures about how organizations work, but it teems with terms, concepts and conjectures that the formal theorist must struggle mightily to make precise. The task of precise pinning down is so daunting that the state of testing the conjectures (trying to prove them) seems unlikely to be reached. The book argues for these conjectures nevertheless, and many of them appear, at some level, to be plausible. Here is one example: 'it is elementary that the advantages of centralization vary with the degree of independence among the members, being... almost certainly great in an integrated task group' (p. 51). To the formal theorist, that is not 'elementary' at all. One requires five or six definitions before one even knows what is being claimed.

Nevertheless, such informal but insightful institution-based essays are an essential challenge to formal theory. The economists' organization theory of the future will grow out of the tension between highly imprecise but widely believed and institutionally grounded claims and the harsh demands of formal argument.

BIBLIOGRAPHY

Barone, E. 1908. The Ministry of Production in the collectivist state. In *Collectivist Economic Planning*, ed. F.A. von Hayek, London: Routledge, 1935, 245–90.

Dobb, M.H. 1940. *Political Economy and Capitalism.* New York: Macmillan.

Hayek, F. von. (ed.) 1935. *Collectivist Economic Planning.* London: Routledge.

Heal, G. 1986. Planning. In *Handbook of Mathematical Economics*, Vol. III, ed. K.J. Arrow and M.D. Intriligator, Amsterdam: North-Holland.

Hurwicz, L. 1960. Optimality and informational efficiency in resource allocation processes. In *Mathematical Methods in the Social Sciences*, ed. K.J. Arrow, S. Karlin and P. Suppes, Stanford: Stanford University Press.

Hurwicz, L. 1971. Centralization and decentralization in economic processes. In *Comparison of Economic Systems*, ed. A. Eckstein, Berkeley: University of California Press.

Hurwicz, L. 1972. On informationally decentralized systems. In *Decision and Organization*, ed. C.B. McGuire and R. Radner, Amsterdam: North-Holland.

Hurwicz, L. 1972. On the dimensional requirements of informationally decentralized Pareto-satisfactory processes. In *Studies in Resource Allocation Processes*, ed. K.J. Arrow and L. Hurwicz, Cambridge: Cambridge University Press, 1977.

Hurwicz, L. 1986. Incentive aspects of decentralization. In *Handbook of Mathematical Economics*, Vol. III, ed. K.J. Arrow and M.D. Intriligator, Amsterdam: North-Holland.

Hurwicz, L. and Marschak, T. 1985. Discrete allocation mechanisms: dimensional requirements for resource-allocation mechanisms when desired outcomes are unbounded. *Journal of Complexity*, December.

Jordan, S.J. 1982. The competitive allocation process is informationally efficient uniquely. *Journal of Economic Theory* 28, January, 1–18.

Lange, O. 1936–7. On the economic theory of socialism. In *On the Economic Theory of Socialism*, ed. B. Lipincott, Minneapolis: University of Minnesota Press, 1938.

Lerner, A.P. 1944. *The Economics of Control.* New York: Macmillan.

Lindahl, E. 1919. Just taxation: a positive solution. In *Classics in the Theory of Public Finance*, ed. R. Musgrave and A. Peacock, London: Macmillan, 1958.

Marschak, T. 1986. Organization design. In *Handbook of Mathematical Economics*, Vol. III, ed. K.J. Arrow and M.D. Intriligator, Amsterdam: North-Holland.

Mount, K. and Reiter, S. 1974. The informational size of message spaces. *Journal of Economic Theory* 8(2), 161–92.

Samuelson, P.A. 1954. The pure theory of public expenditure. *Review of Economics and Statistics* 36, November, 387–9.

Walker, M. 1977. On the informational size of message spaces. *Journal of Economic Theory* 15(2), August, 366–75.

Williamson, O.E. 1975. *Markets and Hierarchicies, Analysis and Antitrust Implications: a Study in the Economics of Internal Organizations.* New York: Free Press.

Perfectly and Imperfectly Competitive Markets

JOHN ROBERTS

In the competition between economic models, the theory of perfect competition holds a dominant market share: no set of ideas is so widely and successfully used by economists as is the logic of perfectly competitive markets. Correspondingly, all other market models (collectively labelled 'imperfectly competitive' and including monopoly, monopolistic competition, dominant-firm price leadership, bilateral monopoly and other situations of bargaining, and all the varieties of oligopoly theory) are little more than fringe competitors.

Although it is not surprising that perfect competition should play a central role as a benchmark for normative purposes, the dominance of perfectly competitive forms of analysis in descriptive and predictive work is remarkable. First, economic theorists seem to be increasingly of the view that something like imperfect competition is the fundamental idea, in that perfect competition should be justified by deriving it from models where imperfectly competitive behaviour is allowed and, in particular, agents recognize the full strategic options open to them and any monopoly power they have. This view has led to a large volume of work over the last twenty-five years that, for the most part, suggests that perfect competition corresponds to an extremely special, limiting case of a more general theory of markets. Second, as the idea of perfect competition has been made more precise and the conditions supporting it have become better understood, it has become completely evident that no important market fully satisfies the conditions of perfect competition and that most would not appear even to come close. This is not to say that models should be descriptively accurate; the only way a map could approach descriptive accuracy would be for it to have a scale of 1:1, but such a map is useless. Still, it is striking that economists so consistently opt for a mode with so little apparent descriptive value. Third, the received theory of perfect competition is a theory of price competition that contains no coherent explanation of price formation. That such a fundamental incompleteness does not severely limit the value of the theory is striking.

Given all this, the dominance of perfectly competitive methods should probably be viewed as a reflection of the weakness of imperfectly competitive analysis. There is in fact no powerful general theory of imperfect competition. Instead, there is a myriad of competing partial equilibrium models of imperfectly competitive markets, and the only general equilibrium theories either rely on questionable assumptions or embody institutional specifications that are no more satisfactory than those associated with perfectly competitive analysis.

Despite the unsatisfactory state of both perfectly and imperfectly competitive market theory, recent work based on game-theoretic methodology holds promise of providing a more satisfactory theory of imperfectly competitive markets, of yielding better insight into why perfectly competitive analysis seems to work so well, and of unifying these theories.

PERFECT COMPETITION. The idea of perfect competition has many aspects: absence of monopoly power; demand and supply curves that, to the individual appear horizontal; negligibility of an individual's quantities relative to aggregates; price-taking behaviour (with respect to the publicly quoted prices); zero profits and equality of returns across all activities; prices equalling marginal costs and factor returns equalling the values of marginal products; and Pareto-efficiency of market allocations and the efficacy of the Invisible Hand. Stigler (1957) has traced the historical development of the idea of perfect competition essentially through the 'imperfect competition revolution' of the 1930s, noting the appearance of many of these features and documenting the increasing recognition of the stringency of the conditions that appeared to be necessary and/or sufficient for perfect competition. Together these include: large numbers; free entry and exit; full information and negligible search costs; product homogeneity and divisibility; lack of collusion; and absence of externalities and of increasing returns to scale.

The theory about which Stigler wrote still largely corresponds to what is presented in intermediate textbooks and probably to the way most economists think about perfect competition when doing applied work. Firms and consumers are treated as making quantity choices at given prices, because with large numbers, it is suggested, individual quantities are 'negligible' relative to the aggregate, upon which prices are assumed to depend. (These arguments derive from Cournot, 1838.) But how prices are determined is not modelled. This approach is justified by informal arguments that prices are actually set by individual agents, but that, with many agents on each side of the market, any individual would be unable to deviate significantly from the prices charged by others without losing all demand or being overwhelmed by buyers. This idea is connected to the work of Bertrand (1883), but is not supported by formal arguments showing that the outcome of such price setting would be perfectly competitive under the assumed structural conditions (large numbers, homogeneity, free entry, etc.).

When Stigler wrote, Arrow, Debreu and MacKenzie had already provided their path-breaking formal analyses of Walrasian general equilibrium, and within two years Debreu published *Theory of Value* (1959), which is still the standard treatment of this subject. In this theory, competition is given a behavioural definition. There is a given list of consumers and of firms and a given list of commodities. A single price for each good is introduced, and perfectly competitive behaviour is then defined. It involves each consumer selecting the net transactions that maximize utility, subject to a budget constraint defined under the assumptions that the consumer can buy or sell unlimited quantities at the specified prices and that the consumer's purchases do not influence the profits he/she receives. As well, each firm selects the inputs and outputs that maximize its net receipts, again given that the firm can buy and sell any quantities it might consider without influencing prices. Finally, equilibrium is a price vector and perfectly competitive choices for each agent at these prices aggregate to a feasible allocation, i.e. such that markets clear.

Three fundamental results are proved for this model. These give conditions on tastes, endowments and technology under which competitive equilibria exist (existence), equilibrium allocations are Pareto-optimal (efficiency), and, with an initial reallocation of resources, any Pareto optimum can be supported as a competitive equilibrium (unbiasedness). The efficiency and existence theorems together formalize Adam Smith's argument of the invisible hand leading self-interested behaviour to serve the common good, while the unbiasedness result indicates that the competitive price system does not inherently favour any group (capitalists, workers, resource owners, consumers, etc.). The non-wastefulness result requires few assumptions beyond those built into the structure of the model: it is enough that not all consumers are satiated. The existence theorem, however, involves much stricter conditions, including especially the absence of any increasing returns to scale. (This is also needed for the unbiasedness result.)

Many of the conditions arising in less formal treatments of perfect competition are embodied in Debreu's formulation. For example, the very definition of a commodity involves homogeneity, and divisibility is explicitly assumed. Strikingly, however, free entry and large numbers play no explicit role in this theory: all the theorems would hold if there were but a single potential buyer and seller of any commodity.

This numbers-independence property relies crucially on the theory being only an *equilibrium theory*, that is, one which specifies what happens only if behaviour is exactly as stipulated and prices are set at equilibrium, market-clearing values. No examination is offered of what would happen if prices were not at their Walrasian levels, nor indeed, of how prices are determined. Further, not even the famous story of a disinterested Walrasian auctioneer and *tâtonnement* (no trade at nonequilibrium prices) supports this equilibrium by giving a consistent model of price formation with rational actors. Instead there would be incentives to misrepresent demands, responding consistently to each price announcement by the auctioneer as if one had different preferences than actually obtain, with the object of effecting monopolistic prices and outcomes (Hurwicz, 1972).

The ability of an individual to manipulate price formation by an auctioneer does disappear once one moves to a model where individuals truly are negligible. Such a model was first introduced by Aumann (1964), where the set of agents is indexed by a continuum endowed with a non-atomic measure. This measure is interpreted as giving the size of a group of agents in comparison with the whole economy. The absence of mass points implies that no individual's excess demands represent a positive fraction of the totals. Thus, any individual's withholding of supply affects neither the magnitude of excess demand (as measured on a per capita basis) nor, correspondingly, whether particular prices clear markets. Thus price-taking is fully rational if prices can be considered to be set by a disinterested auctioneer.

The infinite economy framework captures the large numbers, negligibility and (with an auctioneer) price-taking aspects of perfect competition. Infinite models also provide a setting where numerous other models of production and exchange agree with the Walrasian in their outcomes. However, infinite models clearly are an extreme abstraction, and the real issue is the extent to which they approximate finite economies. This question leads to consideration of sequences of increasingly large finite economies in which each individual becomes relatively small, perhaps with many others like him or her being present. The identification of perfect competition with such sequences of economies and the asymptotic properties of their allocations dates back to Cournot (1838) and Edgeworth (1881) and has become the basis of several major lines of research.

The most complete of these shows that the core converges to the Walrasian allocations (see Hildenbrand, 1974). However, recently attention has focused on the programme initiated by Cournot of obtaining perfect competition as the limit of imperfectly competitive behaviour and outcomes (see Mas-Colell, 1982).

There are three approaches to this problem. One, represented by Roberts and Postlewaite (1976), effectively takes some version of the auctioneer story as given and examines the incentives to respond to price announcements using one's true demands. Here it is shown that if the economy grows through replication or if the sequence of economies under consideration converges to one at which the Walrasian price is locally a continuous function of the data of the economy, then correct revelation of preferences and price-taking is asymptotically a dominant strategy. The second line of work builds more directly on Cournot's model. Agents select quantities and prices somehow arise to clear markets, with some agents (usually the firms) recognizing the impact of their choices on prices and others (consumers) taking prices as given. The central results here are due to Novshek and Sonnenschein (1978), who showed that the free-entry Cournot equilibria converge to the Walrasian allocations as the minimum efficient scale becomes small, provided that a condition of downward sloping demand is met. Finally, the game-theoretic models of noncooperative exchange initiated by Shubik (1973) also lead asymptotically to Walrasian equilibria (see Postlewaite and Schmeidler, 1978). A significant feature of these game-theoretic models is that they explicitly treat out-of-equilibrium behaviour: the outcome of *any* pattern of behaviour is specified, not just what happens in equilibrium. This is an important advance. However, in these models, prices appear only as the ratio of the amount of money bid for a good to the amount of the good offered, and are not directly chosen by agents.

A complementary approach to perfect competition (Ostroy, 1980) relates to marginal productivity theory and to horizontal demands. Central to this approach is a no-surplus condition that, agent by agent, the rest of the economy would be no worse off if the agent's resources and productive capability were removed from the economy. No-surplus allocations correspond to the economy's having Walrasian equilibria at the same prices with or without any single agent (so demands are horizontal). An economy is defined as perfectly competitive if the no-surplus condition is met. This can happen with a finite number of agents, but typically it requires an infinity.

Thus, various pieces of formal theory capture most of the aspects of the intuitive notion of perfect competition, but this theory points to perfect competition being a limiting case associated with many agents in each market or the existence of close substitutes for each firm's output, as well as with properties of continuity of the Walras correspondence and downward sloping demand. Also, this theory lacks models in which prices are explicitly chosen by economic agents. None of these results gives much reason for the success that economists have using perfectly competitive analysis.

IMPERFECT COMPETITION. Formal modelling of markets begins with Cournot's (1838) treatment of quantity-setting, noncollusive oligopoly. Cournot's model yields prices in excess of marginal cost, with this divergence decreasing asymptotically to zero as the number of firms increases. The 19th century saw two other important contributions to imperfect competition theory: Bertrand's (1883) price-setting model which, with constant costs, yields perfectly competitive outcomes from duopoly, and Edgeworth's (1897) demonstration that introducing capacity constraints into this model could prevent existence of (pure strategy) equilibrium.

Thus, even before the important competition revolution, the theory of imperfectly competitive markets was subject to one of the standard complaints still made against it: that it consists of too many models that yield conflicting predictions. This complaint intensified with the proliferation in the 1930s and later of models of firms facing downward-sloping demands. These models usually capture some element of actual competition (or at least appear more realistic than the perfectly competitive alternative). However, it sometimes seems that one can concoct an imperfect competition model that predicts any particular outcome one might wish.

A second complaint against imperfectly competitive analysis is its lack of a satisfactory multiple market formulation.

The first significant contribution to a general equilibrium theory of imperfect competition was Negishi's (1961) model, with later contributions from numerous authors during the 1970s. Although these models differ on important dimensions, the basic pattern in this work involves supplementing the Arrow–Debreu multi-market model of an economy by allowing that some exogenously specified set of firms perceive an ability to influence prices. (These firms may or may not perceive the actual demand relations correctly.) Equilibrium is then a set of choices (prices or quantities) for each imperfect competitor that maximizes its perceived profits, given the behaviour of the other imperfect competitors and the pattern of adjustment of the competitive sectors (under Walrasian, price-taking behaviour) to the choices of the imperfect competitors.

This theory, as it stood in the mid-1970s, was obviously incomplete on several grounds. Most fundamentally, there was no explanation of why some agents should take prices as given while other agents, who formally might be identical to the price-takers, behave as imperfect competitors. Moreover, it then emerged that there were serious flaws in the crucial existence theorems that purported to show that the models were not vacuous.

These theorems obtained profit maximizing choices for the imperfect competitors that were mutually consistent by use of fixed-point arguments based on Brouwer's theorem. To use these methods, the optimal choices of any one agent must depend continuously on the conjectured choices of the others. This role of continuity of reaction functions is analogous to that of continuity of demand functions in the Arrow–Debreu model. However, unlike the continuity of demand, continuity of reaction functions was not derived from conditions on the fundamental data of the economy. Rather, it was either directly assumed or obtained by supposing that the imperfect competitors' perceptions of demand yielded concave profit functions.

Roberts and Sonnenschein (1977) showed that this approach was problematic by displaying extremely simple, nonpathological examples in which reaction functions are discontinuous and no imperfectly competitive equilibrium exists. The source of these failures is nonconcavity of the profit functions, and no standard conditions on preferences ensure the needed concavity: it can fail with only a single consumer or when all consumers have homothetic preferences. (Note, however, that existence ceases to be a problem in general equilibrium Cournot models if the economy, including the number of imperfect competitors, is made large enough through replication.)

These problems with imperfect competition theory perhaps explain some of the popularity of perfect competition models. However, they also suggest two important, positive points. First, the multiplicity of models and the divergence in their predictions indicates that, at least in small numbers situations, institutional details are important. Economists, habituated to the use of perfectly competitive methods, typically are imprecise about such factors as how prices are actually determined, whether decisions are made simultaneously or sequentially, whether individuals select prices, quantities, or both, and what happens when agents' plans are inconsistent. These factors cannot be treated so cavalierly in dealing with imperfectly competitive models and probably ought not to be when actual markets are being analysed. Second, both the failure of existence in models of imperfectly competitive general equilibrium and the unexplained asymmetry of assumed behaviour in these models suggest that a simple grafting of imperfect competitors onto the standard Arrow–Debreu model will not yield a satisfactory theory.

Rather, one ought to start afresh from the foundations with a more careful modelling.

STRATEGIC MODELS OF COMPETITION. An approach to both of these points is provided by the methods of the theory of noncooperative games and especially games in extensive form. Recent work using this approach has resulted in significant improvements in the partial equilibrium theory of imperfect competition, and there is reason to hope that these same methods can provide a satisfactory general equilibrium theory. Moreover, this approach also offers hope of ultimately yielding a unified theory of competition that would encompass both perfect and imperfect competition.

To model a market as a game in extensive form, one must specify the set of participants, the beliefs each has about the characteristics of the other agents, the order in which each acts, the information available to each whenever it makes a decision, the possible actions available at each decision point, the physical outcomes resulting from each possible combination of choices and the valuations of these outcomes by the agents. Thus, such a model involves a complete specification of a particular set of institutions. This aspect might be viewed as a drawback, but it is in fact a potential strength of these methods.

(Note that adopting this approach does not require that price formation be modelled by having prices be chosen by agents in the model. Indeed, Cournot's original model is a well-specified game, but price formation is not explicitly modelled. However, this framework does facilitate and encourage such a specification.)

Given a game, one next specifies a solution concept. In principle, there is great freedom in making this specification, but most researchers opt for the Nash equilibrium or some refinement thereof. Note that adopting the Nash equilibrium does not rule out collusion if opportunities to coordinate and to enforce agreements are modelled as part of the game. Nor does it mean that the agents are acting simultaneously: the order of moves is part of the specification of the game, and the Nash equilibrium applies equally to simultaneous or sequential moves. To illustrate, the von Stackelberg solution corresponds to subgame-perfect Nash equilibrium in a game where the designated leader moves first and the follower observes the leader's choice before making its own. Finally, the Nash criterion does not restrict analysis to one-shot situations; it is equally applicable to models of repeated play.

When von Neumann and Morgenstern's (1944) treatise on game theory first appeared, there was hope among economists that these methods would unify and advance the analysis of imperfect competition. When these hopes were not quickly realized, many economists wrote off game theory as a failure. This position is still reflected in many intermediate textbooks. However, in the last decade these hopes have been revitalized by actual accomplishments of these methods.

The first contribution of this work has been to begin unifying the existing theory of imperfect competition. This has been done on one level by providing a common language and analytical framework in terms of which earlier work can be cast and understood. In this line, game theoretic treatments have made formal sense out of such ideas as reaction curves and kinked demand curves by obtaining equilibria of well-specified, dynamic games that have these features. As well, various of the older theories that appeared to be in conflict have been shown to be consistent in that they arise from a common, more basic model. For example, the Cournot and the von Stackelberg solutions can both be attained as Nash equilibria in a single model where the timing of moves is endogenous. In a similar vein, the Cournot, Bertrand and Edgeworth models have been integrated by showing that equilibrium in a two-stage game where duopolists first select capacities and then compete on price yields the Cournot quantities.

A second contribution has been to provide models embodying aspects of imperfect competition that had been widely discussed in the industrial organization literature but previously lacked formal expression. The best example here is work showing how limit pricing, predatory pricing and price wars can arise as rational behaviour in the presence of informational asymmetries between competitors (see Roberts, 1986). Further examples include explanations of sales and other discriminatory pricing policies, the determination and maintenance of product quality, the use of capacity and other investments in commitment to deter entry, and the opportunities for and limitations on implicit collusion. This work is revolutionizing the field of industrial organization.

The third contribution has been to permit the analysis of realistic models of institutions for exchange that are actually present in the economy. The best-developed example of such work is that on auctions to sell a single object to one of many potential buyers (see Milgrom, 1986), but important work has also been done on multi-object auctions and other monopoly pricing institutions (including posted prices, priority pricing, and nonlinear pricing), bilateral monopoly and bargaining, and bid-ask markets or oral double auctions. In this work, the rules of the institution being modelled, the distribution of information about tastes, costs, etc., held by the various participants, and the preferences of these agents together induce a game in extensive form. This game captures the full strategic options open to all the participants, specifying completely the prices and allocations resulting from any choice of actions. Thus, the Nash equilibrium of this game yields explicit predictions of the choices of prices and of the volume, timing and pattern of trade. Often these predictions are both remarkably tight and in agreement with observed behaviour.

This work is providing a more complete description and a clearer theoretical understanding of the operation of actual markets. Moreover, by providing detailed predictions of the outcomes of equilibrium behaviour under different institutions, it gives the basis for a theory of the choice among market institutions (see, for example, Harris and Raviv, 1981). Finally, it provides an approach to unifying the theories of perfect and imperfect markets and market behaviour. In this work, agents' behaviour is rationally strategic relative to the given economic situation. However, in particular environments this imperfectly competitive behaviour may be very close to perfectly competitive or may yield outcomes that are essentially competitive (see Wilson, 1986). By determining the situations in which this is true, we may finally understand when and why perfectly competitive analyses succeed.

BIBLIOGRAPHY

Aumann, R.J. 1964. Markets with a continuum of traders. *Econometrica* 32, 39–50.

Aumann, R.J. 1975. Values of markets with a continuum of traders. *Econometrica* 43, 611–46.

Bertrand, J. 1883. Théorie mathématique de la richesse sociale. *Journal des Savants* 48, 499–508.

Cournot, A. 1838. *Recherches sur les principes mathématiques de la théorie des richesses.* Paris: M. Rivière.

Debreu, G. 1959. *The Theory of Value.* New York: John Wiley & Sons.

Edgeworth, F.Y. 1881. *Mathematical Psychics.* London: P. Kegan; New York: A.M. Kelley, 1967.

Edgeworth, F.Y. 1897. La teoria pura del monopolio. *Giornale degli Economisti* 15, 13ff.

Harris, M. and Raviv, A. 1981. A theory of monopoly pricing schemes with demand uncertainty. *American Economic Review* 71, 347–65.

Hildenbrand, W. 1974. *Core and Equilibria of a Large Economy.* Princeton: Princeton University Press.

Hurwicz, L. 1972. On informationally decentralized systems. In *Decision and Organization*, ed. C.B. McGuire and R. Radner, Amsterdam: North-Holland, 297–336.

Kalai, E. and Stanford, W. 1985. Conjectural variations strategies in accelerated Cournot games. *International Journal of Industrial Organization* 3, 133–52.

Kreps, D.M. and Scheinkman, J.A. 1983. Quantity precommitment and Bertrand competition yield Cournot outcomes. *Bell Journal of Economics* 14, 326–37.

Mas-Colell, A. (ed.) 1982. *Non-cooperative Approaches to the Theory of Perfect Competition.* New York: Academic Press.

Milgrom, P.R. 1986. Auction theory. In *Advances in Economic Theory*, ed. T. Bewley, Cambridge: Cambridge University Press for the Econometric Society.

Negishi, T. 1961. Monopolistic competition and general equilibrium. *Review of Economic Studies* 28, 196–201.

Novshek, W. and Sonnenschein, H. 1978. Cournot and Walras equilibrium. *Journal of Economic Theory* 19, 223–66.

Ostroy, J. 1980. The no-surplus condition as a characterization of perfectly competitive equilibrium. *Journal of Economic Theory* 22, 183–207.

Postlewaite, A. and Schmeidler, D. 1978. Approximate efficiency of non-Walrasian equilibria. *Econometrica* 46, 127–37.

Roberts, J. 1986. Battles for market share: incomplete information, aggressive strategic pricing, and competitive dynamics. In *Advances in Economic Theory*, ed. T. Bewley, Cambridge: Cambridge University Press for the Econometric Society.

Roberts, J. and Postlewaite, A. 1976. The incentives for price-taking behavior in large exchange economies. *Econometrica* 44, 115–27.

Roberts, J. and Sonnenschein, H. 1977. On the foundations of the theory of monopolistic competition. *Econometrica* 45, January, 101–13.

Shubik, M. 1973. Commodity money, oligopoly, credit and bankruptcy in a general equilibrium model. *Western Economic Journal* 11, 24–38.

Stigler, G. 1957. Perfect competition, historically contemplated. *Journal of Political Economy* 65, 1–17.
von Neumann, J. and Morgenstern, O. 1944. *Theory of Games and Economic Behavior*. Princeton: Princeton University Press.
Wilson, R. 1986. Game theoretic analyses of trading process. In *Advances in Economic Theory*, ed. T. Bewley, Cambridge: Cambridge University Press for the Econometric Society.

Principal and Agent

JOSEPH E. STIGLITZ

The principal–agent literature is concerned with how one individual, the principal (say an employer), can design a compensation system (a contract) which motivates another individual, his agent (say the employee), to act in the principal's interests. The term principal–agent problem is due to Ross (1973). Other early contributions to this literature include Mirrlees (1974, 1976) and Stiglitz (1974, 1975).

A principal–agent problem arises when there is imperfect information, either concerning what action the agent has undertaken or what he should undertake. In many situations, the actions of an individual are not easily observable. It would be very difficult for a landlord to monitor perfectly the weeding activity of his tenant. A bank cannot monitor perfectly the actions of those to whom it lends money. The employer cannot travel on the road with his salesman, to monitor precisely the effort he puts into his salesmanship. In each of these situations, the agent's (tenant's, borrower's, employee's) action affects the principal (landlord, lender, employer). Clearly, if an individual's actions are unobservable, then compensation cannot be based on those actions. In some cases, even if an individual's actions are not directly observable, it may be possible to infer his actions. Thus, if output were a function just of effort [$Q = F(e)$] then even if effort were unobservable, if output were observable, and the relationship between output and effort were known, then effort could be inferred with perfect accuracy.

The principal–agent literature focuses on situations where an individual's actions can neither be observed nor be perfectly inferred on the basis of observable variables; thus, for instance, it is usually assumed that output is a function of effort and an unobservable random variable, θ: $Q = F(e, \theta)$.

Moreover, in many circumstances, the principal wishes the agent to take actions based on information which is available to the agent, not the principal. Indeed, this is the very reason that individuals delegate responsibility. Because of the asymmetry of information, the principal does not know whether the agent undertook the action the principal would himself have undertaken, in the given circumstances. Hence, even if the principal can observe the action, he may not know whether that action was appropriate.

Since, in general, the pay-offs to the agent will differ from those to the principal, the agent will not in general take the action which the principal would like him to take, or that they would contract for in the presence of perfect information. For instance, the employee may not adjust his effort as the situation requires, or he may engage in too much or too little risk taking.

The principal–agent problem is, then, the central problem of economic incentives.

In spite of the importance attached to *economic incentives*, until recently economic theory had little to say on the matter. In the standard theory, individuals were paid for performing a particular task. If they performed the task, they received their compensation; if they failed to perform the task, they did not. Individuals thus always had an incentive to perform the contracted-for service. Only if the employer were so foolish as to pay the worker whether he performed the task or not would an incentive problem arise.

The standard theory was based on the assumption that what action the 'principal' wished his agent to perform was perfectly known, and that the action could be perfectly and costlessly monitored. Neither assumption is plausible and, indeed, relatively few workers are paid solely on the basis of their observed inputs.

ORIGINS OF PRINCIPAL–AGENT PROBLEMS. Principal–agent problems arise whenever one individual's actions have an effect on another individual. The question arises, then, why cannot economic relationships be designed to avoid this kind of dependency? Under what circumstances do these interdependencies arise? For instance, if a landlord were to sell or rent his land to his tenant, then the workers' effort would have no effect on him. If an employer were to sell or rent his capital to his worker, then the workers' effort would again have no effect on him. Traditional neoclassical analysis emphasized the symmetry in economic relationships: one could describe the employer–employee relationship as the employee hiring capital just as well as one could describe it as the employer hiring labour. (This Wicksellian description of economic relationships always seemed peculiar to me; it seemed to suggest the absence within neoclassical analysis of certain important aspects of economic relationships; it is those aspects which are the subject of scrutiny here.)

There are three important reasons for the existence of principal–agent problems. Two have to do with the essential intertemporal nature of certain relationships: insurance and credit. When two individuals enter into an insurance contract, one individual (*a*) promises to pay the other (*b*) a certain amount if event A occurs, while the other (*b*) promises to pay (*a*) a certain amount if event B occurs. If there are actions which one of the individuals can undertake between the date of the contract and the event which will affect the outcome, then there is a principal–agent relationship between the two. This particular form of the principal–agent problem is referred to within the insurance literature as the *moral hazard problem* (see Arrow, 1965), and, by extension, the term has been applied to the principal–agent problem more generally.

Similarly, in credit relationships, one individual gives another some resource (money), in return for a promise to repay that money at some later date. So long as there is some probability of default, which can be affected by the actions of the borrower, there is a *moral hazard* or *principal–agent* problem (provided that that action cannot be perfectly monitored by the lender).

Many economic relationships have an important element of insurance within them. The landlord–tenant sharecropping relationship can be viewed as if the tenant pays a fixed rent, and then receives an insurance policy from the landlord, in which the landlord agrees to pay the tenant a certain amount if output is low (equal to the difference between his share and the fixed rent); and the tenant agrees to pay a premium equal again to the difference between the share and the fixed rent, when output is high.

Indeed, the credit 'problem' can be viewed as a special form of an insurance relationship: the lender provides an insurance policy, such that if the borrower's resources are less than the amount owed, the lender agrees to pay the borrower the difference (which the borrower then immediately repays to the lender). The premium is the difference between the rate of interest on a perfectly safe loan and the rate of interest charged on this risky loan.

Insurance (spreading and transferring risk) provides one of the explanations of sharecropping; were workers to rent the land, they would have to absorb all the risk associated with output variations. With sharecropping, the risk is shared between the landlord and the tenant. Since the wealth of tenants is usually much less than that of landlords, there is some presumption that the landlords are better able to absorb this risk.

But even if the tenants were risk neutral, there might be a principal–agent problem. We suggested above that if the landlord were to rent his land to the tenant, there would be no principal–agent problem. But this is not quite correct. If the tenant did not have sufficient resources to pay the rent before production, then the landlord would have to lend the tenant the money. (If he receives the rent at the end of the period, then it is as if he is lending the individual the money.) And then, if there are actions which the individual can undertake which affect the likelihood of not being able to repay the debt (pay the rent), *then* there is a moral hazard problem.

There is a second reason why renting land might not solve the moral hazard problem. There may be actions which the tenant can take which affect the quality of the land. To the extent that those actions are monitorable, the rental agreement may specify the actions to be undertaken (e.g. concerning what crops are to be grown, or grazing patterns). But these actions are not perfectly monitorable, and thus, even with rental agreements there are important principal–agent problems. (The same issues arise, of course, with the rental of any durable good.)

Again, one should ask, cannot these principal–agent problems be alleviated, e.g. by *selling* the asset. But this entails precisely the two problems we identified before as giving rise to principal–agent relationships: The agent (tenant, employee) may not have sufficient capital (and thus must borrow to make the purchase, creating a credit principal–agent problem); and if there is any risk associated with the future value of the land, it imposes a risk on the agent. Any attempt to alleviate those risks (through insurance) again gives rise to a moral hazard problem.

The third major source of principal–agent relationships is rather different. It arises from the attempt of the principal to extract as much *rent* (surplus) from the agent as possible. The employer does not know how difficult the task is that he would like the worker to perform. He could pay the worker the full value of his output, but that would leave him no profits. He might pay much less, but that might result in the worker refusing to work, if the task is in fact quite difficult; and thus he would lose profits that he might otherwise obtain. This rent extraction problem has been particularly well studied in the context of public utilities: the government does not know the minimum amount of compensation required to keep the utility producing. The rent extraction problem may be alleviated within competitive environments by holding auctions: the individual for whom the asset (franchise) is most valuable will bid the most. But there may not be enough bidders to extract all the rents through an auction mechanism; and at least in the case of utilities, the government may care not only about the rents received, but also about the actions undertaken by the franchisee. (In some cases, the rent extraction problem and the insurance problem are closely related: the average value of rents received may be increased if rents can be varied with the weather, the state of nature; again, we can think of decomposing the rent payment into a fixed rent and an insurance payment.)

This list of reasons for the origins of principal–agent relations is not meant to be exhaustive: yet many of the other reasons cited may be reduced to one of these explanations. For instance, consider the problem of a production line on which there are many workers; the output of the production line depends on all of their efforts. In the absence of risk aversion and credit problems, the incentive problem could be solved by giving each worker the total value of net output. He would purchase the right to the job by paying a fixed fee. With such a compensation scheme, the worker would have full incentives for maximizing the firm's output. But such a compensation scheme imposes on the worker an intolerable level of risk; and the fixed fee he would be required to pay necessitates his borrowing large amounts of money.

THE BASIC PRINCIPAL–AGENT PROBLEM. In the standard principal–agent problem, one looks for that contract (compensation scheme) which maximizes the expected utility of the principal, given that (a) the agent will undertake the action(s) which maximizes his expected utility, given the compensation scheme; and (b) given that he must be willing to accept the contract.

The second set of constraints (which are nothing more than the standard reservation utility constraints) are sometimes referred to as the individual rationality constraints.

There are two standard mathematical formulations. One is a direct generalization of the insurance–moral hazard problem. There are a set of observable events, such as whether an accident occurs. The probability that an event i occurs is a function of the actions undertaken (effort at accident avoidance):

$$p_i = p_i(\mathbf{e}),$$

where $\mathbf{e}$ may be a vector. The wealth of the individual in state i, in the absence of insurance, is w_i, and with insurance it is y_i. Thus

$$h_i = y_i - w_i$$

is the net payment from (to) the insurance company (the principal) in state i. The expected utility of the insured (the agent) is then just

$$U = \sum_i U_i(y_i, \mathbf{e}) p_i(\mathbf{e})$$

while that of the principal is

$$V = \sum_i V_i(h_i) p_i(\mathbf{e}).$$

$\{h_i\}$ is chosen to maximize V subject to $U \geqslant \bar{U}$.

Notice that the employer–employee relationship may be cast in this form: the observable events are the levels of output. Assume for simplicity, that we measure outputs in round numbers (say, bushels of wheat). Then state i refers to the number of bushels produced. p_i then is the probability that i bushels will be produced. Assume that the individual's wealth, apart from this contractual arrangement with his employer, is zero. Then y_i is the individual's pay if output is i. If the employer is risk neutral,

$$V_i(h_i) = qi - h_i = q_i - y_i,$$

where q is the price of output (of a bushel of wheat), assumed to be independent of i.

Although the employer–employee relationship can be cast in this form, it is more naturally represented by a formulation in which the probabilities of the states (weather) are fixed, where the states are unobservable, but where what is affected by the employee is the output in each state.

We can represent this formally in the following way. Let S be a set of state variables (like weather) observable to the agent. Let Q be a set of output variables (assumed observable to the principal and agent). And let A be a set of inputs (actions) by the agent assumed observable only by the agent.

Then a compensation scheme is a payment from the principal to the agent which is a function of all variables that are observable to both the agent and principal,

$$Y = \phi(Q).$$

The agent chooses his actions to maximize his expected utility which depends both on his income and his actions, given

$$\max EU(Y, A, S)$$

where outputs (actions), A, are related to the inputs by a production function

$$Q = Q(A, S).$$

We denote the solution to this by

$$A = H(S).$$

Finally, we can calculate the expected utility of the principal; his utility depends on the agent's actions, the payments he makes to the agent and his state (the actions may affect the principal either directly, or via their effect on outputs, or via their effects on payments),

$$EV = EV(\phi(Q), Q, A, S).$$

The principal's problem is to choose ϕ to maximize his expected utility,

$$\max EV,$$

recognizing the dependence of the agent's action on ϕ and recognizing that he must pay the agent enough to induce him to accept the job,

$$EU \geqslant \bar{U}. \qquad \text{(RU)}$$

POOLING VERSUS SEPARATING EQUILIBRIUM. Much of the literature has focused on situations where the principal wishes to induce the agent to take different actions in different states. That is, in the simplest case where only output is observable by the principal, if $A^*(S)$ is the action desired in state S, then the compensation scheme must be such that

$$EU[\phi(Q(A^*, S)), A^*, S] \geqslant EU[(Q(A, S)), A, S] \qquad \text{for all feasible } A.$$

These constraints are referred to as the self-selection or incentive compatibility constraints.

When the individual takes actions in two different states, so that the observable variables are the same, i.e. so that the principal cannot distinguish which of the two states has occurred, we say that there is a *pooling* equilibrium. When the individual takes actions so that the principal can identify which state has occurred, we say that there is a *separating* equilibrium. (This terminology was introduced within the context of the adverse selection literature by Rothschild and Stiglitz (1976).) A basic result of the principal–agent literature establishes conditions under which the optimal contract involves complete or partial separation.

ADVERSE SELECTION. The variable S can be thought of as a characteristic of an individual, rather than as the state of nature. Then the self-election constraint says that individuals of type S prefer action $A(S)$ to any other feasible action. If the self-selection constraints are satisfied, we can identify who is of what type. The action may consist of nothing more than making a choice. In the adverse selection interpretations of the model, the constraint (RU) needs to be replaced by the set of constraints,

$$U(\phi(Q(A, S)), A, S) \geqslant \bar{U}(S), \qquad \text{for all } s$$

that is, there is a reservation utility level for each individual (an individual rationality constraint for each type). (Note that a similar set of constraints is relevant if the contractual arrangement between the principal and agent is not binding, i.e. the individual can quit after he sees what the state of nature is.)

Some examples follow.

(i) *The partially discriminating monopoly* (see, e.g. Salop, 1977; Stiglitz, 1977). The firm knows that different individuals have different indifference curves between the good he sells and other goods, and different reservation utility levels, but he does not know who is of which type. Q may be the quantity of some commodity chosen by an individual in which case $\phi(Q)$ can be interpreted as the payment to the monopolist. (If one individual unambiguously has stronger preferences for the good, in the sense that at any quantity and payment, the extra amount he is willing to pay for a marginal unit is greater, then some separation is always desirable; this property is called the single crossing property.)

(ii) *Optimal tax structures* (Mirrlees, 1971). The government wishes to impose differential taxation on different individuals; it may want to impose a higher tax on the more able, but cannot tell who is the more able. Neither the individual's productivity nor the number of hours a week he works is observable, but his income is observable. The income tax schedule specifies a level of consumption corresponding to each level of income. The individual chooses (by the amount of work he undertakes) a point on that schedule. A schedule which results in the more able earning (choosing) higher incomes is one which separates. This will be desirable if the indifference curves between consumption and income are flatter for the more able – they require less of an increase in consumption to compensate for an increase in income. This will be true, for instance, if the underlying indifference curves between hours worked and consumption are the same for all individuals.

(iii) *Pareto efficient tax structures* (Stiglitz, 1982a). In the previous problem, the government maximized the sum of utilities, subject to the self-selection constraints, the revenue constraints and the individual rationality constraints (which simply required that the individual desire to work). The revenue constraint was equivalent, in this problem, to the profits (revenues) of the landlord; that is, while in the landlord problem we maximize the revenue, subject to the expected utility of the individual satisfying a certain constraint, here the dual of this problem is analysed. The 'sum of utilities' is equivalent to 'expected utility' – where the probability of each state S is identical. We can directly generalize this by imposing constraints on the level of utility attained by all individuals other than the first; we then maximize the first individual's utility subject to these constraints (and subject to the self-selection constraints, and the revenue constraints). This is the problem of Pareto efficient taxation. It is equivalent to the problem of maximizing a weighted sum of individuals' utilities.

(iv) *Implicit contracts with asymmetric information.* (For surveys, see Hart, 1983; Stiglitz, 1986; Azariadis and Stiglitz, 1983.) With perfect information, the employer would provide insurance to the employee, to stabilize the employee's income. If, for instance, the workers' utility function was separable between hours worked, l, and income y,

$$U = u(y) - v(l),$$

then with complete information, and risk neutral firms, y will be the same in all states, but l will be higher in states where labour productivity is higher. Thus, if the employer knew the state, but the worker did not, the employer would have an incentive always to say that it was a good state (since what he paid the worker was the same, but workers are required to work more in good states). The optimal contract will induce the employer to announce that it is bad when it is in fact bad, i.e. it will separate (at least partially).

QUALITATIVE RESULTS. It is clear that many economic relationships fall within the scope of the 'principal–agent' model. Many of the basic qualitative results emerge from a detailed analysis of the insurance model:

(a) There is a risk-incentive trade-off; since the risks undertaken will be a function of the quantity of insurance purchased, if the latter is observable, the premium will depend on it, and in equilibrium, there will be quantity rationing, i.e., the individual would like to purchase more insurance, at the going benefit premium ratio (Pauly, 1968). The amount of insurance will be greater, the more risk averse the individual.

(b) Indifference curves (between benefits and premia) are not in general quasi-concave, and feasibility sets (the set of insurance premia satisfying the non-negative profit constraint) are not convex; this has important consequences for the existence of competitive equilibria. The amount of insurance purchased may not be a continuous function of the price of insurance; and the level of effort may not be a continuous function of the amount of insurance purchased.

(c) Competitive equilibrium, when it exists, will not in general be Pareto efficient (Arnott and Stiglitz, 1986; Greenwald and Stiglitz, 1986); the profits of one insurance firm are affected both by the terms at which other firms offer insurance contracts (whether for similar accidents or not), and by the prices at which goods (whether complements or substitutes for accident avoidance or accident inducing activities) are sold; there exist a set of Pareto improving subsidies and taxes. In some instances, firms may attempt to internalize some of these 'externalities'. This leads to interlinkage of markets, both across time (the same insurance firm insures the individual over time), and at the same time (the same insurance firm insures the individual for many different risks) (Braverman and Stiglitz, 1982). The frequently observed interlinkage between credit and land markets in less developed countries has been interpreted in this light.

VARIANTS OF THE GENERAL MODEL. Further results have been obtained for various variants of the general model. We discuss a few of the more important versions below:

(i) Adverse selection model. The major qualitative results of this model (other than the specification of the conditions under which pooling or separation occurs, discussed above) entail an analysis of the distortions (relative to perfect information) engendered by the self-selection constraints; in the optimal income tax, the reduction in work (income) of the less able (associated with a positive marginal tax rate); in the asymmetric information implicit contract model, in the existence of overemployment in good states (with the separable utility function and risk neutral firms), or underemployment in bad states (with very risk averse firms). To discriminate among individuals, firms may engage in socially wasteful activities, such as random pricing or long queues. Generally, one group in the population (the most risk averse in the insurance model, the highest ability in the optimal income tax model) chooses a contract which does not distort its behaviour.

(ii) Incentive model with actions taken before state is known. When the random elements have bounded support, then a first best can be achieved simply by imposing a large enough penalty for performances below a given threshold. The individual will exert enough effort to avoid this. (See Mirrlees, 1974; Stiglitz, 1975.)

(iii) Theory of contests. If the output of others performing similar tasks in similar situations is observable, then one will employ compensation schemes based on relative performance; these will do better than individualistic compensation schemes. If there are enough individuals, simple schemes, based only on individuals' rankings, can approximate the first-best outcomes.

(iv) Models in which the utility constraint is not binding. In some cases, when the principal maximizes his expected utility, subject to the workers' reservation utility constraint, the latter constraint will not be binding. Such models give rise to unemployment. A particularly important variant of these models is described next.

(v) Models in which quality is affected by price. If the probability of default increases with the rate of interest charged (either because individuals undertake more risks when the interest rate is higher, or because those who are less risky stop applying for loans at high interest rates), then banks may not raise interest rates, even in the presence of an excess demand for loans. Similarly, if the productivity of a worker increases with the wage paid (either because individuals exert greater effort at higher wages or because those who are recruited at higher wages are more productive), then firms may not lower wages, even in the presence of an excess supply of labour.

(vi) Terminations. In multiperiod models, it has been shown that the optimal contract may entail the termination of a relationship when performance is unsatisfactory; this is shown to be preferable to the imposition of other penalties. (See Stiglitz and Weiss, 1983.)

(vii) Infinite period models. Long-term relationships may ameliorate some of the incentive problems (see Radner, 1981). Over an infinite lifetime, the principal (insurer) can make good inferences concerning the actions of the agent (insured); the relative frequency of accidents will converge to the accident probability corresponding to the individual's effort level. Not surprisingly, then, with low enough discount rates, incentive schemes can be designed which approximate the first best outcomes. The interpretation of this result is, however, subject to some controversy. Since with low discount rates, the change in lifetime income which would be associated with the individual bearing the full risk of the outcome for any period is negligible, it is as if the individual is risk neutral; and with risk neutrality we know that first best optimum can be obtained (if bankruptcy is ignored).

THE SET OF ADMISSIBLE CONTRACTS. One of the important and general results to emerge from the principal–agent literature is that the nature of the equilibrium contract depends on the set of admissible contracts. Contracts can depend only on the available information; typically, it is desirable to use all of the available information, though in practice, many variables which ought to be relevant (have information value) are not included within the compensation scheme.

Similarly, if one could costlessly implement a non-linear incentive scheme, such schemes would, in general, be preferable to linear schemes. Though in practice, again, most observed schemes seem relatively simple (linear, piece-wise linear, etc.), much of the literature has been concerned with characterizing in admittedly simple situations the optimal non-linear scheme.

In a variety of situations, if one could make pay a stochastic function, it would be desirable to do so, even with risk averse individuals. (Arnott–Stiglitz (1987) and Holmstrom (1979) show that with separable utility functions, this will not happen.) The intuition behind this, in the case when actions have to be taken prior to the agent obtaining information about the state, is that the possibility that he receives a low compensation so induces him to work hard that the employer (landlord) can reduce the dependence (on average) of pay on output, and thus reduce the variability of income.

Though optimal schemes may thus appear to be fairly complex, in practice most schemes employed are relatively simple. There is an ongoing controversy between those who seek to consider increasingly complex schedules, dismissing work which has analysed simple linear schedules as ad hoc, and those who seek to explain the kinds of compensation schedules actually employed; these dismiss the complex solutions as being irrelevant. They would argue that efforts should be devoted to understanding why actually employed schemes take on the form they do.

One possible explanation of the use of simple schedules is that they may be more *robust*. That is, as technology changes or the probability distribution of states changes (the exogenous parameters in the principal–agent problem) the optimal compensation scheme changes. But in practice, revisions to compensation schemes are costly, and one must find a scheme that works under a variety of situations. Simple, linear schemes may possess this property of robustness.

Another important characteristic of the set of admissible schemes relates to commitments. Can, for instance, the worker commit himself not to leave, or can the employer commit himself not to terminate the relationship?

A closely related issue is the set of punishments (rewards) which are admissible. It makes a great deal of difference if there are limits on the negative compensations that can be provided in the presence of bad outcomes.

We have noted the role of observability in the design of contracts. In some cases an important distinction may arise between observability and verifiability. The question is associated with how a contract is to be enforced. If the contract is to be enforced through the courts, it must be the case that any violation can be verified by an outside third party. Both the principal and the agent might know that the contract has been violated, i.e. they both may observe that S (and not S') has occurred, and therefore that the payment should be that corresponding to S (and not S'). But unless it can be proved, the principal might attempt to cheat the agent. Knowing this, the agent would refuse to sign a contract based on unverifiable variables.

On the other hand, if the contract is enforced by a reputation mechanism, good behaviour may be enforced so long as the state is observable by both parties.

CONCLUDING REMARK. We have focused here on a discussion of general principles. It should be emphasized, however, that the principal–agent model has provided important insights into the nature of a variety of economic relationships, in labour, land, credit and product markets. These detailed applications of the general theory represent an important area of on-going research.

BIBLIOGRAPHY

Allen, F. 1981. The prevention of default. *Journal of Finance* 36, May 271–6.

Arnott, R. and Stiglitz, J.E. 1982. The welfare economics of moral hazard. Discussion Paper No. 465, Queen's University, Kingston, Ontario, March.

Arnott, R. and Stiglitz, J.E. 1985. Labor turnover, wage structures, and moral hazard: the inefficiency of competitive markets. *Journal of Labor Economics* 3(4), 434–62.

Arnott, R. and Stiglitz, J.E. 1986. Moral hazard and optimal commodity taxation. *Journal of Public Economics* 29(1), February, 1–24.

Arnott, R. and Stiglitz, J.E. 1987. Randomization with asymmetric information: a simplified exposition. *Bell Journal of Economics* 17.

Arrow, K.J. 1965. *Aspects of the Theory of Risk-Bearing.* Helsinki: Yrjö Jahnsson Foundation.

Azariadis, C. and Stiglitz, J.E. 1983. Implicit contracts and fixed price equilibria. *Quarterly Journal of Economics* 98(3), Supplement, 1–22.

Braverman, A. and Stiglitz, J.E. 1982. Sharecropping and the interlinking of agrarian markets. *American Economic Review* 72(4), September, 695–715.

Eaton, J. and Gersovitz, M. 1981. Debt with potential repudiation; theoretical and empirical analysis. *Review of Economic Studies* 48, 289–309.

Fellingham, J.C., Kwon, Y.K. and Newman, D.P. 1982. Ex ante randomization in agency models. *Rand Journal of Economic Studies* 15, 290–301.

Gjesdal, F. 1982. Information and incentives: the agency information problem. *Review of Economic Studies* 49, 373–90.

Green, J. and Stokey, N. 1983. A comparison of tournaments and contests. *Journal of Political Economy* 91, 349–64.

Greenwald, B. and Stiglitz, J.E. 1986. Externalities in economies with imperfect information and incomplete markets. *Quarterly Journal of Economics* 101(4), May, 229–64.

Grossman, S. and Hart, Q. 1983. An analysis of the principal–agent problem. *Econometrica* 51(1), January, 7–45.

Hart, O. 1983. Optimal labor contracts under asymmetric information: an introduction. *Review of Economic Studies* 50, 3–35.

Helpman, E. and Laffont, J.J. 1975. On moral hazard in general equilibrium. *Journal of Economic Theory* 10, 8–23.

Holmstrom, B. 1979. Moral hazard and observability. *Bell Journal of Economics* 10(1), Spring, 74–91.

Holmstrom, B. 1982. Moral hazard in teams. *Bell Journal of Economics* 13, Autumn, 324–40.

Keeton, W.R. 1979. *Equilibrium Credit Rationing*. New York: Garland Publishing.

Lazear, E. and Rosen, S. 1981. Rank order tournaments as optimum labor contracts. *Journal of Political Economy* 89, 841–64.

Mirrlees, J. 1971. An exploration of the theory of optimum income taxation. *Review of Economic Studies* 38(2), April, 175–208.

Mirrlees, J. 1974. Notes on welfare economics, information, and uncertainty. In *Contributions to Economic Analysis*, ed. M.S. Balch, D.L. McFadden and S.Y. Wu, Amsterdam: North-Holland.

Mirrlees, J. 1976. The optimal structure of incentives and authority within an organization. *Bell Journal of Economics* 7(1), Spring, 105–31.

Nalebuff, B. and Stiglitz, J.E. 1983a. Information, competition and markets. *American Economic Review* 72(2), May, 278–84.

Nalebuff, B. and Stiglitz, J.E. 1983b. Prizes and incentives: towards a general theory of compensation and competition. *Bell Journal of Economics* 14, Spring, 21–43.

Pauly, M.V. 1968. The economics of moral hazard: comment. *American Economic Review* 58, June, 531–6.

Radner, R. 1981. Monitoring cooperative agreements in a repeated principal–agent relationship. *Econometrica* 49, September, 1127–48.

Radner, R. and Stiglitz, J.E. 1983. A nonconcavity in the value of innovation. In *Bayesian Models in Economic Theory*, ed. M. Boyer and R. Kihlstrom, Amsterdam: North-Holland.

Ross, S. 1973. The economic theory of agency: the principal's problem. *American Economic Review* 63(2), May, 134–9.

Rothschild, M. and Stiglitz, J.E. 1976. Equilibrium in competitive insurance markets: an essay on the economics of imperfect information. *Quarterly Journal of Economics* 90(4), November, 629–49.

Salop, S. 1977. The noisy monopolist: imperfect information, price dispersion and price discrimination. *Review of Economic Studies* 44, October, 393–406.

Salop, S. and Salop, J. 1976. Self-selection and turnover in the labor market. *Quarterly Journal of Economics* 90, November, 619–28.

Sappington, D. and Stiglitz, J.E. 1987. Information and regulation. In *Public Regulation: New Perspectives on Institutions and Policies*, ed. E. Bailey, Cambridge, Mass.: MIT Press.

Spence, A.M. and Zeckhauser, R. 1971. Insurance, information, and individual action. *American Economic Review* 61(2), May, 380–87.

Stiglitz, J.E. 1974. Incentives and risk sharing in sharecropping. *Review of Economic Studies* 41, April, 219–55.

Stiglitz, J.E. 1975. Incentives, risk, and information: notes toward a theory of hierarchy. *Bell Journal of Economics* 6(2), Autumn, 552–79.

Stiglitz, J.E. 1977. Monopoly non-linear pricing and imperfect information: the insurance market. *Review of Economic Studies* 44, October, 407–30.

Stiglitz, J.E. 1982a. Self-selection and Pareto efficient taxation. *Journal of Public Economics* 17, 213–40.

Stiglitz, J.E. 1982b. Utilitarianism and horizontal equity: the case for random taxation.

Journal of Public Economics 18, 1–33.
Stiglitz, J.E. 1987. On the causes and consequences of the dependence of quality on price. *Journal of Economic Literature* 27, March, 1–48.
Stiglitz, J.E. 1986. Theories of wage rigidity. In *Keynes' Economic Legacy*, ed. J. Butkiewicz, K. Koford and J. Miller, New York: Praeger Publishers, 153–221.
Stiglitz, J.E. and Weiss, A. 1981. Credit rationing in markets with imperfect information. *American Economic Review* 71(3), June, 393–410.
Stiglitz, J.E. and Weiss, A. 1983. Incentive effects of terminations: applications to the credit and labor markets. *American Economic Review* 73, December, 912–27.
Weiss, L. 1976. On the desirability of cheating, incentives and randomness in the optimal income tax. *Journal of Political Economy* 84, 1343–52.

Public Goods

AGNAR SANDMO

The development by Paul Samuelson (1954, 1955) of the modern theory of public goods must be counted as one of the major breakthroughs in the theory of public finance. In these two very short papers Samuelson posed and partly solved the central problems in the normative theory of public expenditure:

(1) How can one define analytically goods that are consumed collectively, that is for which there is no meaningful distinction between individual and total consumption?

(2) How can one characterize an optimal allocation of resources to the production of such goods?

(3) What can be said about the design of an efficient and just tax system which will finance the expenditures of the public sector?

None of these questions was entirely new to the literature of public finance. Indeed, 250 years ago David Hume (1739) noted that there were tasks which, although unprofitable to perform for any single individual, would yet be profitable for society as a whole, and which could therefore only be performed through collective action. The progress made over the next centuries, certainly with regard to problems (1) and (2), was, however, rather modest. From the point of view of the history of ideas, this is hardly surprising. What is required is a satisfactory theory of market failure. But this presupposes a clear understanding of the optimality properties of the market allocation of resources, and this was not achieved until the modern development of Paretian welfare economics which started in the late 1930s. More was undoubtedly achieved with respect to problem (3), reflecting the fact that problems of tax incidence had been a central area of theoretical analysis ever since the time of the classical economists, and that criteria of just taxation had developed independently of any analysis of the expenditure side of the public budget. Still, Samuelson's formulation was a great leap forward, presenting an integrated solution to all three problems, and determining the research agenda for the years to come. It is therefore natural to begin by setting out the basic elements of his model.

In a short survey it is of course impossible to do justice to the large literature in this field. For more comprehensive surveys the reader is referred to Milleron (1972), Atkinson and Stiglitz (1980, lectures 16–17) and the chapters by Oakland and Laffont in Auerbach and Feldstein (1987).

THE SAMUELSON MODEL. The aim of the model is to derive conditions for optimal resource allocation in an economy in which there are two types of goods, private and public. It is worth emphasizing that these terms do not prejudge the respective tasks of the private and public sectors; the analysis at this stage is institution-free and can best be considered as representing the problems of a planner who knows the production possibilities of the economy, the preferences of the consumers and his own ethical values.

The nature of the two types of goods are defined by the equations which give the relationship between individual and aggregate consumption. For private goods the total quantity consumed is equal to the sum of the quantities consumed by the individuals, so that

$$x_j = \sum_{i=1}^{I} x_j^i, \qquad (j = 0, \ldots, J) \tag{1}$$

where the superscript refers to individuals and the subscript to commodities. For public goods the corresponding relationship is one of *equality* between individual and total consumption, namely

$$x_k = x_k^i, \qquad (i = 1, \ldots, I;\ k = J+1, \ldots, J+K). \tag{2}$$

Individual preferences, represented by utility functions, are then defined over the quantities consumed of private and public goods, so that we can write the utility of individual i as

$$\begin{aligned} U^i &= U^i(x_0^i, \ldots, x_J^i, x_{J+1}^i, \ldots, x_{J+K}^i) \\ &= U^i(x_0^i, \ldots, x_J^i, x_{J+1}, \ldots, x_{J+k}), \qquad (i = 1, \ldots, I). \end{aligned} \tag{3}$$

The definition (2) has given rise to some confusion and controversy. Are there actually any goods which can be described by this definition? The usual answer is that there are some cases of 'pure' public goods, like national defence, which can indeed be so described; in such cases consumer benefits are directly related to the total availability of the good in question, and the consumption benefits of any one individual do not depend on the benefits enjoyed by others. This property of public goods is usually referred to as non-rivalry in consumption; given the supply of the good in question, the consumption possibilities of one individual do not depend on the quantities consumed by others, as they do in the case of private goods. However, many goods which it is natural to think of as public, turn out on closer inspection to have elements of rivalry. A road may satisfy the definition of a public good as long as the traffic is low, but with higher density and consequent congestion this will no longer be the case. Accordingly, several studies have been devoted to the analysis of 'impure' public goods, combining in some way the properties of private and public goods in the original Samuelson definition; we shall return to this below. It should be observed, however, that the Samuelson formulation does not assume that the *benefits* derived from the supply of the public good are the same for all, even though *availabilities* are the same. Neither does it assume that the benefits from public goods are independent of the quantities consumed of private goods. And the elements of rivalry in the road congestion example may be captured by introducing externalities in the consumption of a private good – car use – whose benefits depend on the supply of a public good – the road. Thus, the original Samuelson formulation offers great flexibility of interpretation, and we have been provided with an answer to the first of the main problems noted above.

We now turn to the problem of optimality of resource allocation and begin by characterizing a Pareto optimum for this kind of economy. Since the interesting special features of the model are on the consumption side only, we assume that the conditions for efficient production are satisfied, so that the production possibilities for the economy can be summarized in the transformation or production possibility equation

$$F(x_0,\ldots,x_J,x_{J+1},\ldots,x_{J+K})=0. \tag{4}$$

The problems of Pareto optimality may now be formulated as follows: of all allocations satisfying equation (4), find the allocation which maximizes utility for consumer 1, given arbitrary but feasible utility levels of all other consumers. As shown by Samuelson (1955), the solution can be given an instructive graphical solution in the two-dimensional case. We therefore begin with the case where there are two consumers and one private and one public good. In the upper panel of Figure 1 we have drawn the production possibility curve, as well as an indifference curve corresponding to the fixed level of utility for consumer 2; since the two curves intersect, there are obviously a number of allocations which satisfy these two constraints. In the lower panel the curve ab shows the consumption possibilities for consumer 1, the points a and b corresponding to the points of intersection in the upper panel. For any point on U^2 between a and b, it must be the case that the two individuals consume the same amount of the public good, while consumer 1's private good consumption is equal to the vertical difference between the production possibility curve and consumer 2's indifference curve. The best allocation from 1's point of view is then given by the tangency between his indifference curve and the consumption possibility curve in the lower panel. This determines the optimum supply of the public good (x_1^*) and consumer 1's consumption of the private good (x_0^{1*}) as well as the consumption of consumer 2 (x_0^{2*}).

The slope of the consumption possibility curve must of course be equal to the difference of the slopes of the two curves from which it is derived. The tangency point can therefore be characterized in terms of marginal rates of substitution

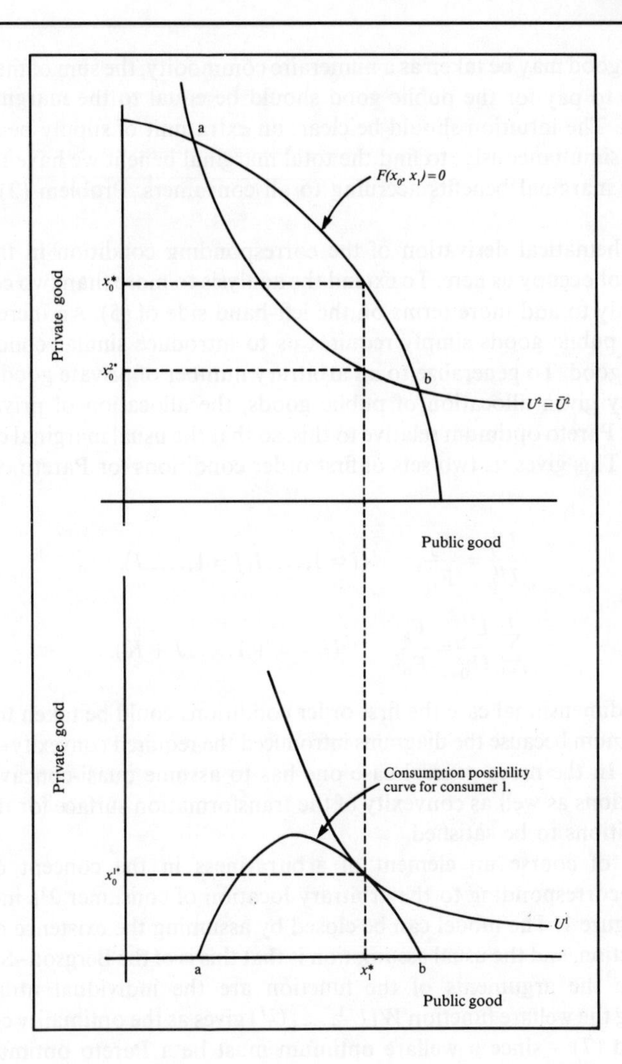

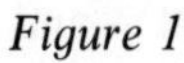

Figure 1

(MRS) and transformation (MRT) as

$$\mathrm{MRS}^1 = \mathrm{MRT} - \mathrm{MRS}^2, \quad \text{or} \quad \mathrm{MRS}^1 + \mathrm{MRS}^2 = \mathrm{MRT}.$$

In more precise mathematical terms this condition can be rewritten (letting subscripts denote partial derivatives) as

$$\frac{U_1^1}{U_0^1} + \frac{U_1^2}{U_0^2} = \frac{F_1}{F_0} \tag{5}$$

In words: the sum of the marginal rates of substitution should be equal to the marginal rate of transformation between the public and private good. Or, since the private good may be taken as a numeraire commodity, the sum of the marginal willingness to pay for the public good should be equal to the marginal cost of production. The intuition should be clear: an extra unit of supply benefits both consumers simultaneously; to find the total marginal benefit we have to take the sum of the marginal benefits accruing to all consumers. Problem (2) has been solved.

The mathematical derivation of the corresponding condition in the general case need not occupy us here. To extend the analysis to more than two consumers, we have only to add more terms on the left-hand side of (5). An increase in the number of public goods simply requires us to introduce similar conditions for every such good. To generalize to an arbitrary number of private goods, we note that for any given allocation of public goods, the allocation of private goods should be a Pareto optimum relative to this, so that the usual marginal conditions must hold. This gives us two sets of first order conditions for Pareto optimality, namely.

$$\frac{U^i_j}{U^i_0}=\frac{F_j}{F_0}, \qquad (i=1,\ldots,I, j=1,\ldots,J), \tag{6}$$

$$\sum_{i=0}^{I}\frac{U^i_k}{U^i_0}=\frac{F_k}{F_0}, \qquad (k=J+1,\ldots,J+K). \tag{7}$$

In the two-dimensional case the first order conditions could be taken to describe a true maximum because the diagrams introduced the required convexity–concavity conditions. In the more general case one has to assume quasi-concavity of the utility functions as well as convexity of the transformation surface for the second order conditions to be satisfied.

There is of course an element of arbitrariness in the concept of Pareto optimality, corresponding to the arbitrary location of consumer 2's indifference curve in Figure 1. The model can be closed by assuming the existence of a social welfare function, and the usual assumption is that this is of the Bergson–Samuelson type, where the arguments of the function are the individual utility levels. Maximizing the welfare function $W(U^1,\ldots,U^I)$ gives as the optimality conditions first (6) and (7) – since a welfare optimum must be a Pareto optimum – and then a set of conditions for optimal distribution of consumption between individuals. This can be written as

$$W_i U^i_0 = W_h U^h_0, \qquad (i, h=1,\ldots,I). \tag{8}$$

The marginal social utility of consumption should be the same for all.

Suppose now that private goods are allocated through a system of perfectly competitive markets, and that the allocation of resources to public goods also satisfies the efficiency conditions (7) as the result of some decision procedure which is yet to be specified. Imagine further that at least part of the provision of public goods is undertaken by the public sector, and that taxes are needed to finance this. What is the ideal tax system for this purpose? We wish the tax system to satisfy conditions (8), but these are conditional on the remaining first order conditions being satisfied. Under competitive conditions the marginal rates of substitution will be equal to consumer prices, taking commodity 0 to be the numeraire good, while marginal rates of transformation will correspond to producer prices. Thus, conditions (6) will be satisfied in a competitive economy provided that consumer prices are equal to producer prices. But this means that there must be no distortionary taxation; the only taxes which are consistent with a fully optimal solution are lump sum taxes in amounts which are independent of all components of demand and supply for consumers and firms. This is of course an insight which is well known from the standard competitive model with private goods only, but it is worth restating in the present context as the answer to problem (3).

This exposition of the basic elements of the Samuelson model can be used to put his contribution into historical perspective. Earlier writers on public finance, for example Mazzola (1890), Sax (1924) and Pigou (1928), did in fact apply marginal utility theory to the problem of the optimal supply of public goods, emphasizing the optimality rule that marginal benefit at the optimum should be equal to marginal cost. They failed, however, to develop a definition of public goods which could be used to characterize the difference between such goods and private goods. For the same reason they were also vague about the nature of the marginal benefit and how to measure it in the absence of market prices. Finally, although there is much interesting discussion by the older writers of the ability to pay and benefit theories of taxation, the efficiency aspect of taxation played a very minor part in their writings, and so they were unable to face the basic problem of how to reconcile the objectives of a just distribution and economic efficiency. With the Samuelson formulation all these issues had been clarified, and the foundation had been laid for further progress.

DISTORTIONARY TAXATION. The above optimality rules hold for the case where taxation is non-distortionary, that is where taxes are imposed to raise revenue and to redistribute incomes without disturbing the efficiency properties of the price mechanism. For a variety of reasons such taxes are hardly feasible, and it is interesting to consider the modifications that will have to be made if taxes are distortionary. Pigou (1928) argued that in this case the marginal social cost of producing a unit of the public good should exceed the direct resource cost by an amount reflecting the efficiency loss due to increased taxation. As pointed out by Atkinson and Stern (1974), however, this argument is not necessarily correct. Their analysis is an interesting exercise in the theory of the second best.

To abstract from problems of redistribution, consider the case where all individuals are identical. There are one public and two private goods, one of which serves as an untaxed numeraire. The representative consumer maximizes his utility function $U(x_0, x_1, x_2)$ subject to the budget constraint

$$x_0 + P_1 x_1 = 0. \tag{9}$$

Thus, there is no lump sum income. Given the optimum of the consumer, the government maximizes the sum of the utility functions (a special case of the welfare function in the previous section) subject to the constraint that the resource cost of the public goods supply equals the tax revenue. Thus, the government maximizes $IU(x_0, x_1, x_2)$ subject to

$$It_1 x_1 = p_2 x_2. \tag{10}$$

Here I is as before the number of consumers, t_1 is the tax per unit of commodity 1 such that $P_1 = p_1 + t_1$. The small p's denote producer prices, which for convenience are taken to be constant, corresponding to constant unit costs of production in terms of the numeraire. The government determines t_1 and x_2 simultaneously.

The analytical solution of the model need not concern us here. To understand the result, one should note that from the formulation of the consumer's problem it follows that demand for the taxed good depends on the supply of the public good. Thus, when the supply of the public good is increased, there will be two effects on the demand for private goods. One is the effect via increased availability of the public good, another is the price effect via increased taxation. It can easily be shown that the condition corresponding to the Samuelson equation (7) in this case becomes

$$\sum_i \mathrm{MRS}^i = \frac{p_2 - t_1 I(\partial x_1/\partial x_2)}{1 + (t_1/x_1)(\partial x_1/\partial t_1)}. \tag{11}$$

If there is no distortionary taxation, the right-hand side becomes simply p_2, which is the marginal rate of transformation, and we are back to the original Samuelson case. An increase in the tax rate lowers the demand for the taxed good, and the corresponding term in the denominator shows that this 'blows up' the cost of the public good; this is the effect alluded to by Pigou. On the other hand, the additional term in the numerator can in principle be of either sign and may therefore reverse Pigou's conclusions. Suppose that $\partial x_1/\partial x_2$ is positive, meaning that increased supply of the public good increases the demand for the taxed good. Then the relevant marginal social cost of the public good may in fact be lower than the pure resource cost. The point is that in this case the effect of the public good supply on demand serves to counteract the tax effect. The commodity tax is distortionary because it lowers consumption and production of the taxed good. If the public goods supply in itself serves to push the quantity of the taxed good back towards its first best optimal level, this could lower the economic cost of production.

TYPES OF PUBLIC GOODS. In line with the original Samuelson formulation we have so far limited the discussion to pure public consumption goods. Various alternative formulations have been discussed in the literature, and we shall briefly discuss some of these.

We have already observed that many consumption goods which may be classified as public turn out also to have important elements of 'privateness'. This has two aspects. In the first case it may be argued that a public good like a national park cannot really be enjoyed by the individual without expenditure on private goods like hiking equipment etc., and that even such an apparently clear case of a public good should be analysed as a mixed case of a private and a public good. To some extent this argument is based on a misunderstanding of the theory. There is no presumption that the benefit that an individual derives from the availability of a public good be independent of his consumption of private goods. Still, it may sometimes be useful to model the interaction between private and public goods consumption in a more explicit manner than is done in the standard formulation. One way in which this can be done takes as its point of departure the consumption technology approach and assumes that there are some final goods like road trips and nature hikes which are intrinsically private, but which are produced by the individual by means of private and public goods inputs. The second aspect of mixed goods is that the benefits enjoyed by any one individual may depend on the consumption of others, as in the cases of a crowded road or a congested national park. This aspect too may be handled by the consumption technology approach by letting other people's consumption of complementary private goods enter every individual's production function for the final good in question. This would be a special case of the Samuelson formulation when in addition it is assumed that some private goods create externalities in consumption. Thus, the advantage of the consumption technology approach to the theory of public goods lies not in greater generality, but in a formulation which captures in a more intuitive fashion a natural way of thinking about public goods. An additional advantage is that the theory becomes more closely related to the practice of cost benefit analysis, where willingness to pay is typically computed not by observing preferences directly, but by calculating the private cost reductions that would follow from an increase in the provision of a public good. The theory is further elaborated in Sandmo (1973); for an alternative formulation of similar ideas see Bradford and Hildebrandt (1977).

Not all public goods are naturally analysed as consumption goods. One of the classical examples, the lighthouse, is more easily interpretable as a producer good or a factor of production. Public factors of production were first introduced in the theoretical literature by Kaizuka (1965), who derives efficiency conditions similar to Samuelson's for the production case. Sandmo (1972) shows how the formulation can be used to derive shadow prices for such goods when the private sector is competitive.

The Samuelson formulation implies that the availability of any public good is the same for all individuals and independent of their decisions about private goods consumption – although, as we have noted, the benefit is not. This ignores the fact that many public goods are only available to individuals residing in a particular location, and that an individual may therefore select the amount available of the public good by moving residence. This was first pointed out by Tiebout (1956) in a paper which has since given rise to a rich literature on local public goods. We shall return below to the demand-revealing aspects of mobility between communities. But it is worth noting here that although the original application of the basic idea was to individual choice among residential communities, there are possibilities of application to other interesting areas as well. In the labour market, workers' choice among firms might be affected by public good aspects of the working environment which are specific to the individual firm. Internationally, public goods which are country-specific might influence the pattern of international migration; in this perspective, almost all public goods would be local, and the original formulation becomes a special case characterized by the geographical immobility of the population.

EQUILIBRIA WITH PUBLIC GOODS. We have concentrated on the theory of public goods as an extension of welfare economics; the central question has been how to characterize optimal or efficient allocations in economies with public goods. But just as in the case of private goods, it is interesting to go on from there to consider the equilibrium allocations that would follow from particular institutional arrangements in the economy and to compare these with the optimality conditions. Thus, the theory of public goods ought to be positive as well as normative, a view emphasized strongly in the influential contributions by Buchanan (1968).

The first clear formulation of a theory of public expenditure which can be given a positive interpretation was presented by Lindahl (1919); an important modern exposition was presented by Johansen (1963). In this formulation, individuals bargain over the level of public goods supply simultaneously with the distribution of the cost between them. The bargaining equilibrium is Pareto optimal, implying that the efficiency conditions (7) are satisfied. In addition, each individual pays a price in terms of private goods which is equal to his marginal willingness to pay. Formally, let π^i_{J+k} be the price which individual i pays for public good k, and let p_{J+k} be the producer price or marginal cost. Then the Lindahl equilibrium would be characterized by the condition

$$\sum_i \pi^i_k = p_k, \qquad (k = J+1, \ldots, J+K). \tag{12}$$

Thus, at first glance the concept of a Lindahl equilibrium seems to establish an analogue to competitive markets for private goods with the interesting difference that prices should differ from one individual to another, depending on his marginal willingness to pay. This also ties in with older notions of the benefit theory of taxation, according to which taxes were seen as payments for public goods, to be levied in accordance with the benefits which each individual derived from them.

At the technical level it may be noted that there is an interesting 'duality' between the definitions of private and public goods on the one hand and the properties of equilibrium prices on the other. In terms of quantities, for private goods the sum of individual quantities consumed *add up to* the quantity produced, while for public goods individual consumption *equals* aggregate production. In terms of prices, on the other hand, for private goods each consumer price *equals* the producer price, while for public goods individualized consumer prices *add up to* the producer price.

There is, however, one crucial difference between a Lindahl equilibrium and a competitive equilibrium for private goods. With private goods, individuals facing given prices have clear incentives to reveal their true preferences by equating their marginal rates of substitution to relative prices, at least if the economy is sufficiently large relative to the individual. Without paying, the individual is excluded from enjoying the benefits of consumption. With public goods this no longer holds. Because an individual has the same quantity of public goods available to him whether he pays or not, he has an incentive to misrepresent his preferences and to be a free-rider on the supply paid for by others. Moreover, this problem is likely to be particularly severe when the number of individuals is large, since his own contribution will then make little difference to the total supply. The connection between Lindahl equilibria and the game-theoretic concept of the core was discussed by Foley (1970); see also the survey by Milleron (1972).

The equilibrium of the Lindahl model is not compatible with individual incentives to reveal preferences truthfully; for this reason Samuelson (1969) has referred to the individual Lindahl prices as pseudo-prices and to the equilibrium as a pseudo-equilibrium. In this case one would conjecture that because all individuals have the same incentives to understate their true marginal willingness to pay, the Lindahl mechanism would result in equilibrium levels of public goods supply which would be too low relative to the optimum. But there is really no need to associate the problem of preference revelation with this procedure alone; as another extreme, one might think of the case where individuals are asked to state their preferences on the assumption that the cost to them is completely independent of their stated willingness to pay, but there is a positive association between this and the quantity supplied. Then there will be incentives to exaggerate the willingness to pay and a consequent tendency towards oversupply. Thus, the general problem which arises is how to design a mechanism that will allow the decision-maker to implement the efficiency condition.

Various solutions to this problem have been discussed in the literature. The most practically oriented solution is that of cost–benefit analysis, which takes as its point of departure that people's preferences for public goods are revealed in the market through their demands for complementary private goods (see above). But in theoretical terms it has been shown that this will only be true on certain rather restrictive assumptions about technology and preferences. Another solution is represented in the literature on local public goods, where it has been suggested that people reveal their preferences for public goods by moving to the community offering them their most preferred combination of taxes and public goods. But whether this process will result in an optimum satisfying the efficiency conditions must clearly depend, first, on how the supply of public goods is determined within each community, and second on whether there are enough communities to satisfy the variations of preferences in the population as a whole. Thus, in general, neither observations of private goods demands nor of individuals' mobility between local communities provide reliable information on preferences.

Presumably as a response to the problem of market failure, decisions on public goods supply are largely made by political processes. In a democracy, the natural decision-making process to study is that of voting, and there is by now a substantial literature on this. Most of this is concerned with the stylized situation where public goods supply is determined by majority voting with the consumers themselves being the voters; thus, 'direct democracy' is assumed. The first paper in this area was that of Bowen (1943), who also considered the question of when a voting equilibrium would be Pareto optimal. Later contributions have emphasized that very restrictive assumptions on preferences are sometimes required for a voting equilibrium to exist, and this – like the so-called single-peakedness assumption – is not always attractive in the public goods context. Nevertheless, voting models have become quite popular in descriptive analyses of public goods decisions, particularly at the local government level.

There has also been a great deal of interest in studying planning procedures whereby individuals find it in their own interest to reveal truthfully their preferences for public goods. The first discussion of such a procedure – although in a somewhat different context – was that of Vickrey (1961), but the more recent developments are due to the work of Clarke (1971) and Groves (1973). It is shown there that truthful preference revelation will result if individuals pay a tax on the marginal unit demanded of the public good which is equal to the difference between the marginal cost and the sum of the marginal benefits received by all other individuals. These procedures are of great theoretical interest, perhaps mainly because they clarify the nature of the free rider problem. However, at present they seem rather far from the state where they could be implemented in practical situations; they would probably be administratively costly to operate, and they also make heavy demands on individual consumers' ability to understand and participate in the process. For a survey of this area see Tulkens (1978).

Doubts have occasionally been voiced on whether the free rider problem has been given too much prominence in the theoretical literature. Johansen (1977) has argued that there is no clear evidence that this is in practice seen as a major problem in public sector decision-making and suggests that individuals are much more likely to reveal their willingness to pay than the literature indicates. This is so both because truthfulness is a strong social norm and because it is a simple strategy which does not rely on complicated strategic considerations. There is also some empirical evidence from experimental situations suggesting that the revealed willingness to pay is not very sensitive to the associated method of cost distribution; see Bohm (1972).

PERSPECTIVES. The Samuelson theory of public goods has been of decisive influence for the theory of public expenditure. One of the results of this is that the normative theory of public goods has become much more satisfactory from a theoretical point of view than the positive theory. This state of affairs may in fact be unavoidable. The normative theory has little need to model institutional details and can thus be given a more unified appearance. A positive theory, on the other hand, must model institutions, and there is no single institution corresponding to the competitive market in the private goods case which can serve as a unifying benchmark. Moreover, development of the positive theory of public goods must necessarily be closely tied to the progress of the positive theory of public sector behaviour in general; it will be interesting to see whether this theory can be developed to provide models which are both realistic and reasonably simple.

BIBLIOGRAPHY

Atkinson, A.B. and Stern, N. 1974. Pigou, taxation and public goods. *Review of Economic Studies* 41(1), January, 119–28.

Atkinson, A.B. and Stiglitz, J.E. 1980. *Lectures on Public Economics.* New York: McGraw-Hill.

Auerbach, A.J. and Feldstein, M. 1987. *Handbook of Public Economics.* Vol. II, Amsterdam; North-Holland.

Bohm, P. 1972. Estimating demand for public goods: an experiment. *European Economic Review* 3(2), March, 111–30.

Bowen, H.R. 1943. The interpretation of voting in the allocation of economic resources. *Quarterly Journal of Economics* 58, November, 27–48.

Bradford, D.F. and Hildebrandt, G.G. 1977. Observable preferences for public goods. *Journal of Public Economics* 8(2), October, 111–31.

Buchanan, J.M. 1968. *The Demand and Supply of Public Goods.* Chicago: Rand McNally.

Clarke, E.H. 1971. Multipart pricing of public goods. *Public Choice* 11, Fall, 17–33.

Foley, D.K. 1970. Lindahl's solution and the core of an economy with public goods. *Econometrica* 38(1), January, 66–72.

Groves, T. 1973. Incentives in teams. *Econometrica* 41(4), July, 617–31.

Hume, D. 1739. *A Treatise of Human Nature.* London: J. Noon; New York: Dutton, 1952.

Johansen, L. 1963. Some notes on the Lindahl theory of determination of public expenditure. *International Economic Review* 4, September, 346–58.

Johansen, L. 1977. The theory of public goods: misplaced emphasis? *Journal of Public Economics* 7, February, 147–52.

Kaizuka, K. 1965. Public goods and decentralization of production. *Review of Economics and Statistics* 47, February, 118–20.

Lindahl, E. 1919. *Die Gerechtigkeit der Besteuerung.* Lund: Gleerup. Partial translation as 'Just taxation – a positive solution'. In *Classics in the Theory of Public Finance*, ed. R.A. Musgrave and A.T. Peacock, London, New York: Macmillan, 1958.

Mazzola, U. 1980. The formation of prices of public goods. In *Classics in the Theory of Public Finance*, ed. R.A. Musgrave and A.T. Peacock, London, New York: Macmillan, 1958.

Milleron, J.-C. 1972. Theory of value with public goods: a survey article. *Journal of Economic Theory* 5(3), December, 419–77.

Pigou, A.C. 1928. *A Study in Public Finance.* 3rd edn, London: Macmillan, 1947; New York: St. Martin's Press, 1956.

Samuelson, P.A. 1954. The pure theory of public expenditure. *Review of Economics and Statistics* 36, November, 387–9.

Samuelson, P.A. 1955. Diagrammatic exposition of a theory of public expenditure. *Review of Economics and Statistics* 37, November, 350–56.

Samuelson, P.A. 1969. Pure theory of public expenditure and taxation. In *Public Economics*, ed. J. Margolis and H. Guitton, London: Macmillan.

Sandmo, A. 1972. Optimality rules for the provision of collective factors of production. *Journal of Public Economics* 1(1), April, 149–57.

Sandmo, A. 1973. Public goods and the technology of consumption. *Review of Economic Studies* 40(4), October, 517–28.

Sax, E. 1924. The valuation theory of taxation. In *Classics in the Theory of Public Finance*, ed. R.A. Musgrave and A.T. Peacock, London, New York: Macmillan, 1958.

Tiebout, C.M. 1956. A pure theory of local expenditures. *Journal of Political Economy* 64, October, 416–24.

Tulkens, H. 1978. Dynamic processes for public goods: an institution-oriented survey, *Journal of Public Economics* 9(3), April, 163–201.

Vickrey, W.S. 1961. Counterspeculation, auctions, and competitive sealed tenders. *Journal of Finance* 16, March, 8–37.

Revelation of Preferences

J.-J. LAFFONT

Competitive rational consumers reveal their preferences through their market behaviour, as was made clear by Samuelson's (1947) revealed preference approach and by the literature on demand theory. Any bundle of commodities less costly than his chosen bundle must be less appreciated by a rational consumer than his chosen bundle.

However, in various circumstances collective decision processes must be used to mitigate market failures (public goods, externalities etc.). To what extent these processes can truthfully elicit agents' preferences, i.e., overcome the decentralization of information, is the issue raised here.

REVELATION. Consider an agent who has preferences, represented by a preordering parameterized by $\theta^i \in \Theta^i$, $R(\theta^i)$, over a set of social states A. It is not difficult to convince oneself that any mechanism, $x\colon \Theta^i \to A$, which induces truthful revelation by agent i is equivalent to giving to the agent a subset $B \subset A$ and letting him maximize over this set. The sufficiency is obvious; the necessity is shown by choosing.

$$A = \bigcup_{\theta^i \in \Theta^i} x(\theta^i).$$

When I agents are present, a mechanism is a mapping

$$x\colon \Theta \equiv \Pi_{i=1}^{I} \Theta^i \to A.$$

It is reasonable in most circumstances to assume that agent i does not know the characteristics θ^j of the other agents. The revelation of preferences is therefore necessarily imbedded in a game of imperfect information for which several solution concepts are possible. A game which induces truthful revelation of preferences is said to be incentive compatible.

IMPLEMENTATION. Consider a social choice function, i.e. a mapping $f\colon \Pi_{i=1}^{I} H^{i} \rightarrow A$. A social choice function f is said to be *implementable* if there exist message spaces M^{i}, $i=1,\ldots,I$, and an outcome function $g\colon \Pi_{i=1}^{I} M^{i} \rightarrow A$ for which the equilibrium messages $m^{i}(\theta^{i}) i=1,\ldots,I$ are such that:

$$g(m^{1}(\theta^{1}),\ldots,m^{I}(\theta^{I}))=f(\theta) \qquad \forall \theta \in \Theta$$

The equilibrium messages depend on the chosen solution concept for the game of imperfect information. The strongest notion of implementation is implementation in dominant strategies. Then, $m^{i}(\theta^{i})$ is the best message of agent i whatever the messages of the other agents, for any i. A weaker notion of implementation is Bayesian implementation. Consider common knowledge prior expectations $\Psi^{i}(\theta^{-i}/\theta^{i})$ describing agent i's expectations about the other agents' characteristics

$$\theta^{-i}=(\theta^{1},\ldots,\theta^{i-1},\theta^{i+1},\ldots,\theta^{I}), \qquad i=1,\ldots,I.$$

For any $\theta^{i} \in \Theta^{i}$, $m^{*i}(\theta^{i})$ is the best message for agent i in the sense of his expected utility computed by using his prior $\Psi^{i}(\theta^{-i}/\theta^{i})$ and by assuming that the others are using the response functions $m^{*j}(\theta^{j})$, $j \neq i$. Then f is implementable in Bayesian equilibrium if there exists a Bayesian equilibrium such that $f(\theta)=g(m^{*1}(\theta^{1}),\ldots,m^{*I}(\theta^{I}))$.

There are many other notions of implementation.

IMPLEMENTATION IN DOMINANT STRATEGY. The *revelation principle* says that any f which is implementable in a dominant strategy can be implemented by a mechanism in which messages are identified with characteristics spaces Θ^{i} – direct mechanisms – and truthful revelation is a dominant strategy equilibrium.

In other words, it is not useful to consider more complex mechanisms than revelation mechanisms. (This neglects problems due to multiple equilibria.) We will therefore concentrate in the sequel on direct revelation mechanisms.

A fundamental result due to Gibbard (1973) and Satterthwaite (1975) tells us that, for more than two states, when no a priori information is available about individuals' preorderings, the only deterministic social choice functions implementable in dominant strategies are dictatorships. To obtain positive results we must either introduce a priori information or weaken the notion of incentive compatibility.

THE VICKREY AUCTION AND THE CLARKE–GROVES MECHANISMS. To fight non-competitive behaviour, Vickrey (1961) proposed an auction which has the remarkable property that each bidder should announce his true willingness to pay for the auctioned object as a dominant strategy. The auction gives the object to the agent who makes the highest bid, but the payment is only the second highest bid.

The solution to the Wicksell–Samuelson free rider problem of public goods provided by Clarke (1971) and Groves (1973) can be viewed as an adaptation of this result. Preferences for public goods are assumed to be restricted to the class of quasi-linear utility functions which permits one to go away from the negative result of the Gibbard–Satterthwaite theorem.

Consider the simple case of a costless indivisible project ($d = 0$ or 1) and call v^i the willingness to pay of agent i, $i = 1, \ldots, I$. The Pareto optimal decision under perfect information is

$$d = 1 \Leftrightarrow \sum_{i=1}^{I} v^i \geqslant 0.$$

The Clark mechanism chooses to realize the project if the sum of the answers $\Sigma_{i=1}^{I} w^i$ is positive and agent i must pay a transfer $\Sigma_{j \neq i} w^j$ if he is pivotal, i.e. his answer changes the sign of the sum. He must pay the cost he imposes on the rest of society, just as in the Vickrey auction, an agent must pay the cost he imposes on the society, which is the second willingness to pay. Groves mechanisms are obtained by adding to the Clarke transfer of agent i an arbitrary function of the answers of the others.

The first best public project decision is implemented. However, the incentive compatible transfers do not sum to zero in general, so that a Pareto optimal allocation is not achieved. This should not come as a surprise. The decentralization of information imposes a cost on allocation rules.

Preferences can be elicited but at the cost of some distortions in allocations rules.

LARGE NUMBERS. The problem of revelation of preferences for private goods is not a serious problem in large economies. Indeed, as a 'negligible' agent cannot affect prices he cannot affect his budget set and therefore the competitive equilibrium is incentive compatible in dominant strategies.

With public goods the problem becomes more and more severe with the number of agents, since everyone can hope to have the others finance the public good. Despite the fact that, as the number of agents increases, the imbalance of transfers in the Groves mechanisms can be made negligible in various senses, the question of the strength of incentives must be raised in such circumstances.

HISTORICAL NOTE. The free rider problem was recognized by Wicksell (1896) and emphasized by Samuelson (1954). The positive results by Groves (1973) and Clarke (1971) and by Aspremont and Gerard-Varet (1979) using Bayesian equilibria have shown that positive results are achievable when prior information is available. These results have played a major role in opening new avenues in the economics of information. The reason is that generalizations of these mechanisms have provided a precise way of evaluating transaction costs due to asymmetric information. Industrial organization, macroeconomics and public economics have been considerably renewed recently by the possibility of taking seriously into account the decentralization of information.

BIBLIOGRAPHY

d'Aspremont, C. and Gerard-Varet, L.A. 1979. Incentives and incomplete information. *Journal of Public Economics* 11, 25–45.

Clarke, E.H. 1971. Multipart pricing of public goods. *Public Choice*, 19–33.

Gibbard, A. 1973. Manipulation of voting schemes. A general result. *Econometrica* 41, 487–601.

Groves, T. 1973. Incentives in teams. *Econometrica* 41, 617–31.

Samuelson, P.A. 1947. *Foundations of Economic Analysis.* Cambridge, Mass.: Harvard University Press.

Samuelson, P.A. 1954. The pure theory of public expenditure. *Review of Economics and Statistics* 37, 350–56.

Satterthwaite, M. 1975. Strategy-proofness and Arrow's conditions: existence and correspondence theorems for voting procedures and social welfare functions. *Journal of Economic Theory* 10, 187–217.

Vickrey, W. 1961. Counterspeculation, auctions and competitive sealed tenders. *Journal of Finance* 16, 1–17.

Wicksell, K. 1896. *Finanztheoretische Untersuchungen und das Steuerwesen.* Jena: Schweders.

Search Theory

P. DIAMOND

Walrasian analysis presumes that resource allocation can be adequately modelled using the assumption of instantaneous and costless coordination of trade. In contrast, Search Theory is the analysis of resource allocation with specified, imperfect technologies for informing agents of their trading opportunities and for bringing together potential traders. The modelling advantages of assuming a frictionless coordination mechanism, plus years of hard work, permit Walrasian analysis to work with very general specifications of individual preferences and production technologies. In contrast, search theorists have explored a variety of special allocation mechanisms together with very simple preferences and production technologies. Lacking more general theories, we examine the catalogue of analyses that have been completed.

Paralleling the Walrasian framework, we first examine individual choice and then equilibrium. There are a large number of variations on the basic search–theoretic choice problem. We explore one set-up in detail, while mentioning some of the variations that have been developed. Coordination of trade involves two separate steps: information gathering about opportunities, and arrangement of individual trades. One simple case is where information gathering is limited to visiting stores sequentially, combining the costs of collecting goods and of gathering information. Alternatively, there can be an information gathering mechanism which is independent of the process of ordering and receiving the good. We begin with models where the only information gathering is associated with visiting stores and then look at the changes that come from additional devices for information spread.

Once two potential traders have met there are several ways of determining whether they trade and the terms of trade if they do. Among these are price setting on a take-it-or-leave-it basis, idealized negotiations where any mutually advantageous trade occurs at a price satisfying some bargaining solution, and more realistic negotiation processes that recognize the time and cost of negotiation, the possibility of a negotiating impasse, and the possible arrival of alternatives for one or the other of the trading partners. We explore the first two mechanisms.

One final distinction in the literature is between one-time purchases of commodities and on-going trade relations. Infrequently purchased consumer goods are the classic example of the former, while the employment relationship is the classic example of the latter. Introducing on-going relationships permits the exploration of delayed learning of the quality of a match and associated rearrangements through quits and firings. Intermediate between these two cases is a situation such as that of frequently purchased consumer goods, where past trades facilitate further trades but do not bring about the closeness of an employment relationship. We discuss mainly the one-shot purchase. The discussion of individual choice and partial equilibrium will be given in terms of a consumer purchase. The parallel discussion of labour markets is only briefly mentioned.

I INDIVIDUAL CHOICE

Consider a consumer in a store who is deciding whether to make a purchase or to visit another store with an unknown price. Denote by $U(p, 1)$ the utility that the consumer receives (net of purchase costs) if the purchase is made in the first store at a price equal to p. This assumes an ability to purchase the optimal number of units at a constant per unit price of p. If the purchase is made at the second store at price p, utility is $U(p, 2)$. This utility is less than $U(p, 1)$ because of the cost and the time delay from visiting a second store. We assume that the entire purchase is made at a single store, that it is impossible to return to the first store and that there are no other stores that can be visited. Ignoring the possibility of making no purchase and no further searches, the alternative to purchasing in store 1 at price p, is a single visit to store 2 where the price will be drawn from a (known) distribution which we denote $F(p)$. The purchase should be made in store 1 if the utility of purchase there is at least as large as the expected utility of purchase in store 2:

$$U(p_1, 1) \geqslant \int U(p, 2)\, dF(p). \qquad \text{(I–1)}$$

As long as the consumer views the distribution of prices in store 2 as independent of the price in the first store, the rule in (I–1) yields a cut-off price, p^*, given by (I–2):

$$U(p^*, 1) = \int U(p, 2)\, dF(p). \qquad \text{(I–2)}$$

For prices above p^*, optimal behaviour calls for visiting the second store, while for prices below p^*, optimal behaviour calls for making a purchase in the first store. Thus p^* is the cut-off price. Implicit in this formulation is the assumption that it is not desirable to make some purchase in store 1 and the remaining purchase in store 2. While this assumption is true for many consumer goods, it is certainly not true for all of them. Without this assumption the decision resembles portfolio choice and has not been explored in the literature. A similar analysis applies to the search for high quality.

If the consumer does not know with certainty the distribution of prices in the second store, the consumer's beliefs about those prices may depend upon the price observed in the first store. We write the subjective distribution of prices in the second store, conditional on an observed price of p_1 in the first store, as $F(p; p_1)$. The purchase should be made in the first store if p_1 satisfies the inequality:

$$U(p_1, 1) \geqslant \int U(p, 2)\, \mathrm{d}F(p; p_1). \tag{I–3}$$

With no restriction on the beliefs of the consumer as to the structure of prices found in both stores, the set of prices resulting in a purchase in store 1 does not necessarily satisfy a cut-off price rule. For example, if either a high or a low observed price implies the same price in both stores, while an intermediate price in store 1 implies a low price in store 2, then the consumer should purchase in store 1 at the high and low prices but not at an intermediate price. Thus, the intermediate price might signal a price war. If the information content of the price found in store 1 is a greater likelihood of similar prices in store 2, the optimality of a cut-off price rule is restored (Rothschild, 1974). For the remainder of this essay we restrict analysis to the case of known distributions. The caveats implicit in this counter example should be kept in mind.

Returning to the set-up with a known distribution, we can increase the options of the shopper by adding the possibility of returning to the first store after observing the price in the second store. Denote by $U(p, 3)$ the utility that is realized if this option is followed. The utility function $U(p, 3)$ is less than $U(p, 2)$, which, in turn, is less than $U(p, 1)$. Once in the second store, the choice is between buying there and returning to the first store with both prices known. Therefore it pays to purchase in the first store in the first period if the price there, p_1, satisfies the inequality;

$$U(p_1, 1) \geqslant \int \max[U(p, 2), U(p_1, 3)]\, \mathrm{d}F(p). \tag{I–4}$$

That is, the purchase should be made in store 1 if utility there is higher than expected utility with optimal behaviour in choosing between the second store and returning to the first store. This is a particularly simple example of the backwards induction that can be used to solve the finite horizon sequential shopping problem. Behaviour in the first store, (I–4), again satisfies a cut-off price rule if the utility function has constant search costs and discount rate.

We now specialize the example by assuming additive, constant search costs c and utility discounting with a discount factor R. That is, $U(p, 2)$ equals $RU(p, 1) - c$, with $R \leqslant 1$. Returning to the choice problem without a return to store 1, we denote by $V(p_1)$ expected utility on observing the price p_1 in store 1, given optimal behaviour:

$$V(p_1)=\max\left[U(p_1)-c+R\int U(p)\,\mathrm{d}F(p)\right]. \qquad \text{(I–5)}$$

The value of being in a store that has price p_1 is the larger of (i) the utility from making the optimal purchase at that price, and (ii) the expected utility if the search cost c is paid and the purchase is made in the second store. Using this function V, we can describe choice in the first period of a new three period search problem with no return to previous stores. The optimal rule is to purchase if

$$U(p_1)\geqslant -c+R\int V(p)\,\mathrm{d}F(p). \qquad \text{(I–6)}$$

That is, purchase is made in the first period if the achievable utility there is at least as large as that achievable with optimal behaviour, beginning with a visit to a randomly selected second store. The latter utility is the discounted expected optimized utility minus the search costs of the visit, recognizing that the second period choice is again a choice between a purchase and a search in the following period. By having $F(p)$ independent of p_1, we are sampling with replacement rather than sampling without replacement from the known distribution of prices. The choice rule given in (I–6) again shows cut-off price behaviour for period one choice. However, the cut-off price is higher in the second period than in the first because of the reduction in options as the end of the search process comes closer. Denoting the cut-off prices in the two periods by p_1^* and p_2^*, they satisfy the two equations:

$$U(p_1^*)= -c+R\int V(p)\,\mathrm{d}F(p) \qquad \text{(I–7a)}$$

$$U(p_2^*)= -c+R\int U(p)\,\mathrm{d}F(p). \qquad \text{(I–7b)}$$

$V(p)$ is at least as large as $U(p)$ since it represents the choice between purchase and searching again. Thus $p_1^*\leqslant p_2^*$, with a strict inequality in problems where the search cost and discount rate are not so large as to always imply a purchase in the current store.

There are additional reasons for cut-off prices to rise over time or equivalently, in a job search setting, for reservation wages to fall over time. In many settings, search costs rise over time. The utility of a purchase or of finding a job can fall over time. In the job setting, these can arise from declining wealth being used to finance consumption while searching for a job and from the shortening period over which any job might be held.

A known finite horizon for the end of search is incorrect in many settings. In addition, with many periods, the backwards induction optimization process is a cumbersome description of individual choice. Fortunately, the infinite horizon stationary case is easy to analyse. In this setting, a parallel analysis to that in (I–7) is a straightforward application of dynamic programming principles. With the assumption of a stationary environment the cut-off price is the same period after period. Denote by p^* the cut-off price and by V the optimized expected value of utility after paying the search cost to enter a store, but before observing its price. Then V equals the utility of purchase, if a purchase is made, plus the probability of not making a purchase times the discounted optimized utility from facing the same problem one period later after paying search cost c:

$$V = \int_0^{p^*} U(p)\,\mathrm{d}F(p) + [1 - F(p^*)][-c + RV]. \tag{I–8}$$

Solving (I–8) for V we have:

$$V = \frac{\int_0^{p^*} U(p)\,\mathrm{d}F(p) - c[1 - F(p^*)]}{1 - R[1 - F(p^*)]} \tag{I–9}$$

The optimal p^* maximizes V and can be calculated by differentiation. More intuitively, we note that a purchase just worth making will give the same utility as will waiting to search again:

$$U(p^*) = -c + RV. \tag{I–10}$$

Rearranging terms, we can write the implicit equation for p^*:

$$(1 - R)U(p^*) = -c + R\int_0^{p^*} [U(p) - U(p^*)]\,\mathrm{d}F(p). \tag{I–11}$$

Using this first order condition we can analyse the comparative statics of optimal search behaviour. Naturally, the cut-off price increases if the search cost increases or if the discount factor becomes smaller. Interestingly, an increase in the riskiness of the distribution of prices (holding constant mean utility from a randomly selected price, $\int U(p)\,\mathrm{d}F$) makes search more valuable and so lowers the cut-off price. This result follows from the structure of optimal choice – decreases in low prices make search more attractive while increases in high prices are irrelevant since no purchase is made at high prices. Analysis of the relationship between the expected number of searches and the distribution of prices is complicated since it depends on the shape of that distribution.

Thus far we have assumed that all stores are ex ante identical; that is, that a choice to search is a choice to draw from the distribution $F(p)$. In many problems one can choose where to search. In that case, one is choosing which distribution $F(p)$ to sample from or, if there are limited draws allowed from a particular distribution, the sequence of distributions from which prices should be sampled. Interestingly, the reservation prices, which tell one whether to purchase or to sample again from a given distribution, also serve to rank distributions.

In the choice problem analysed so far we have used discrete time, with the arrival of one offer in each time period. There are two straightforward generalizations. First, one might have the opportunity to receive more than one offer in any period, with the number of offers received being a function of the chosen level of search costs. In this way one can model the choice of search intensity. Second, the process of attempting to locate stores might have a stochastic rather than a determinate time structure. The simplest such model has the arrival of purchase opportunities satisfying the Poisson distribution law. That is, at any moment of time there is a constant flow probability of an offer arriving, any such offer being an independent draw from the distribution of available prices. Let us denote by a, the arrival rate of these offers; and by c, the constant search cost from being available to receive these offers. Utility is discounted at the constant (exponential) rate r. One can derive the optimal cut-off price and the optimized level of expected utility by analysing the discrete time process as above and passing to the limit. As a more intuitive alternative, let us think of the opportunity to purchase as an asset, where V now represents the value of that asset. The utility discount rate plays the role of an interest rate in asset theory. The asset is priced properly when the rate of discount times the value of the asset equals the expected flow of benefits from holding that asset. The expected flow of benefits is the gain that will come from making a purchase at a price below the cut-off price rather than continuing to search, adjusted for the probability of such an event, less search costs. Thus asset value satisfies

$$rV = a\int_0^{p^*} [U(p) - V]\,\mathrm{d}F(p) - c. \tag{I–12}$$

It is worthwhile making any purchase with a higher utility than that from continued search. Thus the cut-off price satisfies

$$rU(p^*) = a\int_0^{p^*} [U(p) - U(p^*)]\,\mathrm{d}F(p) - c. \tag{I–13}$$

Again one can introduce search intensity by having the Poisson arrival rate be a function of the search cost. In the equilibrium discussions below we will use the choice problem in the form (I–13).

So far we have ignored events after a purchase. In the labour setting this is equivalent to the assumption that taking a job is the end of search. In practice individuals frequently shift from job to job with no intervening period of unemployment. One can model job choice to recognize the possibility of continued search while working. Such an analysis must consider the rules that cover compensation between the parties in the event of a quit or firing, with no compensation and compensatory and liquidated damages being the situations analysed in the literature. The search for a better job is only one aspect of turnover. Also, one can model learning about the quality of match in a particular job as a function of the time on the job and the stochastic realization of experience. With a shadow value for quitting to search for a new job, one then has a second aspect of the theory of turnover.

The formulation of job taking given above has been combined with data on individual experience to examine empirically the determinants of the distribution of spells of unemployment. Since this essay focuses on equilibrium, and the empirical literature has not examined the determinants of the distribution of opportunities, we do not explore this sizeable and interesting literature, nor the estimates of the effect of unemployment compensation on the distribution of unemployment spells. For an example, see Kiefer and Neumann (1979).

In the model above we have assumed that no additional information is received during the search process. In practice, individuals are simultaneously searching for many different consumer goods and often for jobs and investment opportunities as well. The relations among search processes, coming from the arrival of information and the random positions with simultaneous search for many different goods, have not been explored in the literature. Focusing on search for a single good, we have added several new factors to the theory of demand, particularly the cost of attempting to purchase elsewhere and the knowledge and beliefs of shoppers about opportunities elsewhere. In practice, these are important determinants of demand.

II EQUILIBRIUM WITH BARGAINING

The theory of choice above is a simple version of the complex problem people face when making decisions about information gathering and purchases over time. That simplicity yields a choice theory that can be embedded in an equilibrium model. To complete an equilibrium model, we need to model the determination of two endogenous variables: the arrival rate of purchase opportunities and the distribution of their prices. In this section, we consider prices that satisfy the bargaining condition of equal division of the gains from trade. In the next section, we consider take-it-or-leave-it prices set by suppliers. In both cases we assume that there are no reputations, either of soft bargaining or low price setting, that affect the arrival rate of potential customers. We begin by assuming that all buyers are identical and all sellers are identical. This case brings out the role of search in determining the level of prices. Below we consider determinants of the distribution of prices.

Axiomatic bargaining theory relates the terms of trade to the threat points of the two bargainers and the shapes of their utility functions. To avoid complications from the latter, we assume that a single unit is purchased and that utility from purchase equals a constant, u_d, minus the price paid. We also assume that each seller has a single unit to sell. The utility from a sale is the price received less the cost of the good, u_s. One might think of this as a homogeneous used car market. To divide equally the gains from trade, the differences between the utility position with the trade and the utility position without it are equalized for the two parties. The value of purchasing at price p is $u_d - p$; expected utility without a trade is V_d, the optimized expected utility from continued search. We restrict ourselves to an economic environment where all trades take place at the same price. With a degenerate distribution of prices, we can rewrite the value equation (I–12) as

$$rV_d = a_d(u_d - p - V_d) - c_d. \tag{II–1}$$

For suppliers, the utility from a sale is $p - u_s$. The gain from selling now rather than later is $p - u_s$ less the value of having a car for sale, V_s. The carrying cost of having a car available for sale can be incorporated in the search cost. The value equation for suppliers is

$$rV_s = a_s(p - u_s - V_s) - c_s. \tag{II–2}$$

We ignore the sufficient conditions for search to be worthwhile, $(V_d, V_s \geqslant 0)$.

Equal division of the gains from trade implies

$$u_d - p - V_d = \frac{r(u_d - p) + c_d}{r + a_d} = \frac{r(p - u_s) + c_s}{r + a_s} = p - u_s - V_s. \tag{II–3}$$

We have assumed the same utility discount rate for both parties. Thus we have a relationship between the equilibrium price, the arrival rates of trading opportunities, the search costs and the utility from ownership. Solving (II–3) for the equilibrium price, we have:

$$p = \frac{(r + a_s)(ru_d + c_d) + (r + a_d)(ru_s - c_s)}{r(2r + a_s + a_d)}. \tag{II–4}$$

Without direct search costs ($c_d = c_s = 0$), the position of the price between the seller's reservation price of u_s and the demander's reservation price u_d depends on the relative ease of finding alternative trading partners. As it becomes very easy to find buyers (a_s becomes infinite), the price goes to u_d. Alternatively, as it becomes very easy to find suppliers (a_d becomes infinite), the price goes to u_s. Furthermore, an increase in one's search cost pushes the price in an unfavourable direction. In this extremely simplified setting, (II–4) brings out the new element that search theory brings to equilibrium analysis, namely the dependence of equilibrium prices on the abilities of traders to find alternatives. Implicit in Walrasian theory is the idea that a perfectly substitutable trade can be found costlessly and instantaneously. In this restricted sense, there is no consumer surplus in a Walrasian equilibrium.

To complete the theory we need to determine the two endogenous arrival rates of trading partners. Assuming a search process without history, these depend on the underlying technology for bringing together buyers and sellers, and on the stocks of buyers (N_d) and sellers (N_s). We write the arrival rates as $a_d(N_d, N_s)$ and $a_s(N_d, N_s)$. The two arrival rate functions satisfy the accounting identity between the numbers of purchases and of sales:

$$a_d(N_d, N_s)N_d = a_s(N_d, N_s)N_s. \tag{II–5}$$

Next, we must examine the determinants of the stocks of buyers and sellers. This theory can be based on the stocks of traders or the flows of new traders. One extreme example is that the steady state stocks of buyers and sellers are exogenous. One then inserts the functions a_d and a_s in the price equation (II–4).

An alternative extreme to perfect inelasticity is the assumption of perfectly elastic supplies of buyers and sellers at given reservation values for search, $\bar{V}_s$ and $\bar{V}_d$. Assuming reservation values that are consistent with the existence of equilibrium with positive trade, the equality of gains from trade (II–3) implies

$$p = \frac{u_d + u_s + \bar{V}_s - \bar{V}_d}{2}. \tag{II–6}$$

The numbers of traders actively searching adapts to give this simple formula. Substituting from (II–6) in (II–1) and (II–2), we have the necessary values of a_d and a_s and so two equations for N_s and N_d.

For a market with professional suppliers one can consider the case of inelastic demand ($\bar{N}_d$) and a perfectly elastic supply ($\bar{V}_s$). If we assume further that demanders visit suppliers at a rate and cost independent of the number of suppliers, then a_d and c_d are parameters. Solving (II–3) for p in terms of the exogenous variables we now have

$$p = \frac{(r + a_d)(u_s + \bar{V}_s) + ru_d + c_d}{2r + a_d}. \tag{II–7}$$

In this case the response of price to an increase in the cost of the good or in the reservation utility of suppliers is $(r + a_d)/(2r + a_d)$, which is less than one. The speed of the search process relative to the interest rate determines the extent to which search equilibrium is different from Walrasian equilibrium. In a labour setting, an analogue to (II–7) shows how unemployment compensation affects wages by changing search costs.

Efficiency. There are two decisions implicit in the model above – whether to enter the search market and whether to accept a particular trade opportunity. The decision to enter a search market, like the choice of search intensity, affects the ease of trade of others. There is nothing in the process that determines prices which reflects the externalities arising from the impact of changed numbers on the opportunities to trade. Thus, in general, equilibrium will not be efficient and one has the possibility of both too much entry and too little entry.

In order to explore the efficiency of the choice of acceptable trades, we need a reason for waiting for a better deal in the future. This can be done by introducing differences in traders or differences in matches between preferences of demanders and goods on sale. However formulated, we have the proposition that the marginally acceptable trade generates no surplus to the two agents making that trade, yet the marginal trade changes the search environment of others. This involves externalities of the same kind as the entry decision already discussed. Again, in general, equilibrium is not efficient.

Individual differences. There are many patterns of differences among demanders in their evaluations of different goods. We explore two simple cases which have been dubbed quality differences and variety differences. With quality differences, all demanders have the same utility evaluation of goods. One asks how the price of a good varies with the quality of the good. With variety differences, all demanders have the same distribution of utility evaluations of the set of goods in the market, but demanders disagree as to which is better. There is then an issue of 'matching' preferences with goods. One asks how the price in a transaction varies with the quality of the match.

We use q as the index of universally agreed on quality, and denote by $p(q)$ the price paid in a transaction for a good of quality q. By suppressing all other differences, we have the same price in all the purchases of a good of any quality. We denote by $V_s(q)$ the optimized net value to a supplier of having a unit of quality q for sale. Paralleling (II–2), we can calculate the net gain to a supplier of selling his unit. This gain, $p(q) - u_s(q) - V_s(q)$, satisfies

$$p(q) - u_s(q) - V_s(q) = \frac{r[p(q) - u_s(q)] + c_s}{r + a_s}. \qquad \text{(II–8)}$$

For the demander, we denote by V_d the value of entering the search market to make a purchase, and by $u_d(q)$ the utility, gross of purchase price, of purchasing a unit of quality q. Paralleling (I–12), the utility discount rate times the value of being a demander is equal to the net flow of gains from search. The gross flow of gains equals the arrival rate of purchase opportunities times the expected gain from a purchase. The expected gain is the utility of buying the good, less the price that has to be paid for the good, less the shadow value of being a searcher. Denoting the distribution of qualities in a randomly selected trade encounter by $F(q)$, the value of being a demander satisfies

$$rV_d = a_d \int [u_d(q) - p(q) - V_d]\, \mathrm{d}F(q) - c_d. \qquad \text{(II–9)}$$

A full equilibrium analysis of this model would require determination of the distribution $F(q)$ as well as the arrival rates a_d and a_s. $V_s(q)$ would play an important role in determining $F(q)$. Such a model could consider investment in human capital with a search labour market. We will not carry out such an analysis, but focus merely on the relative prices $p(q)$, given a non-degenerate distribution $F(q)$. This problem is kept simple by the uniformity of product evaluations, which results in consumers' purchasing the first unit encountered, just as in the homogeneous case above. In any trade, the gains are shared equally between buyer and seller. Using (II–8) and (II–9) to eliminate V_d and $V_s(q)$ in the equal gain condition (II–3), we have the equilibrium price function

$$(2r + a_s)p(q) = (r + a_s)u_d(q) + ru_s(q) - c_s + (r + a_s) \times \left\{c_d - a_d \int [u_d(z) - p(z)]\, \mathrm{d}F(z)\right\} \Big/ (r + a_d). \qquad \text{(II–10)}$$

This generalization of the homogeneous case, (II–4), shows a price that rises with quality, assuming that cost does,

$$p'(q) = \frac{(r + a_s)u'_d(q) + ru'_s(q)}{2r + a_s}. \tag{II–11}$$

The speed of search, relative to the interest rate, determines the magnitude of deviation from the Walrasian result that, with identical demanders, all transactions give the same utility level, $[p'(q) = u'_d(q)]$.

With pure quality differences, all consumers have the same expected utility from search, while suppliers have expected utilities which vary with the quality of goods for sale. In a symmetric variety model, both demanders and suppliers have the same expected utility from search. The variable q now represents the quality determined by the particular match of demander and good. We view the distribution of these qualities, $F(q)$, as given and the same for all demanders and all goods. Implicitly we are assuming random matching between demanders and different goods. It is now the case that a sufficiently poor match will not result in a trade. We denote by $u_d(q)$ the utility evaluation, gross of purchase price, of buying a good, by $u_s(q)$ the cost of supplying a good, and by $p(q)$ the price when the quality of a match is q. The value of search for a supplier satisfies

$$rV_s = a_s \int_{q_1}^{q_2} [p(q) - u_s(q) - V_s]\, \mathrm{d}F(q) - c_s, \tag{II–12}$$

where q_1 is the lower bound of match qualities at which it is mutually advantageous to carry out a trade. At the lowest acceptable quality, q_1, $p(q_1)$ is equal to $u_s(q_1) + V_s$. The value of search for a demander continues to satisfy (II–9). The assumption that all mutually advantageous trades are taken implies that q_1 also equates the gain from a purchase $u_d(q_1) - p(q_1)$ with the utility from search V_d. Equating the gains from trade for buyer and seller and solving for the price we have

$$2p(q) = u_d(q) + u_s(q) - V_d + V_s. \tag{II–13}$$

Price increases with match quality to reflect the changed cost of supply, $u'_s(q)$, plus half the change in surplus, $[u'_d(q) - u'_s(q)]/2$.

Recapitulating our analysis of search equilibrium with bargaining, we have seen two themes. The first is how the search for trading partners introduces an additional element in the determination of trading prices: namely, the relative ease of the two potential trading partners in finding alternative trades. Secondly, the presence of a costly trade coordination mechanism is naturally replete with externalities, as the availability of traders affects the trading opportunities of others.

In the model used in this section, negotiation is instantaneous while search is slow. A fascinating recent literature explores equilibrium in models where the negotiation process is an explicit game of exchanging bids that can be interrupted by the arrival of an alternative trading partner (cf. Rubinstein and Wolinsky, 1985).

III EQUILIBRIUM WITH PRICE SETTING

In contrast to the bargaining theory used above, we now assume that prices are set on a take-it-or-leave-it basis by suppliers. This rule of (not) bargaining over prices gives the supplier a potential for monopoly power. The search for alternatives limits this monopoly power. The fundamental question is how much. We begin with the assumption that the only source of price information is visiting randomly chosen suppliers sequentially one at a time. We assume many identical suppliers, implying equal profitability of different pricing strategies used in equilibrium. If all buyers have identical positive search costs and identical demand curves that yield a unique profit maximizing price, then the unique equilibrium is the price that would be set by a monopolist. This result assumes a sufficient number of suppliers that buyers will not search for a single low price. This extreme result comes from the uniformity of trading opportunities. The best a buyer can do is wait to make exactly the same deal in the future. Therefore a buyer is always willing to pay a little bit more today than he has to pay in the future. Thus the demand curve for an individual seller coincides with the underlying demand curve in the neighbourhood of the equilibrium price. Even though this result is limited to unrealistic cases, it is interesting that the price is independent of the cost and speed of search, as long as search is not costless and instantaneous.

Given the pervasive reality of price distributions in retail markets, it has been natural for the literature to concentrate on generating equilibria without uniform prices. With differences in demanders, either from differences in underlying characteristics or from differences in their history of past purchases, the equilibrium can involve a distribution of prices and the structure of that distribution will depend upon search costs. In this case, consumers care about the characteristics of other consumers, since these characteristics affect price setting behaviour. Similarly, with differences among suppliers the equilibrium price distribution varies with search costs.

Information gathering. When visiting a store is the only way to learn its price, price quotations are gathered one at a time. Separating the gathering of price information from going to stores does not necessarily change the model. If price quotations are still gathered one at a time, the cost of going to purchase the good can be deducted from the utility of acquiring it, leaving the model unchanged. However, the separation of the gathering of information from the collection of goods opens up the possibility of sometimes receiving price quotations one at a time and sometimes two or more at a time. This possibility destroys the single price equilibrium in the model of identical buyers and sellers. To see this result, note that profit per sale is continuous in price but, with uniform prices, the number of sales is discontinuous in price, since a slight decrease in price wins all sales when a firm's price is one of two that are learned simultaneously. With positive profit made on each sale it would always pay to decrease price slightly below the uniform price of all other suppliers. With constant costs the competitive price is not a possible equilibrium either since a price increase gains profits when one is the only price quote while losing zero profit sales when one is not the only price quote. Thus there is necessarily a distribution of prices in equilibrium. Without price reputations, a store can choose any price it wants without affecting the flow of information about that store. Therefore, with identical firms the equilibrium will satisfy an equal profit condition. There will be low price high volume stores and high price low volume stores. One way to complete this model is to allow purchasers a choice of intensity of search which stochastically generates varying numbers of price quotations per period. We examine three additional models – price guides, advertising and word-of-mouth.

Price guide. In this extension of the model we continue to have consumers seek price information one price at a time. In addition, consumers can purchase a guide to lowest cost shopping, with the purchase cost varying across consumers. A consumer who purchases such a guide is directed to one of the lowest price stores; a consumer who does not, follows the search procedure described above. Assuming free entry of identical firms with U-shaped costs, and an equilibrium where some consumers purchase the price guide and some do not but otherwise consumers are identical, we have a two-price equilibrium. Some of the stores set the price at the competitive equilibrium level. These stores sell to all consumers who purchase price information and those sequential shoppers who are lucky enough to find one of these stores on their first shopping visit. The remaining stores have higher prices, equal to the cut-off price for searching consumers or the profit maximizing price for selling to such a consumer, whichever is lower. The fraction of stores of the two kinds and the aggregate quantity of stores per consumer are determined by the zero profit condition for the two pricing strategies. When more consumers purchase the price guide, there will be more stores setting the competitive price and a drop in the cut-off price of searching consumers. This external benefit to searching consumers implies the inefficiency of the original equilibrium. A very slight subsidization of the cost of the price guide involves a second order efficiency cost to the purchase of guides, no effect on firms (which have zero profits), and a first order gain to searching consumers.

Advertising. It is obviously counterfactual to have all the information flows resulting from actions by shoppers. Advertising is a pervasive modern phenomena. We continue to assume that stores have no price reputations. If the form of advertising is direct communication of prices to individual consumers, we can construct a model that again results in a distribution of prices. Stochastic communication from stores to consumers naturally generates a distribution of the number of price quotes that consumers receive. Any specific model of the stochastic structure of attempted communication will generate a distribution of numbers of price quotes learned by consumers. Free entry, then, implies a particular equilibrium distribution of prices, provided some consumers receive a single price quotation and others receive more than one.

Word-of-mouth. It is natural to model both the seeking of price information and the spreading of price information as costly activities. However, some price information passes between consumers as a costless activity, part of the pleasure of discussing life. The presence of word-of-mouth communication in addition to sequential shopping alters equilibrium. The natural way to model word-of-mouth price communication brings price reputations into the model, since the prices set in one period affect communications about stores in future periods when their prices might be different. In order to isolate the effect of world-of-mouth we consider a very artificial model. Stores set prices which must hold for two periods. Consumers shop in the first or second period but are otherwise identical. In the first period, there is only sequential search, visiting stores one at a time as modelled above. Between the first and second periods there are random contacts between first period shoppers and second period shoppers. In this way, each second period shopper receives information about the price in some positive number of stores. We assume that some people hear of only one store, while others hear of at least two. Then there will be a distribution of prices, with the structure of the distribution depending on the details of the word-of-mouth process. This analysis can be extended by having shoppers tell not only of the prices they paid, but also of prices they have heard from others. Both types of communication require a model of memory. The density of stores has different effects on equilibrium prices for different models of memory. This approach has been used, in a setting of search for quality rather than low price, to argue that doctors' fees can be higher where there are more doctors per capita (Satterthwaite, 1979).

Recapitulating the analysis of search equilibrium with price setting but not price reputation, we have seen two themes. One is the tendency for even low cost search to generate sizeable amounts of monopoly power because of similar incentives for all suppliers. The second is a tendency for equilibrium to have a distribution of prices. Since price distributions are a widespread phenomenon in decentralized economies, it is reassuring that the theory produces such distributions.

IV ADDITIONAL ISSUES

We have considered the search analogue to competitive equilibrium. It was assumed that there were many small firms, whose behaviour was adequately approximated while ignoring their impacts on certain aspects of equilibrium. Search theory has also examined equilibria with small numbers of firms. It may pay a monopolist to have a distribution of prices across his outlets, rather than a single price, as a method of discriminating among consumers with different search costs, even though the need to search for a low price adds to the cost of purchase of the good (Salop, 1977). In a duopoly or oligopoly setting, it is natural to consider randomized pricing strategies which again give rise to a distribution of prices (Shilony, 1977). This may be one of the many factors that go into the empirical fact of sales by retail outlets.

The technology of shopping in the models above is extremely simple. Little has been done to marry the underlying search issues with some of the realities of the geographic distributions of consumers and firms and the normal travels of shoppers. Similarly, little has been done to model the search basis for the role of intermediaries.

Price reputations. All the models mentioned above omit or severely limit the intertemporal links in profitability that arise from price reputations. This is a major hole in the existing literature,. Probably significant progress in this area will have to await the discrimination of cases in which optimal strategies (whether determinate or stochastic) are stationary, from those in which optimal strategies involve building up a reputation which is then run down. In such a setting, analysis will be very sensitive to the assumptions made about consumer knowledge both of existing prices and of price strategies followed by firms. It would be nice to have both an empirical evaluation of the level of consumer ignorance about opportunities, and a theoretical structure capable of examining the relationship between equilibrium and the extent to which consumers are accurately informed.

CONCLUSION

Walrasian theory assumes that consumers are perfectly informed about the prices of all commodities in the economy. This assumption is central for the law of one price, that a homogeneous commodity sells at the same price in all transactions in a given market. This assumption is also central for a variety of inequalities on prices, limiting price differences to be less than transportation costs. These inequalities are consequences of the absence of opportunities for arbitrage profits. In order to make a rigorous arbitrage argument, there must be simultaneous purchase and sale of the same commodity at different prices, net of transportation costs. If the purchase and sale are at different times, there is likely to be risk for the would-be arbitrageur. Similarly, a proper arbitrage argument requires homogeneous commodities. It is improper to apply arbitrage arguments to labour markets, for example, although migration arguments may lead to similar conclusions. In search theory with a known distribution of prices, there is a cost to finding any trading partner, and possibly a large cost to finding one willing to trade at some particular price. This idea captures one aspect of the limitations on the extent of arbitrage arguments.

Realistically, one must recognize that infrequent traders are often ill-informed about the distribution of prices in the market. This introduces two important changes in the basic theory. One is that gathering information changes beliefs about the distribution of prices, as well as revealing the location of possible transactions. The second is the incentive created for sellers to find consumers whose beliefs make them willing to transact at high prices. The differences between the search for suckers and the hunt for the highest value use of resources has not been clearly drawn in the literature, yet this distinction is valid and important for evaluating the functioning of some markets. Search-based theory and empirical work have a long way to go until we have satisfactory answers to a number of allocation questions that are totally ignored in a Walrasian setting. Nevertheless, the theory has already shown how informational realities can seriously alter the conclusions of Walrasian theory.

It would have been highly duplicative to have reviewed search theory of the labour market as well as that of the retail market. For a survey of labour search theory and a partial guide to the literature, see Mortensen (1984). Individual patterns of unemployment spells are the key empirical fact requiring revision of the Walrasian paradigm.

The failure of the profession, thus far, to produce a satisfactory integration of micro and macroeconomics based on the Walrasian paradigm (with or without price stickiness) raises the thought that such an integration might come out of search theory. For a presentation of this view, and discussion of some applications of search ideas to macro unemployment issues, see Diamond (1984).

BIBLIOGRAPHY

Diamond, P. 1984. *A Search-Equilibrium Approach to the Micro Foundations of Macroeconomics.* Cambridge, Mass.: MIT Press.

Kiefer, N. and Neumann, G. 1979. An empirical job search model with a test of the constant reservation wage hypothesis. *Journal of Political Economy* 87, 69–82.

Mortensen, D. 1984. Job search and labor market analysis. In *Handbook of Labour Economics*, ed. R. Layard and O. Ashenfelter, Amsterdam: North-Holland.

Rothschild, M. 1974. Searching for the lowest price when the distribution is not known. *Journal of Political Economy* 82, 689–711.

Rubinstein, A. and Wolinsky, A. 1985. Equilibrium in a market with sequential bargaining. *Econometrica* 53, 1133–50.

Salop, S. 1977. The noisy monopolist: imperfect information, price dispersion and price discrimination. *Review of Economic Studies* 44, 393–406.

Satterthwaite, M. 1979. Consumer information, equilibrium industry price, and the number of sellers. *Bell Journal of Economics* 10(2), 483–502.

Shilony, Y. 1977. Mixed pricing in oligopoly. *Journal of Economic Theory* 14, 373–88.

Signalling

JOHN G. RILEY

If product quality of individual units cannot be observed at the time of purchase, but buyers do eventually learn average quality, goods will be traded at a price which reflects buyers' beliefs about this average. The price will then adjust until buyers' beliefs about average quality are confirmed ex post.

Such a market has two highly undesirable features. First, to the extent that a seller can lower costs by lowering the quality of his product, he has an incentive to do so. Secondly, even when such hidden actions are not possible, if a seller of a product of above average quality has a high opportunity cost, he may be better off withdrawing from the market. Average quality thus falls below that in a world of complete information, and *adverse selection* occurs.

As Akerlof (1970) showed, this process of withdrawal from the market might even continue until only the very worst 'lemons' would actually be traded.

It was Spence (1973) who provided a striking new insight into how the potential gains to trade might still be realized despite the problems created by informational asymmetry. His essential point was that if a seller of a higher quality product could find some activity that was less costly for him than for a seller of a lower quality product, it might pay him to undertake this activity as a *signal* of high quality. On the other side of the market, even if buyers were not aware of the underlying differences in the cost of the activity, they would learn that the signal was associated with higher quality and thus be willing to pay a premium price.

Going beyond the special case of either signalling or not signalling. Spence argued that, as long as the *marginal cost* of some activity was lower for sellers of higher quality, an equilibrium would emerge in which quality could be perfectly inferred by buyers from the level of signalling undertaken by the seller.

In Spence's own work and in most of the ensuing literature, it is assumed that there are many buyers and many sellers of the product. It is therefore natural to focus on this case here. I also follow most of the literature in ignoring possible opportunities for sellers to change product quality without being observed, that is, I shall abstract from problems of *moral hazard*.

Perhaps the most widely analysed application of signalling theory is to insurance markets. In this case risky outcomes are 'sold' by individuals to insurance companies. As Rothschild and Stiglitz (1976) first argued, an individual with a preferred risk is more willing to co-insure since his loss probability is lower. The level of co-insurance is thus a potential signal of risk quality.

A second major application of signalling theory has been to issues in finance. In this case a manager (Ross, 1977) with superior knowledge about a high quality investment opportunity can signal to potential investors by his choice of financing or dividend policy. More recently, Titman and Trueman (1986) have also argued that an entrepreneur can signal project quality by his choice of an independent auditor. Here it is the favourable estimate of actual quality which makes an entrepreneur more willing to spend funds on a high-cost, high-reputation auditor whose report, he anticipates, is likely to be confirming.

Spence's own focus was primarily on the use of education as a signal of productivity. He argues that an individual of higher ability is able to accumulate educational credentials at lower cost. Education thus not only enhances human capital but also has a valuable informational role for higher ability workers.

The basic insight that agents can signal quality via observable actions is intuitively plausible. However, upon closer inspection, the precise characterization of a 'competitive' signalling equilibrium turns out to be subtle. Indeed, a decade after the early challenges posed by Riley (1975), Rothschild and Stiglitz (1976) and Wilson (1977), the issue remains controversial. My goal here is to lay out the central themes of the on-going debate by means of a bare-bones labour market example.

To make the exposition as simple as possible, suppose that marginal productivity in some industry is unaffected by the level of education s. It will be convenient to refer to an individual with productivity θ as being of type θ. Suppose also that the cost of education level s, for a type θ worker is given by

$$C_\theta(s) = s/\theta. \tag{1}$$

Higher quality workers thus have a lower marginal cost of signalling.

If type θ accepts the offer (s, w), that is, a wage w for an education level of at least s, his net payoff is

$$U_\theta(s, w) = w - C_\theta(s). \tag{2}$$

Suppose that there are just two types, θ_1 with productivity 1 and θ_2 with productivity 5. Finally suppose that there is another industry (industry R) which pays a wage $w_R = 2$ to all workers.

At the heart of Spence's analysis is the following description of an equilibrium.

Definition: *Signalling Equilibrium* (*Spence*) 'A signalling equilibrium in the market is a set of conditional probabilistic beliefs for the employer which, when translated into offered wages, employee investment responses and new market data, are confirmed by the new market data relating educational levels to productivity.'

For our simple example, suppose workers who do not signal are offered a wage of 1 and workers who signal at level $s = 5$ are offered a wage of 5. A worker of type θ has a net payoff, if he signals, of

$$U_\theta(5,5) = 5 - 5/\theta = \begin{cases} 0, & \text{if } \theta = 1 \\ 4, & \text{if } \theta = 5 \end{cases}.$$

Low quality workers thus choose to work in industry R and earn a wage of 2. High quality workers, however, are better off signalling.

This equilibrium is depicted in Figure 1 as the pair of offers

$$\{E_1^*, E_2\} = \{(0,2),(5,5)\}.$$

Given our assumptions (see (1) and (2) above), indifference curves for each type are linear. Type 1 workers, with their steeper indifference curves, prefer E_1^* to E_2. Type 2 workers, however, with their flatter (dashed) indifference curves prefer E_2 to E_1^*. The initial beliefs of firms that only high quality workers will choose to signal are thus confirmed by the market.

To complete the description of the equilibrium it is necessary to introduce beliefs about the productivity of a worker who chooses a signal other than $s_2 = 5$. Clearly the equilibrium is sustained by the belief that anyone who chooses a level of s below 5 has low productivity. However, in Spence's world firms (buyers) never test such beliefs.

This is the heart of the critiques by Riley (1975) and Rothschild and Stiglitz (1976). Firms can readily test their beliefs by offering lower wages for slightly lower levels of the signal. Consider Figure 1. With other firms making offers of

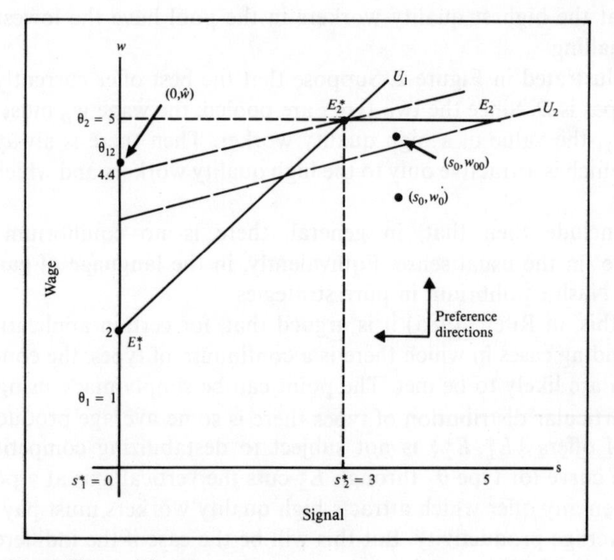

Figure 1 Signalling with two types

E_1^* and E_2 a firm offering (s_0, w_0) finds that no workers are attracted. However as long as the firm recognizes that higher quality workers have lower costs of signalling it knows that by raising the wage it will eventually attract high quality workers. The point (s_0, w_{00}) is one such offer. Since it is strictly profitable, the belief that a worker choosing s_0 would be of low quality is disconfirmed by market data.

This same argument holds for any Spencian equilibrium in which low quality workers are strictly better off not signalling. Therefore the only candidate pair of 'competitive' equilibrium offers is the pair $\{E_1^*, E_2^*\}$ depicted in Figure 1. (We ignore here the purely technical issue of what a seller does when indifferent between offers, and simply assume that he will always choose the one involving the smallest amount of signalling.)

Experimenting with offers in the neighbourhood of E_2^* is not profitable since any wage offer below 5 which is attractive to type 2 workers is also attractive to type 1 workers. However, the market also provides information about the proportion of high quality workers. If this is less than 0.25 so that $\bar{\theta}_{12}$, the average productivity of the two types, is less than $w_R = 2$, it is clear $\{E_1^*, E_2^*\}$ is a competitive equilibrium set of offers. On the other hand, suppose the proportion of high quality workers is sufficiently high that $\bar{\theta}_{12}$ is above the point where type 2's indifference curve through E_2^* intersects the vertical axis. Then, as depicted, there are alternative offers such as $(0, \hat{w})$ which attract both types and are profitable. In this latter case all the signalling equilibria are potentially subject to destabilizing competition.

This suggests that an equilibrium must involve pooling of different types. However, as Rothschild and Stiglitz emphasized, whenever a pool of heterogeneous types choose the same offer, a buyer can always 'skim the cream' by exploiting the fact that the highest quality workers in the pool have the lowest marginal cost of signalling.

This is illustrated in Figure 2. Suppose that the best offer currently available for both types is D. Since the two types are pooled, the wage w_D must be strictly less than θ_2, the value of a high quality worker. Then there is always an offer such as T which is attractive only to the high quality workers and which is strictly profitable.

We conclude then that, in general, there is no equilibrium which is 'competitive' in the usual sense. Equivalently, in the language of game theory, there is no Nash equilibrium in pure strategies.

Despite this, in Riley (1985) it is argued that, for certain applications of the theory including cases in which there is a continuum of types, the conditions for equilibrium are likely to be met. The point can be simply made using Figure 1. For any particular distribution of types there is some average productivity $\bar{\theta}_{12}$. The pair of offers $\{E_1^*, E_2^*\}$ is not subject to destabilizing competition if the indifference curve for type θ_2 through E_2^* cuts the vertical axis at a point above θ_{12}. For then any offer which attracts high quality workers must pay a wage in excess of average productivity. But this will be the case if the indifference curve for type θ_2 through E^* is sufficiently less steep than the corresponding indifference

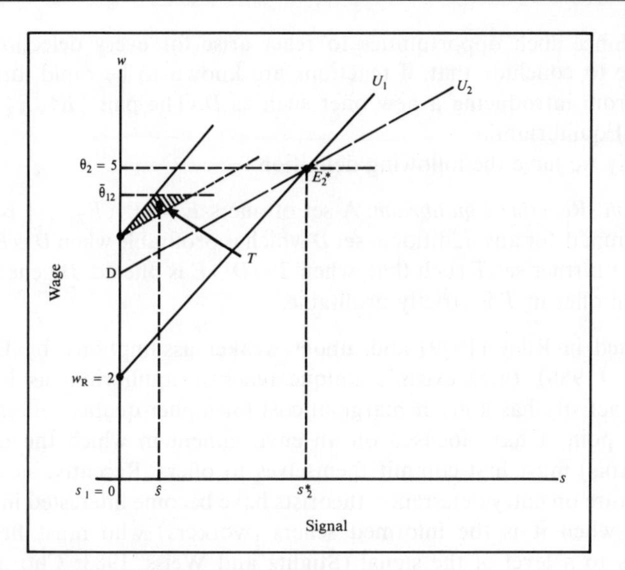

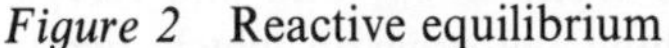
Figure 2 Reactive equilibrium

curve for type 1. That is, the ratio of marginal costs

$$\frac{\partial C_2(s)/\partial s}{\partial C_1(s)/\partial s}$$

is sufficiently small. Thus it is the *rate* at which the marginal cost of signalling declines with productivity which is critical. As long as the proportional rate of decline is sufficiently large, $\{E_1^*, E_2^*\}$ is a competitive equilibrium set of offers.

This still leaves unresolved the theoretically important issue of how competitive markets perform when there is informational asymmetry and the sufficient conditions are not satisfied. One way out of the dilemma has been suggested by Wilson (1977) and further examined by Miyazaki (1977) and Riley (1979). The key idea is that, when competitive behaviour of the type described above does not result in convergence to an equilibrium, agents will begin to learn that certain actions result in predictable responses by others. In particular, certain offers which are profitable, *ceteris paribus*, result in losses when other buyers react.

To illustrate, the essential features of the two type example have been reproduced in Figure 2. Since average productivity, $\bar{\theta}_{12}$, is close to θ_2, there are offers such as D which attract both types away from $\{E_1^*, E_2^*\}$ and which are strictly profitable. But such a 'defection' creates its own profitable opportunities. Any firm reacting with the offer T depicted in the figure succeeds in skimming the cream from the pool and hence garnering additional profits. As a result the initial defector attracts only low quality types and hence loses money.

Note also that, since the reactor makes money on every worker who accepts, the worst that can happen is that other firms introduce preferred reactions so there are no takers for T. The profit of the reactor is thus bounded from below by zero. Since such opportunities to react arise for every defection it seems reasonable to conclude that, if reactions are known to be rapid, firms will be deterred from introducing a new offer such as D. The pair $\{E_1^*, E_2^*\}$ is thus a 'Reactive Equilibrium'.

Formally we have the following definition.

Definition: *Reactive Equilibrium.* A set of offers $E=\{E_1, E_2, \ldots\}$ is a reactive equilibrium if, for any additional set D which is profitable when $D \cup E$ is offered, there is a further set T such that, when $T \cup D \cup E$ is offered, D generates losses and each offer in T is strictly profitable.

As argued in Riley (1979) and, under weaker assumptions, by Engers and Fernandez (1986), there exists a unique reactive equilibrium as long as the signalling activity has a lower marginal cost for higher quality sellers.

To this point I have focused on an environment in which the uninformed buyers (firms) must first commit themselves to offers. Recently, as part of the new literature on entry deterrence, theorists have become interested in modelling signalling when it is the informed sellers (workers) who must first commit themselves to a level of the signal (Stiglitz and Weiss, 1983; Cho and Kreps, 1987). In this literature it is argued that switching the order in which agents move results in a multitude of equilibrium rather than a problem of existence.

The point is easily made using our simple labour market example. Consider Figure 1 once more. Workers believe that they will be treated as low quality types unless they signal at level $s_2=5$. Given such beliefs, low quality workers choose $s=0$ and high quality workers $s=s_2$.

If firms know that workers have these beliefs they will bid wages up to 1 and 5 respectively. As a result the pair $\{E_1^*, E_2^*\}$ is an equilibrium *relative to workers' beliefs.*

But the particular beliefs assumed are not consistent with the underlying model. Suppose a seller were to choose $s=s_0$ rather than s_2. Note that low quality workers are strictly better off at E_1^* than choosing $s=s_0$ even if by doing the latter they would be paid the high wage. Thus if all other workers were to choose $s=0$ or $s=s_2$, it is rational for firms to believe that a worker choosing s_0 is of high quality.

Arguing along these lines Kreps concludes that the Pareto dominating pair of offers $\{E_1^*, E_2^*\}$ is the only 'stable' equilibrium. But taking this argument one step further, suppose a worker were to choose some level $\hat{s}$ between zero and s_2^* as depicted in Figure 2 . With $\bar{\theta}_{12}$ so close to θ_2 it would be rational for a firm to believe that this worker is a random draw from the population. For, given these beliefs, the wage the worker would be paid, $\bar{\theta}_{12}$, is attractive to both high and low quality workers. But then we are forced to conclude that there is no static competitive equilibrium with rational beliefs.

Comparing this with the earlier argument it should be clear that the non-existence problem arises under exactly the same conditions as when the uninformed firms must make the first moves. Once again, however, if an offer cannot be quickly withdrawn there are reactions which seem likely to operate as an effective deterrent. If one firm responds to a signal level $\hat{s}$ with an offer of $\hat{w} \leqslant \bar{\theta}_{12}$, a high quality worker has an incentive to raise his signal above $\hat{s}$ in the expectation that a second firm will 'skim the cream' just as argued above.

To conclude, Spence's initial insight that information could be conveyed by endogenous signalling activity in a competitive environment is theoretically valid. However, the conditions under which signalling equilibria are free of potential dynamic instability are rather more restrictive than he supposed. His assumption that the potential signalling activity should have a lower marginal cost for high quality workers is necessary but not sufficient. None the less it is sufficient that the proportional rate of decline in the marginal cost of signalling with respect to product quality be sufficiently large.

The issue of what happens when this condition fails remains open. It seems to me that it will only be resolved when theorists take up the challenge of modelling dynamics as a process in which agents react with very incomplete information, rather than attempting to build ever more subtle 'rational' beliefs into essentially static models. My conjecture is that the eventual resolution will hinge critically on the length of time for which agents are committed to announced strategies. For environments where it is not possible to withdraw an offer quickly once it is made, I believe that Wilson's insight into the deterrent effect of potential reactions will prove to be correct. However, for environments where agents are not committed to strategies, I believe we will have to accept that there may be no stable equilibrium. Instead market behaviour will have to be modelled as intrinsically uncertain, within prescribable bounds.

BIBLIOGRAPHY

Akerlof, G.A. 1970. The market for 'lemons': qualitative uncertainty and the market mechanism. *Quarterly Journal of Economics* 84, August, 488–500.

Bhattacharya, S. 1980. Nondissipative signalling structures and dividend policy. *Quarterly Journal of Economics* 95, August, 1–24.

Cho, I.-K. and Kreps, D.M. 1987. Signalling games and stable equilibria. *Quarterly Journal of Economics* 102, May, 179–222.

Engers, M. and Fernandez, L. 1986. On the existence and uniqueness of signalling equilibria. *Econometrica* 54.

Leland, H.E. and Pyle, D.H. 1977. Informational asymmetries, financial structure, and financial intermediation. *Journal of Finance* 32, May, 381–7.

Miyazaki, H. 1977. The rat race and internal markets. *Bell Journal of Economics* 8, Autumn, 394–418.

Riley, J.G. 1975. Competitive signalling. *Journal of Economic Theory* 10, April, 174–86.

Riley, J.G. 1979. Informational equilibrium. *Econometrica* 47, March, 331–60.

Riley, J.G. 1985. Competition with hidden knowledge. *Journal of Political Economy* 93, October, 958–76.

Ross, S. 1977. The determinants of financial structure: the incentive signalling approach. *Bell Journal of Economics* 8, Spring, 23–40.

Rothschild, M. and Stiglitz, J.E. 1976. Equilibrium in competitive insurance markets: an essay on the economics of imperfect information. *Quarterly Journal of Economics* 80, November, 629–49.

Spence, A.M. 1973. *Market Signalling: Information Transfer in Hiring and Related Processes.* Cambridge, Mass.: Harvard University Press.

Stiglitz, J.E. and Weiss, A. 1983. Alternative approaches to analyzing markets with asymmetric information: reply. *American Economic Review* 73, March, 246–9.

Titman, S. and Trueman, B. 1986. Information quality and the value of new issues. *Journal of Accounting and Economics* 8.

Wilson, C.A. 1977. A model of insurance markets with incomplete information. *Journal of Economic Theory* 16, December, 167–297.

Teams

ROY RADNER

The economic theory of teams addresses a middle ground between the theory of individual decision under uncertainty and the theory of games. A *team* is made up of a number of decision-makers, with common interests and beliefs, but controlling different decision variables and basing their decisions on (possibly) different information. The theory of teams is concerned with (1) the allocation of decision variables (tasks) and information among the members of the team, and (2) the characterization of efficient decision rules, given the allocation of tasks and information.

For example, in the pre-computer age, airline companies had a number of ticket agents who were authorized to sell reservations on future flights with only partial information about what reservations had been booked by other agents. A team-theoretic issue would be the characterization of best rules for those agents to use under such circumstances, taking account of the joint probability distribution of demands for reservations at the different offices, the losses due to selling too many or too few reservations in total, and so forth. A second issue would be the calculation of the increase in expected profit that would be obtained by providing each agent with better information about the status of reservations at all offices, or by increased centralization of the reservation process. To calculate this increase in expected profit – the *value* of the additional information – one of course needs to know something about the best decision rules with and without the additional information. However, providing this additional information would require additional communication, transmission, processing and storage, all of which would be costly. The value of the information puts an upper bound on the additional cost that should be incurred. The value – and cost – of the information will depend on its structure and on the structure of the team's decision problem, and not just on some simple measure of the 'quantity' of information. (For a study of the airline reservation problem, and other models of sales organization, from a team-theoretic point of view, see Beckmann, 1958 and McGuire, 1961, respectively.)

In this essay we shall sketch a formal model of team theory, the characterization of optimal team decision functions and the evaluation of information in a team. The theory will be illustrated with a discussion of decentralized resource allocation, followed by concluding remarks on the incentive problem.

A FORMAL MODEL. We consider a *team* and *M members*. Each member m controls an *action*, say a_m. The resulting utility to the team depends on the *team action*,

$$a = (a_1, \ldots, a_M),$$

and on the *state of the environment*. (Since the team members have common interests, there is a single utility for the whole team.) The state of the environment comprises all the variables about which team members may be uncertain before choosing their actions. It is determined exogenously, i.e. is not subject to the control or influence of the team members. If we denote the state of the environment by s, then we can denote the utility to the team by $u(a, s)$; the function u will be called the *payoff function* for the team.

Before choosing an action, each team member m receives an information signal, y_m. This information signal is determined by the state of the environment, say $y_m = \eta_m(s)$. (This includes the case of 'noisy' information, if the description of the state of the environment includes a description of the noise.) We shall call η_m the *information function* for member m, and the M-tuple $\eta = (\eta_1, \ldots, \eta_M)$ will be called the *information structure* of the team.

Each team member m will choose his action on the basis of the information signal he receives, according to a decision function, say α_m. Thus

$$a_m = \alpha_m(y_m) = \alpha_m(\eta_m[s]). \tag{1}$$

If we use the symbol α to denote the *team decision function*, i.e., the M-tuple of individual decision functions, then the utility to the team, in *state* s, of using the information structure η and decision function α can be expressed as

$$U(s) = u[\alpha(\eta[s]), s]. \tag{2}$$

To express the team's uncertainty about the state of the environment, we suppose that s is determined according to some probability distribution, ϕ, on the set S of possible states. This probability distribution may be interpreted as 'objective' or 'personal'; in the latter case it represents the beliefs of the team members (Savage, 1954). It is part of the definition of a team that its members have common beliefs, as well as common utility functions.

With the state s distributed according to the probability distribution ϕ, the utility $U(s)$ in (2) is a random variable. We shall assume that the team chooses its decision function so as to maximize the (mathematical) expectation of this utility,

$$E[U(s)] = \sum_s \phi(s) U(s) \equiv \omega(\alpha, \eta, \phi). \tag{3}$$

As a special case, suppose that the information functions of the team members are identical. In this case, the team decision problem is formally identical to a one-person decision problem in which the same person controls all of the actions. An alternative interpretation of this case is that the information is *centralized.* By contrast, if at least two team members have essentially different information functions, then we may say that the information is *decentralized.* With this definition of (informational) decentralization, we see that all organizations but the very smallest are likely to be decentralized to some extent.

The expected utility for the team depends on the team members' decision function, the team information structure and the probability distribution of states of the environment, as well as on the 'structure' of the decision problem, i.e. the way in which the utility (2) depends on the members' action and the state of the environment. This is brought out by the notation in (3). If we want to compare the usefulness of two different information structures, we have to associate with them some corresponding decision function α and probability distribution ϕ. Since the probability distribution (sometimes called the 'prior distribution') represents either objective probabilities or the team members' common beliefs before they receive further information, it is natural to take it as a datum of the problem. On the other hand, since the decision functions can be chosen by the team, it is natural to associate with each information structure the corresponding team decision function that maximizes its expected utility (given the information structure). Thus the optimization problem for the team may be posed in two stages: (1) for a given information structure, characterize the optimal team decision function(s); (2) optimize the information structure, taking account of the costs of – or constraints on – making the information available, and with the proviso that for each information structure the team uses an optimal decision function.

More will be said below about each of these stages of the problem. However, it should be emphasized here that the choice of information structure comprises most of the organizational design choices that are not concerned with conflicts of interests or beliefs among the organization's members. The information structure is, of course, affected by the pattern of observation and communication in the team. In addition, the allocation of tasks within the team is expressed by the information structure. To see this, suppose that each member of the team were assigned an information structure; then a reassignment of decision variables to team members would be formally equivalent to reassigning information functions to decision variables.

OPTIMAL DECISION FUNCTIONS. We shall now consider the characterization of team decision functions that are optimal for a given structure of information. It will be useful to recall here the corresponding problem for a single-person decision (see, e.g., Marschak and Radner, 1972, ch. 2). We may use the same model and notation as in the previous section, but remembering that there is only one member of the team. The following statement provides a general characterization of the optimal decision function: *For each information signal, choose an action that maximizes the conditional expected utility given the particular signal.*

This characterization is easily derived from equations (2) and (3). In equation (3), group the terms in the sum according to the information signal associated with each state; this gives us

$$E[U(s)] = \sum_{y} \sum_{\eta(s)=y} \phi(s)U(s). \tag{4}$$

From (2), if $\eta(s) = y$, then the resulting utility in that state is

$$U(s) = u[\alpha(y), s]. \tag{5}$$

For each signal y, the decision-maker can choose an action $a = \alpha(y)$. Hence, combining (4) and (5) we see that, for each signal y, the decision-maker should choose $a = \alpha(y)$ to maximize

$$\sum_{\eta(s)=y} \phi(s)u(a, s). \tag{6}$$

Let $\psi(y)$ denote the probability of y, and let $\phi(s|y)$ denote the conditional probability of s given y. By definition,

$$\psi(y) = \sum_{y=\eta(s)} \phi(s),$$

and if $y = \eta(s)$,

$$\phi(s|y) = \frac{\phi(s)}{\psi(y)},$$

or

$$\phi(s) = \psi(y)\phi(s|y).$$

Hence (6) can be written as

$$\psi(y) \sum_{\eta(s)=y} \phi(s|y)u(a, s), \tag{7}$$

so that maximizing (6) is equivalent to maximizing

$$\sum_{\eta(s)=y} \phi(s|y)u(a, s), \tag{8}$$

which we recognize as the conditional expected utility using the action a, given the signal y. This proves the above characterization of the best decision function. (Notice that we have implicitly assumed that the signal has positive probability. There is no loss of generality in doing so; we can simply exclude from consideration all signals that have zero probability, since they do not affect the expected utility.)

The characterization of optimal single-person decision functions can be extended to the case of a team, but in a restricted way. Consider a particular team member i. If a team decision function, say $\hat{\alpha}$, is optimal, then surely i's decision function α_i is optimal given that each other member j uses $\hat{\alpha}_j$. Hence i is faced, so to speak, with a one-person decision problem in which the other members' decision functions form part of i's 'environment'. The following is therefore a *necessary* condition for a team decision function to be optimal:

Person-by-Person-Optimality Condition: For each member i, and for each signal y_i with positive probability, the corresponding action $a_i = \alpha_i(y_i)$ maximizes the team's conditional expected utility given the signal y_i and the decision functions of the other members.

Although person-by-person-optimality is necessary for optimality, it need not be sufficient. However, one can prove the following:

Theorem 1. If each member's action is a real finite-dimensional vector chosen from some open rectangle, and if for each state s the team's utility is a concave and differentiable function of the team action, then any team decision function that is person-by-person-optimal is also optimal.

(For a proof of this theorem, and an example in which a person-by-person-optimal decision function fails to be optimal, see Marschak and Radner, 1972, ch. 10, s. 3; for a more complete treatment, see Radner, 1962.)

The person-by-person-optimality condition can be applied to yield more detailed characterizations of optimal team decision functions for special cases, e.g., in which the utility function is quadratic or piecewise-linear (see Marschak and Radner, 1972, ch. 10). A few such applications are illustrated below.

THE EVALUATION OF INFORMATION. As noted at the beginning of this discussion, many of the most interesting questions in organizational design concern the comparison of alternative information structures. One information structure is better than another to the extent that it permits better decisions; on the other hand, this improvement can be obtained only at some additional cost.

We first consider the case in which the utility from the decisions is additively separable from the cost of the information structure; we shall call this the *separable case.* In this case, one is justified in defining the *gross value* of an information structure as the difference between (1) the expected utility derived from its best use and (2) the maximum utility obtainable using no information (beyond that contained in the prior probability distribution of states).

If the team has no information (the null information structure), then its decision function reduces to a single team action. The maximum expected utility that the team can obtain with the null information structure is

$$V_0(\phi) = \max_a \sum_s u(a, s). \tag{9}$$

Hence in the separable case, the gross value of an information structure η is defined as

$$V(\eta, \phi) \equiv \max_\alpha \omega(\alpha, \eta, \phi) - V_0(\phi). \tag{10}$$

(Cf. equation (3).)

Note that the value of an information structure depends on the prior distribution, as well as on the entire structure of the decision problem (available actions, utility function, etc.). This should make one suspect that there is no way to tell whether one information structure is more valuable than another just by examining the two information structures alone.

To examine this question more carefully, it is useful to introduce another representation of information. Consider again for the moment the single-person case; an information structure then consists of a single function from states to information signals. For any given signal, there is a set of states that give rise to that signal. This correspondence between signals and sets of states determines a partition of the set of states; each element of the partition is a set of all states that lead to a particular signal; denote this partition by (S_y). It is obvious that any two information structures that give rise to the same partition are equivalent from the point of view of the decision-maker, and in particular must have the same value. In other words, the names or labels of the signals are unimportant.

Suppose now that the set S of states of the environment, the number M of team members and the set A of team actions are fixed. Consider the family of all team decision problems that can be formulated with the given triple (S, M, A). In other words, consider the set of all pairs (u, ϕ), where u is a utility function for the team, and ϕ is a prior distribution, compatible with (S, M, A). We shall say that one information structure *is as valuable* as another information structure if the value of the first is greater than or equal to the value of the second for all team decision problems compatible with (S, M, A). (Value is defined by equation (10).)

The following criterion provides a simple test for the relation 'as valuable as'. Of two partitions of the set S, we shall say the first is as *fine* as the second if every element of the first partition is a subset of some element of the second (the first can be obtained by 'refining' the second). Let $\eta = (\eta_1, \ldots, \eta_M)$ and $\chi = (\chi_1, \ldots, \chi_M)$ be two team information structures. We shall say that η is as fine as χ if for every team member m, η_m is as fine as χ_m. One can prove (see Marschak and Radner, 1972, Ch. 2, Sec. 6):

Theorem 2. Assume that every team member has at least three alternative actions; then the information structure η is at least as valuable as the information structure χ if and only if, for each member m, η_m is as fine as χ_m.

Theorem 2 can be extended to deal with 'noisy' information (see, e.g., McGuire, 1972).

Since two partitions of a set need not be ranked by the relation 'as fine as', it is clear from Theorem 2 that the relation 'as valuable as' is only a partial ordering of information structures. This implies, in particular, that there is no numerical measure of 'quantity of information' that can rank all information structures in order of value, independent of the decision problem in which the information is used.

If the utility of the team decision and the cost of information are not additively separable, then an alternative definition of the value of information must be used.

For example, suppose that the outcome of the team decision and the cost of the information structure are both measured in dollars, and the team is not risk-neutral, so that the team utility is some (nonlinear) function of the outcome and the cost. Then we can define the value of the information structure as the 'demand price', i.e., the smallest cost that would make the team indifferent between using the information structure and having no information beyond the prior distribution. (For further discussion of the comparison of information structures, see McGuire, 1972. For more on the value of and demand for information, see Arrow, 1972.)

DECENTRALIZATION. We have used the term informational decentralization to refer to a structure of information in which not all members have the same information function. In an economic organization the information structure is generated by processes of observation, communication, storage and computation. For example, suppose that each team member m starts by observing a different random variable, say $\zeta_m(s)$. If there were no communication among the members before actions were taken, then each member's information would be the same as his observation – an extreme form of decentralization. On the other hand, if there were complete communication of their observations among the members, then their information functions would be identical, namely $\zeta = (\zeta_1, \ldots, \zeta_M)$. Alternatively, the latter information structure could be generated by having all members communicate their observations to a central agency, which would then compute the team action and communicate the corresponding individual action to each member. In the last two cases, we would say that the information structure is completely centralized, because all of the members' actions were based on the same information.

Rarely does one encounter in a real organization the extremes of no communication or complete communication just described. Rather, one finds that numerous devices are used to bring about a partial exchange of information. The usefulness of such devices is measured by the excess of additional value (expected utility) they contribute over the costs of installing and operating them. Examples of such devices are the dissemination of reports and instructions, the formation of committees and task forces, and 'management by exception'. Formal models and a comparative analysis of some of these devices are given in Marschak and Radner (1972, ch. 6). In particular, this methodology is used to elucidate the value of two different forms of management by exception.

ALLOCATION OF RESOURCES IN A TEAM. For many economists, the purely competitive market represents the ideal model of economic decentralization. Indeed, in some economic literature, 'decentralization' and 'pure competition' are synonymous. The potential usefulness of market-like mechanisms to decentralize economic decision-making in a socialist economy has also been discussed by students of socialism (Lange and Taylor, 1938; Lerner, 1944; Ward, 1967).

The theory of teams provides a natural framework for the analysis of market mechanism as a device for decentralization. For example, consider the problem of allocating resources to productive enterprises. Suppose that some resources are initially held centrally by a 'resource manager'. Before any exchange of information, the resource manager observes the supplies of centrally available resources, and each enterprise manager observes his respective local conditions of production: technology, supplies of local resources, etc. The action of the resource manager is to allocate the central resources among the enterprises. The action of an enterprise manager includes (say) the choice of techniques and the levels of inputs of local resources. The state of the environment comprises the total supplies of central resources and the local conditions.

At one extreme, the team action could be taken without any communication. In particular, the central resources would be allocated based on the prior probability distribution of local conditions. Regarding the supplies of central resources, each enterprise manager would know only the prior probability distribution of such supplies, and the allocation rule to be used by the resource manager. We might call the resulting information structure 'routine'.

At the other extreme (complete centralization), each enterprise manager might be required to report to the resource manager all of his information about local conditions. The resource manager would then compute both the optimal decisions of the enterprises and the optimal allocation of resources. Accordingly, the resources would be allocated and the enterprise managers would be 'instructed' by the resource manager as to what actions they should take.

In a market mechanism, the resource manager would announce prices (of central resources), and the enterprise managers would respond with demands. In the literature on allocation and price-adjustment mechanisms it is usually assumed that this exchange of messages is iterated until an equilibrium of supply and demand is reached (this may require infinitely many iterations!). In a real application of such a mechanism, only a few iterations would typically be feasible, and equilibrium would not be reached. Thus one could not appeal to the theory of optimality of the equilibria of such processes. Nevertheless, the exchange of information produced by even a few iterations might be quite valuable, i.e., the information structure might be much more valuable than the 'routine' structure, and possibly close in value to that of complete centralization.

Indeed, research done to date on models of such processes suggests that price and demand signals are strikingly efficient in conveying the information needed for good allocation decisions, even out of equilibrium (Radner, 1972; Groves and Radner, 1972; T.A. Marschak, 1959, 1972; Arrow and Radner, 1979; Groves and Hart, 1982; Groves, 1983; Hogan, 1971).

INCENTIVES IN TEAMS. The model of a team assumes that the team members have identical interests and beliefs. Thus no special incentives are required to persuade the individual members to implement honestly the given information structure or to take the decisions prescribed by the optimal team decision function. A full-fledged theory of economic organization should, of course, take account of conflicting interests and beliefs, and the resulting problems of incentives.

This article is not the place to review the growing literature on this subject, but a few comments may be useful here. In general, it is not possible to solve the 'incentive problem' costlessly. (For exceptions to this generalization, see Groves, 1973; Green and Laffont, 1979.) Thus, in an economic organization, there will be two sources of efficiency loss: (1) decentralization of information, having the effect that individual actions will be based on information that is less complete than the information jointly available to the organization as a whole; (2) conflicts of interests and beliefs among the decision-makers, leading to distortions of information and action ('game-playing'). In fact these two sources are not so easily disentangled. For example, under conditions of uncertainty and limited information, it will typically be difficult for a supervisor (or organizer) to determine whether a particular decision-maker is providing correct information or following a prescribed decision rule, since to achieve this would require the supervisor to have all of the information that is available to the subordinate. In other words, informational decentralization leads to de facto decentralization of authority. (For references to the literature on incentives and decentralization in economic organizations see Arrow, 1974; Hurwicz, 1979; Radner, 1975, 1986; and Stiglitz, 1983.)

BIBLIOGRAPHY

Arrow, K.J. 1972. The value of and demand for information. Ch. 6 of McGuire and Radner (1986).

Arrow, K.J. 1974. *The Limits of Organization.* New York: Norton.

Arrow, K.J. and Radner, R. 1979. Allocation of resources in large teams. *Econometrica* 47, 361–85.

Beckmann, M.J. 1958. Decision and team problems in airline reservations. *Econometrica* 26, 134–45.

Green, J. and Laffont, J.-J. 1979. *Incentives in Public Decision-Making.* Amsterdam: North-Holland.

Groves, T. 1973. Incentives in teams. *Econometrica* 41, 617–31.

Groves, T. 1983. The usefulness of demand forecasts for team resource allocation in a stochastic environment. *Review of Economic Studies* 50, 555–71.

Groves, T. and Radner, R. 1972. Allocation of resources in a team. *Journal of Economic Theory* 3, 415–44.

Groves, T. and Hart, S. 1982. Efficiency of resource allocation by uninformed demand. *Econometrica* 50, 1453–82.

Hogan, T.M. 1971. A comparison of information structures and convergence properties of several multisector economic planning procedures. Technical Report No. 10, Center for Research in Management Science, University of California, Berkeley.

Hurwicz, L. 1979. On the interaction between information and incentives in organizations. In *Communication and Control in Society*, ed. K. Krittendorf, New York: Gordon and Breach, 123–47.

Lange, O. and Taylor, F.M. 1938. *On the Economic Theory of Socialism.* Minneapolis: University of Minnesota Press.

Lerner, A. 1944. *The Economics of Control.* New York: Macmillan.

Marschak, T.A. 1959. Centralization and decentralization in economic organizations. *Econometrica* 27, 399–40.

Marschak, T.A. 1972. Computation in organizations: the comparison of price mechanisms and other adjustment processes. Ch. 12 of McGuire and Radner (1986), 237–82.

Marschak, J. and Radner, R. 1972. *Economic Theory of Teams*. New Haven: Yale University Press.

McGuire, C.B. 1961. Some team models of a sales organization. *Management Science* 7, 101–130.

McGuire, C.B. 1972. Comparisons of information structures. Ch. 5 of McGuire and Radner (1986), 101–30.

McGuire, C.B. and Radner, R. 1986. *Decision and Organization*. 2nd edn, Minneapolis: University of Minnesota Press; originally published Amsterdam: North-Holland, 1972.

Radner, R. 1962. Team decision problems. *Annals of Mathematical Statistics* 33, 857–881.

Radner, R. 1972. Allocation of a scarce resource under uncertainty: an example of a team. Ch. 11 of McGuire and Radner (1986), 217–36.

Radner, R. 1975. Economic planning under uncertainty. Ch. 4 of *Economic Planning, East and West*, ed. M. Bornstein, Cambridge, Mass.: Ballinger, pp. 93–118.

Radner, R. 1987. Decentralization and incentives. In *Information, Incentives, and Economic Mechanisms: Essays in Honor of Leonid Hurwicz*, ed. T. Groves, R. Radner and S. Reiter, Minneapolis: University of Minnesota Press.

Savage, L.J. 1954. *The Foundations of Statistics*. New York: Wiley.

Stiglitz, J.E. 1983. Risk, incentives, and the pure theory of moral hazard. *The Geneva Papers on Risk and Insurance* 8, 4–33.

Ward, B. 1967. *The Socialist Economy*. New York: Random House.

Contributors

Costas Azariadis Professor of Economics, University of Pennsylvania. 'Implicit contracts and underemployment equilibria', *Journal of Political Economy* (1975); 'Self-fulfilling prophecies', *Journal of Economic Theory* (1981); 'Employment with asymmetric information', *Quarterly Journal of Economics* (supplement, 1983); 'Sunspots and cycles' *Review of Economic Studies* (1986).

Stephen N.S. Cheung Professor of Economics, University of Hong Kong. *The Theory of Share Tenancy* (1969); 'The structure of a contract and the theory of a non-exclusive resource', *Journal of Law and Economics* 13(1), (1970); 'The fable of the bees: an economic investigation', *Journal of Law and Economics* 16(1), (1973); *The Myth of Socialist Cost* (1978); *Will China Go Capitalist?* (1982); 'The contractual nature of the firm', *Journal of Law and Economics* (1983).

Robert D. Cooter Professor of Law, University of California, Berkeley; Olin Visiting Research Fellow, University of Virginia Law School. 'The cost of Coase', *Journal of Legal Studies* 11, (1982); 'Prices and Sanctions', *Columbia Law Review* 84, (1984); 'A theory of loss allocation for consumer payments', *University of Texas Law Review* 66, (1987); 'Liberty, efficiency and law', *Law and Contemporary Problems* 50, (1987); *Law and Economics* (with Tom Ullen, 1988); 'Towards a market in unmatured tort claims', *University of Virginia Law Review* (1989).

Peter A. Diamond Professor of Economics, Massachusetts Institute of Technology. *Uncertainty in Economics, Readings and Exercises* (with M. Rothschild, 1978; revised edn, 1989); *A Search-Equilibrium Approach to the Micro Foundations of Macroeconomics* (1984).

Roger Guesnerie Ecole Hautes Etudes en Sciences Sociales; Centre National de la Recherche Scientifique. Member, Econometric Society; Member, European

Economic Association. 'Pareto optimality in nonconvex economics', *Econometrica* 43(1), (1975); 'On the direction of tax reform', *Journal of Public Economics* 7 (1977); *Modèles de l'économie publique* (1980); 'Structure of tax equilibria', (with G. Fuchs) *Econometrica* 51 (1983); 'Sunspots and cycles', (with C. Azariadis) *Review of Economic Studies* 53(5), (1986).

Oliver D. Hart Professor of Economics, Massachusetts Institute of Technology. Fellow, Econometric Society; Fellow, American Academy of Arts and Sciences. 'On the optimality of equilibrium when the market structure is incomplete', *Journal of Economic Theory* 11 (1975); 'Monopolistic competition in a large economy with differentiated commodities', *Review of Economic Studies* 46 (1979); 'Take-over bids, the free rider problem and the theory of corporation', (with S. Grossman) *Bell Journal of Economics and Management Science* 11 (1980); 'An analysis of the principal–agent problem', (with S. Grossman) *Econometrica* (1983); 'The costs and benefits of ownership: a theory of vertical and lateral integration', (with S. Grossman) *Journal of Political Economy* (1986); 'One share/one vote and the market for corporate control', (with S. Grossman) *Journal of Financial Economics* (1988).

Edi Karni Professor of Economics, Johns Hopkins University. 'Free competition and the optimal amount of fraud', (with M.R. Darby) *Journal of Law and Economics* 16 (1973); 'On multivariate risk aversion', *Econometrica* 47 (1979); 'On state dependent preferences and subjective probabilities', (with S. Schmeidler and K. Vind) *Econometrica* 51 (1983); 'Risk aversion for state-dependent utility functions: measurement and applications', *International Economic Review* 24 (1983); *Decision Making Under Uncertainty: The Case of State Dependent Preferences* (1985); ''Preference reversal' and the observability of preferences by experimental methods', (with Z. Safra) *Econometrica* 55 (1987).

Yehuda Kotowitz Professor of Economics, University of Toronto. 'Informative advertising and welfare', (with F. Mathewson) *American Economic Review* (1979); 'Advertising, consumer information and product quality', (with F. Mathewson) *Bell Journal of Economics* (1979); 'Patent policy in an open economy', (with M.K. Berkowitz) *Canadian Journal of Economics* 4(1), (1982); 'The Economics of the union controlled firm', (with F. Mathewson) *Economica* 49 (1982); 'Optimal R&D processes and market structure', (with N. Gallini) *Economica* 52 (1985); 'A model of advertising and learning' in *Applied Behavioral Economics* (ed. S. Maital, 1987).

Jean-Jacques Laffont Professor of Economics, University of Toulouse. Council Member, Econometric Society; Council Member, European Economic Association. *Essaies externes et théorie économique* (1977); *Incentives in Public Decision Making* (with Gerry Green, 1980); *Fundamentals of Public Economics* (1988); *Economics of Uncertainty and Information.*

Edward P. Lazear Isidore Brown and Gladys J. Brown Professor of Urban and Labor Economics; Senior Fellow, Hoover Institution. 'Why is there mandatory retirement?', *Journal of Political Economy* (1979); 'Agency, earnings profiles, productivity and hours restrictions', *American Economic Review* (1981); 'Rank-order tournaments as optimum labor contracts', (with Sherwin Rosen) *Journal of Political Economy* (1981); 'Retail pricing and clearance sales', *American Economic Review* (1986); 'Salaries and piece rates', *Journal of Business* 59 (1986); 'Pay equality and industrial politics', *Journal of Political Economy* (1989).

John O. Ledyard Professor of Economics and Social Sciences, California Institute of Technology. Fellow, Econometric Society; President, Public Choice Society; Member, Executive Committee, Economic Science Association. 'A convergent Pareto-satisfactory non-tatonnemont adjustment process for a class of unselfish exchange environments', *Econometrica* 39(3), (1971); Dynamics and land use: the case of forestry', (with L. Moses) in *Public and Urban Economics: Essays in Honor of William Vickrey* (ed R. Grierson, 1976); 'Optimal allocation of public goods: a solution to the "free-rider" problem', (with T. Groves) *Econometrica* 45(4), (1977). 'Incentive compatibility and incomplete information', *Journal of Economic Theory* 18(1), (1978); 'The pure theory of large two candidate elections', *Public Choice* 44 (1984); 'The scope of the hypothesis of Bayesian equilibrium', *Journal of Economic Theory* 39, (1986).

Edmond Malinvaud Professor, Collège de France. President, International Economic Association (1974–7); President, European Economic Association (1988). *Statistical Methods of Econometrics* (1966); *Lectures on Microeconomic Theory* (1972); *French Economic Growth* (with J.J. Carré and P. Dubois, 1975); *The Theory of Unemployment Reconsidered* (1977); *Théorie Macroéconomique* (1981).

Thomas Marschak Professor, School of Business, University of California, Berkeley. Fellow, Econometric Society. 'Centralization and decentralization in economic organizations', *Econometrica* (1959); *Strategy for RAND* (with R. Summers and T.K. Glennan Jr, 1967); 'Centralized versus decentralized resource allocation: the Yugoslav "Laboratory"', *Quarterly Journal of Economics* (1968); 'Computation in organizations: the comparisons of price mechanisms and other adjustment processes', in *Decision and Organization* (ed C.B. Mcguire and R. Radner, 1972); 'Restabilizing responses, inertia supergames, and oligopolistic equilibria', (with R. Selten) *Quarterly Journal of Economics* (1978); 'Price versus direct revelation: informational judgements for finite mechanisms', in *Information, Incentives and Economic Mechanisms* (ed. T. Groves, R. Radner and S. Reiter, 1987).

Roger B. Myerson Harold L. Stuart Professor of Decision Sciences, J.L. Kellogg Graduate School of Management, Northwestern University. 'Incentive compatibilty and the bargaining problem', *Econometrica* 47 (1979); 'Optimal auction design', *Mathematics of Operations Research* 6 (1981); 'Cooperative games with incomplete information', *International Journal of Game Theory* 13 (1984); 'Two-person bargaining problems with incomplete information', *Econometrica* 52 (1984); 'Multistage games with communication', *Econometrica* 54(2), (1986); 'An introduction to game theory', *Studies in Mathematical Economics* (ed. S. Reiter, 1986).

Andrew Postlewaite Professor of Economics and Finance, University of Pennsylvania. 'Approximate efficiency of non-Walrasian Nash equilibria', (with D. Schmeidler) *Econometrica* 46(1), (1978); 'Manipulation via endowments', *Review of Economic Studies* 46(143), (1979); 'Oligopoly and competition in large markets', (with M. Okuno and J. Roberts) *American Economic Review* 70(1), (1980); 'The economics of quality testing and disclosure', (with S. Matthews) *Rand Journal of Economics* 16(3), (1985); 'Implementation in differential information economies', (with D. Schmeidler) *Journal of Economic Theory* 39(1), (1986); 'Pre-play communication in two-person sealed-bid double auctions', (with S. Matthews) *Journal of Economic Theory* (forthcoming).

Roy Radner Distinguished Member of Technical Staff, AT&T Bell Laboratories; Research Professor of Economics, New York University. Member, National Academy of Sciences, USA; Fellow, American Academy of Arts and Sciences; President, Econometric Society, 1972–3; Distinguished Fellow, American Economic Association; Guggenheim Fellow, 1961, 1965. 'Paths of economic growth that are optimal with regard to final states: a turnpike theorem', *Review of Economic Studies* 28 (1961); *Economic Theory of Teams* (with J. Marschak, 1972); 'Existence of equilibrium of plans, prices, and price expectations in a sequence of markets', *Econometrica* 40 (1972); 'Satisficing', *Journal of Mathematical Economics* 2 (1975); 'Equilibrium under uncertainty', in *Handbook of Mathematical Economics* (ed. K.J. Arrow and M. Intriligator, 1981); 'Decision and information', in *Information, Incentives, and Economic Mechanisms* (ed., with T. Groves and S. Reiter, 1987).

Stanley Reiter Morrison Professor of Economics, Mathematics and Managerial Economics, Northwestern University. Guggenheim Fellow; Fellow, Econometric Society; Fellow, American Association for the Advancement of Science. 'The informational size of message spaces', (with K. Mount) *Journal of Economic Theory* 8(2), (1974); 'A stochastic decentralized allocation process: part 1', (with L. Hurwicz and R. Radner) *Econometrica* 43(2), (1975); 'A preface on modelling the regulated United States economy', (with J.R.T. Hughes) *Hofstra Law Review* 9(5), (1981); 'Approximation in a continuous model of computing', (with K. Mount) *Journal of Complexity* 1 (1985); 'Informational incentive and performance in the (new) welfare economics', Papers and Proceedings of the 89th Annual Meeting of the American Economic Association, *The American Economic Review* 67(1), (1977); 'Game forms with minimal message spaces', *Econometrica* (1988).

John Graham Riley Professor of Economics, UCLA. 'Competitive signalling', *Journal of Economic Theory* 10 (1975); 'Informational equilibrium', *Econometrica* 47 (1979); 'The analytics of uncertainty and information', (with J. Hirschleifer), *Journal of Economic Literature* 18 (1979); 'Optimal auctions', (with W. Samuelson), *American Economic Review* (1981); 'Optimal auctions with risk averse buyers', *Econometrica* 71 (1984); 'Monopoly with incomplete information', (with E. Maskin), *Rand Journal* 15 (1984).

John Roberts Jonathan B. Lovelace Professor of Economics, Associate Dean, Stanford University. Fellow, Econometric Society. CORE Faculty Research Fellow (1974–5); Associate Editor, *Econometrica* (1985–7); *Journal of Economic Theory* (1977–); *Games and Economic Behaviour* (1988–). 'Existence of Lindahl equilibrium with a measure space of consumers', *Journal of Economic Theory* 6 (1973); 'On the foundations of the theory of monopolistic competition', (with Hugo Sonnenschein) *Econometrica* 45 (1977); 'Limit pricing and entry under incomplete information: analysis', (with Paul Milgrom) *Econometrica* 50 (1982); 'Predation, reputation and entry deterrence', (with Paul Milgrom) *Journal of Economic Theory* 27 (1982); 'An equilibrium model with involuntary unemployment at flexible, competitive prices and wages', *American Economic Review* 77 (1987); 'An economic approach to influence activities', (with Paul Milgrom) *American Journal of Sociology* 94 (supplement, 1988).

Agnar Sandmo Professor of Economics, Norwegian School of Economics and Business Administration. Fellow, Econometric Society; Vice President, European Economic Association (1988); Editor, *European Economic Review* (1986–); 'Capital risk, consumption and portfolio choice', *Econometrica* (1969); 'Discount rates for public investment under uncertainty', *International Economic Review* (1972); 'Public Goods and the technology of consumption', *Review of Economic Studies* (1973); 'Optimal taxation: an introduction to the literature', *Journal of Public Economics* (1976); 'Welfare implications of the taxation of savings', (with A.B. Atkinson) *Economic Journal* (1980); 'The effects of taxation on saving and risk-taking', *Handbook of Public Economics* 1 (1985).

Vernon L. Smith Regents' Professor of Economics, Research Director, Economic Science Laboratory, University of Arizona. Vice President, Southern Economic Association (1985–6); Founding President, Economic Science Association (1986–7); President, Public Choice Society (1988–90); Fellow, Econometric Society (1988–); President, Western Economic Association (1990–91). 'The theory of investment and production', *Quarterly Journal of Economics* (1959); 'An experimental study of competitive market behavior', *Journal of Political Economy* (1962); 'Corporate financial theory under uncertainty', *Quarterly Journal of Economics* (1970); 'Economics of the primitive hunter culture with applications to pleistocene extinction and the rise of agriculture', *Journal of Political Economy* (1975); 'Bubbles, crashes and endogenous expectations in experimental spot asset markets', (with G. Suchanek and A. Williams) *Econometrica* (1988); *Experimental Economics* (collected works, forthcoming).

Joseph E. Stiglitz Professor of Economics, Stanford University. Fellow, American Academy of Arts and Sciences; Fellow, National Academy of Sciences; John Bates Clark Medal, American Economic Association. *Collected Scientific Papers of P.A. Samuelson* (ed., 1965); *Readings in Modern Theory of Economic Growth* (ed., with H. Uzawa, 1969); *Lectures in Public Finance* (with A.B. Atkinson, 1980); *The Economic Impact of Price Stabilization* (with D. Newbery, 1980).

Charles A. Wilson Professor of Economics, New York University. Fellow, Econometric Society. 'A model of insurance with incomplete information', *Journal of Economic Theory* 16 (1977); 'Anticipated shocks and exchange rate dynamics', *Journal of Political Economy* 87(3), (1979); 'The nature of equilibrium in markets with adverse selection', *The Bell Journal of Economics* 11(2), (1980); 'Equilibrium in dynamic models of pure exchange', *Journal of Economic Theory*, 24(1), (1981); 'The war of attrition in continuous time with complete information', *International Economic Review* 29(4), (1988).

Robert Wilson Professor, Stanford Business School. 'A bidding model of "perfect" competition', *Review of Economic Studies* 4 (1977); 'Sequential equilibria', (with D. Kreps) *Econometrica* 50 (1982); 'Incentive efficiency of double auctions', *Econometrica* 53 (1985); 'Foundations of dynamic monopoly and the Coase conjecture', (with F. Gul and H. Sonnenschein) *Journal of Economic Theory* 39 (1986); 'Priority service: pricing, investment and market organization', (with H. Chao) *American Economic Review* 77 (1987); 'Efficient and competitive rationing', *Econometrica* 57 (1989).

Sidney G. Winter Professor of Economics and Management, Yale School of Organization and Management. Fellow, Econometric Society. *An Evolutionary Theory of Economic Change*, (with Richard R. Nelson, 1982); 'Knowledge and competence as strategic assets', in *The Competitive Challenge: Strategies for Industrial Innovation and Renewal* (ed. D.J. Teece, 1987); 'On Coase, competence and the corporation', *Journal of Law, Economics and Organization* (1988).